CLYMER®

Publisher Shawn Etheridge

EDITORIAL

Managing Editor
James Grooms

Associate Editors
Richard Arens
Steven Thomas

Technical Writers
Jay Bogart
Jon Engleman
Michael Morlan
George Parise
Mark Rolling
Ed Scott
Ron Wright

Group Production Manager
Dylan Goodwin

Senior Production Editors
Greg Araujo
Darin Watson

Production Editors
Julie Jantzer-Ward
Justin Marciniak
Holly Messinger

Associate Production Editor
Susan Hartington

Technical Illustrators
Steve Amos
Errol McCarthy
Mitzi McCarthy
Bob Meyer

MARKETING/SALES AND ADMINISTRATION

Sales Channel & Brand Marketing Coordinator
Melissa Abbott Mudd

Art Director
Chris Paxton

Sales Managers
Justin Henton
Dutch Sadler
Matt Tusken

Business Manager
Ron Rogers

Customer Service Manager
Terri Cannon

Customer Service Representatives
Felicia Dickerson
Courtney Hollars
April LeBlond

Warehouse & Inventory Manager
Leah Hicks

PRISM
BUSINESS MEDIA™
P.O. Box 12901, Overland Park, KS 66282-2901 • 800-262-1954 • 913-967-1719

The following books and guides are published by Prism Business Media

More information available at *clymer.com*

CLYMER®

SUZUKI

VS1400 INTRUDER • 1987-2003

CLYMER®

P.O. Box 12901, Overland Park, Kansas 66282-2901

Copyright ©2003 Prism Business Media Inc.

FIRST EDITION
First Printing September, 1998
Second Printing September, 2001
SECOND EDITION
Updated by James Grooms to include 1999-2003 models
First Printing July, 2003
Second Printing October, 2004
Third Printing August, 2006

Printed in U.S.A.

CLYMER and colophon are registered trademarks of Prism Business Media Inc.

ISBN: 0-89287-874-6

Library of Congress: 2003108286

AUTHOR: Clymer staff.

TECHNICAL PHOTOGRAPHY: Ron Wright. Special thanks to Mike Biggs and Kurk Ringgold for their assistance during the disassembly and assembly of the VS1400.

TECHNICAL ILLUSTRATIONS: Mitzi McCarthy.

TOOLS AND EQUIPMENT: K & L Supply at www.klsupply.com.

COVER: Mark Clifford Photography, Los Angeles, California.

CONTENTS

Manual organization	Serial numbers
Notes, cautions and warnings	Warning and information labels
Safety first	Basic hand tools
Service hints	Precision measuring tools
Washing the bike	Special tools
Torque specifications	Fabricating tools
Special tips	Mechanic's tips
Fasteners	Ball bearing replacement
Lubricants	Seals
Threadlocking compound	Riding safety
Expendable supplies	Storage

Operating requirements	Engine overheating
Troubleshooting instruments	Engine
Starting the engine	Engine noises
Starting difficulties	Engine leakdown test
Poor idle speed performance	Clutch
Poor medium and high speed	Transmission
performance	Final drive
Engine starting system	Handling
Ignition system	Frame noise
Fuel system	Brakes

Routine checks	Battery electrical
Pre-ride inspection	cable connectors
Service intervals	Periodic lubrication
Tires and wheels	Periodic maintenance
Battery	Tune-up

QUICK REFERENCE DATA

MOTORCYCLE INFORMATION

MODEL:_____ YEAR:_____

VIN NUMBER:_____

ENGINE SERIAL NUMBER:_____

CARBURETOR SERIAL NUMBER OR I.D. MARK:_____

TIRE INFLATION PRESSURE (COLD)*

	KPa	psi
Front		
Solo riding	200	29
Dual riding	200	29
Rear		
Solor riding	200	29
Dual riding	228	33

RECOMMENDED LUBRICANTS AND FLUIDS

Fuel	Regular unleaded or low-lead type
U.S. and Canada	87 [(R+M/2 method] or 91 octane or higher
U.K. and all others	85-95 octane
Engine oil	
Grade	API SE, SF or SG
Viscosity	SAE 10W-40
Final drive oil	SAE 90 Hypoid gear oil with
	GL-5 under API classification
Brake fluid	DOT 3 or DOT 4
Clutch hydraulic fluid	DOT 3 or DOT 4
Front fork oil-type	SAE 10W

ENGINE, FORK OIL, FINAL DRIVE UNIT REFILL CAPACITIES

Engine oil	
Oil change	3.7 L (3.9 U.S. qts. or 3.2 Imp. qts.)
Oil and filter chagne	4.3 L (4.5 U.S. qts. or 3.8 Imp. qts.)
Final drive oil	
Capacity at oil change	200-220 ml (6.8-7.4 U.S. oz. or 7.0-7.7 Imp oz.)
Front fork oil capacity (each fork leg)	
Completely dry	354 ml (12.0 U.S. oz. or 12.5 Imp. oz.)
Front fork oil level dimension	
top surface (after completely dry)	
1991-1992	203 mm (7.99 in.)
Cables or pivot pints	Cable lube or SAE 10W/30 motor oil

MAINTENANCE AND TUNE-UP TIGHTENING TORQUES

	N•m	ft.-lb.
Oil drain plug	18-23	13-16.5
Oil filter	Hand tight	Hand tight
Front axle	36-52	26-37.5
Front axle clamp bolt	15-25	11-18
Handlebar		
Mounting bolts	15-25	11-18
Holder nut	80-100	58-72.5
Steering stem nut	80-100	58-72.5
Fork bridge lower clamp bolt	25-40	18-29
Fork cap bolt	45-55	32.5-39.8
Rear axle nut	60-95	43.5-69.5
Rear torque link bolt and nut	40-60	29-43.4
Foot rest mounting bolts	15-25	11-18

MAINTENANCE AND TUNE-UP SPECIFICATIONS

Throttle grip rotational free play	
1987-1993	0.5-1.0 mm (0.02-0.04 in.)
1994-1999	3.0-6.0 mm (0.12-0.24 in.)
2000-on	2.0-4.0 mm (0.08-0.16 in.)
Automatic de-compression cable free play	
Distance between lever and stopper	
Front cylinder	1.5-2.5 mm (0.06-0.10 in.) (dimension A)
Rear cylinder	1.0-2.0 mm (0.04-0.08 in.) (dimension B)
Rear brake pedal	
Height above foot peg	
1987-1995	22 mm (0.87 in.)
1996-on	65 mm (2.6 in,)
Engine cylinder number	
Rear cylinder	No. 1
Front cylinder	No. 2
Firing order	Front, rear
Engine compression	
Standard	1,000-1,400 kPa (142-199 psi)
Service limit	800 kPa (114 psi)
Ignition timing	Non adjustable
Idle speed	950-1,050 rpm
Spark plug type	
1987-1989	NGK DP8EA-9 or ND X24EP-U9
1990-on	NGK DPR8EA-9 or ND X24EPR-U9
Spark plug gap	0.8-0.9 mm (0.031-0.035 in.)
Oil pressure @ 3,000 rpm	3.5 kg/cm^2 (50 psi) to 6.5 kg/cm^2 (92 psi)
Throttle cable ends	
(carburetor synchronization)	18.5 mm (0.73 in.)

CHAPTER ONE

GENERAL INFORMATION

This detailed, comprehensive manual covers the Suzuki 1400 cc Intruder V-twins from 1987-on. The expert text gives complete information on maintenance, tune-up, repair and overhaul. Hundreds of photos and drawings guide you through every step. The book includes all you will need to know to keep your Suzuki running right.

A shop manual is a reference. You want to be able to find information fast. As in all Clymer books, this one is designed with you in mind. All chapters are thumb tabbed. Important items are extensively indexed at the rear of the book. All procedures, tables, photos, etc., in this manual are for the reader who may be working on the bike or using this manual for the first time. All the most frequently used specifications and capacities are summarized in the *Quick Reference Data* pages at the front of the book.

Keep the book handy in your tool box. It will help you better understand how your bike runs, lower repair costs and generally improve your satisfaction with the bike.

Suzuki uses a letter designation on their serial number to indicate the model year of their bikes. Refer to **Table 1** at the end of this chapter for the letter-to-year designation information and the VIN or frame serial numbers.

Table 1 lists model coverage with frame serial numbers.

Table 2 lists general vehicle dimensions.

Table 3 lists decimal to metric equivalents.

Table 4 lists general torque specifications.

Table 5 lists conversion tables.

Table 6 lists technical abbreviations.

Table 7 lists metric tap drill sizes.

Table 8 lists windchill factors.

Tables 1-8 are at the end of this chapter.

MANUAL ORGANIZATION

All dimensions and capacities are expressed in metric and U.S. standard units of measure.

This chapter provides general information and discusses equipment and tools useful both for preventive maintenance and troubleshooting.

Chapter Two provides methods and suggestions for quick and accurate diagnosis and repair of problems. Troubleshooting procedures discuss typical symptoms and logical methods to pinpoint the trouble.

Chapter Three explains all periodic lubrication and routine maintenance necessary to keep the

Suzuki running well. Chapter Three also includes recommended tune-up procedures, eliminating the need to consult chapters on the various assemblies constantly.

Subsequent chapters describe specific systems such as the engine, clutch, transmission, fuel, exhaust, cooling, suspension and brakes. Each chapter provides disassembly, repair and assembly procedures in simple step-by-step form.

If a repair is impractical for a home mechanic, it is indicated. Usually it is faster and less expensive to take such repairs to a dealer or competent repair shop. Specifications concerning a particular system are included at the end of the appropriate chapter.

Some of the procedures in this manual specify special tools. In most cases, the tool is illustrated either in use or alone. Well equipped mechanics may find they can substitute similar tools already on hand or can fabricate their own.

NOTES, CAUTIONS AND WARNINGS

The terms NOTE, CAUTION and WARNING have specific meanings in this manual. A NOTE provides additional information to make a step or procedure easier or clearer. Disregarding a NOTE could cause inconvenience, but would not cause equipment damage or personal injury.

A CAUTION emphasizes areas where equipment damage could result. Disregarding a CAUTION could cause permanent mechanical damage; however, personal injury is unlikely.

A WARNING emphasizes areas where personal injury or even death could result from negligence. Mechanical damage may also occur. WARNINGS *are to be taken seriously*. In some cases, serious injury or death has resulted from disregarding similar warnings.

SAFETY FIRST

Professional mechanics can work for years and never sustain a serious injury. If you observe a few rules of common sense and safety, you can enjoy many safe hours servicing your machine. If you ignore these rules you can hurt yourself or damage the equipment.

1. Never use gasoline as a cleaning solvent.

2. Never smoke or use a torch in the vicinity of flammable liquids, such as cleaning solvent, in open containers.

3. If welding or brazing is required on the bike, remove the fuel tank and shocks to a safe distance, at least 50 feet (15 m) away.

4. Use the proper sized wrenches to avoid damage to fasteners and injury to yourself.

5. When loosening a tight or stuck nut, be guided by what would happen if the wrench should slip. Be careful and protect yourself accordingly.

6. When replacing a fastener, make sure to use one with the same measurements and strength as the old one. Incorrect or mismatched fasteners can result in damage to the bike and possible personal injury. Avoid fastener kits filled with cheap and poorly made nuts, bolts, washers and cotter pins. Refer to *Fasteners* in this chapter for additional information.

7. Keep all hand and power tools in good condition. Wipe greasy and oily tools after using them. They are difficult to hold and can cause injury. Replace or repair worn or damaged tools.

8. Keep your work area clean and uncluttered.

9. Wear safety goggles during all operations involving drilling, grinding, the use of a cold chisel or anytime you feel unsure about the safety of your eyes. Safety goggles should also be worn when using solvent and compressed air to clean parts.

10. Keep an approved fire extinguisher nearby. It must be rated for gasoline (Class B) and electrical (Class C) fires.

11. When drying bearings or other rotating parts with compressed air, never allow the air jet to rotate the bearing or part. The air jet is capable of rotating them at speeds more than those for which they were designed. The bearing or rotating part is very likely to disintegrate and cause serious injury and damage. To prevent bearing damage when using compressed air, hold the inner bearing race by hand.

SERVICE HINTS

Most of the service procedures covered are straightforward and can be performed by anyone reasonably handy with tools. However, consider your capabilities carefully before attempting any operation involving major disassembly of the engine assembly.

Take your time and do the job right. Do not forget that a newly rebuilt engine must be broken-in the same way as a new one. Refer to *Engine Break-In* in Chapter Five.

1. Front, as used in this manual, refers to the front of the bike; the front of any component is the end closest to the front of the bike. The left- and right-hand sides refer to the position of the parts as viewed by a rider sitting on the seat facing forward. For example, the throttle control is on the right-hand side. These rules are simple, but confusion can cause a major inconvenience during service.

2. When servicing the engine or clutch, or when removing a suspension component, secure the bike in a safe manner.

3. Tag all similar internal parts for location and mark all mating parts for position. Record shim number, thickness and alignment when removed. Identify and store small parts in plastic sandwich bags. Seal and label them with masking tape.

4. Place parts from a specific area of the engine like the cylinder head, cylinder, clutch and shift mechanism into plastic boxes to keep them separated.

5. When disassembling transmission shaft assemblies, use an egg flat (the type that restaurants get their eggs in). Set the parts from the shaft in one of the depressions in the same order in which it was removed.

6. Label all electrical wiring and connectors before disconnecting them. Again, do not rely on memory alone.

7. Protect finished surfaces from physical damage or corrosion. Keep gasoline and brake and clutch fluid off painted surfaces.

8. Use penetrating oil on frozen or tight bolts, then strike the bolt head a few times with a hammer and punch (use a screwdriver on screws). Avoid the use of heat where possible, as it can warp, melt or affect the temper of parts. Heat also ruins finishes, especially paints and plastics.

9. Unless specified in the procedure, parts should not require unusual force during disassembly or assembly. If a part is difficult to remove or install, find out why before continuing.

10. To prevent small objects and abrasive dust from falling into the engine, cover all openings after exposing them.

11. Read each procedure completely while looking at the actual parts before starting a job. Make sure you thoroughly understand the procedural steps and then follow the procedure, step by step.

12. Recommendations are occasionally made to refer service or maintenance to a Suzuki dealership or a specialist in a particular field. In these cases, the work will be done more quickly and economically than if you performed the job yourself.

13. In procedural steps, the term replace means to discard a defective part and replace with a new or exchange unit. Overhaul means to remove, disassemble, inspect and replace parts required to major systems.

14. Some operations require the use of a hydraulic press. It would be wiser to have these operations performed by a shop equipped for such work, rather than to try to do the job yourself with makeshift equipment that may damage your machine.

15. Repairs go much faster and easier if your machine is clean before you begin work. There are many special cleaners on the market, like Bel-Ray Degreaser, for washing the engine and related parts. Follow the manufacturer's directions on the container for the best results. Clean all oily or greasy parts with cleaning solvent as you remove them.

WARNING
Never use gasoline as a cleaning agent. It presents an extreme fire hazard. Be sure to work in a well-ventilated area when using cleaning solvent. Keep a fire extinguisher, rated for gasoline fires, handy in any case.

CAUTION
If you use a car wash to clean your bike, do not direct the high pressure water hose at steering bearings, carburetor hoses, suspension components, wheel bearings or electrical components. High pressure water will flush grease out of the bearings or damage the seals.

16. Many of the labor charges for repairs made by dealerships are for the time involved during the removal, disassembly, assembly, and reinstallation of other parts to reach the defective part. It is frequently possible to perform the preliminary operations yourself and then take the defective unit to the dealer for repair at considerable savings.

17. When special tools are required, arrange to get them before you start. It is frustrating and time-consuming to get partly into a job and then be unable to complete it.

18. Make diagrams (or take a Polaroid picture) wherever similar-appearing parts are found. You may think you can remember where everything came from, but mistakes are costly. There is also the possibility that you may be sidetracked and not return to work for days or even weeks and the carefully laid out parts may be disturbed.

19. When assembling parts, be sure all shims and washers are installed exactly as they came out.

20. Whenever a rotating part butts against a stationary part, look for a shim or washer. Use new gaskets if there is any doubt about the condition of the old ones. A thin coat of oil on non-pressure type gaskets may help them seal more effectively.

21. Use heavy grease to hold small parts in place if they tend to fall out during assembly. However, keep grease and oil away from electrical and brake components.

WASHING THE BIKE

Regular cleaning of the bike is an important part of its overall maintenance. After riding your bike in extremely dirty areas, clean it thoroughly. Doing this will make maintenance and service procedures quick and easy. More important, proper cleaning will prevent dirt from falling into critical areas undetected. Failing to clean the bike or cleaning it incorrectly will add to your maintenance costs and shop time because dirty parts wear out prematurely. It's unthinkable that your bike could break because of improper cleaning, but it can happen. When cleaning your Suzuki, you will need a few tools, shop rags, scrub brush, bucket, liquid cleaner and access to water. Many riders use a coin-operated car wash. Coin-operated car washes are convenient and quick, but with improper use the high water pressures can do more damage than good to your bike.

NOTE
A safe biodegradable, nontoxic and nonflammable liquid cleaner that works well for washing your bike as well as for removing grease and oil from engine and suspension parts is Simple Green. Simple Green can be bought through some supermarkets, hardware, garden and discount supply houses. Follow the directions on the container for recommended dilution ratios.

When cleaning your bike, and especially when using a spray type degreaser solution, remember that what goes on the bike will rinse off and drip onto your driveway or into your yard. If possible, use a degreaser at a coin-operated car wash. If you are cleaning your bike at home, place thick cardboard or newspapers underneath the bike to catch the oil and grease deposits as they are rinsed off.

CAUTION
Some of the steps in this procedure relate to a bike that has been subjected to extremely dirty conditions, like mud or severe road dirt. To avoid surface damage, carefully scrub the engine and frame covers with a soft sponge or towel—do not use a brush on these covers as you will scratch the surfaces.

1. Park the bike on level ground on a sidestand.
2. Check the following before washing the bike:
   a. Make sure the gas filler cap is closed and locked.
   b. Make sure the engine oil filler cap is on tight.
   c. Plug the muffler openings.
   d. Cover the air box air inlet openings with plastic or duct tape.
3. Wash the bike from top to bottom with soapy water. Use the soft scrub brush to get excess dirt out of the wheel rims and engine crannies. Concentrate on the upper controls, engine, side covers and gas tank during this wash cycle. Do not forget to wash dirt and mud from underneath the fenders, suspension and engine crankcase.
4. Next, concentrate the on the frame tube members and suspension.
5. Direct the hose underneath the engine and swing arm. Wash this area thoroughly.

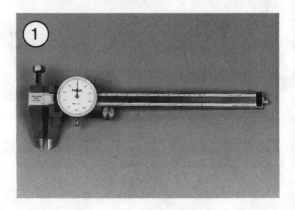

6. Finally, use cold water without soap and spray the entire bike again. Use as much time and care when rinsing the bike as when washing it. Soap deposits will quickly corrode electrical connections and remove the natural oils from tires, causing premature cracks and wear. Make sure you thoroughly rinse off the bike.

7. Tip the bike from side to side to allow any water that has collected on horizontal surfaces to drain off.

8. Remove the plastic cover or duct tape from air box air inlet(s).

9. Unplug the muffler openings.

10. Start the engine and let it idle so the engine will burn off the internal moisture.

11. If you have compressed air, gently blow off any residual water from hard to reach areas.

12. Before taking the bike into the garage, wipe it dry with a soft terry cloth or chamois. Inspect the machine as you dry it for further signs of dirt and grime. Inspect the clearcoat of the frame, swing arm, front forks and other painted pieces. Spray any worn-down spots with WD-40 or Bel-Ray 6-in-1 to prevent rust from building on the bare metal. When the bike is back at your work area you can repaint the bare areas with touch-up paint (clear or color) after cleaning off the WD-40. A quick shot from a touch-up paint can each time you work on the bike will keep it looking sharp and prevent rust from weakening parts.

TORQUE SPECIFICATIONS

The materials used in the manufacture of your Suzuki may be subjected to uneven stresses if the fasteners used to hold the sub-assemblies are not installed and tightened correctly. Improper bolt tightening can cause cylinder head warpage, crankcase leaks, premature bearing and seal failure and suspension failure. An accurate torque wrench (described in this chapter) should be used together with the torque specifications listed at the end of most chapters.

Torque specifications throughout this manual are given in Newton-meters (N•m) and foot-pounds (ft.-lb.).

Existing torque wrenches calibrated in meter kilograms can be used by performing a simple mathematical conversion. All you have to do is move the decimal point one place to the right; for example, 3.5 mkg = 35 N•m. This conversion is accurate enough for mechanical work even though the exact mathematical conversion is 3.5 mkg = 34.3 N•m.

To mathematically convert foot-pounds to Newton meters multiply the foot pounds specification by 1.3558 to achieve a N•m equivalent. For example 150 ft.-lb. × 1.3558 = 203 N•m.

Refer to **Table 5** for standard torque specifications for various size screws, bolts and nuts not listed in the respective chapter tables. To use the table, first determine the size of the bolt or nut. Use a vernier caliper and measure the inside dimension of the threads of the nut (**Figure 1**) and across the threads for a bolt (**Figure 2**).

SPECIAL TIPS

Because of the extreme demands placed on a bike, several points should be kept in mind when performing service and repair. The following items are general suggestions that may improve the overall life of the machine and help avoid costly failures.

1. Use a threadlocking compound such as Three-Bond TB1342 or Loctite 242 on all bolts and nuts, even if they are secured with lockwashers. This type of locking compound does not harden completely and allows easy removal of the bolt or nut. A screw or bolt lost from an engine cover or bearing retainer could easily cause serious and expensive damage before its loss is noticed. Make sure the threads are clean and free of grease and oil. Clean with contact

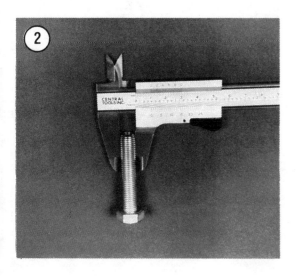

cleaner before applying the locking compound. When applying the threadlocking compound, use a small amount. If too much is used, it can work its way down the threads and enter a bearing or seal. Keep a tube of the various locking compounds in your tool box.

2. When replacing missing or broken fasteners (bolts, nuts and screws), especially on the engine or frame components, always use Suzuki replacement parts. They are specially hardened for each application. The wrong fastener could easily cause serious and expensive damage, not to mention rider injury.

3. When installing gaskets in the engine, always use Suzuki replacement gaskets *without* sealer, unless designated. These gaskets are designed to swell when they come in contact with oil. Gasket sealer will prevent the gaskets from swelling as intended, which can result in oil leaks. These Suzuki gaskets are cut from material of the precise thickness needed. Installation of a too thick or too thin gasket in a critical area could cause engine damage.

FASTENERS

The materials and designs of the various fasteners used on your Suzuki are not arrived at by chance or accident. Fastener design determines the type of tool required to work the fastener. Fastener material is carefully selected to decrease the possibility of physical failure.

Nuts, bolts and screws are manufactured in a wide range of thread patterns. To join a nut and bolt, the diameter of the bolt and the diameter of the hole in the nut must be the same. It is just as important that the threads on both be properly matched.

The best way to tell if 2 fastener threads match is to turn the nut on the bolt (or the bolt into the threaded hole in a piece of equipment) with fingers only. Be sure both pieces are clean. When excessive force is required, check the thread condition on each fastener. If the thread condition is good but the fasteners jam, the threads are not compatible. A thread pitch gauge can be used to determine pitch. Suzuki motorcycles are manufactured with ISO (International Organization for Standardization) metric fasteners. The threads are cut differently than those of American fasteners (**Figure 3**).

Most threads are cut so that the fastener must be turned clockwise to tighten it. These are called right-hand threads. Some fasteners have left-hand threads;

they must be turned counterclockwise to be tightened. Left-hand threads are used in locations where normal rotation of the equipment would tend to loosen a right-hand threaded fastener.

ISO Metric Screw Threads
(Bolts, Nuts and Screws)

ISO (International Organization for Standardization) metric threads come in 3 standard thread sizes: coarse, fine and constant pitch. The ISO coarse pitch is used for almost all common fastener applications. The fine pitch thread is used on certain precision tools and instruments. The constant pitch thread is used mainly on machine parts and not for

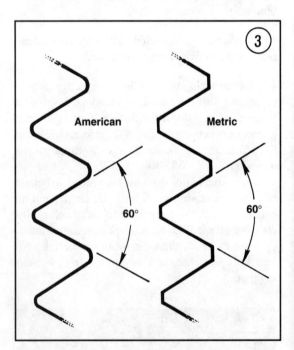

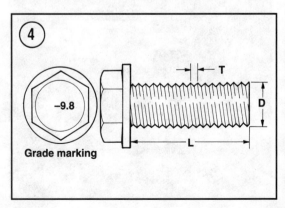

fasteners. The constant pitch thread, however, is used on all metric thread spark plugs.

Metric fasteners are classified by length (L, **Figure 4**), diameter (D) and distance between thread crests (T). A typical bolt might be identified by the numbers $8 \times 1.25—130$, which would indicate that the bolt has a nominal diameter of 8 mm, the distance between thread crests is 1.25 mm and bolt length is 130 mm.

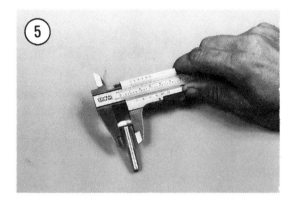

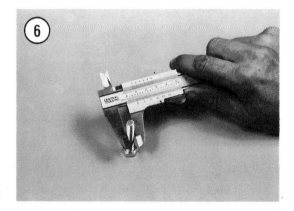

CAUTION
Do not install screws or bolts with a lower strength grade classification than installed originally by the manufacturer. Doing so may cause engine or equipment failure and possible injury.

The measurement across 2 flats on the head of the bolt (**Figure 5**) indicates the proper wrench size to use. **Figure 6** shows how to determine bolt diameter. When buying a bolt from a dealer or parts store, it is important to know how to specify bolt length. The correct way to measure bolt length is by measuring the length starting from underneath the bolt head to the end of the bolt. Always measure bolt length in this manner to avoid buying bolts that are too long.

Machine Screws

There are many different types of machine screws. **Figure 7** shows a number of screw heads requiring different types of turning tools. Heads are also designed to protrude above the metal (round) or slightly recessed in the metal (countersunk). See **Figure 8**.

Nuts

Nuts are manufactured in a variety of types and sizes. Most are hexagonal (6-sided) and fit on bolts, screws and studs with the same diameter and pitch. **Figure 9** shows several types of nuts. The common nut is generally used with a lockwasher. Self-locking nuts have a nylon insert which prevents the nut from loosening; no lockwasher is required. Wing nuts are

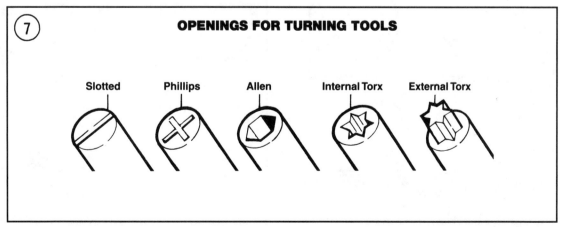

(7) **OPENINGS FOR TURNING TOOLS**

Slotted   Phillips   Allen   Internal Torx   External Torx designed for fast removal by hand and are used for convenience in non-critical locations.

To indicate the size of a metric nut, manufacturers specify the diameter of the opening and the thread pitch. This is similar to bolt specifications, but without the length dimension. The measurement across 2 flats on the nut indicates the proper wrench size to be used.

Self-Locking Fasteners

Several types of bolts, screws and nuts incorporate a system that develops an interference between the bolt, screw, nut or tapped hole threads. Interference is achieved in various ways: by distorting threads, coating threads with dry adhesive or nylon, distort-

ing the top of an all-metal nut, using a nylon insert in the center or at the top of a nut.

Self-locking fasteners offer greater holding strength and better vibration resistance. Some self-locking fasteners can be reused if in good condition. Others, like the nylon insert nut, form an initial locking condition when the nut is first installed; the nylon forms closely to the bolt thread pattern, thus reducing any tendency for the nut to loosen. For greatest safety, discard previously used self-locking fasteners and install new ones during reassembly.

Washers

There are 2 basic types of washers: flat washers and lockwashers. Flat washers are simple discs with a hole to fit a screw or bolt. Lockwashers are de-

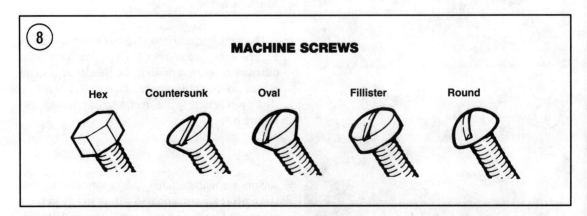

MACHINE SCREWS

Hex   Countersunk   Oval   Fillister   Round

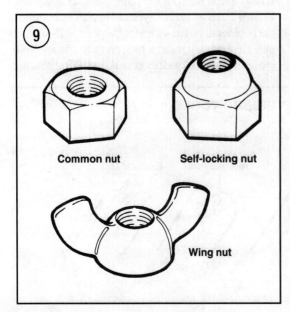

Common nut   Self-locking nut

Wing nut

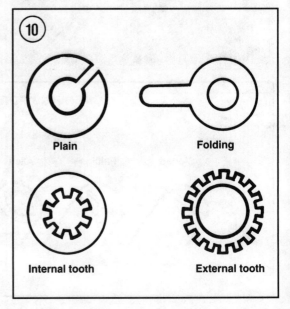

Plain   Folding

Internal tooth   External tooth

signed to prevent a fastener from working loose due to vibration, expansion and contraction. **Figure 10** shows several types of washers. Washers can be used in the following functions:

a. As spacers.

b. To prevent galling or damage of the equipment by the fastener.

c. To help distribute fastener load during torquing.

d. As seals.

Note that flat washers are often used between a lockwasher and a fastener to provide a smooth bearing surface. This allows the fastener to be turned easily with a tool.

NOTE
As much care should be given to the selection and purchase of washers as to bolts, nuts and other fasteners. Beware of washers made of thin and weak materials. These will deform and crush

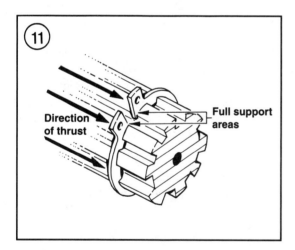

Direction of thrust
Full support areas

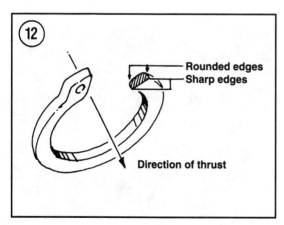

Rounded edges
Sharp edges
Direction of thrust

the first time they are used in a high torque application.

Cotter Pins

Cotter pins are used to secure special kinds of fasteners. The threaded stud, bolt or axle must have a hole in it; the nut or nut lock piece has castellations around which the cotter pin ends wrap. Do not reuse cotter pins.

Circlips

Circlips can be internal or external design. They are used to retain items on shafts (external type) or within tubes (internal type). In some applications, circlips of varying thickness' are used to control the end play of assemblies. These are often called selective circlips. Circlips should be replaced during installation, as removal weakens and deforms them.

Two basic styles of circlips are available: machined and stamped circlips. Machined circlips (**Figure 11**) can be installed in either direction (shaft or housing) because both faces are machined, thus creating two sharp edges. Stamped circlips (**Figure 12**) are manufactured with one sharp edge and one rounded edge. When installing stamped circlips in a thrust situation (transmission shafts, fork tubes, etc.), the sharp edge must face away from the part producing the thrust. When installing circlips, observe the following:

a. Compress or expand circlips only enough to install them.

b. After the circlip is installed, make sure it is completely seated in its groove.

c. Transmission circlips become worn with use and increase side play. For this reason, always use new circlips whenever a transmission is reassembled.

LUBRICANTS

Periodic lubrication assures long life for any type of equipment. The type of lubricant used is just as important as the lubrication service itself, although in an emergency the wrong type of lubricant is better than none at all. The following paragraphs describe the types of lubricants most often used on motorcycle equipment. Be sure to follow the manufacturer's recommendations for lubricant types.

Generally all liquid lubricants are called oil. They may be mineral-based (including petroleum bases), natural-based (vegetable and animal bases), synthetic-based or emulsions (mixtures). Grease is an oil to which a thickening base has been added so that the end product is semi-solid. It is often classified by the type of thickener added; lithium soap is commonly used.

Engine Oil

Motorcycle oil is classified by the American Petroleum Institute (API) and the Society of Automotive Engineers (SAE) in several categories. Oil containers display these classifications on the label. API oil classification is indicated by letters; oils for gasoline engines are identified by an S. Suzuki models described in this manual require SE, SF or SG classified oil.

Viscosity is an indication of the oil's thickness. The SAE uses numbers to indicate viscosity; thin oils have low numbers while thick oils have high numbers. If a W is after the number, it indicates that the viscosity testing was done at low temperature to simulate cold-weather operation. Engine oils fall into the 5 to 50 range.

Multigrade oils (for example 10W-40) are less viscous (thinner) at low temperatures and more viscous (thicker) at high temperatures. This allows the oil to perform efficiently across a wide range of engine operating conditions. The lower the number, the better the engine will start in cold climates. Higher numbers are usually recommended when operating an engine in hot weather.

Grease

Greases are graded by the National Lubricating Grease Institute (NLGI). Greases are graded by number according to the consistency of the grease; these range from No. 000 to No. 6, with No. 6 being the most solid. A typical multipurpose grease is NLGI No. 2. For specific applications, equipment manufacturers may require grease with an additive such as molybdenum disulfide (MOS2).

THREADLOCKING COMPOUND

A threadlocking compound should be used to help secure many of the fasteners used on your bike.

A threadlocking compound will lock fasteners against vibration loosening and seal against leaks. The following threadlocking compounds are recommended for many threadlock requirements described in this manual.

    a. ThreeBond 1342: low strength, frequent repair for small screws and bolts.

    b. ThreeBond 1360: medium strength, high temperature.

    c. ThreeBond 1333B: medium strength, bearing and stud lock.

    d. ThreeBond 1303: high strength, frequent repair.

    e. Loctite 242: low strength, frequent repair.

    f. Loctite 271: high strength, frequent repair.

EXPENDABLE SUPPLIES

Certain expendable supplies are required during maintenance and repair work. These include grease, oil, gasket cement, wiping rags and cleaning solvent. Ask your dealer for the special locking compounds, silicone lubricants and other products which make bike maintenance simpler and easier. Cleaning solvent or kerosene is available at some service stations, paint or hardware stores.

Be sure to follow the manufacturer's instructions and warnings listed on the label of the product you are using. Some cleaning supplies are very caustic and are dangerous if not used properly.

> *WARNING*
> *Having a stack of clean shop rags on hand is important when performing engine and suspension service work. However, to prevent spontaneous combustion from a pile of solvent soaked rags, store them in a sealed*

metal container until they can be washed or properly discarded.

NOTE
To prevent solvent and other chemicals from being absorbed into your skin, wear a pair of petroleum-resistance gloves when cleaning parts. These can be bought through industrial supply houses or well-equipped hardware stores.

SERIAL NUMBERS

Suzuki makes frequent changes during a model year, some minor, some relatively major. When you order parts from the dealer or other parts distributor, always order by VIN and engine serial numbers. The frame serial number is stamped on the right-hand side of the steering head. The engine number is stamped on a raised pad on the left-hand side rear corner of the crankcase (**Figure 13**). The frame or VIN serial number is stamped on the right-hand side of the steering stem (**Figure 14**). The carburetor serial number is on the side of the carburetor body above the float bowl.

Write the numbers down and carry them with you. Compare new parts to old before buying them. If they are not alike, have the parts manager explain the difference to you. **Table 1** lists VIN or frame serial numbers for the models covered in this manual.

WARNING AND INFORMATION LABELS

A number of warning labels have been attached to your Suzuki. These labels contain information that is important to your safety when operating, transporting and storing your bike. Also refer to the

informative labels fastened to the underside of the pillion seat back rest as this information is very useful. Refer to your Owner's Manual for a description and location of each label. If a label is missing, order a replacement label from a Suzuki dealership.

BASIC HAND TOOLS

Many of the procedures in this manual can be carried out with simple hand tools and test equipment familiar to the average home mechanic. Keep your tools clean and in a tool box. Keep them organized with related tools stored together. After using a tool, wipe off dirt and grease with a clean cloth and return the tool to its correct place.

Top quality tools are essential. They are also more economical in the long run. If you are now starting to build your tool collection, avoid the advertised specials featured at some parts houses, discount stores and chain drug stores. These are usually a poor grade tool that can be sold cheaply and that is exactly what they are—cheap. They are usually made of inferior material, and are thick, heavy and clumsy. Their rough finish makes them difficult to clean and they usually do not last very long. If it is ever your misfortune to use such tools, you will probably find out that the wrenches do not fit the heads of bolts and nuts correctly and damage the fasteners.

Quality tools are made of alloy steel and are heat treated for greater strength. They are lighter and better balanced than cheap ones. Their surface is smooth, making them a pleasure to work with and easy to clean. The initial cost of good quality tools may be more but they are cheaper in the long run. Do not try to buy everything in all sizes in the beginning; buy a few at a time until you have the necessary tools.

Screwdrivers

The screwdriver is a very basic tool, but if used improperly, it will do more damage than good. The slot on a screw has a definite dimension and shape. A screwdriver must be selected to conform with that shape. Use a small screwdriver for small screws and a large one for large screws or the screw head will be damaged.

Two basic types of screwdriver are required: common (flat-blade) screwdrivers and Phillips screwdrivers.

Screwdrivers are available in sets which often include an assortment of common and Phillips blades. If you buy them individually, buy at least the following:

  a. Common screwdriver—5/16 × 6 in. blade.
  b. Common screwdriver—3/8 × 12 in. blade.
  c. Phillips screwdriver—size 2 tip, 6 in. blade.
  d. Phillips screwdriver—size 3 tip, 6 and 10 in. blade.

Use screwdrivers only for driving screws. Never use a screwdriver for prying or chiseling metal. Do not try to remove a Phillips or Allen head screw with a common screwdriver (unless the screw has a combination head that will accept either type); you can damage the head so that even the proper tool will be unable to remove it. Keep screwdrivers in the proper condition and they will last longer and perform better. Always keep the tip of a common screwdriver in good condition.

Pliers

Pliers come in a wide range of types and sizes. Pliers are useful for cutting, bending and crimping. Do not use them to cut hardened objects or turn bolts or nuts. **Figure 15** shows several pliers useful in motorcycle repair. Each type of plier has a specialized function. Combination pliers are general purpose pliers used mainly for gripping and bending.

Needlenose pliers are used to hold or bend small objects. Adjustable joint pliers can be adjusted to hold various sizes of objects; the jaws remain parallel to grip around objects such as pipe or tubing. There are many more types of pliers. The ones described here are most suitable for bike repairs.

Locking Pliers

Locking pliers (**Figure 16**) are used to hold objects very tightly like a vise. But avoid using them unless necessary since their sharp jaws will permanently scar any objects which are held. Locking pliers are available in many types for more specific tasks.

Circlip Pliers

Circlip pliers (**Figure 17**) are made for removing and installing circlips. External pliers (spreading)

are used to remove circlips that fit on the outside of a shaft. Internal pliers (squeezing) are used to remove circlips which fit inside a gear or housing.

WARNING
Because circlips can sometimes slip and fly off when removing and installing them, always wear safety glasses when using them.

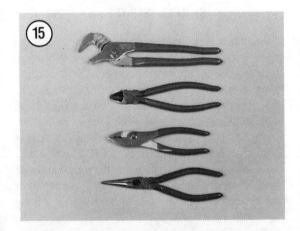

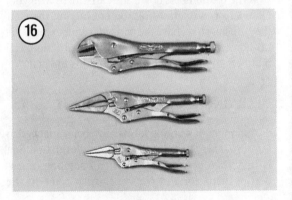

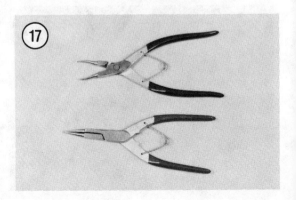

Box, Open-end and Combination Wrenches

Box-end, open-end and combination wrenches are available in sets or separately in a variety of sizes. On open and box end wrenches, the number stamped near the end refers to the distance between 2 parallel flats on the hex head bolt or nut. On combination wrenches, the number is stamped near the center.

Box-end wrenches require clear overhead access to the fastener but can work well in situations where the fastener head is close to another part. They grip on all six edges of a fastener for a very secure grip. They are available in either 6-point or 12-point. The 6-point gives superior holding power and durability but requires a greater swinging radius. The 12-point works better in situations where the swinging radius is limited.

Open-end wrenches are speedy and work best in areas with limited overhead access. Their wide flat

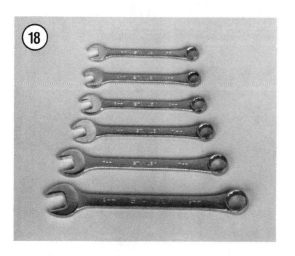

jaws make them unstable for situations where the bolt or nut is sunken in a well or close to the edge of a casting. These wrenches grip only two flats of a fastener so if either the fastener head or the wrench jaws are worn, the wrench may slip off.

Combination wrenches (**Figure 18**) have open-end on one side and box-end on the other with both ends being the same size. Professional mechanics favor these wrenches because of their versatility.

Adjustable Wrenches

An adjustable wrench (sometimes called crescent wrench) can be adjusted to fit nearly any nut or bolt head which has clear access around its entire perimeter. Adjustable wrenches (**Figure 19**) are best used as a backup wrench to keep a large nut or bolt from turning while the other end is being loosened or tightened with a proper wrench.

Adjustable wrenches have only two gripping surfaces which make them more subject to slipping off the fastener and damaging the part and possibly injuring your hand. The fact that one jaw is adjustable only aggravates this shortcoming.

These wrenches are directional. The solid jaw must be the one transmitting the force. If you use the adjustable jaw to transmit the force, it will loosen and possibly slip off.

Adjustable wrenches come in all sizes but one in the 6 to 8 in. and one in the 12 to 14 in. range is recommended.

Socket Wrenches

This type is undoubtedly the fastest, safest and most convenient to use. Sockets which attach to a ratchet handle (**Figure 20**) are available with 6-point or 12-point openings and 1/4, 3/8, 1/2 and 3/4 in. drives. The drive size indicates the size of the square hole which mates with the ratchet handle.

Allen Wrenches

Allen wrenches are available in sets or separately in a variety of sizes. These sets come in U.S. standard and metric size, so be sure to buy a metric set. Allen bolts are sometimes called socket bolts. Sometimes the bolts are difficult to reach and it is suggested that a variety of Allen wrenches to purchase like the

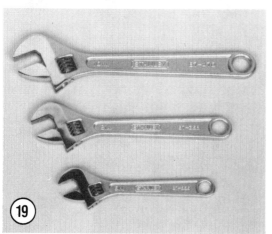

socket driven, T-handle and extension type that are shown in **Figure 21**.

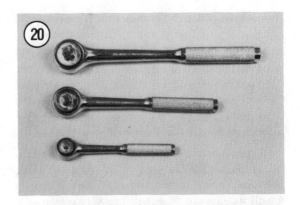

Torque Wrench

A torque wrench is used with a socket to measure how tightly a nut or bolt is installed. They come in a wide price range and with either 1/4, 3/8 or 1/2 in. square drive (**Figure 22**). The drive size indicates the size of the square drive which mates with the socket.

Impact Driver

This tool might have been designed with the motorcycle rider in mind. This tool makes removal of fasteners easy and eliminates damage to bolts and screw slots. Impact drivers (**Figure 23**) and interchangeable bits are available at most large hardware, motorcycle or auto parts stores. Do not buy a cheap one as it will not work as well and require more force than a moderately priced one. Sockets can also be used with a hand impact driver; however, make sure that the socket is designed for use with an impact driver or air tool. Do not use regular hand sockets, as they may shatter during use.

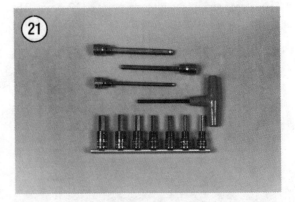

Hammers

The correct hammer is necessary for certain repairs. A hammer with a face (or head) of rubber or plastic or a soft-faced type filled with lead or steel shot is sometimes necessary in engine teardowns. Never use a metal-faced hammer on engine or suspension parts, as severe damage will result in most cases. You can produce the required force with a soft-faced hammer. The shock of a metal-faced hammer, however, is required for using a hand impact driver.

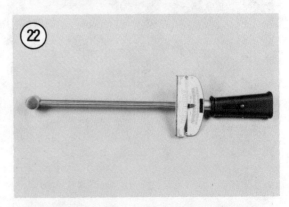

Support Jacks

The correct type of support jack is necessary for many routine service or major component replacement procedures on the bike. When it is necessary to raise either the front or rear end of the vehicle, the K & L MC450 Center Stand available through Suzuki dealerships is suitable for most service procedures on this type of bike. It is adjustable and is very stable for use with the frame configuration of this vehicle.

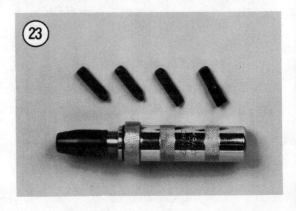

A standard floor jack may also be used for some applications. To protect the engine and frame surfaces, place a piece of wood between the jack pad and the component being supported.

PRECISION MEASURING TOOLS

Measurement is an important part of engine and suspension service. When performing many of the service procedures in this manual, you will be required to make a number of measurements. These include basic checks such as engine compression

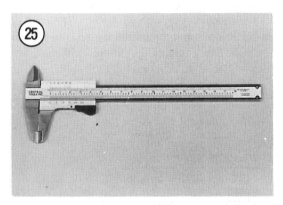

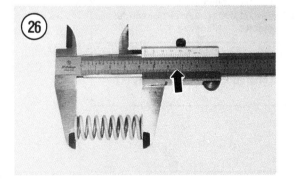

and spark plug gap. As you expand your shop work into engine disassembly and service, measurements will be required to determine the size and condition of the piston and cylinder bore and crankshaft runout and so on. When making these measurements, the degree of accuracy will dictate which tool is required. Precision measuring tools are expensive. If this is your first experience at engine or suspension service, it may be more worthwhile to have the checks and measurements made at a Suzuki dealership, a competent independent motorcycle repair shop or a machine shop. However, as your skills and enthusiasm increase for doing service work, you may want to buy some of these specialized tools. The following is a description of the measuring tools used in this manual.

Feeler Gauge

Feeler gauges come in assorted sets and types (**Figure 24**). The feeler gauge is made of either a piece of a flat or round hardened steel of a specified thickness. Wire gauges are used to measure spark plug gap. Flat gauges are used for other measurements. Feeler gauges are also designed for specialized uses. For example, the end of a gauge is usually small and angled to facilitate checking valve clearances.

Vernier Caliper, Dial Caliper and Digital Electronic Caliper

These tools read inside, outside and depth measurements. The vernier caliper is shown in **Figure 25**. Although this type of tool is not as precise as a micrometer, they allow reasonably accurate measurements, typically to within 0.025 mm (0.001 in.). Common uses of a vernier caliper are measuring the length of the clutch springs, the thickness of clutch plates, shims and thrust washers, brake pad or lining thickness or the depth of a bearing bore. The jaws of the caliper must be clean and free of burrs to obtain an accurate measurement. There are several types of vernier calipers available. The standard vernier caliper has a highly accurate graduated scale on the handle (**Figure 26**) in which the measurements must be calculated. The dial indicator caliper is equipped with a small dial and needle that indicates the measurement reading. The digital electronic type uses an LCD display to show the measurement reading.

Some calipers must be zeroed in prior to making a measurement to ensure an accurate measurement. Refer to the manufacturer's instructions for this procedure.

Outside Micrometers

An outside micrometer is a precision tool used to measure parts using the decimal divisions of the inch or meter accurately (**Figure 27**). While there are many types and styles of micrometers, this section will describe steps on how to use the outside micrometer. The outside micrometer is the most common type of micrometer used when servicing a motorcycle. It is useful in accurately measuring the outside diameter, length and thickness of parts. These include pistons, piston pins, crankshaft, piston rings, transmission shafts and various shims. The outside micrometer is also used to measure the dimension taken by a small hole gauge or a telescoping gauge described later in this section.

Other types of micrometers include the depth micrometer and screw thread micrometer. **Figure 28** illustrates the various parts of the outside micrometer with its part names and markings identified.

Micrometer Range

A micrometer's size indicates the minimum and maximum size of a part that it can measure. The usual sizes are: 0-1 in.(0-25 mm), 1-2 in.(25-50 mm), 2-3 in. (50-75 mm) and 3-4 (75-100 mm). These micrometers use fixed anvils.

Some micrometers use the same frame with interchangeable anvils of different lengths. This allows the installation of the correct length anvil for a particular job. For example, a 0-4 in. interchangeable micrometer is equipped with four different length anvils. While purchasing one or two micrometers to cover a range from 0-4 in, or 0-6 inches is less expensive, its overall frame size makes it less convenient to use.

How To Read a Micrometer

When reading a micrometer, numbers are taken from different scales and then added together. The following sections describe how to read the standard inch micrometer, the vernier inch micrometer, the standard metric micrometer and the metric vernier micrometer.

Standard inch micrometer

The standard inch micrometer is accurate up to one-thousandth of an inch (0.001 in.). The heart of the micrometer is its spindle screw with 40 threads per inch. Every turn of the thimble will move the spindle 1/40 of an inch or 0.025 inch.

DECIMAL PLACE VALUES*

0.1	Indicates 1/10 (one tenth of an inch or millimeter)
0.01	Indicates 1/100 (one one-hundredth of an inch or millimeter)
0.001	Indicates 1/1,000 (one one-thousandth of an inch or millimeter)

* This chart represents the values of figures placed to the right of the decimal point. Use it when reading decimals from one-tenth to one one-thousandth of an inch or millimeter. It is not a conversion chart (for example: 0.001 in. is not equal to 0.001 mm).

Before you learn how to read a micrometer, study the markings and part names in **Figure 28**. Turn the micrometers thimble until its zero mark aligns with the zero mark on the sleeve line. Now turn the thimble counterclockwise and align the next thimble mark with the sleeve line. The micrometer now reads 0.001 in. (one one-thousand) of an inch. Thus, each thimble mark is equal to 0.001 in. Every fifth thimble mark is numbered to help with reading: 0, 5, 15 and 20.

Reset the micrometer so that the thimble and sleeve line zero marks align. Then turn the thimble counterclockwise one complete revolution and align the thimble zero mark with the first line in the sleeve line. The micrometer now reads 0.025 in. (twenty-five thousands) of an inch. Thus each sleeve line represents 0.025 inch.

Now turn the thimble counterclockwise while counting the sleeve line marks. Every fourth mark on the sleeve line is marked with a number ranging from 1 through 9. Manufacturer's usually mark the last mark on the sleeve with a 0. This indicates that you have reached the end of the micrometers measuring range. Each sleeve number represents 0.100 in. For example, the number 1 represents 0.100 in. and the number 9 represents 0.900 inch.

When reading a standard micrometer, you take the following 3 measurements described and add them together. The sum of the 3 readings will give you the measurement in a thousandth of an inch (0.001 in.).

To read a micrometer, perform the following steps and refer to the example in **Figure 29**.

1. Read the sleeve line to find the largest number visible—each sleeve number mark equals 0.100 inch.

2. Count the number of sleeve marks visible between the numbered sleeve mark and the thimble edge—each sleeve mark equals 0.025 inch. If there are no visible sleeve marks, continue to Step 3.

3. Read the thimble mark that lines up with the sleeve line—each thimble mark equals 0.001 inch.

NOTE
If a thimble mark does not line up exactly with the sleeve line but falls between 2 lines, estimate the fraction of decimal amount between the lines.

4. Adding the micrometer readings in Steps 1, 2 and 3 gives the actual measurement.

Vernier inch micrometer

A vernier micrometer can accurately measure in ten-thousandths of an inch (0.0001 in.). While it has the same markings as the standard inch micrometer, a vernier scale scribed on the sleeve (**Figure 30**)

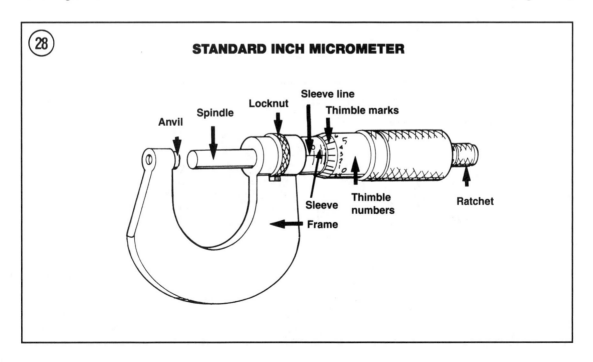

(28) **STANDARD INCH MICROMETER**

Anvil
Spindle
Locknut
Sleeve line
Thimble marks
Sleeve
Thimble numbers
Ratchet
Frame

makes it unique. The vernier scale consists of eleven equally spaced lines marked 0-9 with a 0 on each end. These lines run parallel on the top of the sleeve where each line is equal to 0.0001 inch. Thus, the vernier scale divides a thousandth of an inch (0.001 in.) into ten-thousandths of an inch (0.0001 in.)

To read the vernier micrometer, perform the following steps and refer to the example in **Figure 31**.

1. Read the micrometer in the same way as on the standard inch micrometer. This is the initial reading.

2. If a thimble mark lines up exactly with the sleeve line, reading the vernier scale is not necessary. If a thimble mark does not line exactly with the sleeve line, read the vernier scale in Step 3.

3. Read the vernier scale to find which vernier mark lines up with the one thimble mark. The number of

that vernier mark is the number of ten-thousandths of an inch to add to the initial reading taken in Step 1.

Metric micrometer

The metric micrometer is very similar to the standard inch micrometer. The differences are the graduations on the thimble and sleeve as shown in **Figure 32**.

The standard metric micrometer is accurate measuring to one one-hundredth of a millimeter (0.01 mm). On the metric micrometer, the spindle screw is ground with a thread pitch of one-half millimeter (0.5 mm). Thus, every turn of the thimble will move the spindle 0.5 mm.

The sleeve line is graduated in millimeters and half millimeters. The marks on the upper side of the

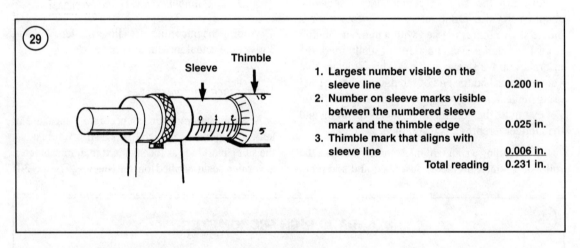

1. Largest number visible on the sleeve line		0.200 in
2. Number on sleeve marks visible between the numbered sleeve mark and the thimble edge		0.025 in.
3. Thimble mark that aligns with sleeve line		<u>0.006 in.</u>
	Total reading	0.231 in.

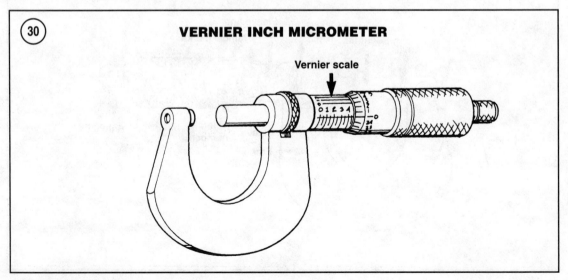

VERNIER INCH MICROMETER

Vernier scale

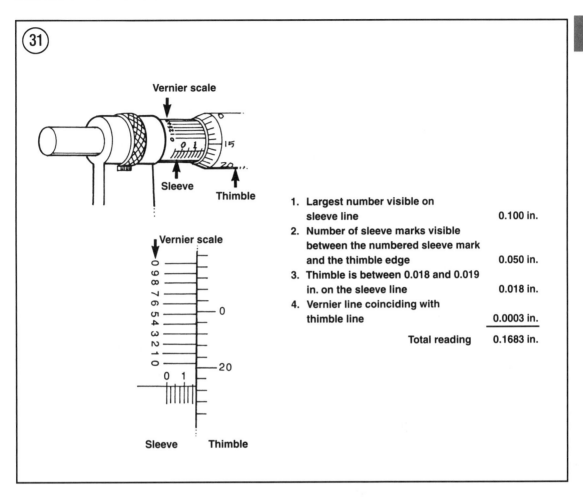

1. Largest number visible on
   sleeve line   0.100 in.
2. Number of sleeve marks visible
   between the numbered sleeve mark
   and the thimble edge   0.050 in.
3. Thimble is between 0.018 and 0.019
   in. on the sleeve line   0.018 in.
4. Vernier line coinciding with
   thimble line   0.0003 in.

                              Total reading 0.1683 in.

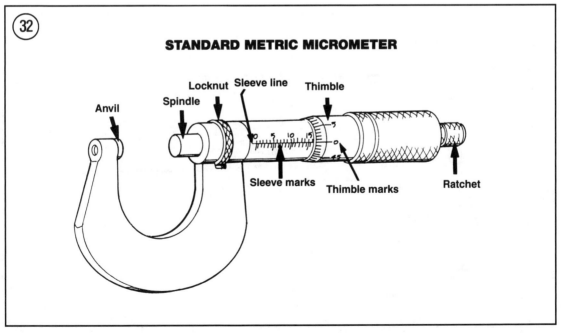

STANDARD METRIC MICROMETER

sleeve line are equal to 1.00 mm . Every fifth mark above the sleeve line is marked with a number. The actual numbers will depend on the size of the micrometer. For example, on a 0-25 mm micrometer, the sleeve marks are numbered 0, 5, 10, 15, 20 and 25. On a 25-50 mm micrometer, the sleeve marks are numbered 25, 30, 35, 40, 45 and 50. This numbering sequence continues with larger micrometers (50-75 and 75-100). Each mark on the lower side of the sleeve line is equal to 0.5 mm.

The thimble scale is divided into fifty graduations where one graduation is equal to 0.01 mm. Every fifth graduation is numbered to help with reading from 0-45. The thimble edge is used to indicate which sleeve markings to read.

To read the metric micrometer add the number of millimeters and half-millimeters on the sleeve line to the number of one one-hundredth millimeters on the thimble. To do so, perform the following steps and refer to the example in **Figure 33**:

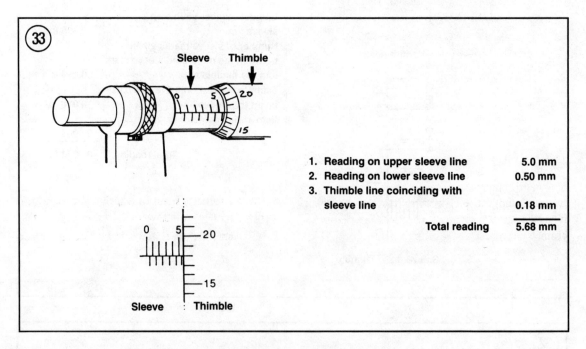

1. Reading on upper sleeve line   5.0 mm
2. Reading on lower sleeve line   0.50 mm
3. Thimble line coinciding with
   sleeve line   0.18 mm

                Total reading   5.68 mm

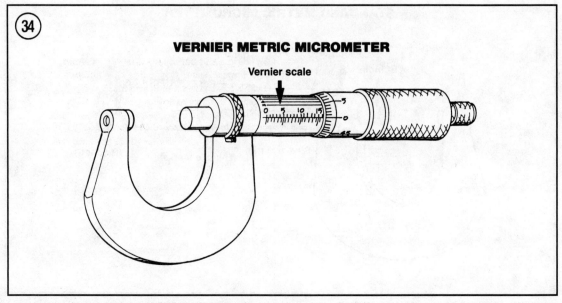

VERNIER METRIC MICROMETER

1. Take the first reading by counting the number of marks visible on the upper sleeve line. Record the reading.

2. Look below the sleeve line to see if a lower mark is visible directly past the upper line mark. If so, add 0.50 to the first reading.

3. Now read the thimble mark that aligns with the sleeve line. Record this reading.

NOTE
If a thimble mark does not align exactly with the sleeve line but falls between the 2 lines, estimate the decimal amount between the lines. For an accurate reading, you must use a metric vernier micrometer.

4. Adding the micrometer readings in Steps 1, 2 and 3 gives the actual measurement.

Metric vernier micrometer

A metric micrometer can accurately measure to two thousandths of a millimeter (0.002 mm). While it has the same markings as the standard metric micrometer, a vernier scale scribed on the sleeve (**Figure 34**) makes it unique. The vernier scale consists of five equally spaced lines 0, 2, 4, 6 and 8. These lines run parallel on the top of the sleeve where each line is equal to 0.002 mm.

To read the metric vernier micrometer, perform the following steps and refer to the example in **Figure 35**:

1. Read the metric vernier micrometer the same way as with the metric standard micrometer. This is the initial reading.

2. If a thimble mark aligns exactly with the sleeve line, reading the vernier scale is not necessary. If a thimble line does not align exactly with the sleeve line, read the vernier scale in Step 3.

3. Read the vernier scale to find which mark aligns with one thimble mark. The number of the vernier mark is the number of thousands of a millimeter to add to the initial reading taken in Step 1.

Micrometer Accuracy Check

The micrometer must be checked frequently to assure accuracy as follows:

1. Make sure the anvil and spindle faces are clean and dry.

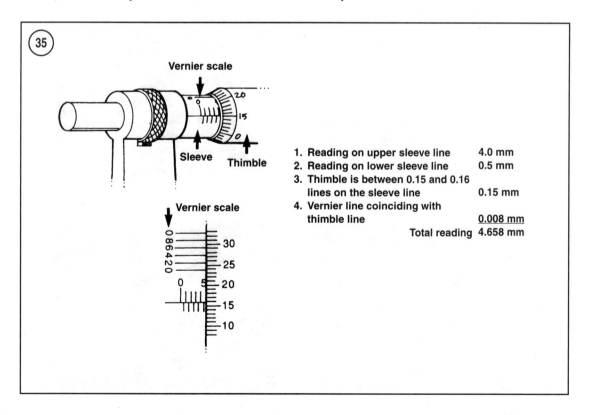

(35)

Vernier scale

Sleeve   Thimble

Vernier scale

1. Reading on upper sleeve line	4.0 mm
2. Reading on lower sleeve line	0.5 mm
3. Thimble is between 0.15 and 0.16 lines on the sleeve line	0.15 mm
4. Vernier line coinciding with thimble line	0.008 mm
	Total reading 4.658 mm

2. To check a 0-1 in. (0-25 mm) micrometer, perform the following:

    a. Turn the thimble until the spindle contacts the anvil. If the micrometer has a ratchet stop, use it to ensure that the proper amount of pressure is applied against the contact surfaces.

    b. Read the micrometer. If the adjustment is correct, the 0 mark on the thimble will be aligned exactly with the 0 mark on the sleeve line. If the 0 marks do not align, the micrometer is out of adjustment.

    c. To adjust the micrometer, follow the manufacturer's instruction provided with the micrometer.

3. To check the accuracy of a micrometer above the 1 inch (25 mm) size, perform the following:

    a. Manufacturers usually supply a standard gauge with their micrometers. A standard is a steel block, disc or rod that is ground to an exact size to check the accuracy of the micrometer. For example, a 1-2 inch micrometer is equipped with a 1 inch standard gauge. A 25-50 mm micrometer is equipped with a 25 mm standard gauge.

    b. Place the standard gauge between the micrometer's spindle and anvil and measure the outside diameter or length in the same manner as you would measure a component from a vehicle. Read the micrometer. If the adjustment is correct, the 0 mark on the thimble will be aligned exactly with the sleeve line. If the 0 marks do not align, the micrometer is out of alignment.

    c. To adjust the micrometer, follow the manufacturer's instruction provided with the micrometer.

Proper Care of a Micrometer

Because the micrometer is a precision instrument, it must be used correctly and with great care. When using and storing a micrometer, refer to the following:

1. Store a micrometer in its box or in a protected place where dust, oil and other debris cannot come in contact with them. Do not store micrometers in a drawer with other tools nor hang them on a tool board.

2. When storing a 0-1 in. (0-25 mm) micrometer, the spindle and anvil must not contact each other. If they do, this may cause rust to form on the contact ends or spindle will be damaged from temperature changes.

3. Do not clean a micrometer with compressed air. Dirt forced under pressure into the tool can cause premature damage.

4. Occasionally lubricate the micrometer with light weight oil to prevent rust and corrosion.

5. Before using a micrometer, check its accuracy. Refer to *Micrometer Accuracy Check* previously described in this section.

Cylinder Bore Gauge

The cylinder bore gauge is a very specialized precision tool. The gauge set shown in **Figure 36** is comprised of a dial indicator, handle and a number of different length adapters to adapt the gauge to different bore sizes. The bore gauge is used to make cylinder bore measurements such as bore size, taper and out-of-round. Depending on the bore gauge, it can sometimes be used to measure brake caliper and master cylinder bore sizes. In some cases, an outside micrometer must be used to calibrate the bore gauge to a specific bore size.

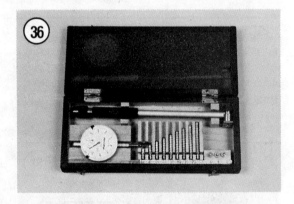

Select the correct length adapter (A, **Figure 37**) for the size of the bore to be measured. Zero the bore gauge according to its manufacturer's instructions, insert the bore gauge into the cylinder, carefully move it around in the bore to make sure it is centered and that the gauge foot (B, **Figure 37**) is sitting correctly on the bore surface. This is necessary in order to obtain a correct reading. Refer to the manufacturer's instructions for reading the actual measurement obtained.

Small Hole Gauges

A set of small hole gauges (**Figure 38**), allows you to measure a hole, groove or slot. The small hole gauge is used for the smallest measurements and the telescoping gauges are used for slightly larger meas-

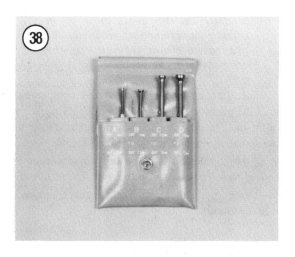

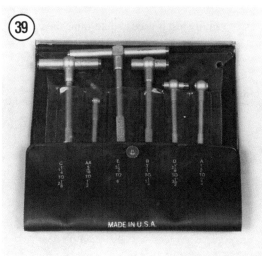

urements. A small hole gauge is required to measure rocker arm bore and brake master cylinder bore diameters. The telescoping gauge does not have a scale for direct readings. An outside micrometer must be used together with the telescoping gauge to determine the bore dimension.

Carefully insert the small hole gauge into the bore of the component to be measured. Tighten the knurled end of the gauge carefully to expand the gauge fingers to the limit within the bore—*do not overtighten* the gauge as there is no built-in release feature. If too tight, the gauge fingers can damage the bore surface. Carefully remove the gauge and measure its outside dimension with a micrometer. See *Outside Micrometer* in this chapter.

Telescoping Gauges

A telescoping gauge (**Figure 39**) is used to measure hole diameters from approximately 8 mm (5/16 in.) to 150 mm (6 in.). For example, they could be used to measure brake caliper bore and cylinder bore diameters. Like the small hole gauge, the telescoping gauge does not have a scale for direct readings. An outside micrometer must be used together with the telescoping gauge to determine the bore dimension.

Select the correct size telescoping gauge for the bore to be measured. Compress the moveable side of the gauge post and carefully install the gauge into the bore of the component to be measured, then release the movable post against the bore. Carefully move the gauge around in the bore to make sure it is centered. Tighten the knurled end of the gauge to hold the movable gauge post in this position. Carefully remove the gauge and measure the outside dimension of the gauge posts with a micrometer. See *Outside Micrometer* in this chapter.

Multimeter or VOM

A VOM (Volt and Ohm Meter) is a valuable tool for all electrical system troubleshooting (**Figure 40**). The voltage application is used to indicate the voltage applied or available to various electrical components. The ohmmeter portion of the meter is used to check for continuity, or lack of continuity, and to measure the resistance of a component. Some tests are easily accomplished using meter with a sweeping needle (analog), but other components must be taken with a digital VOM (DVOM).

In some test procedures, the vehicle's manufacturer will instruct you to use their specific test meter due to the internal design of their meter. They will specify that the resistance reading may differ if another type of test meter is used. Such requirements will be noted throughout the book.

To measure voltage

> *NOTE*
> *Make sure the negative (–) or ground surface you will be using is clean and free of paint and/or grease. If possible, use a non-painted bolt attached directly to the frame.*

1. Make sure the meter battery power source is at full power; if its condition is doubtful, install a new battery(s).
2. Select the meter voltage range to *one scale higher* than the indicated voltage value of the circuit to be tested.
3. Touch the red test probe to the *positive* (+) end and the black test probe to the *negative* (–), or ground, end of the circuit.
4. Refer to the appropriate procedure in the chapter as to what switch(s) must be either turned ON or OFF within the circuit being tested.
5. With the switch(s) in the correct position, read the position of the needle on the VOLTS or VOLTAGE scale of the meter face, or the digital readout, and refer to the specified voltage listed in the test procedure. Refer to the manufacturer's instruction for any special conditions relating to the meter that you are using.

To zero an analog ohmmeter

> *NOTE*
> *Every time an analog ohmmeter is used to measure resistance it must be zeroed to obtain a correct measurement. Most digital ohmmeters are not equipped with a zero ohms adjust feature—when turned on they are automatically set at zero (providing the meter's battery is at full power).*

1. Make sure the meters battery power source is at full power, if its condition is doubtful, install a new battery(s).

2. Make sure the test probes are clean and free of corrosion.
3. Touch the two test probes together and observe the meter needle location on the OHMS scale on the meter face. The needle must be on the "0" mark at the end of the scale.
4. If necessary, rotate the Ohms Adjust knob on the meter in either direction until the needle is directly on the 0 mark on the scale. The meter is now ready for use.

To measure resistance

1. Zero the analog meter as previously described.
2. Disconnect the component from the circuit.

> *NOTE*
> *Polarity is not important when measuring the resistance of a component. Either test probe can be placed at either terminal of the component.*

3. Place the test probe at each end of the component, read the position of the needle on the OHMS scale of the meter face, or the digital readout, and refer to the specified resistance in the test procedure.
4. If the component is not within specification, it should be replaced.
5. If the component is within specification, reinstall it in the circuit.

Continuity test

A continuity test is used to determine the integrity of a circuit, wire or component.

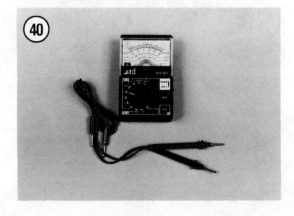

Continuity is indicated by a low resistance reading, usually zero ohms, on the meter. No continuity is indicated by an infinity reading. A broken or open circuit has no continuity, while a complete circuit has continuity. A continuity test is also useful to check components for a short to ground. A shorted component has a complete circuit (continuity) between the component and ground.

NOTE
Every time an analog ohmmeter is used for a continuity check, it must be zeroed to obtain a correct reading.

1. Zero the analog meter as previously described.

NOTE
Polarity is not important when checking the continuity of a component or circuit. Either test probe can be placed at either terminal of the component or circuit.

2. Place the test probe at each end of the component, or circuit and read the position of the needle on the OHMS scale of the meter face, or digital readout.
3. If there is *continuity (low resistance)* the meter will indicate a certain amount of resistance. In this test the resistance value is not important—all you want to know is if the circuit is complete or not.
4. If there is *no continuity (infinite resistance)* the meter needle will not move and will stay at the infinity symbol or the digital readout will indicate infinity.
5. If the component is not within specification, it should be replaced.
6. If the component is within specification, reinstall it in the circuit.

SPECIAL TOOLS

A few special tools may be required for major service. These are shown and described in the appropriate chapters and are available either from a Suzuki dealership or other manufacturers as indicated.

FABRICATING TOOLS

Some of the procedures in this manual require the use of special tools. The resourceful mechanic can, in many cases, think of acceptable substitutes for special tools. This can be as simple as using a few pieces of threaded rod, washers and nuts to remove or install a bearing. If you find that a special tool can be designed and safely made, but requires some type of machine work, contact a local community college or high school that has a machine shop curriculum. Some shop teachers welcome outside work that can be used as practical shop application for advanced students.

MECHANIC'S TIPS

Removing Frozen Nuts and Screws

When fastener rust cannot be removed, several methods may be used to loosen it. First, apply penetrating oil such as Liquid Wrench or WD-40 (available at hardware or auto supply stores). Apply it liberally and let it penetrate for 10-15 minutes. Rap the fastener several times with a small hammer; do not hit it hard enough to cause damage. Reapply the penetrating oil if necessary.

For frozen screws, apply penetrating oil as described, then insert a screwdriver in the slot and rap the top of the screwdriver with a hammer. This loosens the rust so the screw can be removed in the normal way. If the screw head is too chewed up to use this method, grip the head with vise-grip pliers and twist the screw out.

Avoid applying heat unless specifically instructed, as it may melt, warp or remove the temper from parts.

Removing Broken Screws or Bolts

When the head breaks off a screw or bolt, several methods are available for removing the remaining portion. If a large portion of the remainder projects out, try gripping it with vise-grip pliers. If the projecting portion is too small, file it to fit a wrench or cut a slot in it to fit a screwdriver. See **Figure 41**.

If the head breaks off flush, use a screw extractor. To do this, centerpunch the exact center of the remaining portion of the screw or bolt. Drill a small hole in the screw and tap the extractor into the hole. Back the screw out with a wrench on the extractor. See **Figure 42**.

Remedying Stripped Threads

Occasionally, threads are stripped through care-lessness or impact damage. Often the threads can be cleaned up by running a tap (for internal threads on nuts) or die (for external threads on bolts) through the threads. To clean or repair spark plug threads, a spark plug tap can be used.

NOTE
Tap and dies can be bought individually
or in a set.

If an internal thread is damaged, it may be neces-sary to install a Helicoil or some other type of thread

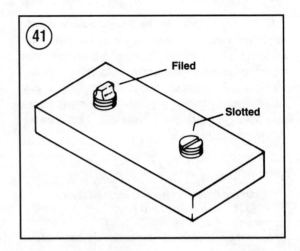

REMOVING BROKEN SCREWS AND BOLTS

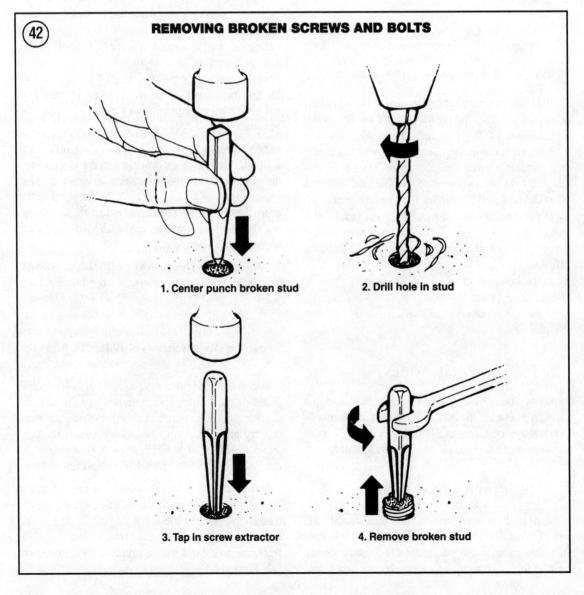

1. Center punch broken stud

2. Drill hole in stud

3. Tap in screw extractor

4. Remove broken stud

insert. Follow the manufacturer's instructions when installing their insert.

If it is necessary to drill and tap a hole, refer to **Table 7** for metric tap drill sizes.

BALL BEARING REPLACEMENT

Ball bearings (**Figure 43**) are used throughout the engine and drive assembly to reduce power loss, heat and noise resulting from friction. Because ball bearings are precision made parts, they must be maintained by proper lubrication and maintenance. When a bearing is found to be damaged, it should be replaced immediately. However, when installing a new bearing, care should be taken to prevent damage to the new bearing. While bearing replacement

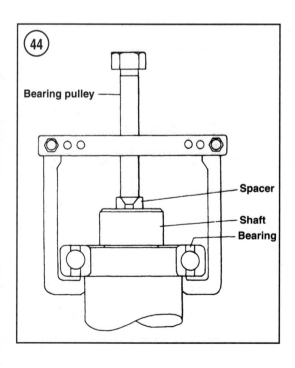

is described in the individual chapters where applicable, the following should be used as a guideline.

NOTE
Unless otherwise specified, install bearings with the manufacturer's mark or number facing outward.

Bearing Removal

While bearings are normally removed only when damaged, there may be times when it is necessary to remove a bearing that is in good condition. However, improper bearing removal will damage the bearing and maybe the shaft or case half. Note the following when removing bearings.

1. When using a puller to remove a bearing from a shaft, take care that shaft is not damaged. Always place a piece of metal between the end of the shaft and the puller screw. In addition, place the puller arms next to the inner bearing race. See **Figure 44.**

2. When using a hammer to remove a bearing from a shaft, do not strike the hammer directly against the shaft. Instead, use a brass or aluminum spacer between the hammer and shaft (**Figure 45**) and make sure to support both bearing races with wood blocks as shown.

3. The most ideal method of bearing removal is with a hydraulic press. However, certain procedures must be followed or damage may occur to the bearing, shaft or bearing housing. Note the following when using a press:

   a. Always support the inner and outer bearing races with a suitable size wood or aluminum spacer (**Figure 46**). If you only support the outer face, pressure applied against the balls and/or the inner race will damage them.

   b. Always make sure the press ram (**Figure 46**) aligns with the center of the shaft. If the ram is not centered, it may damage the bearing and/or shaft.

   c. The moment the shaft is free of the bearing, it will drop to the floor. Secure or hold the shaft to prevent it from falling.

Bearing Installation

1. When installing a bearing in a housing, pressure must be applied to the *outer* bearing race (**Figure**

47). When installing a bearing on a shaft, pressure must be applied to the *inner* bearing race (**Figure 48**).

2. When installing a bearing as described in Step 1, some type of driver will be required. Never strike the bearing directly with a hammer or the bearing will be damaged. When installing a bearing, a piece of pipe or a socket with a diameter that matches the bearing race is required. **Figure 49** shows the correct way to use a driver and hammer when installing a bearing.

3. Step 1 describes how to install a bearing in a case half or over a shaft. However, when installing a bearing over a shaft and into a housing at the same time, a snug fit will be required for both outer and inner bearing races. In this situation, a spacer must be installed underneath the driver tool so that pressure is applied evenly across both races. See **Figure 50**. If the outer race is not supported as shown in **Figure 50**, the balls will push against the outer bearing track and damage it.

Shrink Fit

1. Installing a bearing over a shaft: When a tight fit is required, the bearing inside diameter will be smaller than the shaft. In this case, driving the bearing on the shaft using normal methods may cause bearing damage. Instead, the bearing should be heated before installation. Note the following:

  a. Secure the shaft so that it is ready for bearing installation.

  b. Clean all residue from the bearing surface of the shaft. Remove burrs with a file or sandpaper.

  c. Fill a suitable pot or beaker with clean mineral oil. Place a thermometer (rated higher than 120° C [248° F]) in the oil. Support the thermometer so that it does not rest on the bottom or side of the pot.

  d. Remove the bearing from its wrapper and secure it with a piece of heavy wire bent to hold it in the pot. Hang the bearing in the pot so that it does not touch the bottom or sides of the pot.

  e. Turn the heat on and monitor the thermometer. When the oil temperature rises to approximately 120° C (248° F), remove the bearing from the pot and quickly install it. If necessary, place a socket on the inner bearing race and

tap the bearing into place. As the bearing chills, it will tighten on the shaft so you must work quickly when installing it. Make sure the bearing is installed all the way.

2. Installing a bearing in a housing: Bearings are generally installed in a housing with a slight inter-

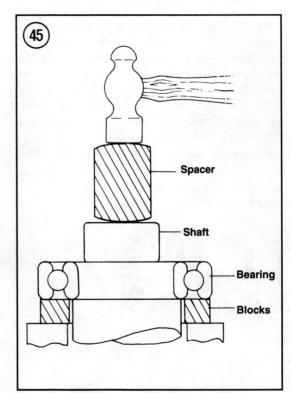

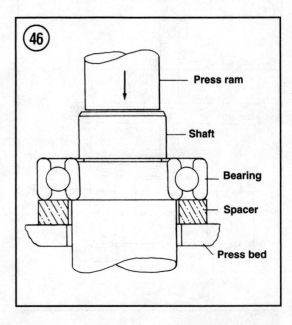

ference fit. Driving the bearing into the housing using normal methods may damage the housing or cause bearing damage. Instead, the housing should be heated before the bearing is installed. Note the following:

CAUTION
Before heating the crankcases in this procedure to remove the bearings, wash the cases thoroughly with detergent and water. Rinse and rewash the cases as required to remove all traces of oil and other chemical deposits.

a. The housing must be heated to a temperature of about 212° F (100° C) in an oven or on a hot plate. An easy way to check that it is at the proper temperature is to drop tiny drops of water on the case; if they sizzle and evaporate

immediately, the temperature is correct. Heat only one housing at a time.

CAUTION
Do not heat the housing with a torch (propane or acetylene)—never bring a flame into contact with the bearing or housing. The direct heat will destroy the case hardening of the bearing and is likely to warp the housing.

b. Remove the housing from the oven or hot plate with a kitchen pot holder, heavy gloves, or heavy shop cloth—it is hot.

NOTE
A suitable size socket and extension works well for removing and installing bearings.

c. Hold the housing with the bearing side down and tap the bearing out. Repeat for all bearings in the housing.

d. Prior to heating the bearing housing, place the new bearing in a freezer, if possible. Chilling a bearing will slightly reduce its outside diameter while the heated bearing housing as-

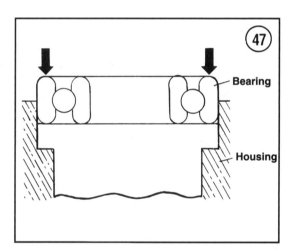

47

Bearing

Housing

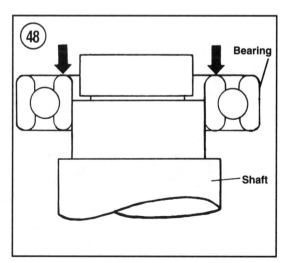

48

Bearing

Shaft

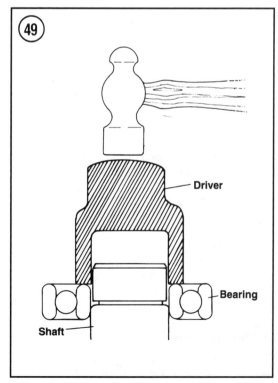

49

Driver

Bearing

Shaft

sembly is slightly larger due to heat expansion. This will make bearing installation much easier.

NOTE
Always install bearings with the manufacturer's mark or number facing outward.

e. While the housing is still hot, install the new bearing(s) into the housing. Install the bearings by hand, if possible. If necessary, lightly tap the bearing(s) into the housing with a socket placed on the outer bearing race. Do not install new bearings by driving on the inner bearing race. Install the bearing(s) until it seats completely.

SEALS

Seals (**Figure 51**) are used to contain oil, water, grease or combustion gasses in a housing or shaft. Improper removal of a seal can damage the housing or shaft. Improper installation of the seal can damage the seal. Note the following:

a. Prying is generally the easiest and most effective method of removing a seal from a housing. However, always place a rag underneath the pry tool to prevent damage to the housing.
b. Waterproof grease should be packed in the seal lips before the seal is installed.
c. Seals should always be installed so that the manufacturer's numbers or marks face out.
d. Seals should be installed with a driver placed on the outside of the seal as shown in **Figure 52**. Make sure the seal is driven squarely into the housing. Never install a seal by hitting against the top of the seal with a hammer.

RIDING SAFETY

General Tips

1. Read your owner's manual regarding safety information and instructions and know your machine.
2. Check the throttle and brake controls before starting the engine.
3. Know how to make an emergency stop.
4. Never add fuel while anyone is smoking in the area or when the engine is running.

5. Never wear loose scarves, belts or boot laces that could catch on moving parts.

6. Always wear eye protection, head protection and protective clothing to protect your entire body.

7. Riding in the winter months requires a good set of clothes to keep your body dry and warm, otherwise your entire trip may be miserable. Even mild temperatures can be very uncomfortable and dangerous when combined with a strong wind or traveling at high speed. See **Table 8** for windchill factors. Always dress according to what the windchill factor is, not the ambient temperature.

8. Never allow anyone to operate the bike without proper instruction. This is for their bodily protection and to keep your machine from damage or destruction.

9. Use the buddy system for long trips, just in case you have a problem or run out of fuel.

10. Never attempt to repair your machine with the engine running except when necessary for certain tune-up procedures.

11. Check all of the machine components and hardware frequently, especially the wheels and the steering.

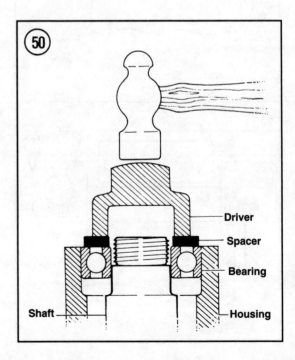

50

Driver

Spacer

Bearing

Shaft

Housing

STORAGE

Several months of inactivity can cause serious problems and general deterioration of your bike. This is especially important in areas with cold winters.

Selecting a Storage Area

Most owners store their motorcycle in their home garage. If you do not have a garage, there are other facilities for rent or lease in most areas. When selecting an area, consider the following points.

1. The storage area must be dry. A heated area is not necessary, but it should be insulated to minimize extreme temperature variations.
2. Avoid buildings with large window areas. If this is not possible, mask the window to keep direct sunlight off the bike.

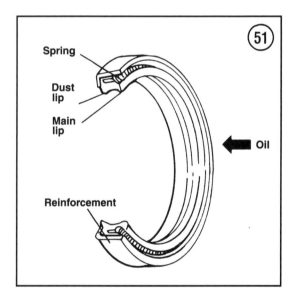

3. Avoid buildings in industrial areas where factories are liable to emit corrosive fumes. Also avoid buildings near large bodies of salt water.
4. Select an area where there is minimum risk of fire, theft or vandalism. Check with your insurance agent to make sure that your insurance covers the motorcycle where it is stored.

Preparing Motorcycle for Storage

Careful preparation will minimize deterioration and make it easier to restore the bike to service later. Use the following procedure.

1. Wash the bike as described in this chapter.
2. Run the engine until it reaches operating temperature. Drain the engine oil regardless of the riding time since the last change. Fill the engine with the recommended type and quantity of fresh oil.
3. Drain all the gasoline from the fuel tank, fuel line and carburetors. Run the engine at idle speed to use up all fuel in the carburetors.
4. Remove the fuel tank, see Chapter Eight, and pour about 250 ml (1/2 pint) of engine oil into the fuel tank. Move the tank around to distribute the oil all over the interior surfaces of the tank, then pour out the excess oil. Reinstall the tank and close the filler cap.

NOTE:
Ground the spark plugs against the cylinder head when turning the engine over in Step 5.

5. Remove the spark plugs and add a small quantity of engine oil into each cylinder. Place a rag over the cylinder head and slowly roll the engine over a few times to distribute the oil, then reinstall the spark plugs.
6. Check the tire pressures, reduce the normal inflation pressure by 20%, and move the machine to the storage area.
7. Place the bike securely on a stand, or wooden blocks, so both wheels are off the ground. If not possible, place a piece of wood (plywood) under the tires to keep moisture from the tire rubber.

After Storage

1. Before returning the motorcycle to service, thoroughly check all fasteners, suspension components

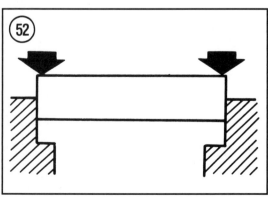

and brake components. Move the front suspension through several complete strokes to make sure the fork seals are not leaking.

2. Pour out any remaining engine oil from the fuel tank, then fill the fuel tank with a fresh tank of gasoline.

3. Check all controls and cables. Replace any cables that are frayed or kinked.

4. Make sure both brakes, the clutch and the throttle operate smoothly. Adjust the controls if necessary.

5. Ensure that all the wiring is correctly routed and all connections are tight and corrosion-free. Check that the STOP button will stop the engine. Check horn operation with the horn button. Make sure none of the wires are positioned against the exhaust pipe.

NOTE:
Ground the spark plugs against the cylinder head when turning the engine over in Step 6.

6. Before starting the engine, remove the spark plugs and turn the engine over a few times to blow out the excess storage oil. Place a rag over the cylinder head to keep the oil off the engine. Install new spark plugs and connect the spark plug leads.

Table 1 MODEL YEAR AND FRAME SERIAL NUMBER

Year and Model	U.S. Models Frame serial numbers
1987 VS1400GLPH/FH	JS1VX51L-H2100001-on
1988 VS1400GLPJ*	JS1VX51L-J2100001-on
1990 VS1400GLPL	JS1VX51L-L2100001-on
1991 VS1400GLPM	JS1VX51L-M2100001-on
1992 VS1400GLPN	JS1VX51L-N2100001-on
1993 VS1400GLPP	JS1VX51L-P2100001-on
1994 VS1400GLPR	JS1VX51L-R2100001-on
1995 VS1400GLPS	JS1VX51L-S2100001-on
1996 VS1400GLPT	JS1VX51L-T2100001-on
1997 VS1400GKPV	JS1VX51L-V2100001-on
1998 VS1400GLPW	JS1VX51L-W2100001-on
1999 VS1400GLPX	NA
2000 VS1400GLPY	NA
2001 VS1400GLPK1	NA
2002 VS1400GLPK2	NA

Year and Model	Non-U.S. Models Frame serial numbers
1987 VS1400GLH	VX51L-100001-on
1988 VS1400GLJ	VX51L-103295-on
1989 VS1400GLK	VX51L-104562-on
1990 VS1400GLL	
Germany	VX51LD-105130-on
All others	VX51L-105125-on
1991 VS1400GLM	
Germany	VX51LD-105902-on
All others	VX51L-105905-on
1992 VS1400GLM	
Germany	VX51LD-108040-on
All others	VX51L-107947-on
1993 VS1400GLP	
Germany	VX51LD-110758-on
Australia	JS1VX51L-P2100001-on
All others	VX51L-110557-on
1994 VS1400GLR	
Australia	JS1VX51L-R2100001-on
All others	VX51L-115246-on
1995 VS1400GLS	
Italy	JS1VX51L-000500001-on
Australia	JS1VX51L-52100001-on
All others	VX51L-121526-on
1996 VS1400GLT	
Italy	JS1VX51L-000500831-on
Australia	JS1VX51L-000500807-on
All others	VX51L-125294-on
1997 VS1400GLV	
Australia, Italy	JS1VX51L-000501373-on
All others	VX51L-129697-on
1998-on VS1400GLW	NA

*The VS1400GL was not available in the U.S. In 1989.

Table 2 VEHICLE GENERAL DIMENSIONS AND WEIGHT

Item and dimension	mm	in.
Overall length	2,330	91.7
Overall width		
GLF models	710	28.0
GLP models	770	30.3
Overall height		
GLF models	1,135	44.7
GLP models	1,220	48.0
Wheelbase	1,620	63.8
Ground clearance	145	5.7
Item and weight	**kg**	**lbs.**
Dry weight		
U.S. (49-state), U.K.		
GLF models	242	533
GLP models	243	535
California		
GLF models	242	533
GLP models	244	537

Table 3 DECIMAL AND METRIC EQUIVALENTS

Fractions	Decimal in.	Metric mm	Fractions	Decimal in.	Metric mm
1/64	0.015625	0.39688	33/64	0.515625	13.09687
1/32	0.03125	0.79375	17/32	0.53125	13.49375
3/64	0.046875	1.19062	35/64	0.546875	13.89062
1/16	0.0625	1.58750	9/16	0.5625	14.28750
5/64	0.078125	1.98437	37/64	0.578125	14.68437
3/32	0.09375	2.38125	19/32	0.59375	15.08125
7/64	0.109375	2.77812	39/64	0.609375	15.47812
1/8	0.125	3.1750	5/8	0.625	15.87500
9/64	0.140625	3.57187	41/64	0.640625	16.27187
5/32	0.15625	3.96875	21/32	0.65625	16.66875
11/64	0.171875	4.36562	43/64	0.671875	17.06562
3/16	0.1875	4.76250	11/16	0.6875	17.46250
13/64	0.203125	5.15937	45/64	0.703125	17.85937
7/32	0.21875	5.55625	23/32	0.71875	18.25625
15/64	0.234375	5.95312	47/64	0.734375	18.65312
1/4	0.250	6.35000	3/4	0.750	19.05000
17/64	0.265625	6.74687	49/64	0.765625	19.44687
9/32	0.28125	7.14375	25/32	0.78125	19.84375
19/64	0.296875	7.54062	51/64	0.796875	20.24062
5/16	0.3125	7.93750	13/16	0.8125	20.63750
21/64	0.328125	8.33437	53/64	0.828125	21.03437
11/32	0.34375	8.73125	27/32	0.84375	21.43125
23/64	0.359375	9.12812	55/64	0.859375	22.82812
3/8	0.375	9.52500	7/8	0.875	22.22500
25/64	0.390625	9.92187	57/64	0.890625	22.62187
13/32	0.40625	10.31875	29/32	0.90625	23.01875
27/64	0.421875	10.71562	59/64	0.921875	23.41562
7/16	0.4375	11.11250	15/16	0.9375	23.81250
29/64	0.453125	11.50937	61/64	0.953125	24.20937
15/32	0.46875	11.90625	31/32	0.96875	24.60625
31/64	0.484375	12.30312	63/64	0.984375	25.00312
1/2	0.500	12.70000	1	1.00	25.40000

Table 4 GENERAL TORQUE SPECIFICATIONS

Fastener size or type	N•m	in.-lb.	ft.-lb.
5 mm screw	4	35	–
5 mm bolt and nut	5	44	–
6 mm screw	9	80	–
6 mm bolt and nut	10	88	–
6 mm flange bolt (8 mm head, small flange)	9	80	–
6 mm flange bolt (10 mm head) and nut	12	106	–
8 mm bolt and nut	22	–	16
8 mm flange bolt and nut	27	–	20
10 mm bolt and nut	35	–	25
10 mm flange bolt and nut	40	–	29
12 mm bolt and nut	55	–	40

Table 5 CONVERSION TABLES

Multiply:	By:	To get the equivalent of:
Length		
Inches	25.4	Millimeter
Inches	2.54	Centimeter
Miles	1.609	Kilometer
Feet	0.3048	Meter
Millimeter	0.03937	Inches
Centimeter	0.3937	Inches
Kilometer	0.6214	Mile
Meter	3.281	Feet
Fluid volume		
U.S. quarts	0.9463	Liters
U.S. gallons	3.785	Liters
U.S. ounces	29.573529	Milliliters
Imperial gallons	4.54609	Liters
Imperial quarts	1.1365	Liters
Liters	0.2641721	U.S. gallons
Liters	1.0566882	U.S. quarts
Liters	33.814023	U.S. ounces
Liters	0.22	Imperial gallons
Liters	0.8799	Imperial quarts
Milliliters	0.033814	U.S. ounces
Milliliters	1.0	Cubic centimeters
Milliliters	0.001	Liters
Torque		
Foot-pounds	1.3558	Newton-meters
Foot-pounds	0.138255	Meters-kilograms
Inch-pounds	0.11299	Newton-meters
Newton-meters	0.7375622	Foot-pounds
Newton-meters	8.8507	Inch-pounds
Meters-kilograms	7.2330139	Foot-pounds
Volume		
Cubic inches	16.387064	Cubic centimeters
Cubic centimeters	0.0610237	Cubic inches
Temperature		
Fahrenheit	(°F – 32) × 0.556	Centigrade
Centigrade	(°C × 1.8) + 32	Fahrenheit

(continued)

Table 5 CONVERSION TABLES (continued)

Multiply	By	To get equivalent of
Weight		
Ounces	28.3495	Grams
Pounds	0.4535924	Kilograms
Grams	0.035274	Ounces
Kilograms	2.2046224	Pounds
Pressure		
Pounds per square inch	0.070307	Kilograms per square centimeter
Kilograms per square centimeter	14.223343	Pounds per square inch
Kilopascals	0.1450	Pounds per square inch
Pounds per square inch	6.895	Kilopascals
Speed		
Miles per hour	1.609344	Kilometers per hour
Kilometers per hour	0.6213712	Miles per hour

Table 6 TECHNICAL ABBREVIATIONS

ABDC	After bottom dead center
ATDC	After top dead center
BBDC	Before bottom dead center
BDC	Bottom dead center
BTDC	Before top dead center
C	Celsius (Centigrade)
cc	Cubic centimeters
CDI	Capacitor discharge ignition
cu. in.	Cubic inches
F	Fahrenheit
ft.-lb.	Foot-pounds
gal.	Gallons
H/A	High altitude
hp	Horsepower
in.	Inches
kg	Kilogram
kg/cm2	Kilograms per square centimeter
kgm	Kilogram meters
km	Kilometer
L	Liter
m	Meter
MAG	Magneto
ml	Milliliter
mm	Millimeter
N•m	Newton-meters
oz.	Ounce
psi	Pounds per square inch
PTO	Power take off
pt.	Pint
qt.	Quart
rpm	Revolutions per minute

Table 7 METRIC TAP DRILL SIZES

Metric (mm)	Drill size	Decimal equivalent	Nearest fraction
3 × 0.50	No. 39	0.0995	3/32
3 × 0.60	3/32	0.0937	3/32
4 × 0.70	No. 30	0.1285	1/8
4 × 0.75	1/8	0.125	1/8
5 × 0.80	No. 19	0.166	11/64
5 × 0.90	No. 20	0.161	5/32
6 × 1.00	No. 9	0.196	13/64
7 × 1.00	16/64	0.234	15/64
8 × 1.00	J	0.277	9/32
8 × 1.25	17/64	0.265	17/64
9 × 1.00	5/16	0.3125	5/16
9 × 1.25	5/16	0.3125	5/16
10 × 1.25	11/32	0.3437	11/32
10 × 1.50	R	0.339	11/32
11 × 1.50	3/8	0.375	3/8
12 × 1.50	13/32	0.406	13/32
12 × 1.75	13/32	0.406	13/32

Table 8 WINDCHILL FACTORS

Estimated wind speed in mph	Actual thermometer reading (°F)											
	50	40	30	20	10	0	−10	−20	−30	−40	−50	−60
	Equivalent temperature (°F)											
Calm	50	40	30	20	10	0	−10	−20	−30	−40	−50	−60
5	48	37	27	16	6	−5	−15	−26	−36	−47	−57	−68
10	40	28	16	4	−9	−21	−33	−46	−58	−70	−83	−95
15	36	22	9	−5	−18	−36	−45	−58	−72	−85	−99	−112
20	32	18	4	−10	−25	−39	−53	−67	−82	−96	−110	−124
25	30	16	0	−15	−29	−44	−59	−74	−88	−104	−118	−133
30	28	13	−2	−18	−33	−48	−63	−79	−94	−109	−125	−140
35	27	11	−4	−20	−35	−49	−67	−82	−98	−113	−129	−145
40	26	10	−6	−21	−37	−53	−69	−85	−100	−116	−132	−148
*	Little danger (for properly clothed person)			Increasing danger				Great danger				
				• Danger from freezing of exposed flesh •								

*Wind speeds greater than 40 mph have little additional effect.

CHAPTER TWO

TROUBLESHOOTING

Diagnosing mechanical problems is relatively simple if you use orderly procedures and keep a few basic principles in mind. The first step in any troubleshooting procedure is to define the symptoms closely and then localize the problem. Subsequent steps involve testing and analyzing those areas that could cause the symptoms. A haphazard approach may eventually solve the problem, but it can be very costly with wasted time and unnecessary parts' replacement.

Proper lubrication, maintenance and periodic tune-ups as described in Chapter Three will reduce the necessity for troubleshooting. Even with the best of care, however, all motorcycles are prone to problems that will require troubleshooting.

Never assume anything. Do not overlook the obvious. If the engine will not start, the engine stop switch or start switch may be shorted out or damaged. When trying to start the engine, you may have flooded it.

If the engine suddenly quits, what sound did it make? Consider this and check the easiest, most accessible problem first. If the engine sounded as if it ran out of fuel, check to see if there is fuel in the tank. If there is fuel in the tank, is it reaching the carburetors? Is the fuel pump operating correctly? If

not, the fuel shutoff valve vacuum hose may be disconnected or plugged, preventing fuel from flowing from the fuel tank through the shutoff valves and to the carburetors.

If nothing obvious turns up in a quick check, look a little further. Learning to recognize and describe symptoms will make repairs easier for you or a mechanic at the dealership. Describe problems accurately and fully.

Gather as many symptoms as possible to aid in diagnosis. Note whether the engine lost power gradually or all at once, what color smoke came from the exhaust and so on. Remember that the more complicated a machine is, the easier it is to troubleshoot because symptoms point to specific problems.

After defining the vehicle's symptoms, areas that could cause the problem are tested and analyzed. Guessing at the cause of a problem may provide the solution, but it can easily lead to frustration, wasted time and a series of expensive, unnecessary parts replacements.

You do not need fancy equipment or complicated test gear to determine whether repairs can be attempted at home. A few simple checks could save a large repair bill and lost time while the bike sits in a dealer's service department. On the other hand, be realistic and do not attempt repairs beyond your abilities. Dealership service departments tend to charge heavily for putting together a disassembled engine that may have been abused. Some will not even take on such a job. Use common sense so that you do not get in over your head.

OPERATING REQUIREMENTS

An engine needs 3 basics to run properly: correct fuel/air mixture, compression and a spark at the right time. If one basic requirement is missing, the engine will not run. Four-stroke engine operating principles are described in Chapter Four under *Engine Principles*.

If the bike has been sitting for any time and refuses to start, check and clean the spark plugs. If the plugs are not fouled, look to the fuel delivery system. This includes the fuel tank, fuel shutoff valve, fuel pump, in-line fuel filter and fuel lines. If the bike sat for a while with fuel in the carburetors, fuel deposits may have gummed up carburetor jets and air passages. Gasoline tends to lose its potency after standing for long periods. Condensation may contaminate it with water. Drain the old gas and try starting with a fresh tankful.

TROUBLESHOOTING INSTRUMENTS

Chapter One lists the instruments needed and instruction on their use.

STARTING THE ENGINE

When your engine refuses to start, frustration can cause you to forget basic starting principles and procedures. The following outline will guide you through basic starting procedures. In all cases, make sure that there is an adequate supply of fuel in the tank.

NOTE
If you have been working on the bike and have removed the seat(s), be sure to reinstall the rider's seat prior to starting the engine. The ignition system's ignitor unit is attached to the underside of the rider's seat and the electrical

connectors are disconnected when the seat is removed.

Starting Notes

1. A sidestand switch ignition cut-off system is used on all models. The position of the sidestand will affect starting. Note the following:

 a. The engine cannot start when the sidestand is down and the transmission is in gear.

 b. The engine can start when the sidestand is down and the transmission is in NEUTRAL. The engine will stop if the transmission is put into gear with the sidestand down.

 c. The engine can be started when the sidestand is up and the transmission is in NEUTRAL or in gear with the clutch lever pulled in.

2. Before starting the engine, shift the transmission into NEUTRAL and confirm that the engine stop switch is in the RUN position.

3. Turn the MAIN (ignition) switch to the ON position and confirm the following:

 a. The neutral indicator light is ON (when the transmission is in NEUTRAL).

 b. The engine oil pressure warning light is ON.

4. The engine is now ready to start. Refer to the appropriate starting procedure in this section.

CAUTION
*Once the engine starts, the red oil pressure warning light should go off in a few seconds. If the light stays on longer than a few seconds, stop the engine immediately. Check the oil level as described in Chapter Three. If the oil level is okay, the oil filter may be plugged, the oil pressure may be too low or the oil pressure switch may be shorted. Check the oiling system and correct the problem before re-starting the engine. If the oil pressure switch is okay, the system is warning you that some type of stoppage has occurred in the lubrication system and that the oil is not being delivered to engine components. Severe engine damage will occur if the engine is run with low oil pressure. Refer to **Engine Lubrication** in this chapter.*

Starting a Cold Engine

1. Shift the transmission into NEUTRAL.

2. Turn the fuel shutoff valve to the ON position.

3. Move the ENGINE STOP switch to the RUN position.

4. Turn the ignition switch to the ON position.

5. Turn the choke lever all the way *clockwise* to the full ON position.

6. With the throttle completely closed, push the START button.

7. When the engine starts, work the throttle slightly to keep it running.

8. Idle the engine approximately for a minute or until the throttle responds cleanly, then turn the choke lever all the way *counterclockwise* to the full OFF position. The engine should be sufficiently warmed to prevent stalling.

Starting a Warm or Hot Engine

1. Shift the transmission into NEUTRAL.

2. Turn the fuel valve to the ON position.

3. Move the ENGINE STOP switch to the RUN position.

4. Turn the ignition switch to the ON position.

5. Make sure the choke lever is all the way *counterclockwise* to the full OFF position.

6. Open the throttle slightly and push the START button.

Starting a Flooded Engine

If the engine will not start and there is a strong gasoline smell, the engine may be flooded. If so, open the throttle all the way and operate the starter. Do not open the choke. Holding the throttle open allows more air to reach the engine.

> *NOTE*
> *If the engine refuses to start, check the carburetor overflow hose attached to the fitting at the bottom of each float bowl. If fuel runs out the end of one or both hoses, the float is stuck open, allowing the carburetor to overfill. If this problem exists, remove the carburetor(s) and correct the problem as described in Chapter Eight.*

STARTING DIFFICULTIES

If the engine turns over but is difficult to start, or will not start at all, it does not help to run down the battery with the electric starter. Check for obvious problems even before getting out your tools. Go down the following list step-by-step. Do each one while remembering the 3 engine operating requirements described under *Operating Requirements* earlier in this chapter.

If the engine still will not start, refer to the appropriate troubleshooting procedures that follow in this chapter.

1. Is the choke lever in the right position? Move the choke lever all the way *clockwise* to the full ON position for a cold engine or *counterclockwise* to its full OFF position for a warm or hot engine.

> *WARNING*
> *Do not use an open flame to check for fuel in the tank. A serious explosion is certain to result.*

2. Is there fuel in the tank? Open the fuel filler cap and rock the bike. Listen for fuel sloshing around. Fill the tank if necessary. Has it been a while since the engine was run? If in doubt, drain the fuel tank and fill it with fresh fuel.

3. If you suspect that the cylinders are flooded, or there is a strong smell of gasoline, open the throttle all the way and operate the START button. If the cylinders are severely flooded (fouled or wet spark plugs), remove the spark plugs and dry the base and electrode thoroughly with a soft cloth, or use an aerosol electrical contact cleaner. Reinstall the plugs and attempt to start the engine.

4. Check the carburetor overflow hoses on the bottom of each float bowl. If fuel is running out of a

hose, the fuel inlet valve is stuck open. Turn the fuel off and tap the carburetor a few times. Then turn on the fuel valve. If fuel continues to run out of the hose, remove and repair the carburetor(s) as described in Chapter Eight. Check the carburetor vent hoses to make sure they are clear. Check the end of the hoses for contamination.

> *NOTE*
> *Now that you have determined that fuel is reaching the carburetor, the fuel system could still be the problem. The jets (pilot and main) could be clogged or the air filter could be severely restricted. However, before removing the carburetor, continue with Step 5 to make sure that the ignition provides an adequate spark.*

5. Make sure the ENGINE STOP switch is not stuck or working improperly or that the wire is broken and shorting out. If necessary, test the engine stop switch as described under *Switches* in Chapter Nine.

6. Are the spark plug wires on tight? Loosen the bolts and remove the cylinder head side covers (**Fig-**

ure 1). Push the spark plug wires and boots (**Figure 2**) on and slightly rotate them to clean the electrical connection between the plug and the connector. Push or screw the plug caps into the high-tension leads. Reinstall the covers.

> *NOTE*
> *If the engine will still not start, continue with the following.*

7. Perform a spark test as described under *Engine Fails to Start (Spark Test)* in this chapter. If there is a strong spark, perform Step 8. If there is no spark or if the spark is very weak, test the ignition system as described under *Ignition System* in this chapter.

> *NOTE*
> *If the fuel and ignition system are working properly, the one remaining area to check is the mechanical system. Unless the engine seized or there is some other type of mechanical problem, mechanical problems affecting the top end generally occur over time, depending on maintenance and vehicle use. Isolate the mechanical problem to one of these areas: top end, bottom end, clutch or transmission. Engine top and bottom end components are covered in Step 8. Clutch and transmission problems are covered elsewhere in this chapter.*

8. Check cylinder compression as follows:
   a. Turn the fuel valve to the OFF position so fuel will not flow to the carburetors.

> *NOTE*
> *Refer to Chapter Three for spark plug removal information.*

   b. Remove and ground the spark plugs shell against the cylinder head (**Figure 3**).

> *CAUTION*
> *To prevent damage to the ignition system, ground the spark plugs when performing the following steps.*

   c. Put your finger tightly over the spark plug hole.
   d. Operate the START button. When the piston comes up on the compression stroke, pressure in the cylinder should force your finger from

the spark plug hole. If your finger pops off, the cylinder probably has sufficient compression to start the engine. Repeat for the other cylinder.

NOTE
You may still have a compression problem even though it seems acceptable from the previous test. Check engine compression with a compression gauge as described under **Tune-up** *in Chapter Three.*

e. Install the spark plugs and caps.

**Engine Fails to Start
(Spark Test)**

An engine that refuses to start or is difficult to start is very frustrating. More often than not, the problem is very minor and can be found with a simple and logical troubleshooting approach.

Perform the following spark test to determine if the ignition system is operating properly.

CAUTION
Before removing the spark plugs in Step 1, clean all dirt and debris away from the plug base. Dirt that falls into the cylinder will cause rapid engine wear.

1. Refer to Chapter Three and remove both spark plugs (**Figure 2**).

NOTE
A spark tester is a useful tool for testing the ignition systems spark output. **Figure 4** *shows the Motion Pro Ignition System Tester (part No. 08-122). This tool is inserted in the spark plug cap and its base is grounded against the cylinder head. The tool's air gap is adjustable, and it allows you to see and hear the spark while testing the intensity of the spark. This tool is available through most motorcycle dealerships.*

2. Insert the spark plug, or spark tester (**Figure 4**), into its cap and touch the base against the cylinder head to ground it. Position the spark plug or spark tester so you can see the electrode.

NOTE
If not using a spark tester, always use a new spark plug for this test procedure.

WARNING
Mount the spark plug, or tester, away from the spark plug hole in the cylinder so that the spark or tester cannot ignite the gasoline vapors in the cylinder. If the engine is flooded, do not perform this test. Fuel that is ejected through the spark plug hole can be ignited by the firing of the spark plug.

3. Turn the ignition switch to the ON position.

WARNING
Do **not** *hold the spark plug, wire or connector or a serious electrical shock may result.*

WARNING
If the engine is flooded, do not perform this test. Fuel that is ejected through the spark plug holes can be ignited by the firing of the spark plugs.

4. Turn the engine over with the electric starter. A fat blue spark should be evident across the spark plug electrode or spark tester terminals. Repeat for the other cylinder.
5. If the spark is good, check for one or more of the following possible malfunctions:
   a. Obstructed fuel line or fuel filter or malfunction fuel pump (models so equipped).
   b. Low compression or engine damage.
   c. Flooded engine.
6. If the spark is weak or if there is no spark, refer to *Engine is Difficult to Start* in this chapter.

NOTE
If the engine backfires when you are attempting to start it, the ignition timing may be incorrect. A signal generator rotor, loose signal generator or a defective ignition component will change the ignition timing. Refer to **Ignition System** *in this chapter for more information.*

Engine Is Difficult To Start

The following section groups the 3 main engine operating systems with probable causes.

Electrical System

On all motorcycles, the electrical system is a common source of engine starting problems. Trouble usually occurs at the wiring harness and connectors.

1. *Spark plugs*:
   a. Fouled spark plug(s).
   b. Incorrect spark plug gap.
   c. Incorrect spark plug heat range; see Chapter Three.
   d. Worn or damaged spark plug electrodes.
   e. Damaged spark plug(s).
   f. Damaged spark plug cap(s) or secondary wire(s).

> *NOTE*
> *Refer to **Reading Spark Plugs** in Chapter Three for additional information.*

2. *Ignition coil*:
   a. Loose or damaged secondary or primary wire leads.
   b. Cracked ignition coil body.
   c. Loose or corroded ground wire.
3. *Switches and wiring*:
   a. Dirty or loose-fitting terminals.
   b. Damaged wires or connectors.
   c. Damaged start switch.
   d. Damaged engine stop switch.
   e. Damaged ignition switch.
4. *Electrical components*:
   a. Damaged pickup coil.
   b. Damaged ignitor unit.
   c. Malfunctioning decompression control system.

Fuel System

A contaminated fuel system will cause engine starting and performance related problems. It only takes a small amount of dirt in the fuel valve, fuel line or carburetors to cause problems.

1. *Air filter*:
   a. Clogged air filter(s).
   b. Clogged air filter housing(s).
   c. Leaking or damaged air filter housing-to-carburetor air boots.
2. *Fuel shutoff valve*:
   a. Clogged fuel hose.
   b. Clogged fuel valve filter.
3. *Fuel tank*:
   a. No fuel.
   b. Clogged fuel filter(s).
   c. Contaminated fuel.
4. *Carburetor*:
   a. Clogged or damaged choke system.
   b. Clogged main jet(s).
   c. Clogged pilot jet(s).
   d. Loose slow jet(s) or main jet(s).
   e. Clogged pilot jet air passages.
   f. Incorrect float level(s).
   g. Leaking or otherwise damaged float(s).
   h. Severely worn or damaged needle valve(s).
5. *Fuel pump*:
   a. Fuel pump filter clogged.
   b. Fuel pump electrical connector faulty, corroded or disconnected.

Engine Compression

Check engine compression with a compression gauge as described in Chapter Three.

1. *Cylinder and cylinder head*:
   a. Loose spark plug(s).
   b. Missing spark plug gasket(s).
   c. Leaking cylinder head gasket.
   d. Leaking cylinder block base gasket.
   e. Severely worn or seized piston(s), piston rings and/or cylinder walls.
   f. Loose cylinder block and/or cylinder head fasteners.
   g. Cylinder head incorrectly installed and/or torqued down.
   h. Warped cylinder head.
   i. Blown head gasket.
   j. Blown cylinder block base gasket.

k. Loose cylinder fasteners.
2. *Piston and piston rings*:
   a. Worn piston rings.
   b. Damaged piston rings.
   c. Piston seizure or piston damage.
3. *Crankcase and crankshaft*:
   a. Seized connecting rod(s).
   b. Damaged crankcases.
   c. Damaged oil seals.

POOR IDLE SPEED PERFORMANCE

If the engine starts but off-idle performance is poor (engine hesitation, cutting out, etc.), check the following:
1. Clogged or damaged air filter(s).
2. *Carburetor*:
   a. Clogged pilot jet(s).
   b. Loose pilot jet(s).
   c. Damaged choke system.
   d. Incorrect throttle cable adjustment.
   e. Incorrect carburetor adjustment.
   f. Flooded carburetor (visually check carburetor overflow hose for fuel).
   g. Vacuum piston doesn't slide smoothly in carburetor bore.
3. *Fuel*:
   a. Water and/or alcohol in fuel.
   b. Old fuel.
4. *Engine*:
   a. Low engine compression.
5. *Electrical system*:
   a. Damaged spark plug(s).
   b. Damaged ignition coil(s).
   c. Damaged signal generator rotor and/or signal generator.
   d. Damaged ignitor unit.

POOR MEDIUM AND HIGH SPEED PERFORMANCE

Refer to Engine is *Difficult to Start*, then check the following:
1. Carburetor(s):
   a. Incorrect fuel level.
   b. Incorrect jet needle clip position (if adjustable).
   c. Clogged or loose main jet(s).
2. Clogged air filter(s).
3. *Other considerations*:

a. Overheating.
b. Clutch slippage.
c. Brake drag.
d. Engine oil viscosity too high or oil level too high.

ENGINE STARTING SYSTEM

This section describes troubleshooting procedures for the electric starting system. Jumper cables, an ohmmeter and a fully charged battery are required to troubleshoot the starting system.

Description

An electric starter motor is mounted horizontally in front of the front cylinder block. **Figure 5** shows a schematic of the starting system and its components.

The electric starting system requires a fully charged battery to provide the large amount of current required to operate the starter motor. The alternator and a voltage regulator/rectifier, connected in circuit with the battery, keep the battery charged while the engine is running. The battery can also be charged externally.

The starter relay, located under the left-hand frame side cover, carries the heavy electrical current to the motor. Depressing the START switch allows current to flow through the starter relay coil. The starter relay contacts close and allow current to flow from the battery through the starter relay to the starter motor.

NOTE
The automatic compression release control system is combined with the starting system.

CAUTION
Do not operate an electric starter motor continuously for more than 5 seconds. Allow the motor to cool for at least 15 seconds between attempts to start the engine.

Troubleshooting

Before troubleshooting the starting circuit, make sure that:
   a. The battery is fully charged.

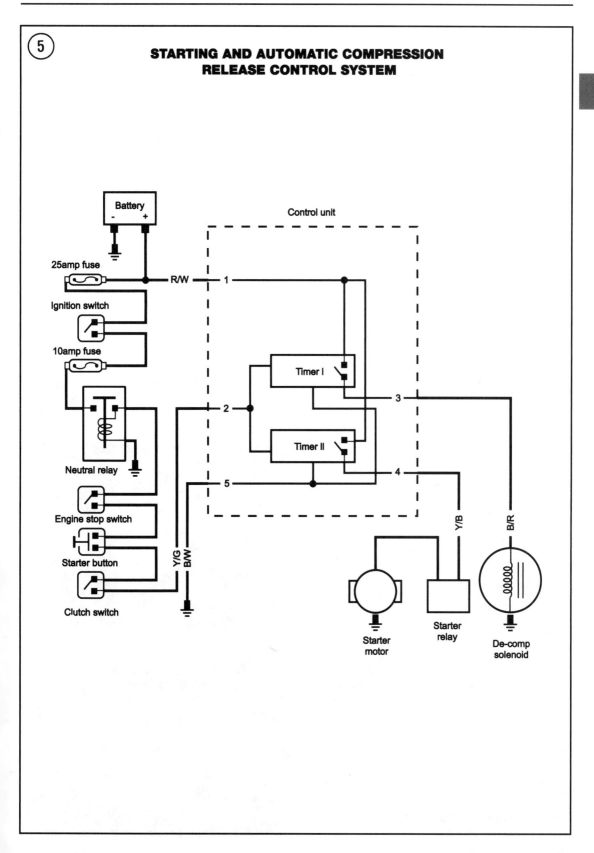

⑤ STARTING AND AUTOMATIC COMPRESSION
RELEASE CONTROL SYSTEM

2

b. Battery cables are the proper size and length. Replace cables that are undersize or damaged.

c. All electrical connections are clean and tight. Especially the battery terminals.

d. The wiring harness is in good condition, with no worn or frayed insulation or loose harness sockets.

e. The fuel system is filled with an adequate supply of fresh gasoline.

Starter Troubleshooting

If the starter does not operate, perform the following. After completing each test, reconnect any electrical connector that was disconnected before beginning the next test. When operating the starter switch, turn the engine stop switch to RUN and the main switch to ON.

1. Check the main fuse mounted in the fuse panel under the left-hand frame cover.

2. Remove the seat and the left-hand side frame cover as described in Chapter Thirteen.

3. Move the hoses out of the way, remove the screw (A, **Figure 6**), remove the fuse panel cover (B, **Figure 6**), pull the fuse (**Figure 7**) out and visually inspect it. If the fuse is blown (**Figure 8**), refer to *Fuses* in Chapter Nine. If the main fuse is good, reinstall it.

4. Test the battery as described under *Battery* in Chapter Three.

If the battery voltage reading is not within the prescribed range, clean and recharge the battery as described under *Battery* in Chapter Three. Replace a damaged battery.

5. Disconnect the MAIN (ignition) switch electrical connector. Test the main switch as described under *Switches* in Chapter Nine. Note the following:

a. If the main switch tested correctly, perform Step 6.

b. If the main switch did not test correctly, replace the main switch and retest.

6. Disconnect the START switch electrical connectors from the wiring harness. Test the start switch as described under *Switches* in Chapter Nine. Note the following:

a. If the start switch tested correctly, perform Step 7.

b. If the start switch did not test correctly, replace the start switch and retest.

7. Disconnect the ENGINE STOP switch electrical connectors from the wiring harness. Test the engine stop switch as described under *Switches* in Chapter Nine. Note the following:

a. If the engine stop switch tested correctly, perform Step 8.

b. If the engine stop switch did not test correctly, replace the engine stop switch and retest.

8. Disconnect the side stand interlock switch electrical connectors from the wiring harness. Test the side stand interlock switch as described under *Switches* in Chapter Nine. Note the following:

a. If the switch tested correctly, perform Step 9.

b. If the side stand interlock switch did not test correctly, replace the switch and retest.

9. Disconnect the starter relay electrical connector and the two large electrical connectors going to the battery and starter. Connect an ohmmeter and 12-volt battery to the starter relay terminals (**Figure 9**). When the battery is connected there should be continuity (low to zero ohms), when the battery is disconnected, there should be no continuity (infinity).

a. If the starter circuit relay tested correctly, perform Step 10.

b. If the starter circuit relay did not test correctly, replace the relay and retest.

10. If you have not found the starting system problem, recheck the wiring system for dirty or loose-fitting terminals or damaged wires; clean and repair as required. If all the connectors and wires are in good condition, the starter motor is probably faulty. Remove and repair the starter motor as described under *Starter* in Chapter Nine.

11. Make sure all connectors disassembled during this procedure are free of corrosion and are reconnected properly.

CHARGING SYSTEM

A malfunction in the charging system generally causes the battery to remain undercharged. **Figure 10** shows a schematic of the charging system.

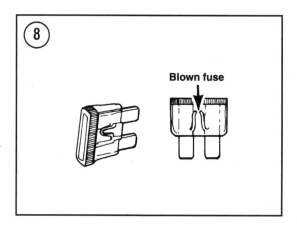

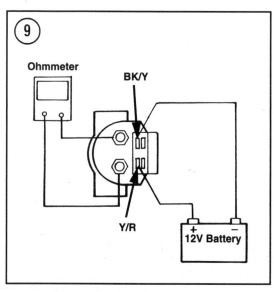

Troubleshooting

Before testing the charging system, visually check the following.

1. Check the battery connections at the battery. If polarity is reversed, check for a damaged regulator/rectifier.

2. Remove the screws and the battery cover (**Figure 11**) and check for loose or corroded battery cable connectors.

3. Inspect all wiring between the battery and alternator stator for worn or cracked insulation or loose connections. Replace wiring or clean and tighten connections as required.

4. Check battery condition. Clean and recharge as required. See *Battery* in Chapter Three.

5. Perform the *Charging System Output Test* listed under *Charging System* in Chapter Nine.

6. Test the regulator/rectifier as described under *Regulator/Rectifier* as described in Chapter Nine.

IGNITION SYSTEM

All models are equipped with a transistorized ignition system. This solid state system uses no contact breaker point or other moving parts. **Figure 12** shows a schematic of the ignition system and its components.

Because of the solid state design, problems with the transistorized system are rare. If a problem occurs, it generally causes a weak spark or no spark at all. An ignition system with a weak spark or no spark is relatively easy to troubleshoot. It is difficult, however, to troubleshoot an ignition system that only malfunctions when the engine is hot or under load. The troubleshooting procedure in **Figure 13** will help isolate an ignition system malfunction.

FUEL SYSTEM

Many riders automatically assume that the carburetors are at fault when the engine does not run properly. While fuel system problems are not uncommon, carburetor adjustment is seldom the answer. In many cases, adjusting the carburetors only compounds the problem by making the engine run worse.

Fuel system troubleshooting should start at the fuel tank and work through the system, reserving the carburetor assembly as the final point. Most fuel

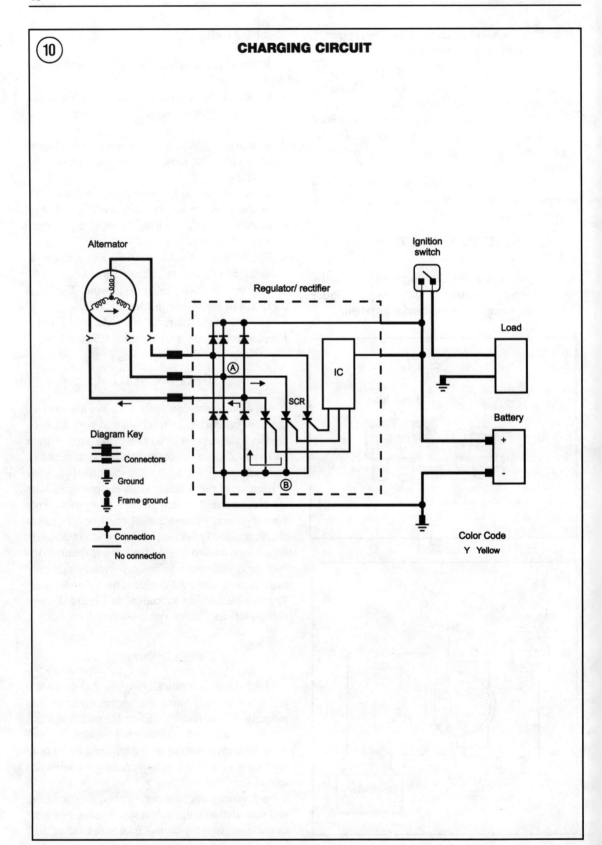

CHARGING CIRCUIT

(10)

Alternator

Regulator/ rectifier

Ignition switch

Load

IC

SCR

A

B

Y   Y   Y

Diagram Key

Connectors

Ground

Frame ground

Connection

No connection

Battery

+

-

Color Code

Y   Yellow

system problems result from an empty fuel tank, a plugged fuel filter or fuel valve, fuel pump failure or sour fuel. Fuel system troubleshooting is covered thoroughly under *Engine Is Difficult To Start, Poor Idle Speed Performance and Poor Medium and High Speed Performance* in this chapter.

The carburetor choke system can also present problems. A choke stuck open will show up as a hard starting problem; one that sticks closed will result in a flooding condition. Check choke operation by turning the choke lever from full clockwise to full counterclockwise. The choke lever should move freely without binding or sticking in one position. If necessary, remove the choke as described under *Carburetor Disassembly* in Chapter Eight and inspect its plunger and spring for severe wear or damage.

ENGINE OVERHEATING

Engine overheating is a serious problem in that it can quickly cause engine seizure and damage. The following section groups 5 main systems with probable causes that can lead to engine overheating.

1. *Ignition system*:
   a. Incorrect spark plug gap.
   b. Incorrect spark plug heat range; see Chapter Three.
   c. Faulty ignitor unit/incorrect ignition timing.
2. *Engine compression system*:
   a. Cylinder head gasket leakage.
   b. Heavy carbon buildup in combustion chamber.
3. *Engine lubrication system*:
   a. Incorrect oil level
   b. Incorrect oil viscosity.
   c. Oil level low

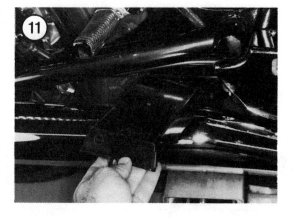

d. Faulty oil pump.
   e. Plugged oil cooler and/or oil cooler lines.
   f. Oil not circulating properly.
4. *Fuel system*:
   a. Clogged air filter element(s).
   b. Carburetor fuel level too low.
   c. Incorrect carburetor adjustment or jetting.
   d. Loose carburetor hose clamps.
   e. Leaking or damaged carburetor-to-air filter housing air boot(s).
   f. Incorrect air-fuel mixture.
   g. Inoperative fuel pump.
5. *Engine load*—Check for:
   a. Dragging brake(s).
   b. Damaged drive train components.
   c. Slipping clutch.
   d. Engine oil level too high.

ENGINE

Engine troubles generally indicate something wrong in a suspect system, such as ignition, fuel or starting.

Preignition

Preignition is the premature burning of fuel and is caused by hot spots in the combustion chambers. The fuel ignites before it is supposed to. Glowing deposits in the combustion chambers, inadequate cooling or an overheated spark plug(s) can all cause preignition. This is first noticed as a power loss but will eventually result in extended damage to the internal parts of the engine because of higher combustion chamber temperatures.

Detonation

Commonly called park knock or fuel knock, detonation is the violent explosion of fuel in the combustion chamber before the proper time of combustion. Severe damage can result. Use of low octane gasoline is a common cause of detonation.

Even when using a high octane gasoline, detonation can still occur. Other causes are over-advanced ignition timing, lean fuel mixture at or near full throttle, inadequate engine cooling, or the excessive accumulation of carbon deposits in the combustion chamber (cylinder head and piston crowns).

Power Loss

Several factors can cause a lack of power and speed. Look for a clogged air filter or fouled or damaged spark plugs. A piston or cylinder that is galled, incorrect piston clearance or worn or sticky piston rings may be responsible. Look for loose bolts, defective gaskets or leaking machined mating surfaces on the cylinder head, cylinder block or crankcase.

Piston Seizure

This is caused by incorrect bore clearance, piston rings with an improper end gap, compression leak, incorrect air-fuel mixture, spark plugs of the wrong heat range or incorrect ignition timing. Overheating from any cause may result in piston seizure.

Piston Slap

Piston slap is an audible slapping or rattling noise resulting from excessive piston-to-cylinder clearance. When allowed to continue, piston slap will eventually cause the piston skirt to shatter.

To prevent piston slap, clean the air filter on a regular schedule. When you hear piston slap, disassemble the engine top end and measure the cylinder bore and piston diameter and check for excessive clearance. Replace parts that exceed wear limits or show damage.

ENGINE NOISES

1. *Knocking or pinging during acceleration*—Can be caused by using a lower octane fuel than recommended or a poor grade of fuel. Incorrect carburetor jetting and a too hot spark plug can cause pinging. Refer to *Correct Spark Plug Heat Range* in Chapter Three. Check also for excessive carbon buildup in the combustion chamber or a faulty ignition system ignitor unit.

2. *Slapping or rattling noises at low speed or during acceleration*—Can be caused by piston slap, i.e., excessive piston-cylinder wall clearance. Also check for bent connecting rods, worn piston pins and/or piston pin holes in the pistons.

3. *Knocking or rapping while decelerating*—Usually caused by excessive rod bearing clearance.

4. *Persistent knocking and vibration or other noise*—Usually caused by worn main bearings. If the main bearings are okay, consider the following:
   a. Loose engine mounts.
   b. Cracked frame.
   c. Leaking cylinder head gasket(s).
   d. Exhaust pipe leakage at cylinder head(s).
   e. Stuck piston ring(s).
   f. Broken piston ring(s).
   g. Partial engine seizure.
   h. Excessive small end connecting rod bearing clearance.
   i. Excessive connecting rod big end side clearance.
   j. Excessive crankshaft runout.
   k. Worn or damaged primary drive gear.

5. *Rapid on-off squeal*—Compression leak around cylinder head gasket or spark plug.

ENGINE LEAKDOWN TEST

An engine leakdown test can isolate engine problems caused by leaking valves, blown head gaskets or broken, worn or stuck piston rings. A cylinder leakage test is performed by applying compressed air to the cylinder and then measuring the percent of leakage. A cylinder leakage tester (**Figure 14**) and an air compressor are required to perform this test.

Follow the manufacturer's directions along with the following information when performing a cylinder leakdown test.

1. Start and run the engine until it reaches normal operating temperature. Then turn off the engine.

2. Remove the air filter assemblies. Open and secure the throttle so that it is at its wide open position.

3. Set the piston for the cylinder being tested to TDC on its compression stroke.

4. Remove one of the spark plug caps and the spark plug as described in Chapter Three.

> *NOTE*
> *The engine may turn over when air pressure is applied to the cylinder. To prevent this from happening, shift the transmission into fifth gear and apply the rear brake.*

5. Install the leakdown tester into the cylinder spark plug hole (**Figure 15**).

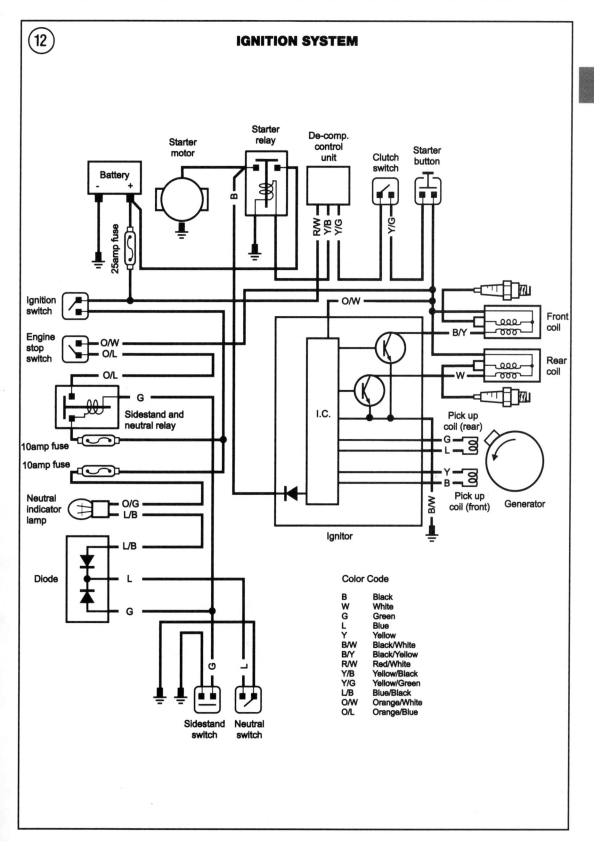

⑬

IGNITION SYSTEM DIAGNOSIS

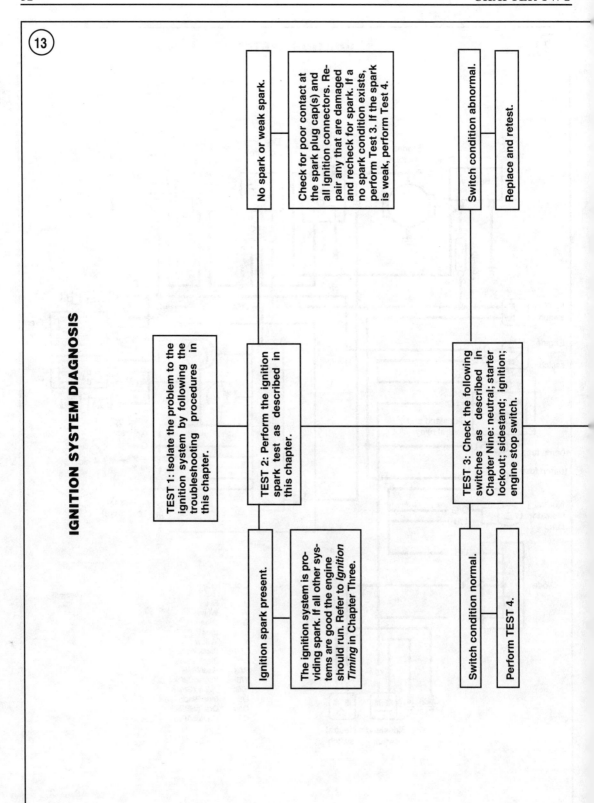

TEST 1: Isolate the problem to the ignition system by following the troubleshooting procedures in this chapter.

TEST 2: Perform the ignition spark test as described in this chapter.

Ignition spark present.

The ignition system is providing spark. If all other systems are good the engine should run. Refer to *Ignition Timing* in Chapter Three.

No spark or weak spark.

Check for poor contact at the spark plug cap(s) and all ignition connectors. Repair any that are damaged and recheck for spark. If a no spark condition exists, perform Test 3. If the spark is weak, perform Test 4.

TEST 3: Check the following switches as described in Chapter Nine: neutral; starter lockout; sidestand; ignition; engine stop switch.

Switch condition normal.

Perform TEST 4.

Switch condition abnormal.

Replace and retest.

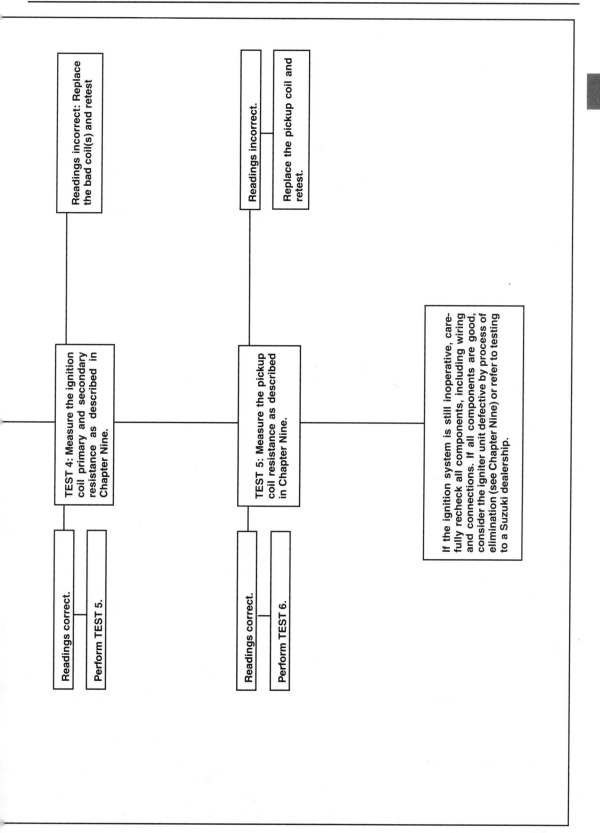

TEST 4: Measure the ignition coil primary and secondary resistance as described in Chapter Nine.

Readings correct.

Perform TEST 5.

Readings incorrect: Replace the bad coil(s) and retest

TEST 5: Measure the pickup coil resistance as described in Chapter Nine.

Readings correct.

Perform TEST 6.

Readings incorrect.

Replace the pickup coil and retest.

If the ignition system is still inoperative, carefully recheck all components, including wiring and connections. If all components are good, consider the igniter unit defective by process of elimination (see Chapter Nine) or refer to testing to a Suzuki dealership.

6. Make a cylinder leakdown test following the testers manufacturer's instructions. Listen for air leaking while noting the following:
   a. Air leaking through the exhaust pipe points to a leaking exhaust valve.
   b. Air leaking through the carburetor points to a leaking intake valve.
   c. Air leaking through the crankcase breather tube indicates worn piston rings.
7. Repeat Steps 3-6 for the remaining cylinder.
8. Any cylinder with 10% cylinder leak down requires further service.

CLUTCH

The 2 most common clutch problems are:
   a. Clutch slipping.
   b. Clutch dragging.

All clutch troubles, except for bleeding the hydraulic system, require partial engine disassembly to identify and cure the problem. Refer to Chapter Six for procedures.

Clutch Slipping

1. *Clutch wear or damage:*
   a. Loose, weak or damaged clutch spring.
   b. Worn friction plates.
   c. Warped steel plates.
   d. Severely worn clutch hub and/or clutch housing.
   e. Incorrectly assembled clutch.
2. *Engine oil:*
   a. Low oil level.
   b. Oil additives present in engine oil.
   c. Low viscosity oil.

Clutch Dragging

1. *Clutch wear or damage:*
   a. Warped steel plates.
   b. Swollen friction plates.
   c. Warped pressure plate.
   d. Incorrect clutch spring tension.
   e. Incorrectly assembled clutch.
   f. Loose clutch nut.
   g. Damaged clutch boss.
2. *Engine oil:*
   a. Oil level too high.

   b. High viscosity oil.

TRANSMISSION

The most common transmission problems are:
   a. Difficult shifting.
   b. Gears pop out of mesh.

Transmission symptoms can be hard to distinguish from clutch symptoms. Be sure that the clutch is not causing the trouble before working on the transmission.

Difficult Shifting

If the shift shaft does not move smoothly from one gear to the next, check the following.
1. *Shift shaft:*
   a. Incorrectly installed shift lever.
   b. Stripped shift lever-to-shift shaft splines.
   c. Bent shift shaft.
   d. Damaged shift shaft return spring.
   e. Damaged shift shaft where it engages the shift drum.
   f. Loosen shift return spring pin.
   g. Shift drum positioning lever binding on pivot bolt.
2. *Stopper lever:*
   a. Seized or damaged stopper lever roller.
   b. Broken stopper lever spring.
   c. Loose stopper lever mounting bolt.
3. *Shift drum and shift forks:*
   a. Bent shift fork(s).
   b. Damaged shift fork guide pin(s).
   c. Seized shift fork (on shaft).
   d. Broken shift fork or shift fork shaft.
   e. Damaged shift drum groove(s).
   f. Damaged shift drum bearing.

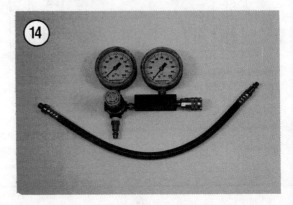

Gears Pop Out Of Mesh

If the transmission shifts into gear but then slips or pops out, check the following:

1. *Shift shaft*:
    a. Incorrect shift lever position/adjustment.
    b. Stopper lever fails to move or set properly.
2. *Shift drum*:
    a. Incorrect thrust play.
    b. Severely worn or damaged shift drum groove(s).
3. Bent shift fork(s).
4. *Transmission*:
    a. Worn or damaged gear dogs.
    b. Excessive gear thrust play.
    c. Worn or damaged shaft circlips or thrust washers.

Transmission Overshifts

If the transmission overshifts when shifting up or down, check for a weak or broken shift mechanism arm spring or a weak or broken shift drum positioning lever.

FINAL DRIVE

Excessive Final Drive Noise

1. Low oil level.
2. Worn or damaged pinion and ring gears.
3. Excessive pinion to ring gear backlash.
4. Worn or damaged drive pinion and splines.
5. Scored driven flange and wheel hub.
6. Scored or worn ring gear shaft and driven flange.

Oil Leakage

1. Loose or missing cover bolts.
2. Damaged final drive oil seals.
3. Clogged breather.
4. Oil level too high.

Rear Wheel Does Not Rotate Freely

1. Bent drive shaft.
2. Damaged ring gear and pinion bearing.
3. Stuck pinion and ring gear.

HANDLING

Poor handling will reduce overall performance and may cause you to crash. If you are experiencing poor handling, check the following items:

1. If the handlebars are hard to turn, check for the following:
    a. Low tire pressure.
    b. Incorrect clutch hydraulic hose routing.
    c. Incorrect front brake hydraulic hose routing.
    d. Incorrect throttle cable routing.
    e. Incorrect handlebar switch cable routing.
    f. Steering stem adjustment is too tight.
    g. Bent steering stem.
    h. Improperly lubricated steering stem bearings.
    i. Damaged steering stem bearings.
    j. Bearing race in steering stem severely worn or dented.
2. If there is excessive handlebar shake or vibration, check for the following:
    a. Loose or damaged handlebar holder bolts.
    b. Incorrect handlebar holder and bolt installation.
    c. Bent or cracked handlebar.
    d. Loose steering stem nut.
    e. Worn wheel bearing(s).
    f. Dry rotted tire.
    g. Severely worn front tire.
    h. Damaged rim or loose spokes.
    i. Loose, missing or broken engine mount bolts and mounts.
    j. Cracked frame, especially at the steering head.
    k. Incorrect tire inflation pressure for prevailing riding conditions.
3. If the rear suspension is too soft, check for the following:
    a. Incorrect shock absorber adjustment.

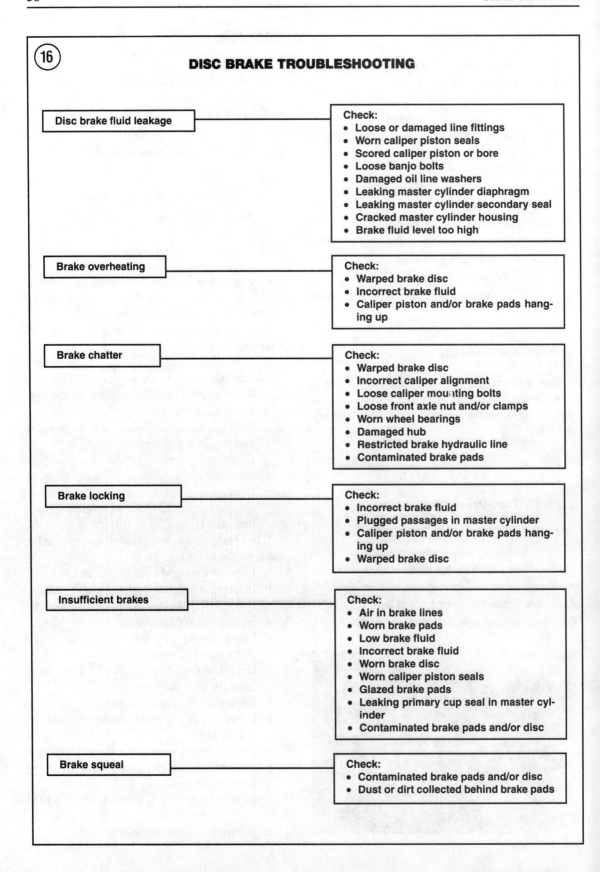

b. Leaking shock absorber.

c. Sagged shock spring.

d. Loose or damaged shock mount bolts and nuts

4. If the rear suspension is too hard, check for the following:

   a. Incorrect shock absorber adjustment.

   b. Rear tire inflation pressure too high.

5. *Frame*—Check the following:

   a. Damaged frame.

   b. Cracked or broken engine mount brackets.

FRAME NOISE

Noises traced to the frame or suspension are usually caused by loose, worn or damaged parts. Various noises that are related to the frame are listed below:

1. *Disc brake noise*—A screeching sound during braking is the most common disc brake noise. Some other disc brake associated noises can be caused by:

   a. Glazed brake pad surface.

   b. Severely worn brake pads.

   c. Warped brake disc(s).

   d. Loose brake disc mounting bolts.

   e. Loose or missing brake caliper mounting bolts.

   f. Damaged caliper(s).

   g. Cracked wheel flange or bosses, where the brake disc mounts to the wheel.

2. *Front fork noise*—Check for the following:

   a. Contaminated fork oil.

   b. Fork oil level too low.

c. Broken fork spring.

d. Worn front fork bushings.

3. *Rear shock absorber noise*—Check for the following:

   a. Loose shock absorber mounting bolts and nuts.

   b. Cracked or broken shock spring(s).

   c. Damaged shock absorber.

4. Some other frame associated noises can be caused by:

   a. Cracked or broken frame.

   b. Broken swing arm or shock linkage.

   c. Loose engine mounting bolts.

   d. Damaged steering bearings.

   e. Loose mounting bracket(s).

BRAKES

The front and rear brake units are critical to riding performance and safety. Inspect the brake frequently and repair any problem immediately. When replacing or refilling the disc brake fluid, use only DOT 4 brake fluid from a closed and sealed container. See Chapter Thirteen for additional information on brake fluid selection and disc brake service. The troubleshooting procedures in **Figure 16** will help you isolate the majority of disc brake troubles.

When checking brake pad wear, check that the brake pads in each caliper contact the disc squarely. If one of the brake pads is wearing unevenly, suspect a warped or bent brake disc or damaged caliper.

CHAPTER THREE

LUBRICATION, MAINTENANCE AND TUNE-UP

A motorcycle, even in normal use, is subjected to tremendous heat, stress and vibration. When neglected, any bike becomes unreliable and actually dangerous to ride.

To gain the utmost in safety, performance and useful life from the Suzuki Intruder, it is necessary to make periodic inspections and adjustments. Frequently minor problems are found during these inspections that are simple and inexpensive to correct at the time. If they are not found and corrected at this time they could lead to major and more expensive problems later on.

Start with regular maintenance, lubrication and a simple tune-up. Tackle more involved jobs as you become more acquainted with the bike.

Table 1 lists factory recommended maintenance and lubrication schedules.

Table 2 lists tire inflation pressure.

Table 3 lists battery capacity and charging time.

Table 4 lists recommended lubricants and fluids.

Table 5 lists engine, fork and drive unit refill capacity.

Table 6 lists maintenance and tune-up tightening torque specifications.

Table 7 lists maintenance and tune-up specifications.

Tables 1-7 are at the end of this chapter.

ROUTINE CHECKS

The following simple checks should be performed at each gas stop.

Engine Oil Level

Refer to *Engine Oil Level Check* under *Periodic Lubrication* in this chapter.

Fuel

All Intruder engines are designed to use gasoline that has a pump octane number (R+M)/2 of 85 or higher or gasoline with a research octane number of 89 or higher. The pump octane number is normally displayed at service station gas pumps. Using a gasoline with a lower octane number can cause pinging or spark knock which can lead to engine damage. Unleaded fuel is recommended because it reduces engine and spark plug deposits.

When choosing gasoline and filling the fuel tank, note the following:

a. When filling the tank, do not overfill it. Fuel expands in the tank due to engine and ambient heat. Stop adding fuel when the fuel level reaches the bottom of the filler tube inside the fuel tank.

b. To help meet clean air standards in some areas of the United States and Canada, oxygenated fuels are being used. Oxygenated fuel is conventional gasoline that is blended with an alcohol or ether compound. When using an oxygenated fuel, make sure that it meets the minimum octane rating as previously specified.

c. Because oxygenated fuels can damage plastic and paint, make sure not to spill fuel onto the fuel tank during fuel stops.

d. An ethanol (ethyl or grain alcohol) gasoline that contains more than 10 percent ethanol by volume may cause engine starting and performance related problems.

e. A methanol (methyl or wooden alcohol) gasoline that contains more than 5 percent methanol by volume may cause engine starting and performance related problems. Gasoline that contains methanol must have corrosion inhibitors to protect the metal, plastic and rubber parts in the fuel system from damage.

f. Suzuki states that you can use a gasoline containing no more than 15 percent MTBE (Methyl Tertiary Butyl Ether) by volume.

g. If your bike is experiencing fuel system damage or performance related problems from the use of oxygenated fuel, consult with a mechanic in an area where this type of fuel is widely sold and used.

General Inspection

1. Quickly inspect the engine for signs of oil or fuel leakage.
2. Check the tires for embedded stones. Pry them out with a suitable small tool.
3. Make sure all lights work.

> *NOTE*
> *At least check the brake light. It can burn out at any time. Motorists cannot stop as quickly as you and need all the warning you can give.*

Tire Pressure

Tire pressure must be checked with the tires cold. Correct tire pressure varies with the load you are carrying or if you have a passenger. See **Table 2**.

Brake Operation

Check that both brakes operate with full hydraulic advantage. Check the brake fluid levels as described under *Disc Brake Fluid Level Inspection* in this chapter. Check that there is no brake fluid leakage from the master cylinders, front and rear calipers or brake lines.

Throttle

Sitting on the bike, with the brake ON, the transmission in NEUTRAL and the engine idling, move the handlebars from side to side, making sure the idle does not increase or decrease by itself. Check that the throttle opens and closes smoothly in all steering positions. Shut off the engine.

Engine Stop Switch

The engine stop switch is designed primarily as an emergency switch. It is part of the right-hand switch assembly next to the throttle housing and it has 2 operating positions: OFF and RUN. When the switch is in the OFF position, the engine will not start or run. When pressing the starter button in the RUN position, the engine should start and run with the ignition switch on and the clutch lever pulled in. With the engine idling, move the switch to OFF. The engine should turn off.

Sidestand Check Switch System Inspection

1. Place wooden block(s) under the engine to support the bike securely with the rear wheel off the ground.
2. Check the sidestand spring. Make sure the spring is in good condition and has not lost tension.
3. Swing the sidestand down and up a few times. The sidestand should swing smoothly and the spring should provide proper tension in the raised position.
4. While sitting on the motorcycle, shift the transmission into NEUTRAL and move the sidestand up.

5. Start the engine and allow it to warm up. Then pull in the clutch lever and shift the transmission into gear.

6. Lower the sidestand with your foot. The engine should stop as the sidestand is lowered.

7. If the sidestand check switch did not operate as described, test the sidestand check switch as described in Chapter Nine

Crankcase Breather Hose

Inspect the hose for cracks and deterioration and make sure that the hose clamps are tight.

Evaporative Emission Control System (California Models)

Inspect the hoses to make sure they are not kinked or bent and that they are securely connected to their respective parts.

Lights and Horn

With the engine running, check the following.

1. Pull the front brake lever on and check that the brake light comes on.

2. Push the rear brake pedal down and make sure the brake light comes on soon after you depresse the pedal.

3. With the engine running, check to see that the headlight and taillight are on.

4. Move the dimmer switch up and down between the HI and LO positions and check to see that the headlight elements are working in the headlight(s).

5. Push the turn signal switch to the left and right positions and check that all 4 turn signals are working.

6. Push the horn button and make sure that the horn blows loudly.

7. If during the test, the rear brake pedal traveled too far before the brake light came on, adjust the rear brake light switch as described in this chapter.

8. If the horn or any of the lights failed to operate properly, refer to Chapter Nine.

PRE-RIDE INSPECTION

The following checks should be performed prior to the first ride of the day.

1. Inspect all fuel lines and fittings for wetness.

2. Make sure the fuel tank is full of fresh gasoline.

3. Make sure the engine oil level is correct. Add oil if necessary.

4. Make sure the final drive unit oil level is correct. Add oil if necessary.

5. Check the operation of the front brake. Add hydraulic fluid to the front brake master cylinder if necessary.

6. Check the operation of the rear brake. Add hydraulic fluid to the rear brake master cylinder if necessary.

7. Check the operation of the clutch. Add hydraulic fluid to the clutch master cylinder if necessary.

8. Check the throttle and the rear brake pedal. Make sure they operate properly with no binding.

9. Inspect the front and rear suspension; make sure they have a good solid feel with no looseness.

10. Check tire pressure. Refer to **Table 2**.

11. Check the exhaust system for damage.

12. Check the tightness of all fasteners, especially engine mounting hardware.

SERVICE INTERVALS

The services and intervals shown in **Table 1** are recommended by the factory. Strict adherence to these recommendations will ensure long service from the Suzuki. If the bike is run in an area of high humidity, perform the lubrication services more frequently to prevent rust damage.

For convenience when maintaining your motorcycle, most of the services shown in these tables are described in this chapter. However, some procedures which require more than minor disassembly or adjustment are covered elsewhere in the appropriate chapter. The *Table of Contents and Index* can help you locate a particular service procedure.

TIRES AND WHEELS

Tire Pressure

Tire pressure must be checked and adjusted to maintain the tire profile, good traction and handling and to get the maximum life out of the tire. A simple, accurate gauge can be purchased for a few dollars and should be carried in your motorcycle tool kit. Tire pressure must be checked when the tires are cold. The appropriate tire pressures are shown in **Table 2**.

> *NOTE*
> *After checking and adjusting the air pressure, install the air valve cap. The cap prevents small pebbles and dirt from collecting in the valve stem; this could allow air leakage or result in incorrect tire pressure readings.*

> *NOTE*
> *A loss of air pressure may be due to a loose or damaged valve core. Put a few drops of water on the top of the valve core. If the water bubbles, tighten the valve core and recheck. If air is still leaking from the valve after tightening it, replace the valve core or inner tube as required.*

Tire Inspection

The tires take a lot of punishment so inspect them periodically for excessive wear. Inspect the tires for the following:

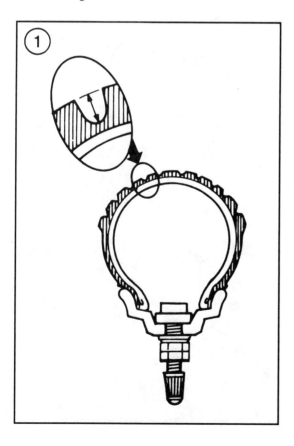

a. Deep cuts and imbedded objects (such as stones or nails). If you find a nail or other object in a tire, mark its location with a light crayon prior to removing it. This will help to locate the hole for repair. Refer to Chapter Ten for tire changing and repair information.
b. Flat spots.
c. Cracks.
d. Separating plies.
e. Sidewall damage.

Tire Wear Analysis

Abnormal tire wear should be analyzed to determine its causes. The most common causes are the following:

a. Incorrect tire pressure: Check tire pressure as described in this chapter.
b. Overloading.
c. Incorrect wheel balance: The tire/wheel assembly should be balanced when installing a new tire and or tube and then re-balanced each time the tire is removed and reinstalled.
d. Worn or damaged wheel bearings.

Incorrect tire pressure is the biggest cause of abnormal tire wear. Under-inflated tires will result in higher tire temperatures, hard or imprecise steering and abnormal tire wear. Overinflated tires will result in a hard ride and abnormal tire wear. Examine the tire tread, comparing wear in the center of the contact patch with tire wear at the edge of the contact patch. Note the following:

a. If a tire shows excessive wear at the edge of the contact patch, but the wear at the center of the contact patch is okay, the tire has been underinflated.
b. If a tire shows excessive wear in the center of the contact patch, but the wear at the edge of the contact patch is okay, the tire has been overinflated.

Tread Depth

Check local traffic regulations concerning minimum tread depth. Measure the tread depth at the center of tire and to the center of the tire tread (**Figure 1**) using a tread depth gauge or a small ruler. Suzuki recommends to replace original equipment tires when the front tire tread depth is 1.6 mm (1/16 in.) or less, when the rear tread depth is 2.0 mm (3/32 in.) or less, or when tread wear indicators appear at the designated area on the tire indicating the minimum tread depth.

Rim Inspection and Runout

Frequently inspect wheel rims or cracks, warpage or dents. A damaged rim may be sufficient to cause an air leak or knock it out of alignment.

Wheel rim runout is the amount of "wobble" a wheel shows as it rotates. You can check runout with the wheels on the bike by simply supporting the bike with the wheel off the ground. Slowly turn the wheel while you hold a pointer solidly against a fork leg or the swing arm with the other end against the wheel rim. Just be sure any wobble you observe isn't caused by your own hand.

NOTE
A more accurate method of measuring runout is described in Chapter Ten.

The maximum allowable runout with the tire installed on the rim is as follows:

    a. 2 mm (1/16 in.) axial play (side-to-side).

    b. 2 mm (1/16 in.) radial play (up-and-down).

BATTERY

The battery is an important component in the bike's electrical system, yet most electrical system problems can be traced to battery neglect. The battery should be cleaned and inspected at periodic intervals. All models are equipped with a maintenance free sealed battery and the electrolyte level cannot be checked.

On all models covered in this manual, the negative side is grounded. When removing the battery, disconnect the negative (–) cable first, then the positive (+) cable. This minimizes the chance of a tool shorting to ground when disconnecting the battery positive cable.

Negative Cable Disconnection
(For Service Procedures Only)

1. Place the bike on the sidestand.

2. Remove the screw on each side and remove the battery cover (**Figure 2**).

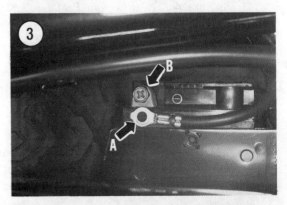

3. On the right-hand side, remove the screw and disconnect the battery negative (–) lead.

4. Move the lead (A, **Figure 3**) out of the way so it will not accidentally contact the battery negative terminal (B, **Figure 3**).

5. Attach the black negative (–) cable. Tighten the bolt securely.

6. Coat the battery connection with dielectric grease or petroleum jelly to retard corrosion.

7. Install the battery cover (**Figure 2**) and the screw on each side. Tighten the screws securely.

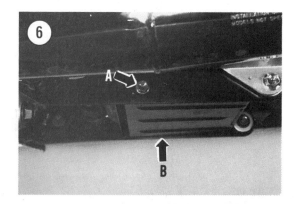

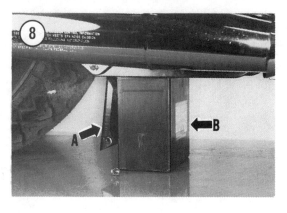

Removal and Installation

1. Place the bike on the sidestand.

2. Remove the screw on each side and remove the battery cover (**Figure 2**).

3. On the right-hand side, remove the screw and disconnect the battery negative (–) lead (**Figure 4**).

4. On the left-hand side, remove the screw and disconnect the battery positive (+) lead (**Figure 5**).

5. Remove the bolt on one side (A, **Figure 6**) securing the battery case floor (B, **Figure 6**) in place.

6. Either hold the battery case floor or place wooden block(s) under it to support the floor when the other bolt is removed.

7. Remove the bolt (**Figure 7**) from the other side of the case.

8. Lower the battery case floor (A, **Figure 8**) and slide the battery (B, **Figure 8**) out of the case. Remove the battery.

9. Inspect the battery as described in this section.

10. Position the battery with the negative (–) battery terminal on the right-hand side of the frame.

11. Carefully move the battery (B, **Figure 8**) up into the battery case and hinge the case floor (A, **Figure 8**) up into position. Install one of the bolts (**Figure 7**) only finger tight at this time.

12. Install the bolt (A, **Figure 6**) on the other side, then tighten both bolts securely.

CAUTION
Be sure the battery cables are connected to their proper terminals. Connecting the battery backwards will reverse the polarity and damage the rectifier.

13. Attach the red positive (+) cable and bolt (**Figure 5**), then the black negative (–) cable (**Figure 4**). Tighten the bolts securely.

14. Coat the battery connections with dielectric grease or petroleum jelly to retard corrosion.

15. Install the battery cover (**Figure 2**) and the screw on each side. Tighten the screws securely.

Inspection and Testing

The battery electrolyte level cannot be serviced. *Never* attempt to remove the sealing bar cap (A, **Figure 9**) from the top of the battery. This bar cap was installed and sealed after the initial filling of electrolyte, and must not to be removed thereafter.

The battery does not require periodic electrolyte inspection or water refilling.

> *WARNING*
> *Even though the battery is a sealed type, protect your eyes, skin and clothing when servicing it. Electrolyte is very corrosive and can cause severe chemical skin burns and permanent injury when spilled. The battery case may be cracked and leaking electrolyte. If any electrolyte is spilled or splashed on clothing or skin, immediately neutralize it with a solution of baking soda and water, then flush with an abundance of clean water. Electrolyte splashed into the eyes is extremely harmful. Safety glasses should always be worn while working with a battery. If you get electrolyte in your eyes, and force your eyes open and flood them with cool, clean water for approximately 15 minutes.*

1. Remove the battery as described in this chapter.
2. Inspect the battery cover, case and floor surfaces for contamination or damage. Clean with a solution of baking soda and water.
3. Set the battery on a stack of newspapers or shop cloths to protect the surface of the workbench.
4. Check the battery case for cracks or other damage. If the battery case is warped, discolored or has a raised top, the battery has been suffering from overcharging or overheating.
5. Check the battery terminal bolts, spacers and nuts for corrosion or damage. Clean parts thoroughly with a solution of baking soda and water. Replace severely corroded or damaged parts.
6. If corroded, clean the top of the battery with a stiff bristle brush using the baking soda and water solution.
7. Check the battery cable clamps for corrosion and damage. If corrosion is minor, clean the battery cable clamps with a stiff wire brush. Replace severely worn or damaged cables.
8. Connect a voltmeter between the battery negative and positive leads (**Figure 10**). Note the following:
   a. If the battery voltage is 13.0-13.2 volts (at 20° C [68° F]), the battery is fully charged
   b. If the battery voltage is below 12.3 volts (at 20° C [68° F]), the battery is undercharged and requires charging.

   c. If the battery voltage is less than 12.0 volts (at 20° C [68° F]), the battery is unserviceable and must be replaced.
9. If the battery is undercharged, recharge it as described in this chapter. Then test the charging system as described in Chapter Two.

Charging

If recharging is required on the maintenance free battery, a digital voltmeter and a special type of charger with a built-in ammeter must be used. It is recommended that the battery be recharged by a Suzuki dealership to avoid damage to a good battery that only requires recharging. The following procedure is included if you choose to recharge this type of battery.

If a battery not in use loses its charge within a week after charging, the battery is defective. A good battery should only self-discharge approximately 1 percent each day.

> *WARNING*
> *During charging, highly explosive hydrogen gas is released from the battery. The battery should be charged only in a well-ventilated area, away from all open flames (including pilot lights on some gas home appliances). Do not allow any smoking in the area. Never check the charge of the battery by arcing across the terminals; the resulting spark can ignite the hydrogen gas.*

> *CAUTION*
> *Always remove the battery from the bike before connecting charging equipment. Always disconnect the battery cables*

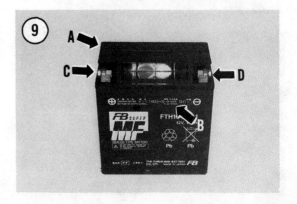

from the battery. During the charging procedure the charger may destroy the diodes within the voltage regulator/rectifier if the cables were left connected.

1. Remove the battery from the bike as described in this chapter.

2. Set the battery on a stack of newspapers or shop cloths to protect the surface of the workbench.

NOTE
*If the instructions (B, **Figure 9**) or label on the battery is damaged or missing, refer to **Table 3** for amperage and charge time specifications.*

3. Connect the positive (+) charger lead to the positive (+) battery terminal (C, **Figure 9**) and the negative (–) charger lead to the negative (–) battery terminal (D, **Figure 9**).

4. Set the charger at 12 volts. If the output of the charger is variable, set it to its lowest setting.

5. The charging time depends on the discharged condition of the battery. Use the suggested charging amperage and length of time charge on the battery label. A battery should be charged at a slow charge rate of 1/10th its given capacity.

6. Turn the charger ON.

7. After the battery has been charged for the pre-determined time, turn the charger off, disconnect the leads and measure the battery voltage. Refer to the following:

   a. If the battery voltage is 13.0-13.2 volts (at 20° C [68° F]), the battery is fully charged.

   b. If the battery voltage is below 12.3 volts (at 20° C [68° F]), the battery is undercharged and requires charging.

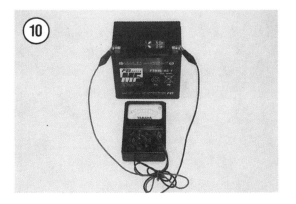

8. If the battery remains stable for one hour, the battery is charged.

9. Install the battery into the bike as described in this chapter.

New Battery Installation

When replacing the old battery with a new one, charge it completely before installing it in the bike. Failure to do will reduce the life of the battery. Using a new battery without an initial charge will cause permanent battery damage. That is, the battery will never be able to hold more than an 80% charge. Charging a new battery after it has been used will not bring its charge to 100%. When purchasing a new battery from a dealership or parts store, verify its charge status. If necessary, have them perform the initial or booster charge before picking up the battery.

NOTE
***Recycle your old battery.** When you replace the old battery, be sure to turn in the old battery at that time. The lead plates and the plastic case can be recycled. Most motorcycle dealerships will accept your old battery in trade when you purchase a new one. Never place an old battery in your household trash since it is illegal, in most states, to place any acid or lead (heavy metal) contents in landfills. There is also the danger of the battery being crushed in the trash truck and spraying acid on the truck or landfill operator.*

BATTERY ELECTRICAL CABLE CONNECTORS

To ensure good electrical contact between the battery and the electrical cables, the cables must be clean and free of corrosion.

1. If the electrical cable terminals are badly corroded, disconnect them from the bike's electrical system.

2. Thoroughly clean each connector with a wire brush and then with a baking soda solution. Rinse thoroughly with clean water and wipe dry with a clean cloth.

3. After cleaning, apply a thin layer of dielectric grease to the battery terminals before reattaching the cables.

4. If disconnected, attach the electrical cables to the bike's electrical system.

5. After connecting the electrical cables, apply a light coating of dielectric grease to the electrical terminals of the battery to retard corrosion and decomposition of the terminals.

PERIODIC LUBRICATION

Engine Oil

Oil is graded according to its viscosity, which is an indication of how thick it is. The Society of Automotive Engineers (SAE) system distinguishes oil viscosity by numbers. Thick oils have higher viscosity numbers than thin oils. For example, an SAE 5 oil is a thin oil while an SAE 90 oil is relatively thick. If the oil has been tested in cold weather it is denoted with a W after the number as SAE 10W.

Grease

A good quality grease (preferably waterproof) should be used. Water does not wash grease from parts as easily as it washes off oil. In addition, grease maintains its lubricating qualities better than oil on long and strenuous rides.

Cleaning Solvent

Use a high flash point solvent to remove dirt, grease and oil during service.

> *WARNING*
> *Never use gasoline as a cleaning solvent. Gasoline is extremely volatile and contains tremendously destructive potential energy. The slightest spark from metal parts hitting each other, or a tool slipping, could cause a fatal explosion.*

Engine Oil Level Check and Adding Oil

Check the engine oil level with the dipstick attached to the oil fill cap located on the rear corner of the right-hand crankcase.

1. Place the bike on the sidestand on level ground.
2. Start the engine and let it idle for 1-2 minutes.
3. Shut off the engine and let the oil settle for 1-2 minutes.
4. Hold the bike in the true vertical position. A false reading will be given if the bike is tipped to either side.
5. On the right-hand side, unscrew the oil fill cap/dipstick (**Figure 11**) from the right-hand crankcase.
6. Use a clean lint-free cloth and wipe the dipstick clean of all residual oil on it.
7. Rest the oil fill cap/dipstick onto the crankcase opening. DO NOT screw it into the threaded hole as you will get a false reading.
8. Remove the oil fill cap/dipstick and observe the oil level (A, **Figure 12**). The oil level should be between the 2 lines. If the level is below the lower F

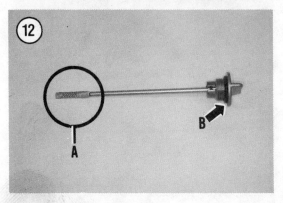

line, add the recommended engine oil to correct the level.

9. Insert a funnel into the oil fill hole and fill the engine with the correct viscosity and quantity of oil. Refer to **Table 4** and **Table 5**.

10. Check the oil fill cap/dipstick O-ring gasket (B, **Figure 12**) for hardness or deterioration and replace if necessary.

11. Install the oil fill cap/dipstick and tighten securely.

Engine Oil and Oil Filter Change

Change the engine oil and the oil filter at the factory-recommended oil change interval indicated in **Table 1**. This assumes that the motorcycle is operated in moderate climates. In extreme climates, oil should be changed every 30 days. The time interval is more important that the mileage interval because acids formed by combustion blowby will contaminate the oil even if the motorcycle is not run for several months. If the motorcycle is operated under dusty conditions, the oil will get dirty more quickly and should be changed more frequently.

Suzuki recommends the use of Suzuki Performance 4 Motor Oil that is a very high performance motor oil which has a special friction modifier added. If this type of oil is not used, use only a high-quality detergent motor oil with an API classification of SE or SF. The API classification is printed on the label of the plastic bottle. Try to use the same brand of oil at each change. Use of any oil additive is not recommended as it may cause clutch slippage. Refer to **Figure 13** for correct oil viscosity to use under anticipated ambient temperatures (not engine oil temperatures).

To change the engine oil and filter you need the following:

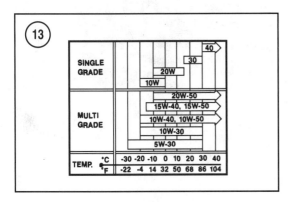

a. Drain pan.

b. Funnel.

c. Open-end wrench (drain plug).

d. Suzuki oil filter wrench or equivalent.

e. Oil.

f. New oil filter element.

g. Socket-type oil filter wrench. See following NOTE.

NOTE
Because of the small working area around the oil filter, use a socket type oil filter wrench to remove it.

NOTE
Never dispose of motor oil in the trash, on the ground, or down a storm drain. Many service stations accept used motor oil and waste haulers provide curbside used motor oil collection. Do not combine other fluids with motor oil to be recycled. To locate a recycler, contact the American Petroleum Institute (API) at www.recycleoil.org.

NOTE
Warming the engine allows the oil to heat up; thus it flows freely and carries contamination and any sludge out with it.

1. Start the engine and let it reach operating temperature; 15-20 minutes of stop-and-go riding is usually sufficient.

2. Turn the engine off and place the bike on level ground on the sidestand.

3. Place a drain pan under the center rear portion of the crankcase and remove the drain plug (**Figure 14**). Remove the oil fill cap/dipstick (**Figure 11**) to speed the flow of oil.

4. Inspect the sealing washer on the crankcase drain plug. Replace if its condition is in doubt.

5. Thoroughly clean the area surrounding the drain plug threaded opening prior to installing the drain plug. This will avoid introducing any foreign matter into the crankcase.

6. Install the drain plug and washer and tighten to the torque specification listed in **Table 6**.

NOTE
Before removing the oil filter, clean off all road dirt and any oil residue around it.

7. Move the drain pan under the oil filter at the front of the engine.

NOTE
Because the right-hand frame rail and the oil cooler hose are so close to the oil filter there is very little working room for oil filter removal and installation. The easiest way to remove the oil filter is to use a Suzuki oil filter wrench (part No. 09915-40611) and a box-end wrench.

8. Use an oil filter wrench and unscrew the oil filter (**Figure 15**) from the engine. Place the old filter in a reclosable plastic bag and close it to prevent residual oil from draining out. Discard the used oil filter properly.

9. Clean off the oil filter mating surface of the crankcase with a shop rag and cleaning solvent. Remove any sludge or road dirt. Wipe it dry with a clean, lint-free cloth.

10. Apply a light coat of clean engine oil to the O-ring seal on the new oil filter.

11. Screw on the new oil filter by hand until the O-ring seal contacts the crankcase mating surface. Tighten the oil filter 2 full turns, then stop. Do not overtighten or the filter can leak.

12. During oil filter removal, some oil may get onto the crankcase. Prior to starting the engine, wipe off any spilled oil with a shop cloth. If necessary, spray some aerosol electrical contact cleaner on the crankcase to remove the oil residue.

13. Insert a funnel into the oil fill hole and fill the engine with the correct viscosity and quantity of oil. Refer to **Table 4** and **Table 5**.

14. Check the oil fill cap/dipstick O-ring gasket (B, **Figure 12**) for hardness or deterioration, replace if necessary.

15. Install the oil fill cap/dipstick and tighten securely.

16. Start the engine, let it run at idle speed and check for leaks.

17. Turn the engine off and check the oil level as described in this chapter; adjust as necessary.

WARNING
Prolonged contact with oil may cause skin cancer. Wash your hands thoroughly with soap and water as soon as possible after handling or coming in contact with motor oil.

Engine Oil Pressure Test

This procedure checks engine oil pressure and should be performed after reassembling the engine or when troubleshooting the lubrication system.

To perform this test, the following special tool assembly, or equivalent, is required:

    a. Oil pressure gauge: Suzuki part No. 09915-74510.

    b. Adapter: Suzuki part No. 90015-74530.

1. Check the engine oil level as described in this chapter. Add oil if necessary.

2. Place a drain pan under the oil pressure inspection bolt.

3. Unscrew the oil pressure inspection bolt (**Figure 16**) from the lower crankcase.

4. Install the adapter, then the gauge into the oil pressure inspection bolt hole. Make sure the fitting is tight to avoid an oil loss.

> *CAUTION*
> *Keep the gauge hose away from the exhaust pipe during this test. If the hose makes contact, it could melt and spray hot oil onto the hot exhaust pipe, resulting in a dangerous fire.*

> *NOTE*
> *Suzuki does not designate what degree range constitute summer or winter temperatures. They do specify that the engine oil temperature should be at 60° C (140° F).*

5A. In summer temperatures: start the engine and allow to idle for 10 minutes at 2,000 rpm.

5B. In winter temperatures: start the engine and allow to idle for 20 minutes at 2,000 rpm.

6. After the engine has warmed up for the specified time period, increase the engine speed to 3,000 rpm and note the gauge reading. Refer to the specified oil

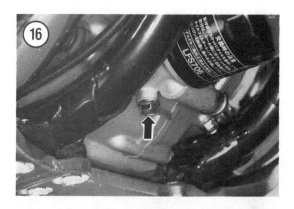

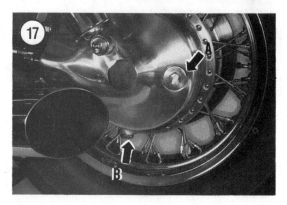

pressure listed in **Table 7**. If the oil pressure is lower than specified check the following:
  a. Clogged oil filter.
  b. Oil leak from oil passageway.
  c. Damaged oil seal(s).
  d. Defective oil pump.
  e. Combination of the above.

7. If the oil pressure is higher than specified check the following:
  a. Oil viscosity too heavy (drain oil and install lighter weight oil).
  b. Clogged oil passageway.
  c. Improperly installed oil filter.
  d. Combination of the above

8. Shut off the engine and remove the test equipment.

9. Apply a light coat of silicone seal to the oil pressure inspection bolt threads, then install the bolt onto the crankcase and tighten securely.

10. Check oil level and adjust if necessary.

Final Drive Oil Level Check

Check the final drive case oil level when the oil is cool. If the bike has run, allow it to cool down (minimum of 10 minutes), then check the oil level. When checking or changing the final drive oil, do not allow any dirt or foreign matter to enter the case opening.

1. Place the bike on the sidestand on a level surface.
2. Wipe the area around the oil filler cap clean and unscrew the oil filler cap (A, **Figure 17**).
3. The oil level is correct when the oil is up to the lower edge of the filler cap hole. If the oil level is low, add hypoid gear oil until the oil level is correct. Refer to **Table 4** for correct oil viscosity and type.
4. Inspect the O-ring seal on the oil filler cap. Replace if it is deteriorated or starting to harden.
5. Install the oil filler cap and tighten securely.

Final Drive Oil Change

The factory-recommended oil change interval is listed in **Table 1**.

To drain the oil you will need the following:
  a. Drain pan.
  b. Funnel.
  c. Approximately 200-220 ml (6.8-7.4 U.S. oz./ [6.7-7.4 Imp. oz.]) of hypoid gear oil.

Discard old oil as outlined under *Engine Oil and Filter Change* in this chapter.

1. Ride the bike until normal operating temperature is obtained. Usually 15-20 minutes of stop-and-go riding is sufficient.

2. Place the bike on the centerstand.

3. Place a drain pan under the drain plug.

4. Remove the oil filler cap (A, **Figure 17**) and the drain plug (B, **Figure 17**).

5. Let the oil drain for at least 15-20 minutes to ensure that the majority of the oil has drained out. Tip the bike to the left-hand side to drain out any residual oil.

6. Inspect the sealing washer on the drain plug; replace the sealing washer if necessary.

7. Install the drain plug and tighten it securely.

8. Insert a funnel into the oil filler cap hole.

9. Add hypoid gear oil until the oil level is correct. Refer to **Table 4** for correct oil viscosity and type to use under anticipated ambient temperatures.

NOTE
In order to measure the correct amount of fluid, use a plastic baby bottle. These have measurements in milliliters (ml) and fluid ounces (oz.) on the side.

10. Install the oil filler cap (A, **Figure 17**) and tighten securely.

11. Test ride the bike and check for oil leaks. After the test ride recheck the oil level as described in this chapter and readjust if necessary.

General Lubrication

At the service intervals listed in **Table 1**, lubricate the following items with engine oil:

    a. Sidestand pivot point.
    b. Brake pedal.
    c. Brake lever.
    d. Clutch lever.

Control Cable Lubrication

Clean and lubricate the throttle cable at the intervals indicated in **Table 1**. In addition, the cable should be checked for kinks and signs of wear and damage or fraying that could cause the cables to fail or stick. Cables are expendable items and will not last forever under the best of conditions.

The most positive method of control cable lubrication involves the use of a cable lubricator like the one shown in **Figure 18**. A can of cable lube or a general lubricant is required. Do not use chain lube as a cable lubricant.

CAUTION
If the stock cable has been replaced with nylon-lined cables, do not oil them as described in the following procedure. Oil and most cable lubricants will cause the liner to expand, pinching the liner against the cable. Nylon lined cables are normally used dry. When servicing nylon-lined cables, follow the cable manufacturer's instructions.

NOTE
The main cause of cable breakage or cable stiffness is improper lubrication. Maintaining the cables as described in this section will assure long service life.

1. Remove the screws securing the right-hand switch assembly together and separate the switch (A, **Figure 19**) to gain access to the throttle cable end.

2. Remove the fuel tank as described in Chapter Eight. This is necessary to gain access to the lower end of the cable being lubricated.

3. Disconnect the throttle cable end (B, **Figure 19**) from the grip assembly.

4. Remove the screw and disconnect the throttle cable from the switch assembly.

5. Attach a cable lubricator to the end of the cable following the manufacturer's instructions (**Figure 18**).

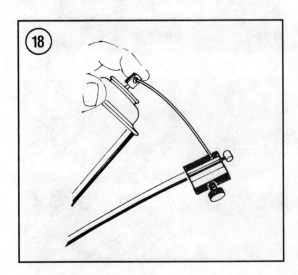

NOTE
Place a shop cloth at the end of the cable
to catch the oil as it runs out.

6. Insert the lubricant can nozzle into the lubricator, press the button on the can and hold down until the lubricant begins to flow out of the other end of the cable. If you cannot get the cable lube to flow through the cable at one end, remove the lubricator, disconnect the cables from the carburetor assembly and try at the opposite end of the cable.

7. Disconnect the lubricator.

8. Apply a light coat of grease to the cable ends before reconnecting it. Reconnect the cable and adjust as described in this chapter.

9. After lubricating the throttle cable, operate the throttle grip at the handlebar. It should open and close smoothly with no binding.

Brake System

The following brake components should be lubricated with silicone grease (specified for brake use) whenever the components are removed for service:

   a. Master cylinder rubber boots (inside).

   b. Brake caliper boots (inside).

   c. Brake caliper pin bolt sliding surface.

Brake Pedal Pivot Shaft Lubrication

The brake pedal should be removed, as described in Chapter Twelve, periodically and the pivot shaft lubricated with grease.

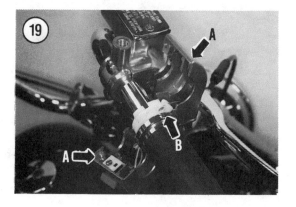

Steering Head Bearings

The steering head bearings should be cleaned and lubricated at the intervals specified in **Table 1**. Because the steering stem must be removed to clean the bearings, refer to *Steering Head* in Chapter Ten.

Speedometer Cable Lubrication

Lubricate the speedometer cable every year or whenever the speedometer needle operation becomes erratic.

1. Unscrew the speedometer cable sleeve nut from the base of the meter assembly and at the front wheel.

2. Remove the cable from the sheath.

3. If the existing grease is contaminated, thoroughly clean off old grease. Wipe the cable with a cloth dipped in cleaning solvent and thoroughly dry with a lint-free cloth.

4. Thoroughly coat the cable with a good grade of multipurpose grease and reinstall it in the sheath.

5. Insert the cable into the meter and tighten the sleeve nut.

6. Insert the cable into the speedometer drive gear and slowly rotate the front wheel until the cable end is indexed properly into the drive gear. Tighten the sleeve nut.

Swing Arm Bearing Assembly Lubrication

Frequent lubrication of the swing arm bearings is vital to maintain the rear suspension in peak condition. The swing arm bearing assemblies should be lubricated at the intervals specified in **Table 1**. Use a good grade of water-proof grease. Do not forget to lubricate the swing arm after each trip to the coin-operated car wash.

The swing arm must be removed and partially disassembled to lubricate the needle bearings and collars as described in Chapter Eleven.

To clean, examine and lubricate the swing arm bearings and bushings, remove the swing arm as described in Chapter Eleven. Clean, inspect and lubricate the bearings while they are still installed in the swing arm. Do *not* remove the bearings as they are damaged during removal.

PERIODIC MAINTENANCE

Throttle Operation

The throttle operation should be checked at the interval indicated in **Table 1**.

Check for smooth throttle operation from fully closed to fulled opened and then return to automatic fully closed position. The throttle should return to the fully closed position without any hesitation.

Check the throttle cable for damage, wear or deterioration. Make sure the throttle cable is not kinked at any place.

If the throttle does not return to the fully closed position smoothly and the exterior of the cable sheaths appears to be in good condition, lubricate the throttle cables as described in this chapter. Also apply a light coat of grease to the throttle cable spool.

If cable lubrication does not solve the problem, replace the throttle cable as described in Chapter Eight.

Throttle Grip Rotational Free Play and Operation

Check the throttle cable free play at the interval indicated in **Table 1**. The throttle grip rotational free play is listed in **Table 7**.

In time, the throttle cable free play will become excessive from cable stretch. This will delay throttle response and affect low speed operation. On the other hand, if there is no throttle cable free play, an excessively high idle can result.

1. Shift the transmission into NEUTRAL.
2. Start the engine and allow it to idle.
3. With the engine at idle speed, slowly twist the throttle to raise engine speed.
4. Determine the amount of rotational movement (free play) required to raise the engine speed from idle. If the rotational free play is incorrect, perform this procedure.
5. Shut off the engine.
6. Slide the rubber sleeve (**Figure 20**) off the cable adjuster.
7. Loosen the locknut (A, **Figure 21**) and turn the adjuster (B, **Figure 21**) in either direction until the correct amount of free play is achieved.
8. Tighten the locknut (B).
9. Restart the engine and repeat Steps 2-4 to make sure the adjustment is correct.

10. If the correct throttle rotational free play cannot be achieved using this method, replace the cables as described in Chapter Eight.

11. Check the throttle cables from grip to carburetor. Make sure they are not kinked or chafed. Replace as necessary.

> *WARNING*
> *With the engine idling, move the handlebar from side to side. If the idle speed increases during this movement, the throttle cable may need adjusting or may be incorrectly routed through the frame. Correct this problem immediately. Do **not** ride the bike in this unsafe condition.*

12. Test ride the bike, slowly at first, and make sure the throttle cables are operating correctly. Readjust if necessary.

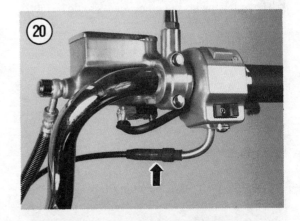

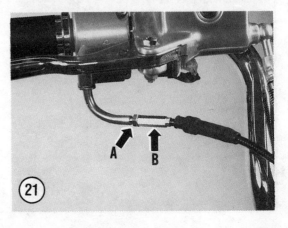

Automatic Compression Release Cable Free Play Check and Adjustment

Check the free play automatic compression release cable at the interval listed in **Table 1**. Incorrect cable free play will result in starting difficulties and/or engine damage.

1. Remove the fuel tank as described in Chapter Eight.

2. Loosen the bolts securing the right-hand front cylinder head side cover and the left-hand rear cylinder head side cover. Remove both covers.

3. On the front cylinder, insert a flat feeler gauge between the lever and the stopper on the cable bracket (**Figure 22**). Refer to dimension A listed in **Table 7**.

4. If adjustment is necessary, continue with Step 5.

NOTE
*Refer to **Figure 23** for the following steps.*

5. Loosen the cable locknut and adjust nut (A, **Figure 23**) and locate the cable outer end tube (B). Check that the cable (C, **Figure 23**) has sufficient free play so the other cable can be adjusted.

6. Loosen the solenoid cable locknut and adjust nut (D, **Figure 23**) and locate the cable outer tube end (E).

7. Rotate adjust nut (D, **Figure 23**) until the clearance between the lever and the stopper on the cable bracket, dimension A, is same as listed in **Table 7**. This dimension locates the decompression solenoid plunger at the top end of its travel. Hold onto the adjust nut (D, **Figure 23**) and tighten the locknut (D, **Figure 23**). Recheck the clearance and readjust if necessary.

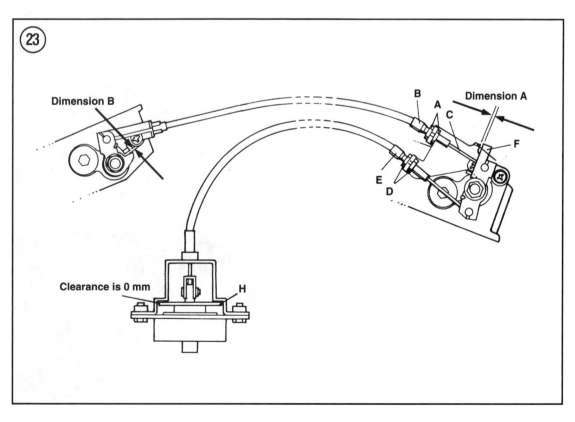

8. While maintaining the dimension A clearance, rotate adjust nut (A, **Figure 23**) until the clearance (**Figure 24**) between the lever and the stopper, dimension B, is same as listed in **Table 7**. Hold onto the adjust nut (A, **Figure 23**) and tighten the locknut. Recheck the clearance and readjust if necessary.

9. Install the right-hand front cylinder head side cover and the left-hand rear cylinder head side cover and tighten the bolts securely.

Disc Brakes

Check the hydraulic brake fluid in each disc brake master cylinder at the interval listed in **Table 1**. The brake pads should also be checked for wear at the same time. Bleeding the system, servicing the brake system components and replacing the brake pads are covered in Chapter Thirteen.

Disc Brake Fluid Level

Keep the hydraulic brake fluid in the reservoir at its maximum level at the upper line. Refer to **Figure 25** for the front brake and A, **Figure 26** for the rear brake. If necessary, correct the level by adding fresh brake fluid.

> *WARNING*
> *Use brake fluid clearly marked DOT 4 and specified for disc brakes. Others may cause brake failure. Do not intermix different brands or types of brake fluid as they may not be compatible. Do not intermix silicone based (DOT 5) brake fluid as it can cause brake component damage leading to brake system failure.*

> *CAUTION*
> *Be careful when adding brake fluid. Do not spill it on plastic, painted or plated surfaces as it will destroy the finish. Wash off the area immediately with soapy water and thoroughly rinse it off with clean water.*

1. Place the bike on level ground on the sidestand.

2. Clean any dirt from the area around the cover prior to removing the cover.

3. On the front master cylinder, perform the following:

a. Position the handlebar so the front master cylinder is horizontal.

b. Remove the screws securing the cover (**Figure 27**). Remove the cover and diaphragm.

4. On the rear master cylinder, perform the following:

a. Remove the screws and the trim cover (B, **Figure 26**)

b. Clean the top of the master cylinder reservoir of all dirt and foreign matter.

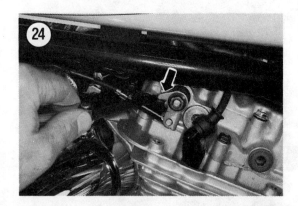

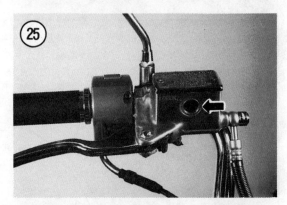

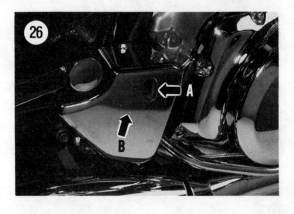

c. Remove the screws securing the top cover (**Figure 28**). Remove the cover and diaphragm.

NOTE
To control the flow of brake fluid, punch a small hole into the seal of a new container of brake fluid next to the edge of the pour spout. This will help eliminate fluid spillage when adding fluid to small reservoirs.

WARNING
Use brake fluid clearly marked DOT 4 from a sealed container. Other types may cause brake failure. Always use the same brand name; do not intermix as many brands are not compatible. Do not intermix silicone based (DOT 5) brake fluid as it can cause brake component damage leading to brake system failure.

5. Refill the master cylinder reservoir to maintain the correct fluid level as indicated on the side of the reservoir.

6. On the front master cylinder, install the diaphragm and cover (**Figure 27**) and tighten the screws securely.

7. On the rear master cylinder, perform the following:

    a. Install the diaphragm and cover (**Figure 28**) and tighten the screws securely.

    b. Install the trim cover and tighten the screws securely.

Disc Brake Hoses

Check the brake hoses between each master cylinder and each brake caliper assembly.

If there is any leakage, tighten the connections and bleed the brakes as described under *Bleeding the System* in Chapter Twelve. If tightening the connection does not stop the leak or if the brake hose(s) is damaged, cracked or chafed, replace the brake hose(s) and bleed the system as described in Chapter Twelve.

Disc Brake Pad Wear

Inspect the brake pads for excessive or uneven wear, scoring and oil or grease on the friction surface.

1. Remove the dust cover from the brake caliper.
2. Look into the caliper assembly and check the wear lines on the brake pads.

NOTE
Figure 29 *is shown with the brake pads removed from the caliper for clarity. The wear line is visible without removing the pads.*

3. Replace both pads if the wear line (**Figure 29**) on the pads reaches the brake disc.

4. If this condition exists, replace the pads as described in Chapter Twelve.

Disc Brake Fluid Change

Every time the reservoir cap is removed, a small amount of dirt and moisture enters the brake fluid. The same thing happens if a leak occurs or any part of the hydraulic system is loosened or disconnected. Dirt can clog the system and cause unnecessary wear. Water in the brake fluid vaporizes at high temperature, impairing the hydraulic action and reducing the brake's stopping ability.

To maintain peak performance, change the brake fluid as indicated in **Table 1**. To change brake fluid, follow the *Bleeding the System* procedure in Chapter Twelve. Continue adding new fluid to the master cylinder and bleeding out at the caliper until the fluid leaving the caliper is clean and free of contaminants.

> *WARNING*
> *Use brake fluid from a sealed container clearly marked DOT 3 or DOT 4 only (specified for disc brakes). Others may cause brake failure. Do not intermix different brands or types of brake fluid as they may not be compatible. Do not intermix a silicone based (DOT 5) brake fluid as it can cause brake component damage leading to brake system failure.*

Rear Brake Pedal Height Inspection and Adjustment

Adjust the brake pedal height at the interval listed in **Table 1**. The pedal height will change with brake pad wear as the hydraulic fluid level lowers in the master cylinder.

The top of the brake pedal should be positioned above the top surface of the footpeg. Refer to **Table 7** for the specified dimension.

1. Make sure the brake pedal is in the at-rest position.

2. To change height position, remove the trim cap from the Allen adjust bolt.

3. Use an Allen wrench (A, **Figure 30**) and turn the adjust bolt (B, **Figure 30**) until the correct height is achieved.

4. Install the trim cap into the bolt.

Rear Brake Light Switch Adjustment

1. Turn the ignition switch to the ON position.

2. Depress the brake pedal. The brake light should come on after the brake pedal is depressed approximately 10 mm (0.4 in.). If necessary, adjust the bolt (**Figure 31**) as follows.

> *NOTE*
> *Figure 32 shows the small adjust bolt and nut with the front footrest assembly partially removed. Do not remove the assembly for this procedure.*

3. To make the light come on earlier, loosen the locknut (A, **Figure 32**) and turn the adjusting bolt (B, **Figure 32**) until the brake light illuminates just before a pressure rise is felt when the brake pedal is depressed. Tighten the locknut securely.

4. Check that the brake light comes on when the pedal is depressed and goes off when the pedal is released. Readjust if necessary.

5. Turn the ignition switch to the OFF position.

Clutch Fluid Level Check

The clutch is hydraulically operated and requires no routine adjustment.

The hydraulic fluid in the clutch master cylinder should be checked as listed in **Table 1** or whenever the level drops, whichever comes first. Bleeding the clutch system and servicing clutch components are covered in Chapter Six.

> *CAUTION*
> *If the clutch operates correctly when the engine is cold or in cool weather, but operates erratically (or not at all) after the engine warms-up or when riding in hot weather, there is air in the hydraulic line and the clutch system must be bled. Refer to **Bleeding the System** in Chapter Six.*

The fluid level in the reservoir should be up to the upper mark within the reservoir. This upper level mark is only visible when the master cylinder top cover is removed. If the fluid level reaches the lower level mark (A, **Figure 33**), visible through the view-

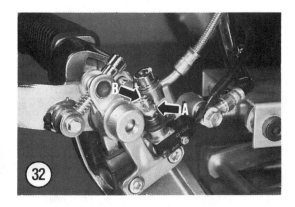

ing port in the master cylinder reservoir, the fluid level must be corrected by adding fresh hydraulic (brake) fluid.

1. Place the bike on level ground and position the handlebars in the straight-ahead position so the master cylinder reservoir is in its normal riding position.

2. Clean any dirt from the area around the top cover prior to removing the cover.

3. Remove the screws securing the top cover and remove the top cover (B, **Figure 33**) and the diaphragm.

> *NOTE*
> *To control the flow of hydraulic fluid, punch a small hole into the seal of a new container of hydraulic (brake) fluid next to the edge of the pour spout. This will help eliminate fluid spillage when adding fluid to small reservoirs.*

> *WARNING*
> *Use hydraulic brake fluid from a sealed container clearly marked DOT 3 or DOT 4 only. Do not intermix different brands or types of hydraulic fluid as they may not be compatible. Do not intermix a silicone based (DOT 5) hydraulic fluid as it can cause clutch component damage leading to clutch release system failure.*

4. Add hydraulic until the level is to the upper level line within the master cylinder body. Use fresh hydraulic fluid from a sealed container.

5. Reinstall the diaphragm and the top cover (B, **Figure 33**). Tighten the screws securely.

Clutch Hydraulic Line

Check the clutch hydraulic line between the master cylinder and the clutch slave cylinder. If there is any leakage, tighten the connections and bleed the clutch as described under *Bleeding the System* in Chapter Six. If this does not stop the leak or if a clutch line is obviously damaged, cracked or chafed, replace the clutch line and bleed the system as described in Chapter Five.

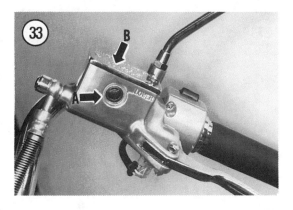

Camshaft Chain Tensioner Adjustment

There is no cam chain tensioner adjustment on this engine. Camshaft chain tension is maintained automatically on each cylinder.

Exhaust System

1. Inspect the exhaust system for cracks or dents which could alter performance.
2. Check all exhaust system fasteners and mounting points for loose or damaged parts.
3. Make sure all mounting bolts and nuts are tight. Refer to **Figure 34** and **Figure 35**. If loose, refer to Chapter Eight for torque specifications.

Air Filter Elements
Removal/Installation

Remove and clean the air filter elements at the interval indicated in **Table 1** and replace whenever they are damaged or start to deteriorate.

The air filter removes dust and abrasive particles before the air enters the carburetors and engine. Without the air filter, very fine particles could enter into the engine and cause rapid wear of the piston rings, cylinder bores and bearings. They also might clog small passages in the carburetors. Never run the bike without the elements installed.

Proper air filter servicing can ensure long service from your engine.

Front air filter

1. Remove both seats and the frame right-hand front side cover as described in Chapter Thirteen.
2. Remove the fuel tank and tank bracket as described in Chapter Eight.
3. Disconnect the battery negative (–) lead as described in this chapter.
4. Remove the screws securing the throttle cable connector (**Figure 36**).
5. Move the throttle cables and connector (A, **Figure 37**) out of the way.
6. Unhook the top cover (B, **Figure 37**) and remove it.
7. Remove the element from the front air box.

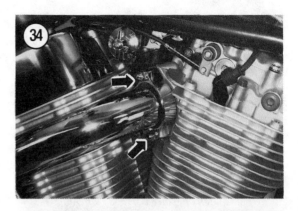

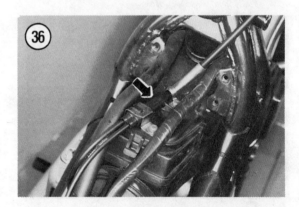

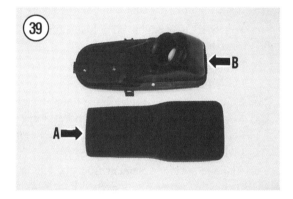

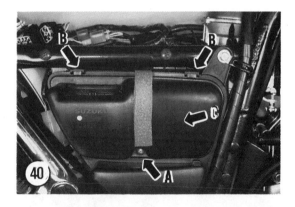

NOTE
The top grid in the box is not removable—do not try to remove it as the lower portion of the air box will be damaged.

8. Check the top grid of the air box (**Figure 38**) for any foreign matter that may have passed through a broken filter element. Remove all debris.

9. Check the air intake opening in the cover for any trapped debris that may restrict air intake flow. Clean out if necessary.

10. Inspect, clean and reoil the element (A, **Figure 39**) as described in this chapter.

11. Inspect the sealing surface of the top cover (B, **Figure 39**) for damage, replace if necessary.

12. Install the air filter element and make sure it is correctly seated into the air box.

13. Install the top cover and seat it correctly so there is no air leak.

14. Install all items removed.

Rear air filter

1. Remove both seats and the frame right-hand side cover as described in Chapter Thirteen.

2. Remove the fuel tank as described in Chapter Seven.

3. Disconnect the battery negative (–) lead as described in this chapter.

4. Loosen the screw (A, **Figure 40**) and hinge the air filter cover up to release the upper hooks (B, **Figure 40**). Remove the cover (C, **Figure 40**).

5. Remove the element from the rear air box.

NOTE
The side grid in the box is not removable—do not try to remove it as the air box will be damaged.

6. Check the grid of the air box (**Figure 41**) for any foreign matter that may have passed through a broken filter element. Remove all debris.

7. Check the air intake opening in the cover for any trapped debris that may restrict air intake flow. Clean out if necessary.

8. Inspect, clean and reoil the element (A, **Figure 42**) as described in this chapter.

9. Inspect the sealing surface of the cover (B, **Figure 42**) for damage, replace if necessary.

10. Install the air filter element and make sure it is correctly seated into the air box (**Figure 43**).

11. Install the cover, seat it correctly so there is no air leak, then install the screw and tighten securely.

12. Install all items removed.

Air Filter Element Cleaning and Reoiling (Front and Rear)

Service the air filter element in a well-ventilated area, away from all sparks and flames.

WARNING
*Do **not** clean the air filter element with gasoline.*

1. Clean both filter elements with a filter solvent to remove oil and dirt. Allow the element to air dry.

2. Thoroughly and carefully inspect the filter element. Refer to A, **Figure 39** for the front air filter and A, **Figure 42** for the rear air filter. If it is torn or broken in any area, replace the air filter element(s). If the element is okay, continue with Step 3.

3. Fill a clean pan with liquid detergent cleaner and warm water.

4. Submerge the filter elements into the cleaning solution and gently work the cleaner into the filter pores. Soak and squeeze (gently) the filter elements to clean them.

CAUTION
Do not wring or twist the filter element when cleaning it. Doing so could damage the filter and allow unfiltered air to enter the engine and cause severe and rapid wear.

5. Rinse the filter elements under warm water while soaking and gently squeezing them.

6. Repeat Step 4 and Step 5 two or three times or until there are no signs of dirt being rinsed from the filter elements.

7. After cleaning the filter elements, inspect them carefully and replace any that are torn or broken. Do not run the engine with a damaged filter element as it may allow dirt to enter the engine and cause severe engine wear.

8. Set the filter element aside and allow it to dry thoroughly.

CAUTION
Make sure the filter elements are completely dry before oiling them.

9. Properly oiling an air filter element is a messy job. Wear a pair of disposable rubber gloves when performing this procedure. Oil one filter element at a time as follows:

   a. Purchase a box of gallon size storage bags. The bags can be used when cleaning the filter as well as for storing engine and carburetor parts during disassembly service procedures.

   b. Place the filter element into a storage bag.

   c. Pour SAE 30W engine oil or foam air filter oil onto the filter element to soak it.

   d. Gently squeeze the filter element to let the air out of the bag and close the bag.

   e. Gently squeeze and release the filter element to soak filter oil into the filter's pores. Repeat until all of the filter element 's pores are saturated with the oil.

   f. Remove the filter element from the bag and check the pores for uneven oiling. This is

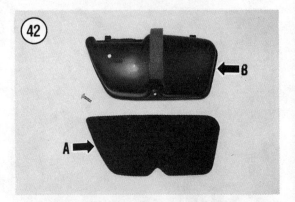

indicated by light or dark areas. If necessary, soak the filter and squeeze it again.

g. When the filter element oiling is even, squeeze the filter element a final time.

h. Repeat for the other filter element.

i. Pour the leftover engine or filter oil from the bag back into the oil container for reuse.

j. Dispose of the plastic bag correctly.

10. Install the air filter elements as described in this chapter.

> *WARNING*
> *Prolonged contact with oil may cause skin cancer. Wash your hands thoroughly with soap and water as soon as possible after handling or coming in contact with motor oil.*

Fuel Line Inspection

Inspect the fuel line from the fuel tank (**Figure 44**) to the fuel shutoff valve (**Figure 45**) and then to the carburetors and the fuel pump. If any are cracked or starting to deteriorate they must be replaced. Make

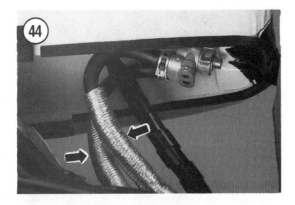

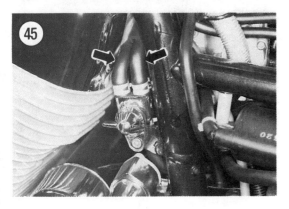

sure the hose clamps are in place and holding securely.

> *WARNING*
> *A damaged or deteriorated fuel line presents a very dangerous fire hazard to both the rider and the vehicle if fuel should spill onto a hot engine or exhaust pipe.*

Vacuum Line Inspection

Inspect the condition of all vacuum lines for cracks or deterioration; replace if necessary. Make sure the hose clamps are in place and holding securely.

Crankcase Breather (U.S. Only)

Inspect the breather hose from the cylinder head breather cover to the front air filter air case. If it is cracked or starting to deteriorate it must be replaced. Make sure the hose clamps are in place and holding securely.

Evaporative Emission Control System (California Models Only)

Fuel vapor from the fuel tank is routed into a charcoal canister when the engine is stopped. When the engine is started these vapors are drawn, through the vacuum controlled valves, into the carburetors and into the engine to be burned. Make sure all vacuum hoses are correctly routed and attached. Inspect the hoses and replace any if necessary.

Refer to Chapter Eight for detailed information on the Evaporative Emission Control System and for vacuum hose routing.

Wheel Bearings

There is no factory-recommended mileage interval for cleaning and repacking the wheel bearings. They should be inspected and serviced, if necessary, every time the wheel is removed or whenever there is a likelihood of water contamination. The correct service procedures are covered in Chapter Ten and Chapter Eleven.

Front Suspension Check

1. Apply the front brake and pump the forks up and down as vigorously as possible. Check for smooth operation and check for any fork oil leaks around the oil seal area on each fork leg.

2. Make sure the lower fork bridge clamp bolt (**Figure 46**) is tight on both fork assemblies.

3. Remove the top cap bolt (**Figure 47**) and make sure the spring stopper is tight on both fork assemblies. Check the O-ring seal for hardness or deterioration, replace if necessary.

4. Remove the trim caps and make sure the bolts securing the handlebar holders to the upper fork bridge are tight.

5. Remove the front axle trim cap from the left-hand fork leg.

6. Make sure the front axle (A, **Figure 48**) and front axle pinch bolt (B, **Figure 48**) are tight.

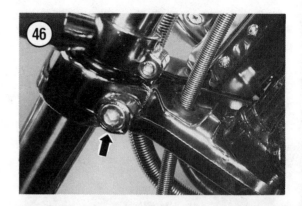

> *CAUTION*
> *If any of the previously mentioned bolts and nuts are loose, refer to Chapter Ten for correct procedures and torque specifications.*

Rear Suspension Check

1. Support the bike with the rear wheel off the ground.

2. Push hard on the rear wheel (sideways) to check for side play in the rear swing arm bearings. Support the bike with both wheels on the ground.

3. Remove the trim cap from the upper bolt, then check the tightness of the shock absorber's upper and lower mounting bolts and nuts (**Figure 49**).

4. On the right-hand side, remove the trim cap covering the swing arm pivot bolt nut.

5. Make sure the pivot bolt nut (**Figure 50**) on the swing arm pivot bolt is tight.

6. On the right-hand side, remove the trim cap covering the rear axle nut.

7. Make sure the rear axle nut (**Figure 51**) is tight.

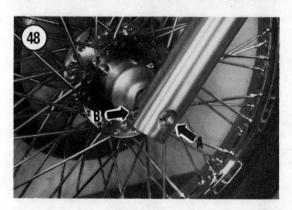

> *NOTE*
> *Figure 52 is shown with the rear wheel removed for clarity.*

8. Make sure the 3 nuts (**Figure 52**) securing the final drive unit to the swing arm are tight. Only 2 of the nuts are visible in **Figure 52**. Be sure to check all 3 nuts for tightness.

9. Remove the trim cap from the rear brake torque arm special Allen bolt and the rubber cap from the nut. Remove the cotter pin.

10. Check the tightness of the rear brake torque arm Allen bolt (**Figure 53**) and nut. Install a new cotter pin and bend the ends over completely.

> *CAUTION*
> *If any of the previously mentioned bolts and nuts are loose, refer to Chapter Eleven for correct procedures and torque specifications.*

11. Install all trim caps removed.

Rear Suspension Adjustment

The rear shock can be adjusted to suit the load and your ride preference. The spring preload can be adjusted by the hidden adjuster at the base of the shock absorber.

The adjuster has 5 positions with the No. 1 position (softest), being the standard factory setting. Rotate the adjuster (**Figure 54**) from the No. 1, all the way to the No. 5, position (stiffest) depending on your riding requirements.

Always adjust both shock absorbers to the same setting to maintain safe stable handling.

Steering Head Adjustment Check

Check the steering head bearings for looseness at the interval listed in **Table 1**.

1. Support the bike with the front wheel off the ground.

2. Hold onto the front fork tube and gently rock the fork assembly back and forth. If you feel looseness, refer to Chapter Ten.

Nuts, Bolts and Other Fasteners

Constant vibration can loosen many of the fasteners on the motorcycle. Check the tightness of all fasteners, especially those on:

a. Engine mounting hardware.
b. Engine crankcase covers.
c. Handlebar and front forks.
d. Gearshift lever.
e. Brake pedal and lever.
f. Final drive unit nuts.
g. Exhaust system.
h. Lighting equipment.

TUNE-UP

Perform a complete tune-up at the interval listed in **Table 1** of normal riding. More frequent tune-ups may be required if the bike is ridden in stop-and-go traffic. The purpose of the tune-up is to restore the performance lost due to normal wear and deterioration of parts.

The spark plugs should be routinely replaced at every other tune-up or if the electrodes show signs of erosion. In addition, this is a good time to clean the air filter elements. Have all known new parts on hand before you begin.

Because the different systems in an engine interact, the procedures should be done in the following order:

a. Run a compression test.
b. Change spark plugs.
c. Synchronize the carburetors.
d. Set the idle speed.

Table 7 summarizes tune-up specifications.

To perform a tune-up on your Suzuki, you will need the following tools and equipment:

a. 18 mm (5/8 in.) spark plug wrench.
b. Socket wrench and assorted sockets.
c. Compression gauge.
d. Spark plug feeler gauge and gap adjusting tool.
e. Carburetor synchronization tool.

Air Filter Element

Clean or replace the air filter element, as described in this chapter, prior to performing the following tune-up procedures.

Valve Clearance Measurement and Adjustment

The rocker arms are equipped with hydraulic valve lash adjusters, thus eliminating any routine valve clearance adjustment procedure.

Compression Test

Periodic check the cylinder compression. Record the results and compare them to the results at the next interval. A running record will show trends in deterioration so that corrective action can be taken before complete failure.

The results when properly interpreted, can indicate general cylinder, piston ring and valve condition.

1. Warm the engine to normal operating temperature, then shut it off. Make sure the choke valves are completely open.
2. Remove both spark plugs and ground them against the cylinder leads.
3. Connect the compression tester to one cylinder following the manufacturer's instructions.

> *CAUTION*
> *Do not turn the engine over more than absolutely necessary.*

4. Crank the engine over until there is no further rise in pressure.
5. Remove the tester and record the reading. Repeat for the other cylinder.
6. When interpreting the results, actual readings are not as important as the difference between the readings. The recommended cylinder compression pressure and service limits are listed in **Table 7**. If the

compression readings between the cylinders differ less than 10 psi (69kPA), the rings and valves are in good condition.

If a low reading (10% or more) is obtained it indicates valve or ring trouble. To determine which, pour about a teaspoon of engine oil through the spark plug hole onto the top of the piston. Turn the engine over once to distribute the oil, then take another compression test and record the reading. If the compression increases significantly, the valves are good but the rings are defective. If the compression does not increase, the valves require servicing.

Spark Plug Selection

Spark plugs are available in various heat ranges, hotter or colder than the plugs originally installed at the factory.

Select a plug of the heat range designed for the loads and conditions under which the bike will be run. Use of incorrect heat ranges can cause the plug to foul, overheating and piston damage.

In general, use a hot plug for low speeds and low temperatures. Use a cold plug for high speeds, high engine loads and high temperatures. The plug

should operate hot enough to burn off unwanted deposits, but not so hot that it is damaged or causes preignition. A spark plug of the correct heat range will show a light tan color on the portion of the insulator within the cylinder after the plug has been in service.

The reach (length) of a plug is also important. A longer than normal plug could interfere with the piston, causing permanent and severe damage.

Refer to **Table 7** for the recommended spark plug heat ranges.

Spark Plug Removal

A spark plug can be used to help determine the operating condition of its cylinder when properly read. As each spark plug is removed, label it with its cylinder number.

If anything turns up during the inspection step, you will want to know which cylinder it came from . The cylinders are numbered as follows: rear cylinder No. 1 and front cylinder No. 2.

1. Loosen the bolts securing the right-hand front cylinder head side cover (**Figure 55**) and the left-hand rear cylinder head side cover (**Figure 56**).
2. Grasp each spark plug lead (**Figure 57**) and carefully pul it off the plug. If the boot is stuck to the plug, twist it slightly to break it loose.

> *CAUTION*
> *If any dirt falls into the cylinder when the plugs are removed, it could cause serious engine damage.*

3. Use compressed air and blow away any dirt that may have passed by the rubber boot on the spark plug lead and accumulated in the spark plug well.
4. Remove the spark plugs with an 18 mm spark plug wrench. Keep the spark plugs in the order than they were removed. If anything turns up during the inspection step, you will then know which cylinder it came from.

> *NOTE*
> *If plugs are difficult to remove, apply penetrating oil around base of plugs and let it soak in about 10-20 minutes.*

5. Inspect the spark plug carefully. Look for broken center porcelain, excessively eroded electrodes and excessive carbon or oil fouling and make sure these plugs are replaced. If deposits are light, the plug

may be cleaned in solvent with a wire brush or in a special spark plug sandblast cleaner. Regap the plug as explained in this chapter.

> *NOTE*
> *Spark plug cleaning with the use of a sand-blast type device is not recommended. While this type of cleaning is thorough, the plug must be perfectly free of all abrasive cleaning material when done. If not, it is possible for the cleaning material to fall into the engine during operation and cause damage.*

Spark Plug Gapping and Installation

A new plug should be carefully gapped to ensure a reliable, consistent spark. You must use a special spark plug gapping tool with a wire feeler gauge.

1. Remove the new plug from the box. Do not screw on the small piece that is sometimes loose in the box. They are not used with the stock plug caps.
2. Insert a wire feeler gauge between the center and the side electrode of each plug (**Figure 58**). The correct gap is listed in **Table 7**. If the gap is correct, you will feel a slight drag as you pull the feeler gauge through. If there is no drag or the gauge won't pass through, bend the side electrode(s) with the gapping tool (**Figure 59**) to set the proper gap.

> *NOTE*
> *Antiseize compound may be purchased at most automotive parts stores.*

3. Apply a light coat of antiseize compound to the threads of the spark plug before installing it. Do not use engine oil on the plug threads.
4. Screw each spark plug in by hand until it seats. Very little effort is required. If force is necessary, you may have the plug cross-threaded; unscrew it and try again.

> *NOTE*
> *If a spark plug is difficult to install, the cylinder head threads may be dirty or slightly damaged. To clean the threads, apply grease to the threads of a spark plug tap and screw it carefully into the cylinder head. Turn the tap slowly until it is completely installed. If the tap cannot be installed, the*

threads are severely damaged and must be repaired.

5. Tighten the spark plugs an additional 1/2 turn after the gasket has made contact with the head. If you are reinstalling old, regapped plugs and are reusing the old gasket, only tighten an additional 1/4 turn.

> *CAUTION*
> *Do not overtighten. Besides making the plug difficult to remove, the excessive torque will squash the gasket and destroy its sealing ability.*

6. Install the spark plug leads; make sure the leads are on tight.
7. Install the right-hand front cylinder head side cover (**Figure 55**) and the left-hand rear cylinder head side cover (**Figure 56**) and tighten the screws securely.

Reading Spark Plugs

Much information about engine and spark plug performance can be determined by careful examination of the spark plugs. This information is more valid after performing the following steps.

1. Ride the bike a short distance at full throttle in any gear.
2. Move the engine stop switch to the OFF position before closing the throttle and simultaneously pull in the clutch or shift to NEUTRAL; coast and brake to a stop.
3. Remove one spark plug at a time and examine it. Compare it to **Figure 60**.

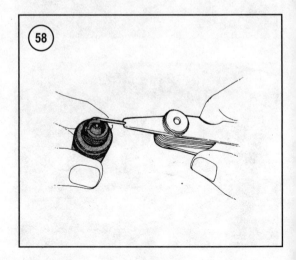
(58)

Normal condition

Good engine, carburetion and ignition conditions are indicated by plugs with light tan- or gray-colored deposits and no abnormal gap wear or erosion. The plug in use is of the proper heat range and may be serviced and returned to use.

Carbon fouled

Soft, dry, sooty deposits covering the entire firing end of the plug are evidence of incomplete combustion. Even though the firing end of the plug is dry, the plug's insulation decreases. An electrical path is formed that lowers the voltage from the ignition system. Engine misfiring is a sign of carbon fouling. Carbon fouling can be caused by one or more of the following:

a. Too rich fuel mixture.

b. Spark plug heat range too cold.

c. Clogged air filter.

d. Improperly operating ignition component.

e. Ignition component failure.

f. Low engine compression.

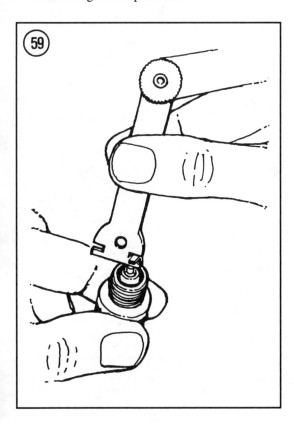

g. Prolonged idling.

Oil fouled

The tip of an oil fouled plug has a black insulator tip, a damp oily film over the firing end and a carbon layer over the entire nose. The electrodes will not be worn. Common causes for this condition are:

a. Incorrect carburetor jetting.

b. Low idle speed or prolonged idling.

c. Ignition component failure.

d. Spark plug heat range too cold.

e. Engine still being broken in.

f. Valve guides worn.

g. Piston rings worn or broken.

Oil fouled spark plugs may be cleaned in an emergency, but it is better to replace them. It is important to correct the cause of fouling before the engine is returned to service.

Ignition Timing

The engine is equipped with a fully transistorized ignition system consisting of two pickup coils, an ignitor unit, one ignition coil and 2 spark plugs. This solid state system uses no breaker points, and there are no means of adjusting ignition timing. Suzuki does not provide any ignition timing procedures.

Since there are no components to wear, adjusting the ignition timing is not necessary nor possible. If you suspect an ignition related problem, inspect the ignition coil, pickup coil and ignitor unit as described in Chapter Nine.

Incorrect ignition timing can cause a drastic loss of engine performance and efficiency. It may also cause overheating.

Carburetor Idle Speed Adjustment

Prior to making this adjustment, the air filter elements must be clean and the engine must have adequate compression. See Compression Test in this chapter. Otherwise this procedure cannot be done properly.

1. Start the engine and let reach normal operating temperature. Make sure the choke lever (**Figure 61**) is in the off position.

2. Connect a portable tachometer following its manufacturer's instructions.

SPARK PLUG CONDITION

NORMAL
- Identified by light tan or gray deposits on the firing tip.
- Can be cleaned.

GAP BRIDGED
- Identified by deposit buildup closing gap between electrodes.
- Caused by oil or carbon fouling. If deposits are not excessive, the plug can be cleaned.

OIL FOULED
- Identified by wet black deposits on the insulator shell bore and electrodes.
- Caused by excessive oil entering combustion chamber through worn rings and pistons, excessive clearance between valve guides and stems or worn or loose bearings. Can be cleaned. If engine is not repaired, use a hotter plug.

CARBON FOULED
- Identified by black, dry fluffy carbon deposits on insulator tips, exposed shell surfaces and electrodes.
- Caused by too cold a plug, weak ignition, dirty air cleaner, too rich a fuel mixture or excessive idling. Can be cleaned.

LEAD FOULED
- Identified by dark gray, black, yellow or tan deposits or a fused glazed coating on the insulator tip.
- Caused by highly leaded gasoline. Can be cleaned.

WORN
- Identified by severely eroded or worn electrodes.
- Caused by normal wear. Should be replaced.

FUSED SPOT DEPOSIT
- Identified by melted or spotty deposits resembling bubbles or blisters.
- Caused by sudden acceleration. Can be cleaned.

OVERHEATING
- Identified by a white or light gray insulator with small black or gray brown spots and with bluish-burnt appearance of electrodes.
- Caused by engine overheating, wrong type of fuel, loose spark plugs, too hot a plug or incorrect ignition timing. Replace the plug.

PREIGNITION
- Identified by melted electrodes and possibly blistered insulator. Metallic deposits on insulator indicate engine damage.
- Caused by wrong type of fuel, incorrect ignition timing or advance, too hot a plug, burned valves or engine overheating. Replace the plug.

3. On the rear carburetor, turn the idle adjust knob (**Figure 62**) in or out to adjust idle speed.

4. The correct idle speed is listed in **Table 7**.

5. Open and close the throttle a couple of times; check for variations in idle speed. Readjust if necessary.

> *WARNING*
> *With the engine running at idle speed, move the handlebar from side to side. If the idle speed increases during this movement, the throttle cable may need adjusting or it may be incorrectly routed through the frame. Correct this problem immediately. Do not ride the bike in this unsafe condition.*

Carburetor Idle Mixture

The idle mixture (pilot screw) is preset at the factory and should not be reset unless the carburetors have been overhauled. If so, refer to Chapter Eight.

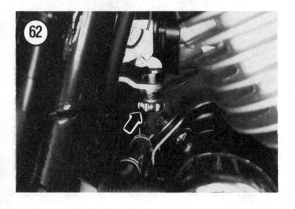

Carburetor Cable Synchronization

Synchronizing the carburetor cables makes sure that one cylinder does not try to run faster than the other, cutting power and gas mileage. The only accurate way to synchronize the carburetors is to use a set of vacuum gauges that measure the intake vacuum of both cylinders at the same time.

Refer to **Figure 63** for this procedure.

These 2 separate procedures relate to the synchronization of the carburetors after the synchronizing cable (3) has been removed or is incorrectly adjusted or if the front throttle cable (2) and/or rear throttle cable (1) have been replaced.

> *NOTE*
> *Prior to synchronizing the carburetors, the air filter elements must be clean and the engine must have adequate compression.*

Synchronizing cable balancing

1. Warm the engine to normal operating temperature.

2. Check the idle speed as described in this chapter and adjust if necessary. Shut off the engine.

3. Remove both seats as described in Chapter Thirteen.

4. Remove the mounting nuts and remove the ignition igniter unit from the underside of the seat (**Figure 64**). Reconnect the igniter unit to the main wiring harness.

5. Remove the fuel tank as described in Chapter Eight.

6. Install an auxiliary fuel tank onto the motorcycle and attach to the main fuel hose leading to the fuel pump.

> *NOTE*
> *Carburetor synchronization cannot be performed with the stock fuel tank in place because of the lack of room required to install the gauges and make adjustments. An auxiliary fuel tank is required to supply fuel to the carburetors during this procedure.*

> *NOTE*
> *An auxiliary fuel tank can be purchased from a motorcycle dealership or mail order house, or made from a small*

displacement motorcycle, ATV or a lawn mower fuel tank.

> *WARNING*
> *When supplying fuel by temporary means, make sure the auxiliary fuel tank is secure and that all fuel lines are tight with no leaks.*

7. Remove the vacuum port screw (**Figure 65**, just behind the horn) for the No. 2 carburetor (front cylinder).

8. Connect a vacuum line from the carb-synch tool to the carburetor vacuum port, following the manufacturer's instructions. If necessary, install an adapter to the vacuum port to ensure a good vacuum seal.

9. Start the engine. Turn the idle adjust screw to increase engine speed to 1,000 rpm.

10. Turn the No. 2 balance screw on the gauge so the vacuum acting on the No. 2 tube moves the ball to the centerline of the No. 2 tube. After the steel ball has stabilized in the center of the tube, disconnect the No. 2 hose and connect the hose for the No. 1 tube to the same vacuum port.

11. Turn the balance screw on the No. 1 gauge so the vacuum acting on the No. 1 tube will move the ball to the centerline of the No. 1 tube. After the steel ball has stabilized in the center of the No. 1 tube, the balancer is now calibrated.

12. Shut off the engine.

13. Remove the screws securing the frame mounted fuel shutoff valve to the frame. Move the shutoff valve out of the way.

14. Reconnect the No. 2 vacuum line from the carb-synch tool to the No. 2 carburetor vacuum port.

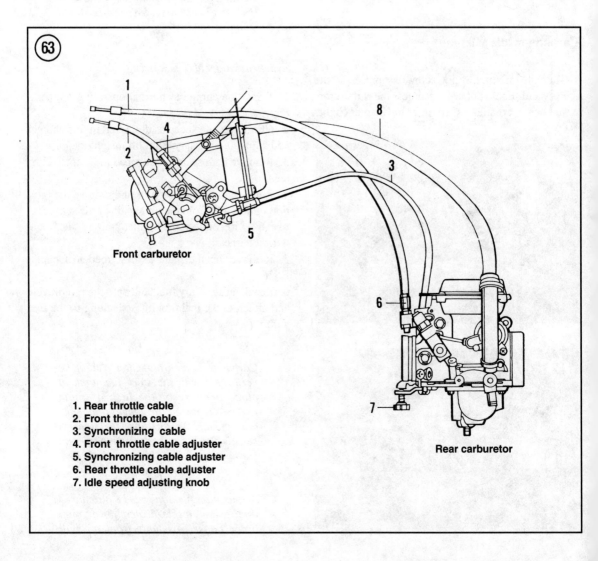

Front carburetor

Rear carburetor

1. Rear throttle cable
2. Front throttle cable
3. Synchronizing cable
4. Front throttle cable adjuster
5. Synchronizing cable adjuster
6. Rear throttle cable adjuster
7. Idle speed adjusting knob

15. Remove the vacuum port screw (**Figure 66**, between the shut off valve and frame) from the No. 1 carburetor (rear cylinder).

16. Connect the No. 1 vacuum line from the carb-synch tool to the No. 1 carburetor vacuum port, following the manufacturer's instructions. If necessary, install an adapter to the vacuum port to ensure a good vacuum seal.

17. Restart the engine and maintain the same idle speed of 1,000 rpm.

18. Check the gauge readings. If the difference in gauge readings is 10 mm Hg (0.4 in. Hg) or less be-

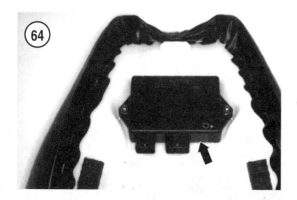

tween the 2 cylinders, the carburetors are considered synchronized.

19. If the carburetors are not synchronized, proceed as follows:

    a. With the engine at idle speed of 1,000 rpm, loosen the locknut and turn the synchronizing cable adjuster (5, **Figure 63**) and the throttle stop screw (7, **Figure 63**) to synchronize the front-to-rear carburetors.

NOTE
To gain the utmost in performance and efficiency from the engine, adjust the carburetors so the gauge readings are as close to each other as possible.

    b. After the carburetors are balanced, tighten the locknut on the synchronizing cable adjuster.

    c. Reset the idle speed as listed in **Table 7** and shut off the engine.

NOTE
Make sure the vacuum port screws are tight to prevent a vacuum leak.

20. Install the vacuum port screws. Refer to **Figure 65** for the No. 2 carburetor and **Figure 66** for the No. 1 carburetor.

21. Disconnect the auxiliary fuel tank and install the standard fuel tank.

22. Disconnect the igniter unit from the main wiring harness.

23. Install the ignition igniter unit onto the underside of the seat and tighten the nuts securely.

24. Install both seats as described in Chapter Thirteen.

Throttle cable balancing

Refer to **Figure 63** for this procedure.

NOTE
This procedure is only necessary if the throttle cables have been replaced.

1. Remove the bolts securing the fuel tank front mounting bracket (**Figure 67**) and remove the bracket.

2. Remove the screw securing the throttle cable joint (**Figure 68**) to the air filter housing and remove the joint from the clip on the air filter housing.

3. Separate the throttle cable joint (**Figure 69**).

4. At the carburetors, loosen locknut on the front carburetor throttle cable (2, **Figure 63**) and the locknut on the rear carburetor throttle cable (1).

5. At the carburetors, turn the throttle cable adjuster (4) on the front carburetor and the throttle cable adjuster (6) on the rear carburetor until the throttle cable ends protrude from the throttle cable joint (**Figure 70**) the exact same amount.

6. Tighten both throttle cable locknuts securely and reconnect the throttle cable joint.

7. Install the throttle cable joint into the clip on the air filter housing and install the screw. Tighten the screw securely.

8. Install the fuel tank mounting bracket and bolts. Tighten the bolts securely.

9. Refer to *Synchronizing Cable Balancing* in the previous procedure and calibrate the balancer at 2,000 rpm this time, not 1,000 rpm as used in the previous procedure.

10. Connect the vacuum lines from the carb-synch tool to the vacuum ports, following the manufacturer's instructions. Be sure to route the vacuum lines to the correct cylinder.

11. Start the engine and increase the engine speed to 2,000 rpm.

12. Check the gauge readings. If the difference in gauge readings is 10 mm Hg (0.4 in. Hg) or less

   a. After the carburetors are balanced, tighten the locknut on the front carburetor throttle cable adjuster.

   b. Reset the idle speed as listed in **Table 7** and shut off the engine.

13. Disconnect the carb-synch tool vacuum lines from the carburetors.

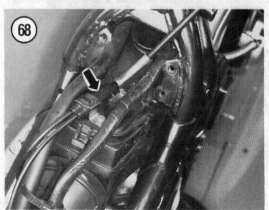

NOTE
Make sure the vacuum port screws are
tight to prevent a vacuum leak.

14. Install the vacuum port screws. Refer to **Figure 65** for the front carburetor and **Figure 66** for the rear carburetor.

15. Disconnect the auxiliary fuel tank and install the standard fuel tank.

16. Disconnect the igniter unit from the main wiring harness.

17. Install the ignition igniter unit onto the underside of the seat and tighten the nuts securely.

18. Install both seats as described in Chapter Thirteen.

Table 1 MAINTENANCE AND LUBRICATION SCHEDULE

Weekly/fuel stop
  Check tire pressure cold; adjust to suit load and speed
  Check brakes for a solid feel
  Check brake pedal play; adjust if necessary
  Check throttle grip for smooth operation and return
  Check for smooth but not loose steering
  Check axles, suspension, control nuts, bolts and fasteners; tighten if necessary
  Check engine oil level; add oil if necessary
  Check final gear oil level; add oil if necessary
  Check lights and horn operation, especially brake light
  Check for any abnormal engine noise and leaks
  Check kill switch operation
Initial 600 miles (1,000 km)
  Check throttle free play; adjust if necessary
  Change engine oil and replace oil filter
  Check idle speed; adjust if necessary
  Check automatic compression release cable; adjust if necessary
  Check brake pad wear
  Check brake fluid level; add fluid if necessary
  Check brake hydraulic hoses for leakage or damage
  Check clutch fluid level; add fluid if necessary
  Check clutch hydraulic hoses for leakage or damage
  Change final gear case oil
  Check brake light operation; adjust if necessary
  Check steering play; adjust if necessary
  Check tire condition and inflation pressure
  Check evaporative emission control system (California models)
  Check and tighten all nuts, bolts and fasteners
12 months/4,000 miles (6,000 km)
  All above checks and the following
  Clean and inspect air filter elements
  Check spark plugs, set gap; replace if necessary
  Check brake light switch operation; adjust if necessary
  Lubricate all pivot points
  Check and tighten all nuts, bolts and fasteners

(continued)

Table 1 MAINTENANCE AND LUBRICATION SCHEDULE (continued)

Yearly/7,500 miles (12,000 km)
  All above checks and the following
  Replace spark plugs
  Check shock absorbers for oil leakage
  Check all fuel lines for leakage, chafing of damage; replace if necessary
  Check front fork
Every two years
  Change brake fluid
  Change clutch fluid
  Lubricate wheel bearings
  Lubricate speedometer cable
Every 4 years
  Replace all fuel hoses
  Replace all evaporative emission control system hoses (California models)
  Replace the clutch hydraulic hose assembly
  Replace all brake hydraulic hoses

Table 2 TIRE INFLATION PRESSURE (COLD)*

	kPa	psi
Front		
Solo riding	200	29
Dual riding	200	29
Rear		
Solo riding	200	29
Dual riding	228	33

*Tire inflation pressure for factory equipped tires. Afternarket tires may require different inflation pressure.

Table 3 BATTERY CAPACITY AND CHARGING TIME

Capacity	12 volt, 14 amp hour
Charging time	
Standard charge	1.4 A × 5.0 hrs
Quick charge	7.0 A × 1.0 hrs

Table 4 RECOMMENDED LUBRICATS AND FLUIDS

Fuel	Regular unleaded or low-lead type
U.S. and Canada	87 [(R+M/2 method] or 91 octane or higher
U.K. and all others	85-95 octane
Engine oil	
Grade	API SE, SF or SG
Viscosity	SAE 10W-40
Final drive oil	SAE 90 Hypoid gear oil with
	GL-5 under API classification
Brake fluid	DOT 3 or DOT 4
Clutch hydraulic fluid	DOT 3 or DOT 4
Front fork oil-type	SAE 10W

Table 5 ENGINE, FORK OIL, FINAL DRIVE UNIT REFILL CAPACITIES

Engine oil	
Oil change	3.7 L (3.9 U.S. qts. or 3.2 Imp. qts.)
Oil and filter chagne	4.3 L (4.5 U.S. qts. or 3.8 Imp. qts.)
Final drive oil	
Capacity at oil change	200-220 ml (6.8-7.4 U.S. oz. or 7.0-7.7 Imp oz.)
Front fork oil capacity (each fork leg)	
Completely dry	354 ml (12.0 U.S. oz. or 12.5 Imp. oz.)
Front fork oil level dimension	
top surface (after completely dry)	
1991-1992	203 mm (7.99 in.)
Cables or pivot pints	Cable lube or SAE 10W/30 motor oil

Table 6 MAINTENANCE AND TUNE-UP TIGHTENING TORQUES

	N•m	ft.-lb.
Oil drain plug	18-23	13-16.5
Oil filter	Hand tight	Hand tight
Front axle	36-52	26-37.5
Front axle clamp bolt	15-25	11-18
Handlebar		
Mounting bolts	15-25	11-18
Holder nut	80-100	58-72.5
Steering stem nut	80-100	58-72.5
Fork bridge lower clamp bolt	25-40	18-29
Fork cap bolt	45-55	32.5-39.8
Rear axle nut	60-95	43.5-69.5
Rear torque link bolt and nut	40-60	29-43.4
Foor rest mounting bolts	15-25	11-18

MAINTENANCE AND TUNE-UP SPECIFICATIONS

Throttle grip rotational free play	
1987-1993	0.5-1.0 mm (0.02-0.04 in.)
1994-1999	3.0-6.0 mm (0.12-0.24 in.)
2000-on	2.0-4.0 mm (0.08-0.16 in.)
Automatic de-compression cable free play	
Distance between lever and stopper	
Front cylinder	1.5-2.5 mm (0.06-0.10 in.) (dimension A)
Rear cylinder	1.0-2.0 mm (0.04-0.08 in.) (dimension B)
Rear brake pedal	
Height above foot peg	
1987-1995	22 mm (0.87 in.)
1996-on	65 mm (2.6 in,)
Engine cylinder number	
Rear cylinder	No. 1
Front cylinder	No. 2
Firing order	Front, rear
Engine compression	
Standard	1,000-1,400 kPa (142-199 psi)
Service limit	800 kPa (114 psi)
Ignition timing	Non adjustable
Idle speed	950-1,050 rpm
Spark plug type	
1987-1989	NGK DP8EA-9 or ND X24EP-U9
1990-on	NGK DPR8EA-9 or ND X24EPR-U9
Spark plug gap	0.8-0.9 mm (0.031-0.035 in.)
Oil pressure @ 3,000 rpm	3.5 kg/cm^2 (50 psi) to 6.5 kg/cm^2 (92 psi)
Throttle cable ends	
(carburetor synchronization)	18.5 mm (0.73 in.)

CHAPTER FOUR

ENGINE UPPER END

The engine is a V-twin air/oil-cooled, 4-stroke design. The cylinders are offset and set at a 45° angle. The cylinders fire on alternate crankshaft rotations. Each cylinder is equipped with a single camshaft and 4 valves. The crankshaft is supported by 2 main bearings in a vertically split crankcase.

Both engine and transmission share a common case and the same wet sump oil supply. The clutch is a wet-type located inside the right crankcase cover. Refer to Chapter Six for clutch and external gearshift mechanism and to Chapter Seven for transmission and internal gearshift mechanism service procedures.

This chapter provides complete procedures and information for removal, inspection, service and reassembly of the engine. Before beginning work, read Chapter One in the front section of this book. You will do a better job with this information fresh in your mind.

Before removing and disassembling the crankcase, clean the entire engine and frame with a good grade commercial degreaser, like Gunk or Bel-Ray engine degreaser. It is easier to work on a clean engine and you will do a better job.

The text makes frequent references to the left- and right-hand side of the engine. This refers to the engine as it sits in the vehicle's frame, not as it sits on your workbench.

Table 1 lists the general engine specifications.

Table 2 lists engine top end service specifications.

Table 3 lists engine top end tightening torques.

Tables 1-3 are at the end of the chapter.

ENGINE PRINCIPLES

Figure 1 explains how the engine operates. This will be helpful when troubleshooting or repairing the engine.

SERVICING ENGINE IN FRAME

This procedure describes engine removal and installation. If the engine requires crankcase disassembly, it will be easier to remove as many sub-assemblies from the engine before removing the engine from the frame. By following this method, the frame can be used as a holding fixture when servicing the engine. Attempting to disassemble the complete engine while placed on a workbench is more time consuming. You may need an assistant to

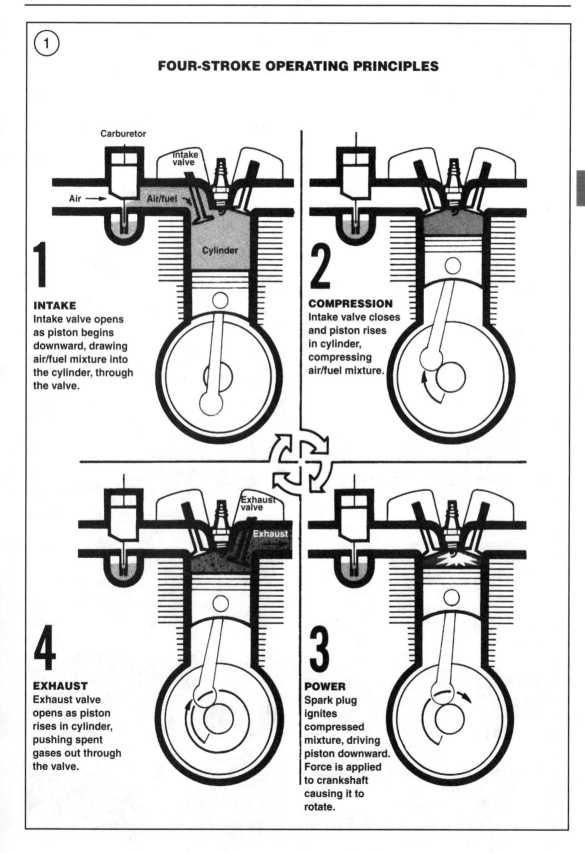

FOUR-STROKE OPERATING PRINCIPLES

1 INTAKE
Intake valve opens as piston begins downward, drawing air/fuel mixture into the cylinder, through the valve.

2 COMPRESSION
Intake valve closes and piston rises in cylinder, compressing air/fuel mixture.

4 EXHAUST
Exhaust valve opens as piston rises in cylinder, pushing spent gases out through the valve.

3 POWER
Spark plug ignites compressed mixture, driving piston downward. Force is applied to crankshaft causing it to rotate.

help hold the engine while you loosen many of the larger nuts and bolts.

The following components can be serviced while the engine is mounted in the frame (the bike's frame is a great holding fixture for breaking loose stubborn bolts and nuts):

NOTE
The cylinder heads and cylinders cannot be removed with the engine in the frame. They are removed as an assembly after the engine is removed.

a. Carburetor assembly (Chapter Eight).
b. Alternator (Chapter Nine).
c. Starter clutch assembly (Chapter Nine).
d. Primary drive gear (this chapter).
e. Secondary gear assembly (this chapter).
f. External shift mechanism (Chapter Six).
g. Clutch (Chapter Six).
h. Starter motor (Chapter Nine).

ENGINE

Removal/Installation

1. Drain the engine oil as described in Chapter Three.
2. Remove both seats, the frame side covers and frame head side covers as described in Chapter Thirteen.
3. Remove the fuel tank and the front mounting bracket as described in Chapter Eight.
4. Remove the horn as described in Chapter Nine.
5. Remove the exhaust system as described in Chapter Eight.
6. Disconnect the decompression cable from the rear cylinder head (**Figure 2**) and the front cylinder head (**Figure 3**).

NOTE
Unless the carburetors are going to be removed for service, they can be disconnected from the cylinder heads and allowed to remain on the frame.

7. Partially remove the carburetor assembly as described in Chapter Eight. Perform only the steps necessary to disconnect the carburetors from the intake pipes on the cylinder heads.
8. Remove the battery and battery case as described in Chapter Nine.

9. Remove the bolts securing the secondary drive gear cover (**Figure 4**) and remove the cover and spacers.

10. Remove the screw securing the swing arm trim panel (A, **Figure 5**) and remove the panel.

11. Loosen the clamping band (B, **Figure 5**) securing the rubber boot to the engine and move the rubber boot away from the engine and onto the swing arm (**Figure 6**).

12. Remove the clutch slave cylinder as described in Chapter Six.

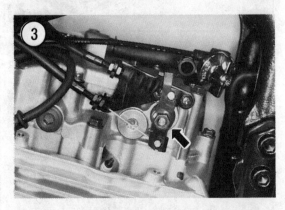

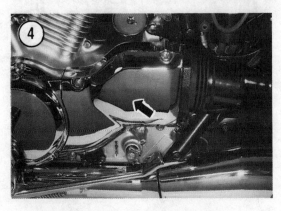

13. Loosen the bolts and remove all 4 cylinder head chrome covers.

14. Disconnect the spark plug leads and move them out of the way.

15. Disconnect the following electrical wires from the engine:

    a. Starter motor and oil pressure switch.

    b. Alternator stator and the pulse generator.

    c. Decompression solenoid.

    d. Ignition switch.

    e. Voltage regulator/rectifier.

    f. Neutral switch.

    g. Starter relay.

    h. Sidestand check switch.

    i. Ground.

16. Remove the ignition switch as described in Chapter Nine.

17. Remove the fuel shutoff valve from the frame as described in Chapter Eight.

18. Remove the front footpeg assembly as described in Chapter Thirteen.

19. Partially remove the rear brake remote reservoir as described in Chapter Twelve. It is not necessary to remove the reservoir completely; just move it out of the way. Also remove the bolts and the mounting bracket from the frame.

20. Remove the oil cooler and hoses from the engine and frame as described in Chapter Five.

21. Disconnect the vacuum hose from the front cylinder head.

NOTE
A good source for the rubber, or vinyl, used in the next step is an old discarded automobile floor mat. Use the thin portions of the mat.

22. To protect the left-hand side of the frame from scratches or gouges during engine removal and installation, wrap the frame members with rubber, or vinyl, sheets and secure with tie wraps.

23. Place wooden block(s) on a small hydraulic jack to protect the crankcase, then move the jack into position under the engine and support it securely (A, **Figure 7**).

24. Take a final look all over the engine to make sure everything has been disconnected.

25. Make sure the hydraulic jack is still in place and supporting the engine securely.

26. Loosen, but do not remove, all engine mounting bolts and nuts.

27. Remove the Allen bolts and nuts securing the right-hand rear mounting bracket to the frame and subframe (**Figure 8**). Remove the bracket.

28. On California models, remove the evaporation canister assembly as described in Chapter Eight.

29. Remove the cap nut from the front through bolt.

30. Remove the cap nut (A, **Figure 9**), Allen bolts (B, **Figure 9**), washers and nuts securing the subframe to the frame at the rear.

31. Remove the front hex bolts (**Figure 10**) securing the subframe to the frame at the front crossover.

32. Remove the Allen bolts (**Figure 11**), washers and nuts securing the subframe to the frame at the upper front side.

33. Remove the cap nut (**Figure 12**) from the front through bolt.

34. Remove the subframe (B, **Figure 7**) from the engine and frame.

35. Withdraw the rear lower through bolt (**Figure 13**).

36. Withdraw the front through bolt (**Figure 14**).

37. Withdraw the rear through bolt.

38. Check that everything is disconnected or routed away from the engine.

39. Slowly move the engine forward to disengage the engine output shaft from the drive shaft universal joint. If necessary, use a screwdriver and disengage the drive shaft's universal joint from the output shaft.

CAUTION
Due to the size and weight of the engine, the following steps require the aid of a helper to remove the engine assembly from the frame safely.

40. Slightly lower the engine on the jack and continue to move the engine forward and toward the right-hand side to clear the remaining frame members.

41. Take the engine to a workbench for further disassembly.

42. Inspect the subframe and the main frame mounting area for wear or damage.

43. Install by reversing these removal steps, noting the following:

   a. Apply a light coat of molybdenum disulfide grease to the splines of the output shaft and the universal joint prior to engaging these 2 parts.

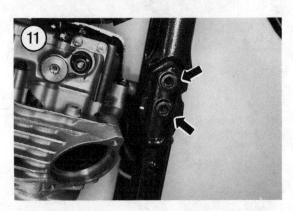

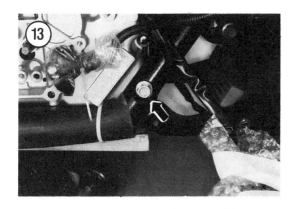

b. Tighten the engine mounting bolts to the torque specifications in **Table 3**.

c. Fill the engine with the recommended type and quantity of oil as described in Chapter Three.

d. Start the engine and check for oil leaks.

FRONT CYLINDER HEAD COVER AND CAMSHAFT

Removal

1. Remove the engine from the frame as described in this chapter.

2. Remove the spark plugs from both cylinder heads.

3. Loosen the bolts securing the remaining cylinder head side cover and remove the cover.

> *NOTE*
> *To help keep track of the cylinder head cover and breather cover bolts, draw the cover outline on a piece of cardboard. Label it for the front or rear cylinder head, then punch holes to correspond with each bolt location. After removal, insert the bolts in their appropriate locations). This will make installation easier.*

4. Remove the bolts securing the breather cover (**Figure 15**) and remove the cover and gasket (**Figure 16**).

> *NOTE*
> *Do not remove the bolt (A, **Figure 17**) securing the compression release shaft.*

5. Using a crisscross pattern, loosen and then re-move the bolts securing the cylinder head cover (**Figure 18**). Do not forget the single bolt (B, **Figure 17**) within the breather cover area.

6. Loosen the cylinder head cover by tapping around the perimeter with a rubber or soft faced mallet.

7. Remove the front cylinder head cover. Do not lose the locating dowels.

8. Straighten the tab on the camshaft sprocket bolt lockwasher and remove the exposed bolt.

9. If removed, temporarily install the alternator ro-tor and bolt and tighten securely.

> *CAUTION*
> *If the rear camshaft has been removed, pull up on the camshaft chain and keep it taut, when rotating the crankshaft. Otherwise, the chain may become kinked and cause damage to the crankcases, the camshaft chain and the timing sprocket on the crankshaft.*

10. Install a socket and wrench on the alternator rotor bolt or the 36 mm hex fitting on the rotor. Rotate the engine clockwise, as viewed from the left-hand side, until the other sprocket bolt is visible.

11. Straighten the tab on the other camshaft sprocket bolt lockwasher and remove the exposed bolt and the lockwasher.

12. Disengage the camshaft drive chain from the camshaft sprocket and remove the camshaft.

13. Tie a piece of wire from the camshaft chain to an external portion of the engine or insert a long drift or socket extension through the camshaft drive chain to prevent the camshaft chain from falling down into the crankcase.

> *CAUTION*
> *If the crankshaft must be rotated with the camshaft removed, pull up on the camshaft chain and keep it taut, when rotating the crankshaft. Otherwise, the chain may become kinked and cause damage to the crankcases, the camshaft chain and the timing sprocket on the crankshaft.*

14. Inspect the camshaft as described in this chapter.

15. Inspect the cylinder head cover as described in this chapter.

Installation

> *CAUTION*
> *If the engine has been completely disassembled, first install the rear cylinder camshaft and cylinder head cover then install the front. If only the front cylinder camshaft was removed, the **Rear Cylinder** must be positioned at TDC on the compression stroke prior to installing the front camshaft. This is necessary for the correct camshaft timing of both cylinders.*

> *CAUTION*
> *Whenever the cylinder head cover is removed, the hydraulic tappets located within the rocker arms must be bled of any air that may have entered during the cover removal procedure. Failure to do so will result in a loud clicking noise and may result in engine damage.*

> *NOTE*
> *During this procedure, reference is made to the RT timing marks for the rear cylinder. This is correct, since the*

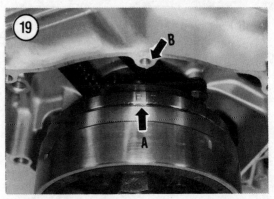

*camshaft timing for both the front and rear cylinders is based on the **Rear Cylinder** being at TDC on its compression stroke.*

1. Remove all 3 tappets from the rocker arms and bleed each one as described in this chapter. Reinstall the tappets into the rocker arms.

2. Check the timing mark for the *rear cylinder*. The RT mark on the alternator rotor (A, **Figure 19**) must align with the crankcase mark (B, **Figure 19**). If the

timing marks align, proceed to Step 3. If the alignment is correct, perform the following steps:

    a. Pull up on the front camshaft chain to keep it taut, and meshed with the crankshaft sprocket as described in substep B. Then rotate the crankshaft.

    b. Use a socket and wrench on the alternator rotor bolt. Rotate the engine clockwise, as viewed from the left-hand side, until the *rear cylinder* is at top dead center (TDC) on its compression stroke. Align the RT mark on the alternator rotor (A, **Figure 19**) with alignment mark on the crankcase (B, **Figure 19**).

    c. To confirm that the rear cylinder is at TDC on the compression stroke, insert a plastic or wooden dowel into the spark plug hole and touch the top of the piston. If you contact the piston top immediately the piston is in the correct location. If the dowel continues to travel down into the cylinder, the piston is *not* positioned correctly. If positioned incorrectly, rotate the engine an additional 360° clockwise and recheck piston position for TDC on the compression stroke.

    d. Again check that the RT mark on the alternator rotor (A, **Figure 19**) is aligned with alignment mark on the crankcase (B, **Figure 19**).

3. Unlock the cam chain tensioner by installing the tensioner lock tool as described under *Cylinder Head and Cylinder Assembly* in this chapter. The tensioner lock tool must be kept in place until after the cylinder head cover is installed and tightened on the engine.

4. Apply a light coat of molybdenum disulfide grease to the camshaft bearing surfaces in the cylinder head.

5. If both camshafts are removed, be sure to install the camshafts correctly. The camshafts are marked with F (front cylinder) or R (rear cylinder) (**Figure 20**) on the sprocket mounting boss.

6. Position the camshaft sprocket so the locating pin hole is midway between the 9 and 10 o'clock position (**Figure 21**) and engage the camshaft sprocket with the drive chain.

7. Apply a *light* coat of cold grease to the locating pin and install it (**Figure 22**) into the end of the camshaft.

NOTE
When installing the camshaft onto the sprocket be careful not to knock the locating pin out of the camshaft.

8. Position the front camshaft with the locating pin midway between the 9 and 10 o'clock position, then install the front camshaft into the cylinder head and into the camshaft sprocket.

9. Make sure the camshaft is still positioned correctly with the locating pin midway between the 9 and 10 o'clock position (A, **Figure 23**) and the timing marks on the end of the camshaft are aligned with the top surface of the cylinder head (B, **Figure 23**).

10. After the camshaft has been installed onto the sprocket, again check that the RT mark on the alternator rotor (A, **Figure 19**) is still aligned with alignment mark on the crankcase (B, **Figure 19**).

NOTE
Install the lockwasher in Step 11 so that it covers the locating pin in the end of the camshaft.

11. Install a new lockwasher (A, **Figure 24**) and the camshaft sprocket bolt (B, **Figure 24**) in the exposed hole. Tighten the bolt finger-tight at this time.

12. Use a socket and wrench on the alternator rotor bolt. Rotate the engine clockwise, as viewed from the left-hand side, until the other sprocket bolt hole is exposed.

CAUTION
Apply ThreeBond TB1360 or Loctite No. 271 to the sprocket bolt threads prior to installation.

13. Install the other camshaft sprocket bolt (**Figure 25**) in the exposed hole.

14. Hold down the end of camshaft opposite the camshaft sprocket and tighten the sprocket bolt to the torque specification listed in **Table 3**. Bend up the tab of the lockwasher against the bolt head (**Figure 26**).

15. Rotate the engine clockwise, as viewed from the left-hand side, until the bolt installed in Step 10 is exposed. Remove this bolt and apply the thread locking agent to the threads prior to installation.

16. Reinstall the camshaft sprocket bolt. Hold down the end of camshaft opposite the camshaft sprocket and tighten the sprocket bolt to the torque specifica-

tion listed in **Table 3**. Bend up the tab of the lockwasher against the bolt head (**Figure 26**).

17. Make sure the camshaft shoulder is properly indexed into the groove in the cylinder head.

18. Apply a light coat of molybdenum disulfide grease to the bearing surfaces and lobes of the camshaft.

19. Fill the pocket in the cylinder head where the camshaft lobes ride with fresh engine oil.

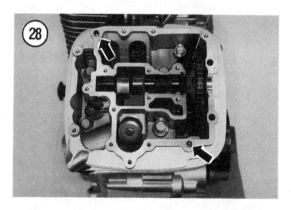

20. Remove the camshaft end plug from the cylinder head cover. Do not apply any sealant to the end plug.

21. Apply a light coat of molybdenum disulfide grease to the camshaft bearing surfaces in the cylinder head cover.

22. Clean the sealing surface of both the cylinder head and cover as follows:

    a. Remove the old gaskets and clean off all gasket sealer residue from the cylinder head and cover.

    b. Clean the surface with aerosol electrical contact cleaner and wipe dry with a lint-free cloth.

    c. Apply a coat of ThreeBond No. 1104, or equivalent, to the sealing surface of the cylinder head cover. Do not apply sealant to the round camshaft bearing journal surfaces.

23. Install the camshaft end plug (**Figure 27**) into the cylinder head cover and make sure it is seated correctly.

24. If removed, install both locating dowels (**Figure 28**) into the cylinder head.

NOTE
Do not pull on the tensioner lock tool when installing it through the cylinder head cover in Step 25. If the tensioner lock tool pulls loose and releases the cam chain tensioner, the lock tool must be reinstalled as described under **Cylinder Head and Cylinder Assembly** *in this chapter.*

25. Carefully feed the tensioner lock tool through the cylinder head cover opening. Then install the cylinder head cover over the camshaft and onto the cylinder head. Push it down until it bottoms out. Check that the camshaft end plug is seated evenly between the cylinder head and cylinder head cover.

26. Install and tighten the cover bolts in a crisscross pattern, starting with the center bolts (surrounding the camshaft) and working outward. Tighten in 2-3 stages to the torque specification listed in **Table 3**.

27. Carefully pull the tensioner lock tool out from the camshaft drive chain tensioner and though the opening in the cylinder head cover.

28. Remove the oil plug and gasket (**Figure 29**).

29. Use a pump-type oil can and fill the cylinder head cover rocker arm passage with fresh engine oil. Fill with approximately 50 ml (1.7 U.S. oz.) of oil.

Install the oil plug and new gasket and tighten securely.

30. Install a new gasket (**Figure 16**) and the breather cover (**Figure 15**).

31. Install the cylinder head side cover and tighten the bolts.

32. Install the spark plugs into both cylinder heads.

33. Install the engine into the frame as described in this chapter.

REAR CYLINDER HEAD COVER AND CAMSHAFT

Removal

1. Remove the engine from the frame as described in this chapter.

2. Loosen the bolts securing the remaining cylinder head side cover and remove the side cover.

3. If not already removed, remove the spark plug from both cylinders. This will make it easier to rotate the engine.

> NOTE
> *To help keep track of the cylinder head cover and breather cover bolts, draw the cover outline on a piece of cardboard. Label it for the front or rear cylinder head, then punch holes to correspond with each bolt location. After removal, insert the bolts in their appropriate locations. This will make installation easier.*

> NOTE
> *Do not remove the bolt (A, **Figure 30**) securing the compression release shaft.*

4. Using a crisscross pattern, loosen and then remove the bolts securing the cylinder head cover (B, **Figure 30**).

5. Loosen the cylinder head cover by tapping around the perimeter with a rubber or soft faced mallet.

6. Remove the rear cylinder head cover. Don't lose the locating dowels.

7. Straighten the tab on the camshaft sprocket bolt lockwasher and remove the exposed bolt.

> CAUTION
> *If the front camshaft has been removed, pull up on the camshaft chain and keep it taut when rotating the crankshaft.*

> *Otherwise, the chain may become kinked and cause damage to the crankcases, the camshaft chain and the timing sprocket on the crankshaft.*

8. Install a socket and wrench on the alternator rotor bolt or the 36 mm hex fitting on the rotor. Rotate the engine clockwise, as viewed from the left-hand side, until the other sprocket bolt is visible.

9. Straighten the tab on the other camshaft sprocket bolt lockwasher and remove the exposed bolt and the lockwasher.

10. Disengage the camshaft drive chain from the camshaft sprocket and remove the camshaft.

11. Tie a piece of wire from the camshaft chain to an external portion of the engine or insert a long drift or socket extension through the camshaft drive chain to prevent the camshaft chain from falling down into the crankcase.

> CAUTION
> *If the crankshaft must be rotated with the camshaft removed, pull up on the camshaft chain and keep it taut when rotating the crankshaft. Otherwise, the chain may become kinked and cause damage to the crankcases, the camshaft chain and the timing sprocket on the crankshaft.*

12. Inspect the camshaft as described in this chapter.

13. Inspect the cylinder head cover as described in this chapter.

Installation

> CAUTION
> *Whenever the cylinder head cover is removed, the hydraulic tappets located*

within the rocker arms must be bled of any air that may have entered during the cover removal procedure. Failure to do so will result in a loud clicking noise and may result in engine damage.

1. Remove all 3 tappets from the rocker arms and bleed each one as described in this chapter. Reinstall the tappets into the rocker arms.

2. Check the timing mark for the *rear cylinder*. The RT mark on the alternator rotor (A, **Figure 31**) must align with the crankcase mark (B, **Figure 31**). If the timing marks align, proceed to Step 3. If the alignment is correct, perform the following steps:

a. Pull up on the front camshaft chain to keep it taut and meshed with the crankshaft sprocket. Then rotate the crankshaft as described in substep B.

b. Use a socket and wrench on the alternator rotor bolt. Rotate the engine clockwise, as viewed from the left-hand side, until the *rear cylinder* is at top dead center (TDC) on its compression stroke. Align the RT mark on the alternator rotor (A, **Figure 31**) with the alignment mark on the crankcase (B, **Figure 31**).

c. To confirm that the rear cylinder is at TDC on the compression stroke, insert a plastic or wooden dowel into the spark plug hole and touch the top of the piston. If you contact the piston top immediately the piston is in the correct location. If the dowel continues to travel down into the cylinder, the piston is *not* positioned correctly. If positioned incorrectly, rotate the engine an additional 360° clockwise and recheck piston position for TDC on the compression stroke.

d. Again check that the RT mark on the alternator rotor (A, **Figure 31**) is aligned with the alignment mark on the crankcase (B, **Figure 31**).

3. Unlock the cam chain tensioner by installing the tensioner lock tool as described under *Cylinder Head and Cylinder Assembly* in this chapter. The tensioner lock tool must be kept in place until after the cylinder head cover is installed and tightened on the engine.

4. Apply a light coat of molybdenum disulfide grease to the camshaft bearing surfaces in the cylinder head.

5. If both camshafts are removed, be sure to install the camshafts correctly. The camshafts are marked with an F (front cylinder) or R (rear cylinder) on the sprocket mounting boss (**Figure 20**).

6. Apply a light coat of cold grease to the locating pin and install it (**Figure 22**) into the end of the camshaft.

7. Position the camshaft sprocket so the locating pin hole is midway between the 1 o'clock position (**Figure 32**) and engage the camshaft sprocket with the drive chain.

NOTE
When installing the camshaft onto the sprocket be careful not to knock the locating pin out of the camshaft.

8. Position the front camshaft with the locating pin midway between the 1 o'clock position, then install the rear camshaft into the cylinder head and into the camshaft sprocket (**Figure 33**).

9. Check that the camshaft is still positioned correctly with the locating pin at the 1 o'clock position (A, **Figure 34**) and the timing marks on the end of the camshaft are aligned with the top surface of the cylinder head (B, **Figure 34**).

10. After the camshaft has been installed onto the sprocket, again check that the RT mark on the alter-

nator rotor (A, **Figure 31**) is still aligned with the alignment mark on the crankcase (B, **Figure 31**).

NOTE
Install the lockwasher in Step 11 so that it covers the locating pin in the end of the camshaft.

11. Install a new lockwasher (A, **Figure 35**) and camshaft sprocket bolt (B, **Figure 35**) in the exposed hole. Tighten the bolt only finger-tight at this time.

12. Rotate the engine clockwise, as viewed from the left-hand side, until the other sprocket bolt hole is exposed.

CAUTION
Apply ThreeBond TB1360 or Loctite No. 271 to the sprocket bolt threads prior to installation.

13. Install the other camshaft sprocket bolt in the exposed hole.

14. Hold down the end of camshaft opposite the camshaft sprocket and tighten the sprocket bolt to the torque specification listed in **Table 3**. Bend up the tab of the lockwasher against the bolt head (**Figure 26**).

15. Rotate the engine clockwise, as viewed from the left-hand side, until the bolt installed in Step 11 is exposed. Remove this bolt and apply a thread locking agent to the threads prior to installation.

16. Reinstall the camshaft sprocket bolt. Hold down the camshaft end opposite the camshaft sprocket and tighten the sprocket bolt to the torque specification listed in **Table 3**. Bend up the tab of the lockwasher against the bolt head.

17. Make sure the camshaft shoulder is properly indexed into the groove in the cylinder head.

18. Apply a light coat of molybdenum disulfide grease to the bearing surfaces and lobes of the camshaft.

19. Apply a light coat of molybdenum disulfide grease to the camshaft bearing surfaces in the cylinder head cover.

20. Fill the pocket in the cylinder head where the camshaft lobes ride with fresh engine oil.

21. Remove the camshaft end plug from the cylinder head cover. Do not apply any sealant to the end plug.

22. Clean the sealing surface of both the cylinder head and cover as follows:

a. Remove the old gaskets and clean off all gasket sealer residue from the cylinder head and cover.

b. Clean the surface with aerosol electrical contact cleaner and wipe dry with a lint-free cloth.

c. Apply a coat of ThreeBond No. 1104, or equivalent, to the sealing surface of the cylinder head cover. Do not apply sealant to the rounded camshaft bearing journal surfaces.

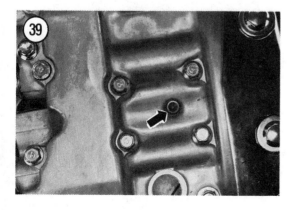

23. Install the camshaft end plug (**Figure 36**) into the cylinder head cover and make sure it is seated correctly.

24. If removed, install both locating dowels (**Figure 37**) into the cylinder head.

25. Remove the cylinder head plug (**Figure 38**).

NOTE
Do not pull the tensioner lock tool when installing it through the cylinder head cover in Step 26. If the tensioner lock tool pulls loose and releases the cam chain tensioner, the tool must be reinstalled as described under **Cylinder Head and Cylinder Assembly** *in this chapter.*

26. Carefully feed the tensioner lock tool through the cylinder head cover opening. Then install the cylinder head cover over the camshaft and onto the cylinder head. Push it down until it bottoms out. Check that the camshaft end plug is seated evenly between the cylinder head and cover.

27. Tighten the bolts in a crisscross pattern, starting with the center bolts (surrounding the camshaft) and working outward. Tighten in 2-3 stages to the torque specification listed in **Table 3**.

28. Install the cylinder head side cover and tighten the bolts.

29. Remove the oil plug and gasket (**Figure 39**).

30. Use a pump-type oil can and fill the cylinder head cover rocker arm passage with fresh engine oil. Fill with approximately 50 ml (1.7 U.S. oz.) of oil. Install the oil plug and new gasket and tighten securely.

31. Carefully pull the tensioner lock tool (**Figure 40**) out from the camshaft drive chain tensioner and though the opening in the cylinder head cover.

32. Install the cylinder head cover plug and tighten securely.

33. Install the spark plugs into both cylinder heads.

34. Install the engine into the frame as described in this chapter.

Cylinder Head Cover Inspection (Front and Rear Cylinders)

1. Remove all traces of gasket material from the cylinder head cover gasket surfaces.

2. After the cylinder head cover is thoroughly cleaned, place the cover on an inspection surface like

a piece of plate glass and check for any warpage at several points with a flat feeler gauge.

3. Measure for warpage by inserting a flat feeler gauge between the cylinder head cover gasket surface and the plate glass. Replace the cylinder head cover if the gasket surface is warped to the service limit listed in **Table 2**.

4. On the front cylinder head cover, perform the following:

    a. Make sure the small and large openings in the breather area are clear. Clean if necessary with a piece of wire and compressed air.

    b. Inspect the gasket (A, **Figure 41**) for damage or deterioration and replace if necessary.

    c. Inspect the breather cover (B, **Figure 41**) for cracks or damage and replace if necessary.

5. Inspect the exterior of both cylinder head covers for wear, cracks or damage; replace if necessary.

6. Disassemble and inspect the rocker arms as described in this chapter.

CAMSHAFT

Camshaft Inspection

1. Inspect the camshaft bearing journals (A, **Figure 42**) for wear.

2. Measure both camshaft bearing journals with a micrometer (**Figure 43**). Compare to the dimensions given in **Table 2**. If worn to the service limit, the camshaft must be replaced.

3. Check the camshaft lobes (B, **Figure 42**) for wear. The must not be scored and the edges should be square. Slight damage may be removed with a silicone carbide oilstone. Use No. 100-120 grit stone initially, then polish with a No. 280-320 grit stone.

4. Even though the camshaft lobe surface appears to be satisfactory, with no visible wear, the camshaft lobes must be measured with a micrometer (**Figure 44**). Compare to the dimensions given in **Table 2**. If worn to the service limit, the camshaft must be replaced.

5. Place the camshaft on a set of V-blocks and check its runout with a dial indicator. Compare to the dimension given in **Table 2**. If the runout exceeds the service limit, the camshaft must be replaced.

6. Make sure the locating pin installed in the end of the camshaft is a tight fit. If loose, replace the pin.

7. Inspect the camshaft bearing surfaces in the cylinder head and cylinder head cover. They should not be scored or excessively worn. Replace the cylinder head and cylinder head cover as a set, if the bearing surfaces are worn or scored.

8. Inspect the camshaft sprocket teeth (A, **Figure 45**) for wear; replace if necessary.

9. Make sure the camshaft sprocket bolt holes (B, **Figure 45**) and locating pin hole (C, **Figure 45**) are not elongated or damaged. If damaged, replace the camshaft sprocket.

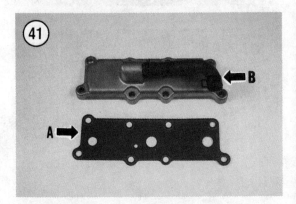

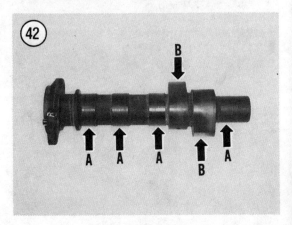

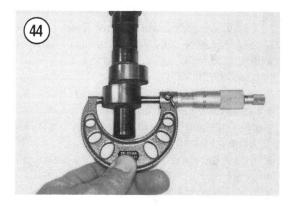

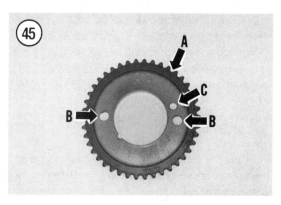

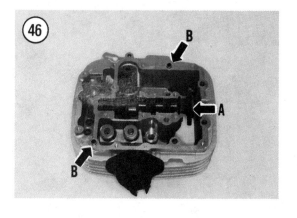

Camshaft Bearing Clearance Measurement

NOTE
This procedure is shown with the cylinder head removed for clarity. Bearing clearance can be performed with the cylinder head installed on the cylinder or as shown in this procedure.

1. Wipe all oil residue from the comshaft bearing journals and bearing surfaces in the cylinder head and cylinder head cover.

2. Install the camshaft (A, **Figure 46**) into the cylinder head with the lobes facing down. Do not attach the drive sprocket to the camshaft.

3. Make sure the locating dowels (B, **Figure 46**) are in place in the cylinder head.

4. Place a strip of Plastigage material on top of each camshaft center and end bearing journals, parallel to the camshaft.

5. Install the cylinder head cover.

6. Install the bolts securing the cylinder head cover.

7. Tighten the bolts in a crisscross pattern, starting with the center bolts (surrounding the camshaft) and working outward. Tighten in 2-3 stages to the torque specification listed in **Table 3**.

CAUTION
Do not rotate the camshafts with the Plastigage material in place.

8. Loosen the cylinder head bolts in 2-3 stages in a crisscross pattern, then remove the bolts.

9. Carefully remove the cylinder head cover.

10. Measure the width of the flattened Plastigage material at its widest point (**Figure 47**), according to its manufacturer's instructions.

CAUTION
Be sure to remove all traces of Plastigage material from the bearing journals in the cylinder head cover. If any material is left in the engine it can plug up an oil control orifice and cause severe engine damage.

11. Remove all Plastigage material from the camshaft and the bearing surfaces in the cylinder head cover.

12. If the oil clearance is greater than specified in **Table 2**, and the camshaft bearing journals are within specification in replace the cylinder head and cylinder head cover as a set.

13. Remove the camshaft from the cylinder head.

14. Repeat for the other camshaft and cylinder head assembly.

ROCKER ARM ASSEMBLIES

Refer to **Figure 48** for this procedure.

> *NOTE*
> *This procedure is performed on the rear cylinder head cover. All steps also relate to the rocker arm assemblies in the front cylinder head cover.*

Removal

> *NOTE*
> *The rocker arms and shafts are different and must be kept separate to avoid the intermixing of parts.*

1. Remove the cylinder head cover as described in this chapter.

2. Loosen the intake rocker arm shaft (A, **Figure 49**).

3. Remove the intake rocker arm shaft, gasket, thrust washer, intake rocker arm and wave washer.

4. Remove the trim cap and gasket (B, **Figure 49**) from the end of exhaust rocker arm shaft.

5. Screw a 6 mm bolt (A, **Figure 50**) into the end of the exhaust rocker arm shaft.

6. Remove the exhaust rocker arm shaft, thrust washer, exhaust rocker arm and wave washer (B, **Figure 50**).

7. Remove the bolt and washer (A, **Figure 51**) securing the compression release shaft (B, **Figure 51**). Withdraw the compression release shaft and spring from the cylinder head cover.

8. Wash all parts in solvent and thoroughly dry with compressed air.

Inspection

1. Inspect the rocker arm pad where it rides on the cam lobe (A, **Figure 52**) and where the tappets ride on the valve stems (**Figure 53**). If the pad is scratched or unevenly worn, inspect the camshaft lobe for scoring, chipping or flat spots. Replace the rocker arm if defective as well as the camshaft if it is damaged.

2. On the exhaust valve rocker arm, inspect the pad (**Figure 54**) where the compression release shaft arm rides. If the pad is scratched or unevenly worn, replace the rocker arm.

3. Remove the tappets from the rocker arms and inspect them as described in the following procedure.

4. Inspect the tappet receptacle(s) (B, **Figure 52**) in the rocker arm for wear. If worn or damaged, replace the rocker arm.

5. Measure the inside diameter of the rocker arm bore (**Figure 55**) and check against the specification in **Table 2**. Replace if wear exceeds the service limit.

6. Inspect the rocker arm shaft for signs of wear or scoring. Measure the outside diameter (**Figure 56**) with a micrometer and check against the specification in **Table 2**. Replace if worn to the service limit.

7. Make sure the oil holes in the rocker arm shaft are clean and clear. If necessary, clean out with a piece of wire and thoroughly clean with solvent. Dry with compressed air.

8. Check the gaskets and washers for breakage or distortion; replace if necessary.

9. Check the rocker arms and shafts for fractures, wear or damage; replace if necessary.

10. Check the compression release shaft, spring and bolt for wear or damage and replace as necessary. There are no service specifications for these parts.

11. Inspect the compression release shaft oil seal for hardness or leakage. If necessary, replace the oil seal.

Installation

1. Coat the compression release shaft and the shaft receptacle in the cylinder head with assembly oil or clean engine oil.

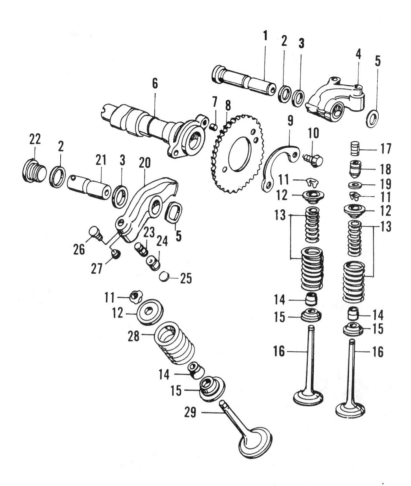

1. Rocker arm shaft (intake)
2. Gasket
3. Thrust washer
4. Rocker arm (intake)
5. Wave washer
6. Camshaft
7. Dowel pin
8. Camshaft sprocket
9. Lockwasher
10. Bolt
11. Keepers
12. Valve spring retainer
13. Valve spring set (intake)
14. Valve stem seal
15. Spring seat
16. Valve (intake)
17. Tappet chamber
18. Tappet
19. O-ring
20. Rocker arm (exhaust)
21. Rocker arm shaft (exhaust)
22. Plug
23. Tappet chamber
24. Tappet
25. O-ring
26. Compression release pin
27. Gasket
28. Valve spring (exhaust)
29. Valve (exhaust)

2. Install the shaft (A, **Figure 57**) with its flat end facing up (B, **Figure 57**).

3. Install the spring and nut (A, **Figure 58**) and position the end of the spring on the cylinder head boss as shown in B, **Figure 58**. Tighten the nut securely.

4. Coat the rocker arm shaft, rocker arm bore and the shaft receptacles in the cylinder head with assembly oil or clean engine oil.

> *NOTE*
> *The rocker arms and shafts are not identical. Refer to the marks made during removal to install these parts correctly.*

5. For the *exhaust* rocker arm assembly, **Figure 59** shows the correct order of parts as they must be installed into the cylinder head.

  a. Install a 6 mm bolt onto the end of the exhaust rocker arm shaft.

  b. Insert the rocker arm shaft (A, **Figure 60**) part way into the cylinder head cover and install the thrust washer (B, **Figure 60**).

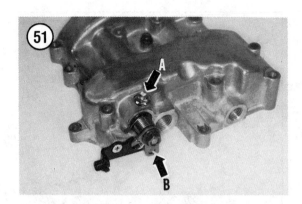

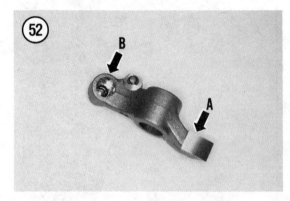

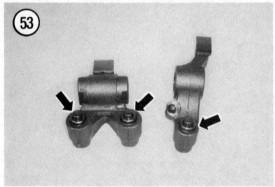

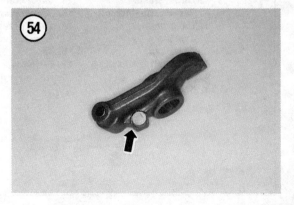

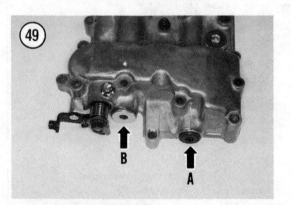

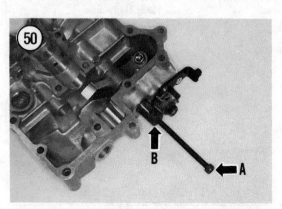

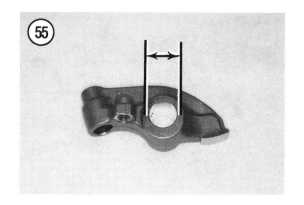

c. Position the rocker arm (A, **Figure 61**) and push the rocker arm shaft through but not past it, allowing room for installation of the wave washer.

d. Install the wave washer (B, **Figure 61**), then push the rocker arm shaft through the wave washer and stop.

e. Align the rocker arm shaft hole (A, **Figure 62**) with the cylinder head cover bolt hole (B, **Figure 62**), then push the rocker arm shaft in until it stops.

NOTE
The following alignment check is important. If the bolt hole in the rocker arm shaft is not aligned properly at this time, you will be unable to install the cylinder head cover mounting bolt during the cover installation procedure.

f. Insert a bolt in through the cylinder head cover bolt hole and through the rocker arm shaft to make sure the bolt hole is aligned correctly.

g. Install the gasket and plug and tighten to the torque specification listed in **Table 3**.

6. For the *intake* rocker arm assembly, **Figure 63** shows the correct order of parts as they are to be installed into the cylinder head as follows:

   a. Install a gasket (A, **Figure 64**) onto the rocker arm shaft.

   b. Insert the rocker arm shaft (B, **Figure 64**) part way into the cylinder head cover and install the thrust washer (C, **Figure 64**).

   c. Position the rocker arm (A, **Figure 65**) and push the rocker arm shaft through but not past it, allowing room for installation of the wave washer.

   d. Install the wave washer (B, **Figure 65**), then push the rocker arm shaft through the wave washer until it stops.

   e. Tighten the rocker arm shaft to the torque specification listed in **Table 3**.

HYDRAULIC TAPPETS (VALVE LASH ADJUSTERS)

For the proper operation, the hydraulic tappet must be free of air in the high-pressure chamber. The Suzuki air bleeding tool (part No. 09913-10740) or equivalent must be used to bleed the tappets.

The hydraulic tappets must be bled every time the cylinder head covers are removed as air can enter the tappets during the removal and installation procedures.

Inspection and Bleeding

1. Remove the tappets from the rocker arms.

2. Inspect the tappet and O-ring (**Figure 66**) for wear, scratches or damage.

3. Install the tappet (A, **Figure 67**) into the air bleeding tool (B, **Figure 67**).

4. Compress and stroke the plunger with your finger (**Figure 68**) to force the oil out of the tappet body.

5. Wash the tappet in kerosene and dry thoroughly.

6. Compress and stroke the plunger with your finger and check for smooth operation and lack of friction. The plunger must move in and out smoothly with no drag.

CAUTION
Only use kerosene to bleed the tappets. Never use any solvent, oil or any other type of petroleum based fluid for this procedure as they will cause engine

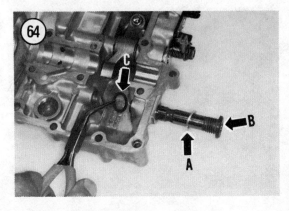

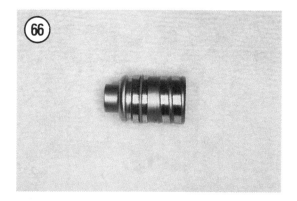

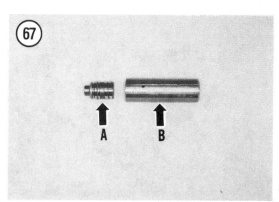

A   B

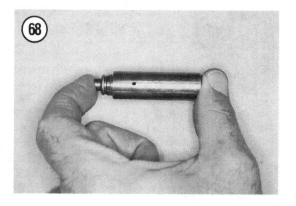

damage. The minimal amount of kerosene that remains in the tappets will mix with the engine oil and not be a problem.

7. Bleed the tappet as follows:

   a. Wear disposable latex gloves during this procedure to protect your hands from the kerosene.

   b. Fill a small flat container (A, **Figure 69**) with clean kerosene.

   c. Place the tappet (B, **Figure 69**) into the air bleeding tool (C, **Figure 69**).

   d. Submerge the tappet and air bleeding tool horizontally in the container of kerosene.

   e. Compress and stroke the plunger with your finger until all air bubbles are removed from the tappet chamber. The chamber is now full of kerosene.

   f. Remove the tappet from the tool and compress the plunger with your finger. The stroke should be between 0-0.5 mm (0.02 in.). If the stroke is more than specified, bleed the tappet again and recheck the stroke.

   g. After bleeding the tappet again, if the stroke is not within the specified range, replace the tappet.

8. Repeat Step 7 for all tappets.

9. Install the tappets in the rocker arm receptacles.

CYLINDER HEAD AND CYLINDER

The cylinder head and cylinder must be removed from the crankcase as an assembly. After removal from the crankcase, they are then separated.

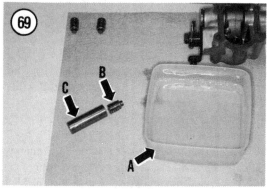

CAUTION
Removal and installation of the cylinder and cylinder head assembly requires the aid of an assistant. The combined cylinder and cylinder head is a long bulky assembly and must be pulled straight up and off the piston without causing damage to the cylinder wall or piston. Have the assistant secure the crankcase assembly while you remove the cylinder and cylinder head assembly from the crankcase.

Removal

NOTE
This procedure is shown on the front cylinder and cylinder assembly. Removal of the rear cylinder and cylinder head are identical.

1. Remove the engine from the frame as described in this chapter.
2. Remove the following exterior assemblies from the crankcase assembly:
   a. Alternator (Chapter Eight).
   b. Primary drive gear (Chapter Five).
   c. Secondary gear assembly (Chapter Five).
   d. Rear cylinder camshaft chain and tensioner guide (Chapter Five).
   e. External shift mechanism (Chapter Six).
   f. Clutch (Chapter Six).
3. Remove the cylinder head cover and camshaft as described in this chapter.
4. Using a crisscross pattern, loosen then remove the bolts and washers (**Figure 70**) securing the cylinder head and cylinder to the crankcase.

CAUTION
Remember the small cooling fins are fragile and may be damaged if tapped or pried on too hard. Never use a metal hammer.

5. Loosen the cylinder head and cylinder by tapping around the perimeter base of the cylinder with a rubber or soft faced mallet.
6. Untie the wire, or remove the drift or long socket extension securing the camshaft chain.
7. Carefully lift the cylinder head and cylinder assembly (**Figure 71**) and remove the assembly from the piston and the crankcase. Guide the camshaft

chain through the opening in the cylinder head and cylinder and secure it to the exterior of the engine.

8. Remove the cylinder base gasket and discard it. Do not lose the locating dowels.

9. If only one cylinder head and assembly is going to be removed, place a clean shop cloth into the opening in the crankcase to prevent the entry of foreign matter.
10. Remove the oil control jet(s) from the camshaft chain cavity in the crankcase.

11. Repeat the procedure for the other cylinder head and cylinder assembly if necessary.

Disassembly

1. Remove the front and rear nuts (**Figure 72**).
2. Loosen the cylinder head from the cylinder by tapping around the perimeter of the cylinder head with a rubber or soft faced mallet.
3. Carefully remove the cylinder head from the cylinder.

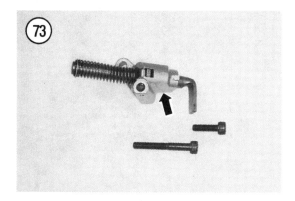

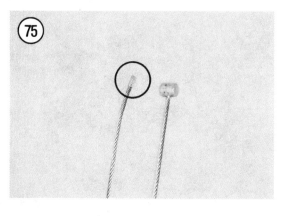

4. Remove the cylinder head gasket. Don't lose the locating dowels.
5. Remove the camshaft chain guide from the cylinder.

NOTE
The camshaft chain tensioners are unique and must be installed in the correct cylinder. If they are not marked with a F (front) or R (rear), identify them with a permanent marking pen or scratch the letter on the body with a scribe (Figure 73).

6. Remove the bolts (A, **Figure 74**) securing the camshaft chain tensioner (B, **Figure 74**) and remove the tensioner from the cylinder.
7. Inspect the cylinder head, cylinder and camshaft chain tensioner as described in this chapter.

Assembly

A special tool is required to hold the camshaft chain tensioner spring in the compressed position. The special Suzuki tool, tensioner lock tool (part No. 09918-53810) can be substituted with a homemade tool made from a length of control cable with one end flattened as shown in **Figure 75**. The cable must be long enough to exit through the top of the cylinder head cover during assembly so it can be easily removed.

NOTE
The camshaft chain tensioners are unique and must be installed in the correct cylinder. Refer to the marks noted during removal.

1. Install the correct camshaft chain tensioner into the cylinder and install the bolts (**Figure 76**). Tighten the bolts securely.

NOTE
The camshaft chain tensioner spring must be compressed, and remain compressed, prior to installing the camshaft chain guide.

2. On the camshaft tensioner assembly, release the ratchet with a small screwdriver, then push in on the end of the tensioner to compress the spring. See **Figure 76**). Hold the tensioner in the compressed position and install the flattened end of the throttle

control cable into the ratchet area (**Figure 77**). The cable end will keep the ratchet unlocked and the spring compressed.

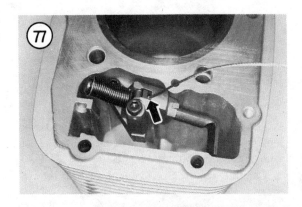

> *NOTE*
> *The front and rear cylinder head gaskets have a different hole pattern. Be sure to install the correct gasket on the correct cylinder.*

> *NOTE*
> *The camshaft chain guides are unique and must be installed in the correct cylinder. They are marked with an F (front) or R (rear).*

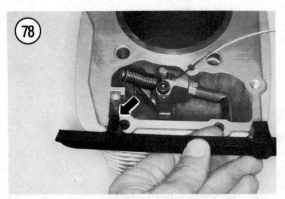

3A. On the front cylinder, perform the following:
   a. Position the camshaft chain guide with the locator notch (**Figure 78**) at the top.
   b. Place the cylinder on a wooden block (A, **Figure 79**) so the guide can pass unobstructed through the cylinder.
   c. Install the camshaft chain guide into the cylinder. Make sure it is correctly seated in the locator notch at the top of the cylinder (B, **Figure 79**).
   d. Install a new cylinder head gasket (A, **Figure 80**). Make sure all of the gasket holes match the holes in the cylinder.
   e. If removed, install the 2 locating dowels (B, **Figure 80**) in the cylinder.

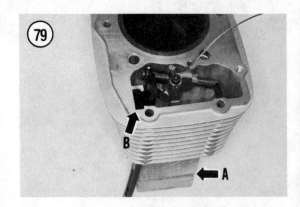

3B. On the rear cylinder, perform the following:
   a. Position the camshaft chain guide with the locator notch (**Figure 81**) at the top.
   b. Install the camshaft chain guide into the cylinder. Make sure it is correctly seated in the locator notch at the top of the cylinder (**Figure 82**).

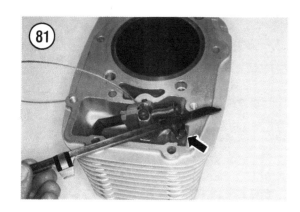

c. Place the cylinder on a wooden block (**Figure 83**) to protect the end of the guide.

d. Install a new cylinder head gasket (A, **Figure 84**). Make sure all of the gasket holes match the holes in the cylinder.

e. If removed, install the 2 locating dowels (B, **Figure 84**) in the cylinder.

CAUTION
The cylinder head and cylinder should fit together without force. If they do not fit together completely, do not attempt to pull them together with the bolts and nuts in the next step. Separate the 2 parts and investigate the cause of the interference. Do not risk damage by trying to force the parts together.

4. Carefully install the cylinder head onto the cylinder. Guide the tensioner lock tool up through the camshaft chain opening in the cylinder head (**Figure 85**). Push the 2 parts together until they bottom out.

5. Install the front and rear nuts (**Figure 86**).

6. Since the nuts are in a recessed area it is impossible to tighten them with a torque wrench and socket. Use the Motion Pro Torque Wrench Adapter (A, **Figure 87**) (part No. 08-134), available from most motorcycle dealerships, on the nut, then place the torque wrench (B, **Figure 87**) onto the tool. Follow the manufacturer's instructions when using the tool. Tighten the nuts to the torque specification listed in **Table 3**.

Installation

NOTE
This procedure is shown on the front cylinder and cylinder assembly.

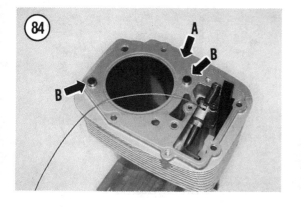

Installation of the rear cylinder and cylinder head are identical unless otherwise indicated.

1. If used, remove the shop cloth from the opening in the crankcase.

2. Apply a liberal coat of clean engine oil to the cylinder wall especially at the lower end where the piston will be entering.

3. Lubricate the piston and piston rings with engine oil.

4. Make sure the crankcase and cylinder surfaces are clean prior to installing a new base gasket.

> *NOTE*
> *The front and rear cylinder base gaskets have a slightly different hole pattern. Be sure to install the correct gasket on the correct location on the crankcase.*

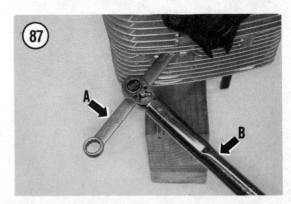

5A. On the rear cylinder, perform the following:
  a. If the oil control jets were removed, make sure the oil hole is open and the O-ring is installed. Install the oil control jets into the crankcase. Push both jets down until they bottom (**Figure 88**).
  b. Install a new cylinder base gasket (A, **Figure 89**).
  c. If removed, install the locating dowels (B, **Figure 89**).

5B. On the front cylinder location on the crankcase, perform the following:
  a. If the oil control jet was removed, make sure the oil hole is open and that O-ring is installed. Install the oil control jet into the crankcase and push it down until it bottoms (**Figure 90**).
  b. Install a new cylinder base gasket (A, **Figure 91**).
  c. If removed, install the locating dowels (B, **Figure 91**).

> *NOTE*
> *Make a piston holding fixture out of a piece of wood 2 in. (51 mm) thick. This thickness will hold the piston in place for the following procedures.*

6. Place the piston holding fixture under the piston (**Figure 92**).

7. Make sure the end gaps of the piston rings are staggered and not lined up with each other. Lubricate the piston rings and the inside of the cylinder bore with assembly oil or fresh engine oil.

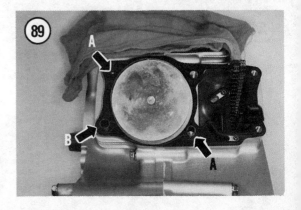

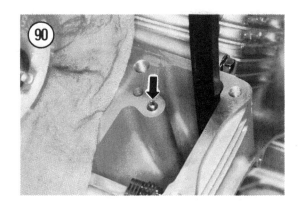

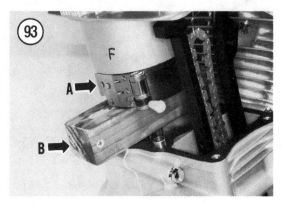

8. Install a piston ring compressor tool onto the piston.

NOTE
The following step requires the aid of an assistant. The cylinder head and cylinder assembly are long and also quite heavy. Trying to hold onto the cylinder head and cylinder assembly by yourself, while guiding it onto the piston could cause damage to the piston and/or piston rings.

9. Move the cylinder head and cylinder assembly into position on the crankcase.

10. Carefully feed the camshaft chain and wire up through the opening in the cylinder head and cylinder and tie it to the exterior of the assembly.

NOTE
Figure 93 *shows the front cylinder.*

11. Start the cylinder down over the piston.

12. Remove the piston ring compressor (A, **Figure 93**) and the piston holding fixture (B, **Figure 93**).

13. Slide the cylinder head and cylinder assembly down until it bottoms out on the crankcase.

14. Look down into the camshaft chain cavity and make sure the camshaft chain, camshaft tensioner assembly guide and the chain guide are all positioned correctly and that the camshaft chain is not binding.

15. Make sure the camshaft chain guide is correctly seated in the crankcase groove. Refer to **Figure 94** for the rear cylinder and **Figure 95** for the front cylinder.

16. Install a washer (**Figure 96**) onto each bolt and install all 4 bolts (**Figure 97**) securing the cylinder head and cylinder to the crankcase. Using a crisscross pattern, tighten the bolts in 2-3 stages to the torque specification listed in **Table 3**.

17. Install the camshaft and the cylinder head cover as described in this chapter.

18. Install the following exterior assemblies from the crankcase assembly:
    a. Alternator: Chapter Nine.
    b. Primary drive gear: Chapter Five.
    c. Secondary gear assembly: Chapter Five.
    d. Rear cylinder camshaft chain and tensioner guide: Chapter Five.
    e. External shift mechanism: Chapter Six.
    f. Clutch: Chapter Six.

19. Install the engine into the frame as described in this chapter.

Cylinder Head Inspection

1. Remove all traces of gasket material from the cylinder head upper and lower mating surfaces. Do not scratch the gasket surface.

2. Without removing the valves, remove all carbon deposits from the combustion chamber (A, **Figure 98**) and valve ports with a wire brush.

3. Inspect the threads of the studs (B, **Figure 98**) for damage. Clean up with an appropriate size metric die if necessary. Make sure the stud is tightly secured into the cylinder head.

4. Examine the spark plug threads in the cylinder head for damage. If damage is minor or if the threads are dirty or clogged with carbon, use a spark plug thread tap to clean the threads following the manufacturer's instructions. If thread damage is severe, refer further service to a dealer or competent machine shop.

5. After the carbon is removed from the combustion chamber and the valve ports and the spark plug thread hole are repaired, clean the entire head in cleaning solvent. Blow dry with compressed air.

6. Clean away all carbon from the piston crown. Do not remove the carbon ridge at the top of the cylinder bore.

7. Check for cracks in the combustion chamber and exhaust port. A cracked head must be replaced.

8. Inspect the camshaft bearing area in the cylinder head for damage, wear or burrs. Clean up if damage is minimal; replace the cylinder head if necessary.

9. Inspect the threaded holes in the cylinder head for damage. Clean up with an appropriate size metric tap if necessary.

10. Inspect the cooling fins for cracks or damage.

11. Check the rubber intake manifold for cracks, deterioration or damage. Replace if necessary.

12. After the head is thoroughly cleaned, place a straightedge across the cylinder head/cylinder gasket surface (**Figure 99**) at several points. Measure the warp by inserting a flat feeler gauge between the straightedge and the cylinder head at each location. Maximum allowable warpage is 0.010 in. (0.25 mm). If warpage exceeds this limit, the cylinder head must be replaced.

13. Inspect the valve and valve guides as described in this chapter.

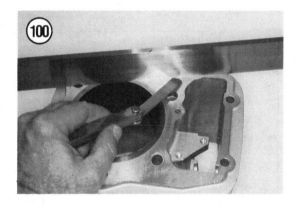

14. Repeat for the other cylinder head.

Cylinder Inspection

1. Soak the old cylinder head gasket with solvent. Use a broad-tipped dull chisel to scrape off all gasket residue gently. Do not gouge the sealing surface as oil and air leaks will result.

2. After the cylinder has been thoroughly cleaned, place a straightedge across the gasket surface at several points. Measure warp by attempting to insert a feeler gauge between the straightedge and cylinder at each location (**Figure 100**). Maximum allowable warpage is listed in **Table 2** . Warpage or nicks in the cylinder top surface could cause an air leak and result in overheating. If warpage exceeds the limit, the cylinder head must be resurfaced or replaced. Consult a Suzuki dealership or machine shop experienced in this type of work.

3. Measure the cylinder bore with a cylinder gauge (**Figure 101**) or inside micrometer at the points shown in **Figure 102**.

4. Measure in 2 axes in line with the piston-pin and at 90° to the pin. If the taper or out-of-round is 0.004 in. (0.10 mm) or greater, the cylinder must be rebored to the next oversize and a new piston and rings installed. Rebore both cylinders even if only one is worn.

> *NOTE*
> *The new pistons should be obtained before the cylinders are rebored so that the pistons can be measured. Slight manufacturing tolerances must be taken into account to determine the actual size and working clearance. Piston-to-cylinder wear limit is listed in Table 2.*

5. If the cylinders are not worn past the service limit, thoroughly check the bore surface for scratches or gouges. If damaged in any way, the bore will require boring and reconditioning.

6. If the cylinders require reboring, remove all dowel pins from the cylinders, then take them to a dealership or machine shop for service.

7. After the cylinders have been serviced, perform the following:

> *CAUTION*
> *A combination of soap and hot water is the only solution that will completely*

clean cylinder walls. Solvent and kerosene cannot wash fine grit out of cylinder crevices. Any grit left in the cylinders will act as a grinding compound and cause premature wear to the new rings.

a. Wash each cylinder bore in hot soapy water. This is the only way to clean the cylinders of the fine grit material left from the bore and honing procedure.

b. Also wash out any fine grit material from the cooling cores surrounding each cylinder.

c. After washing the cylinder walls, run a clean white cloth through each cylinder wall. It should not show any traces of grit or debris. If the rag is the slightest bit dirty, the wall is not thoroughly cleaned and must be rewashed.

d. After the cylinder is cleaned, lubricate the cylinder walls with clean engine oil to prevent the cylinder liners from rusting.

8. Inspect the cooling fins for cracks or damage.

9. Repeat for the other cylinder.

Camshaft Chain Tensioner and Chain Guide Inspection

1. Inspect all parts of the camshaft chain tensioner adjuster for wear or damage (**Figure 103**).

2. Make sure the ratchet (**Figure 104**) operates correctly.

3. If any part of the tensioner adjuster body or rack is worn or damaged, replace the entire assembly. Replacement parts are not available.

4. Inspect the camshaft chain guides (**Figure 105**) for wear or deterioration. Replace if necessary.

VALVES AND VALVE COMPONENTS

General practice among those who do their own service is to remove the cylinder heads and take them to a machine shop or dealership for inspection and service. Since the cost is relative to the required effort and equipment, this may be the best approach even for the experienced mechanics.

Refer to **Figure 106** for this procedure.

Valve Removal

1. Remove the cylinder head as described in this chapter.

CAUTION
To avoid loss of spring tension, do not compress the springs any more than necessary to remove the keepers.

2. Compress the valve springs with a valve spring-compressor (**Figure 107**). Remove the valve keepers, release the compressor and remove it.

3. Remove the valve spring retainer and valve springs.

4. Prior to removing the valve, remove any burrs from the valve stem (**Figure 108**). Otherwise the valve guide will be damaged.

5. Remove the valve.

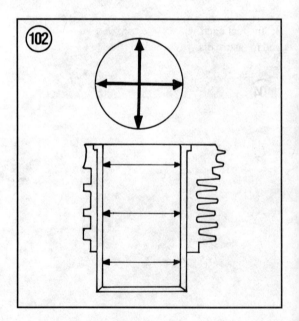

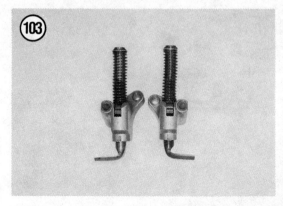

6. Remove the valve stem seal (A, **Figure 109**) and spring seat (B, **Figure 109**) from the valve guide.

7. Repeat Steps 2-6 for the remaining valves.

8. Mark all parts as they are disassembled so they are installed in their same locations. The exhaust valve, with a single spring, is adjacent to the exhaust port and the 2 intake valves, with dual springs, are located next to the intake manifold.

Valve Inspection

1. Clean the valves with a soft wire brush and solvent.

2. Inspect the contact surface of each valve (**Figure 110**) for burning or pitting. Unevenness of the contact surface is an indication that the valve is not serviceable. The valve contact surface cannot be ground and must be replaced if defective.

3. Inspect each valve stem for wear and roughness and measure the valve stem runout as shown in **Fig-**

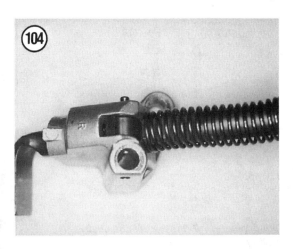

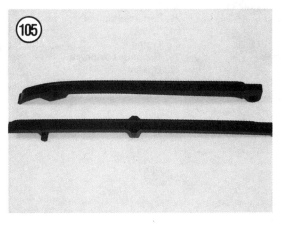

ure **111**. The runout should not exceed the service limit listed in **Table 2**.

4. Check the valve head runout with a V-block and dial indicator as shown in **Figure 112**. Runout should not exceed the service limit listed in **Table 2**.

5. Measure each valve stem for wear (**Figure 113**). If the measured diameter is less than the specification in **Table 2**, replace the valve.

6. Measure each valve seat width (**Figure 114**). If the seat width is not within the specification in **Table 2**, replace or recondition the valve.

7. Remove all carbon and varnish from each valve guide with a stiff spiral wire brush.

8. Insert each valve in its guide. Hold the valve with the head just slightly off the valve seat and rock it sideways in 2 directions, perpendicular to each other as shown in **Figure 115**. If the valve stem deflection measurement exceeds the limit listed in **Table 2**, measure the valve stem. If the valve stem is worn, replace the valve. If the valve stem is within tolerance, refer to *Valve Guide Inspection* in this chapter.

9. Measure each valve spring free length with a vernier caliper (**Figure 116**). All should be within the length specified in **Table 2** with no bends or distortion (**Figure 117**). On intake valves, replace defective springs in pairs (inner and outer).

10. Check the valve spring retainer and valve keepers. If they are in good condition they may be reused; replace as necessary.

11. Inspect the valve seats (**Figure 118**) in the cylinder head. If worn or burned, they must be reconditioned as described in this chapter.

12. Inspect the valve stem end for pitting and wear. If pitted or worn, the end may be resurfaced providing the finished end length (**Figure 119**) is not less than the length listed in **Table 2**. Replace the valve(s) if the finished length is less than specified.

Valve Installation

1. Install the spring seat (**Figure 120**). Do not confuse the valve spring retainer (A, **Figure 121**) with the spring seat (B, **Figure 121**). The inner diameter is different.

2. Apply clean engine oil to the new valve stem seal. Install a new seal on each valve guide (**Figure 122**) and push it down until it bottoms out.

3. Coat the valve stems with molybdenum disulfide grease. To avoid damage to the valve stem seal, turn the valve slowly while inserting the valve into the

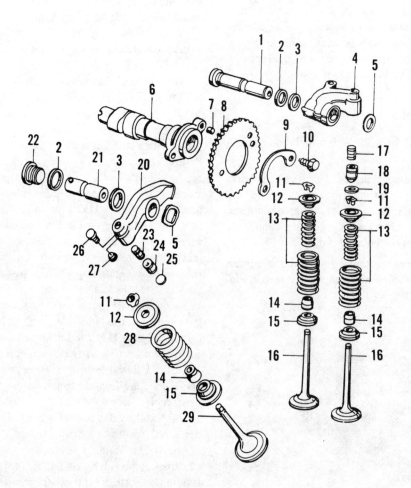

1. Rocker arm shaft (intake)	11. Keepers	21. Rocker arm shaft (exhaust)
2. Gasket	12. Valve spring retainer	22. Plug
3. Thrust washer	13. Valve spring set (intake)	23. Tappet chamber
4. Rocker arm (intake)	14. Valve stem seal	24. Tappet
5. Wave washer	15. Spring set	25. O-ring
6. Camshaft	16. Valve (intake)	26. Decompression pin
7. Dowel pin	17. Tappet chamber	27. Gasket
8. Camshaft sprocket	18. Tappet	28. Valve spring (exhaust)
9. Lockwasher	19. O-ring	29. Valve (exhaust)
10. Bolt	20. Rocker arm (exhaust)	

cylinder head. Push the valve all the way in until it bottoms.

4. Install the valve springs with the closer wound coils (**Figure 123**) going on first against the spring seat.

5A. On the intake valves, install the inner valve spring (**Figure 124**) and the outer valve spring (**Figure 125**) with the closer wound coils toward the cylinder head.

5B. On the exhaust valve, install the valve spring (**Figure 126**) with the closer wound coils toward the cylinder head.

6. Install the valve spring retainer (**Figure 127**) on top of the valve spring(s).

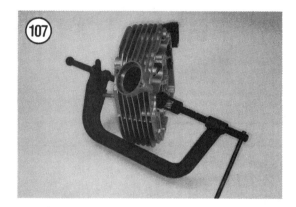

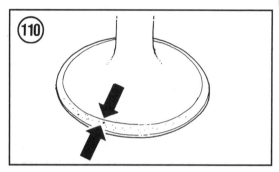

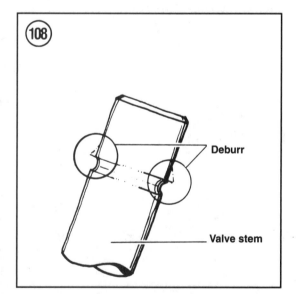

Deburr

Valve stem

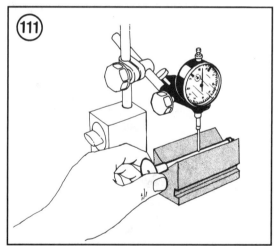

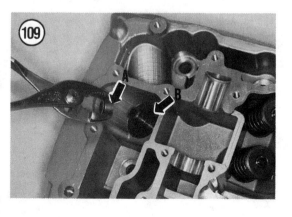

CAUTION
To avoid loss of spring tension, do not compress the springs any more than necessary to install the keepers.

7. Compress the valve springs with a spring compressor (**Figure 107**) and install the valve keepers. Make sure the keepers fit snug into the rounded groove in the valve stem.

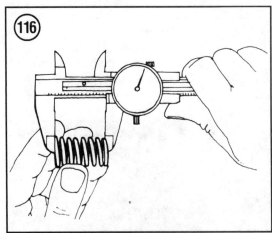

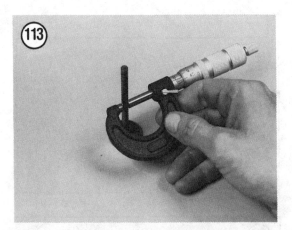

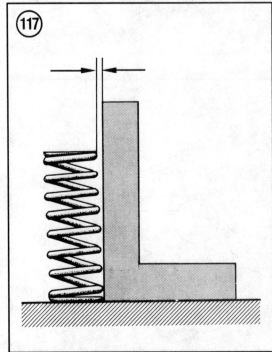

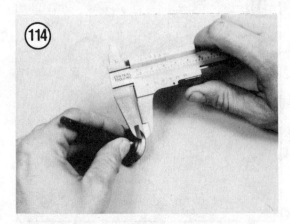

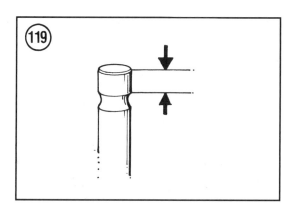

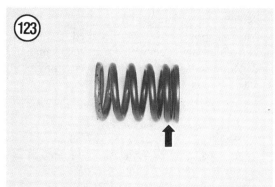

4

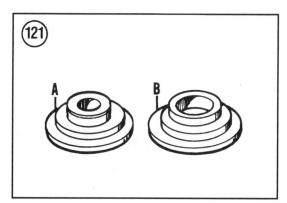

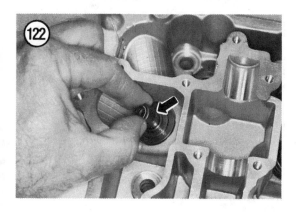

8. Remove the compression tool.

9. After all springs have been installed, gently tap the end of the valve stem with a soft faced hammer. This will ensure that the keepers are properly seated.

> *CAUTION*
> *If the valve stem end has been resurfaced, make sure that the valve stem face (A, **Figure 128**) is above the valve retainers (B, **Figure 128**).*

10. Repeat for all valve assemblies and for the other cylinder head if necessary.

11. Install the cylinder head(s) as described in this chapter.

Valve Guide Inspection

Measure the inside diameter of the valve guide and compare this to the specification in **Table 2**. If the measurement exceeds the specification replace the valve guide. Subtract the valve guide diameter from the valve stem outside diameter to determine the valve stem-to-guide clearance (**Table 2**). If necessary, refer valve guide replacement to a machine shop.

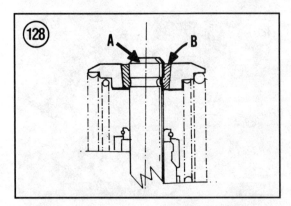

Valve Seat Inspection

1. Remove the valves as described in this chapter.

2. To check the valve seal with Prussian Blue or machine's dye, perform the following:

  a. Thoroughly clean all carbon deposits from the valve face with solvent or detergent, then thoroughly dry.

  b. Spread a thin layer of Prussian Blue or machinist's dye evenly on the valve face.

  c. Moisten the end of a suction cup valve tool (**Figure 129**) and attach it to the valve. Insert the valve into the guide.

  d. Using the suction cup tool, tap the valve up and down in the cylinder head. Do not rotate the valve or a false indication will result.

  e. Remove the valve and examine the impression left by the Prussian Blue or machinist's dye. If the impression left in the dye (on the valve or in the cylinder head) is not even and continuous and the valve seat width (**Figure 130**) is not within the specified tolerance listed in

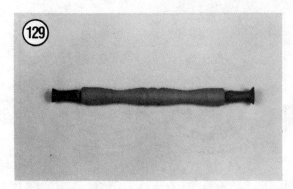

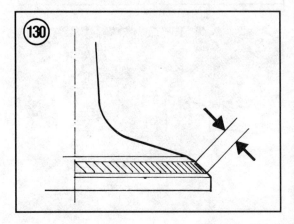

Table 2, the cylinder head valve seat must be reconditioned.

3. Closely examine the valve seat (**Figure 118**) in the cylinder head. It should be smooth and even with a polished seating surface.

4. If the valve seat is okay, install the valves as described in this chapter.

5. If the valve seat is not correct, have the valve seat(s) reconditioned.

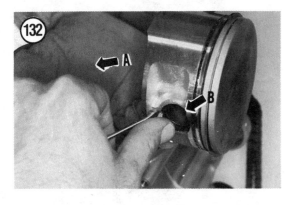

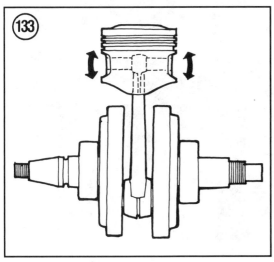

Valve Seat Reconditioning

Special valve cutters and considerable expertise are required to recondition the valve seats properly. You can save considerable money by taking just the cylinder heads to a dealership or machine shop to have the valve seats reconditioned.

PISTONS AND PISTON RINGS

Piston
Removal/Installation

1. Remove the cylinder head and cylinder assemblies as described in this chapter.

2. Lightly mark the top of the pistons with an F (front) or R (rear) so they will be installed into the correct cylinder (**Figure 131**).

3. Stuff clean shop cloths (A, **Figure 132**) into the cylinder bore crankcase opening to prevent objects from falling into the crankcase.

4. If necessary, remove the piston rings as described in this chapter.

5. Before removing the piston, hold the rod tightly and rock the piston as shown in **Figure 133**. Any rocking motion (do not confuse with the normal sliding motion) indicates wear on the piston pin, piston pin bore or connecting rod small-end bore (more likely a combination of these). Mark the piston and pin so they will be reassembled into the same set.

6. Remove the circlips (B, **Figure 132**) from each side of the piston pin bore with a small screwdriver or scribe. To prevent the circlip from springing out, hold your thumb over one edge during removal.

7. Use a proper size wooden dowel or socket extension and push out the piston pin.

> *CAUTION*
> *Be careful when removing the pin to avoid damaging the connecting rod. If it is necessary to tap the pin gently to remove it, be sure the piston is properly supported so lateral shock is not transmitted to the connecting rod lower bearing.*

8. If the piston pin is difficult to remove, heat the piston and pin with a butane torch. The pin will probably push right out. Heat the piston to only about 140° F (60° C), (too warm to touch, but not

---

excessively hot). If the pin is still difficult to push out, use a homemade tool as shown in **Figure 134**.

9. Lift the piston from the connecting rod and inspect it as described in this chapter.

10. If the piston is going to be left off for some time, place a piece of foam insulation tube over the end of the rod to protect it.

11. Apply molybdenum disulfide grease to the inside surface of the connecting rod piston pin bore.

12. Oil the piston pin with assembly oil or fresh engine oil and install it in the piston until its end extends slightly beyond the inside of the boss (**Figure 135**).

13. Correctly position the piston onto the connecting rod. Refer to arrow mark (**Figure 136**) on top of the piston crown. Install the piston with the arrow toward the exhaust side of the cylinder.

14. Place the piston over the connecting rod.

15. Align the piston pin with the hole in the connecting rod. Push the piston pin through the connecting rod until it is centered in the piston.

> *CAUTION*
> *If it is necessary to tap the piston pin into the connecting rod, do so gently with a block of wood or a soft-faced hammer. Make sure you support the piston to prevent the lateral shock from being transmitted to the connecting rod lower bearing.*

> *NOTE*
> *In the next step, install the piston pin circlips with their gap facing away from the cutout in the piston (**Figure 137**).*

16. Install a new piston pin circlip in one side of the piston. Make sure the circlip seats in the piston groove completely. Repeat for the other circlip.

17. Check the installation by rocking the piston back and forth around the pin axis and from side to side along the axis. It should rotate freely back and forth but not from side to side.

18. If removed, install the piston rings as described in this chapter.

19. Repeat Steps 1-18 for the other piston.

Piston Inspection

1. Carefully clean the carbon from the piston crown (**Figure 138**) with a chemical remover or with a soft scraper. Do not remove or damage the carbon ridge

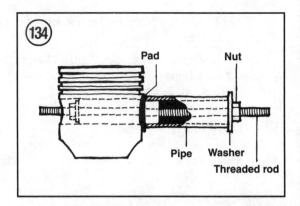

Pad   Nut
Pipe   Washer
Threaded rod

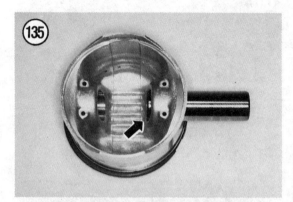

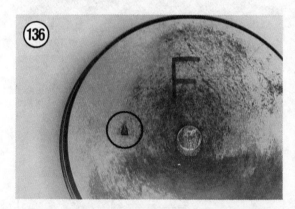

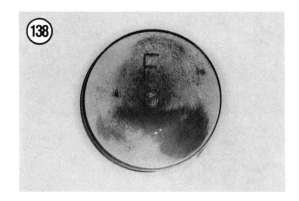

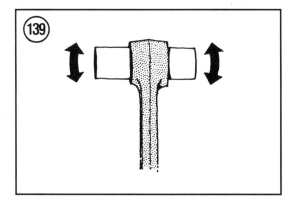

around the circumference of the piston above the top ring. If the piston, rings and cylinder are found to be dimensionally correct and can be reused, removal of the carbon ring from the top of the piston or the carbon ridge from the top of the cylinder will promote excessive oil consumption. Mark the piston crown with a F or R mark as soon as it is cleaned in order to keep it correctly located during installation.

CAUTION
Do not wire brush the piston skirts.

2. Examine each ring groove for burrs, dented edges and wide wear. Pay particular attention to the top compression ring groove as it usually wears more than the other grooves.

3. If damage or wear indicates piston replacement, select a new piston as described under *Piston Clearance Measurement* in this chapter.

4. Oil the piston pin and install it in the connecting rod. Slowly rotate the piston pin and check for radial and axial play (**Figure 139**). If any play exists, the piston pin should be replaced, providing the rod bore is in good condition.

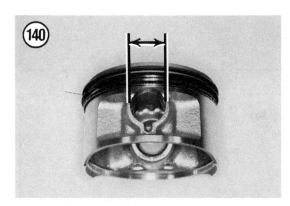

5. Measure the inside diameter of the piston pin bore (**Figure 140**) with a snap gauge and measure the outside diameter of the piston pin with a micrometer (**Figure 141**). Compare to the specification in **Table 2**. Replace the piston and piston pin as a set if either or both are worn.

6. Check the oil control holes (**Figure 142**) in the piston for carbon or oil sludge buildup. Clean the holes with a small diameter drill bit and blow out with compressed air.

7. Check the piston skirt for galling and abrasion which may have been caused by piston seizure. If light galling is present, smooth the affected area with No. 400 emery paper and oil or a fine oilstone. However, if galling is severe or if the piston is deeply scored, replace it.

8. Check the circlip groove on each side for wear, cracks or other damage. If the grooves are questionable, check the circlip fit by installing a new circlip into each groove and then attempt to move the circlip from side-to-side. If the circlip has any side play, the groove is worn and the piston must be replaced.

9. If damage or wear indicate piston replacement, select a new piston as described under *Piston Clearance Measurement* in this chapter.

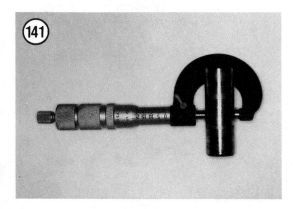

Piston Clearance Measurement

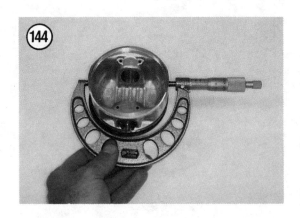

1. Make sure the piston and cylinder walls are clean and dry.

2. Measure the diameter of the cylinder bore at a point 1/2 in. (13 mm) from the upper edge using a bore gauge (**Figure 143**).

3. Measure the diameter of the piston across the skirt (**Figure 144**) at a right angle to the piston pin. Measure at a distance 0.60 in. (15 mm) up from the bottom of the piston skirt.

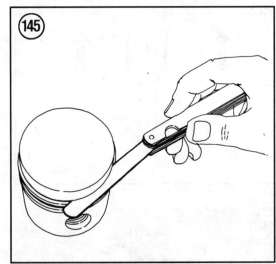

4. Subtract the diameter of the piston from the cylinder bore diameter and compare to the specification listed in **Table 2**. If clearance is excessive, the piston should be replaced and the cylinder should be rebored to the next oversize. Purchase the new piston first; measure its diameter and add the specified clearance to determine the proper cylinder bore diameter.

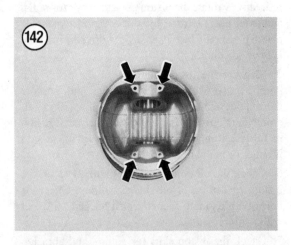

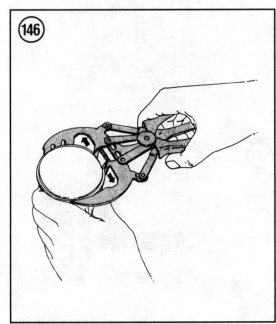

Piston Ring
Removal/Installation

> *WARNING*
> *The edges of all piston rings are very sharp. Be careful when handling them to avoid cutting your fingers.*

1. Measure the side clearance of each ring in its groove using a flat feeler gauge (**Figure 145**) and compare to the specification in **Table 2**. If the clearance is greater than specified, the rings must be replaced. If the clearance is still excessive with the new rings, the piston must also be replaced.

2. Remove the old rings with a ring expander tool (**Figure 146**) or by spreading the ends with your thumbs just enough to slide the ring up over the piston (**Figure 147**). Repeat for the remaining rings.

3. Carefully remove all carbon buildup from the ring grooves with a broken piston ring (**Figure 148**).

4. Inspect the grooves carefully for burrs, nicks or broken and cracked lands. Recondition or replace the piston if necessary.

5. Check the end gap of each ring. To check the ring, insert the ring, one at a time, into the bottom of the cylinder bore and push it in about 20 mm (3/4 in.) with the crown of the piston to ensure that the ring is square in the cylinder bore. Measure the gap with a flat feeler gauge (**Figure 149**) and compare to dimensions in **Table 2**. If the gap is greater than specified, the rings should be replaced. When installing new rings, measure their end gap in the same manner as for old ones. If the gap is less than specified, carefully file the ends with a fine-cut file until the gap is correct.

6. Check the free end gap of each ring with a vernier caliper (**Figure 150**) and compare to the dimension in **Table 2**. If the gap is greater than specified, the rings should be replaced. When installing new rings, measure their free end gap prior to installation.

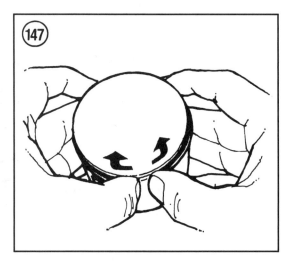

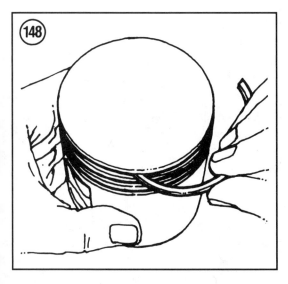

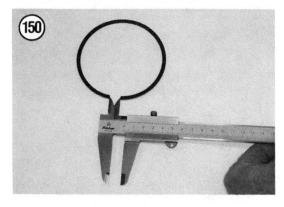

NOTE
It is not necessary to measure the oil control ring expander spacer. If the oil control ring rails show wear, all 3 parts of the oil control ring should be replaced as a set.

7. Measure the thickness of each compression ring with a micrometer (**Figure 151**). If the thickness is less than specified, replace the ring(s).

8. Roll each ring around its piston groove as shown in **Figure 152** to check for binding. Minor binding is probably caused by dirty or nicked grooves. Small nicks may be cleaned up with a fine-cut file.

NOTE
Install the compression rings with their markings facing up.

9. Install the piston rings - first, the bottom, then the middle, then the top ring - by carefully spreading the ends with your thumbs and slipping the rings over the top of the piston. Remember that the piston rings must be installed with the manufacturer's marks on them toward the top of the piston or there is the possibility of oil pumping past the rings. Install the rings in the order shown in **Figure 153**.

10. Make sure the rings are seated completely in their grooves all the way around the piston and that the ends are distributed around the piston as shown in **Figure 154**. The important thing is that the ring gaps are not aligned with each other when installed to prevent compression pressure from escaping.

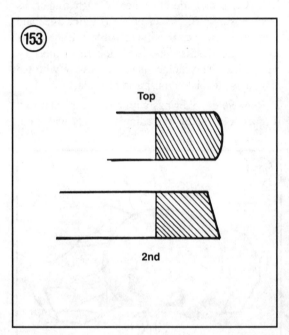

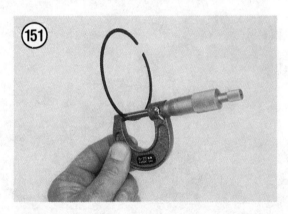

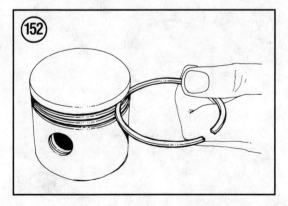

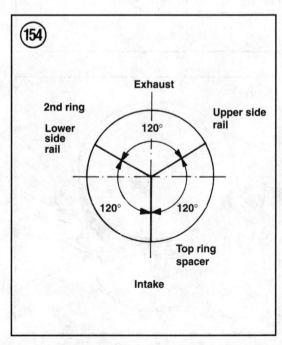

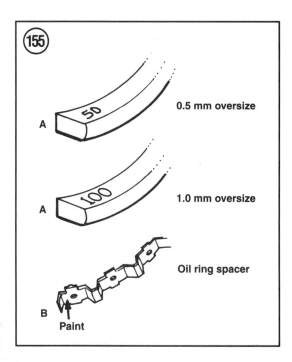

11. If installing oversize compression rings, check the number (A, **Figure 155**) to make sure the correct rings are being installed. The ring numbers should be the same as the piston oversize number.

12. If installing oversize oil rings, check the paint color spot (B, **Figure 155**) to make sure the correct rings are being installed. The paint color spots indicates the following size:

    a. No color: standard size.

    b. Red: 0.5 mm oversize.

    c. Yellow: 1.0 mm oversize.

13. If new rings are installed, measure the side clearance of each ring in its groove with a flat feeler gauge (**Figure 145**) and compare to specification given in **Table 2**.

14. After the rings are installed, apply clean engine oil to the rings. Rotate the rings several complete revolutions in their respective grooves. This will assure proper oiling when the engine is first started.

Table 1 GENERAL ENGINE SPECIFICATIONS

Engine type	4-stroke, SOHC, 3 valve head, 45 V-twin
Cooling system	Air/oil cooled
Bore and stroke	94.0 98.0 mm (3.701-3.858 in.)
Displacement	1360 cc (83.0 cu.in.)
Compression ratio	9.3:1
Ignition timing	2° BTDC @ 1,500 rpm
	30° BTDC @ 4,000 rpm
Firing order	Front, rear
Lubrication system	Wet sump

Table 2 ENGINE TOP END SERVICE SPECIFICATIONS

Item	New mm (in.)	Service limit mm (in.)
Cylinder head warp limit	0.05 (0.002)	0.05 (0.002)
Cylinder head cover warp limit	0.05 (0.002)	0.05 (0.002)
Camshaft		
Lobe height		
Intake	35.683-35.723	35.41
	(1.4048-1.4064)	(1.394)
Exhaust	36.883-36.923	35.61
	(1.4521-1.4537)	(1.378)
	(continued)	

Table 2 ENGINE TOP END SERVICE SPECIFICATIONS (continued)

Item	New mm (in.)	Service limit mm (in.)
Journal holder (cylinder head and cylinder head cover) inner diameter		
Front cylinder head		
Right-hand side	20.012-20.025 (0.7879-0.7884)	–
Left-hand side	25.010-25.025 (0.9847-0.9852)	–
Rear cylinder head		
Left-hand side	20.012-20.025 (0.7879-0.7884)	–
Right-hand side	25.010-25.025 (0.9847-0.9852)	–
Journal out diameter		
Front cylinder head		
Right-hand side	19.959-19.80 (0.7858-0.7866)	–
Left-hand side	24.959-24.985 (0.9826-0.9835)	–
Rear cylinder head		
Left-hand side	19.959-19.980 (0.7858-0.7866)	–
Right-hand side	24.959-24.985 (0.9826-0.9835)	–
Journal oil clearance		
Intake and exhaust	0.032-0.066 (0.0013-0.0026)	0.150 (0.0060)
Runout	–	0.10 (0.004)
Camshaft chain 20-pitch (pin) measurement	–	128.9 (5.075)
Rocker arms and shafts		
Rocker arm bore diameter		
Intake	14.000-14.018 (0.5511-0.5519)	–
Exhaust	16.000-16.018 (0.6299-0.6306)	–
Rocker arm shaft outer diameter		
Intake	13.966-13.984 (0.5498-0.5506)	–
Exhaust	15.966-15.984 (0.6286-0.6293)	–
Valves and valve springs		
Valve head diameter		
Intake	33 (1.3)	–
Exhaust	40 (1.6)	–
Valve lift		
Intake	8 (0.31)	–
Exhuast	7.000-7.012 (0.2756-0.2761)	–
Valve guide inside diameter		
Intake	5.500-5.512 (0.2165-0.2170)	–
Exhaust	7.000-7.012 (0.2756-0.2761)	–
Valve stem outside diameter		
Intake	5.475-5.490 (0.2156-0.2161)	–
Exhaust	6.945-6.960 (0.2734-0.2740)	–
	(continued)	

Table 2 ENGINE TOP END SERVICE SPECIFICATIONS (continued)

Item	New mm (in.)	Service limit mm (in.)
Valve stem-to-guide clearance		
Intake	0.010-0.037	–
	(0.0004-0.0015)	
Exhaust	0.040-0.070	–
	(0.0016-0.0028)	
Valve stem deflection (intake and exhaust)	–	0.35 (0.014)
Valve stem runout (intake and exhaust)	–	0.05 (0.002)
Valve head runout	–	0.03 (0.001)
Valve stem end length (intake and exhaust)	–	2.6 (0.10)
Head thickness		
(Intake and exhuast)	–	0.5 (0.02)
Seat width		
(Intake and exhaust)	0.9-1.3 (0.04-0.05)	–
Valve spring free length		
Intake		
Inner spring	–	35.0 (1.38)
Outer spring	–	37.8 (1.49)
Exhaust	–	40.5 (1.59)
Cylinder		
Bore diameter	94.000-94.015	94.080
	(3.7008-3.7013)	(3.7039)
Cylinder-to-piston clearance	0.050-0.060	0.120
	(0.0020-0.0024)	(0.0047)
Out-of-round	–	0.05 (0.002)
Top surface warp limit	–	0.05 (0.002)
Piston		
Diameter	93.945-93.960	93.880
	(3.6986-3.6992)	(3.6960)
Piston pin bore	23.000-23.006	23.030
	(0.9055-0.9057)	(0.9067)
Piston pin diameter	22.996-23.000	22.980
	(0.9054-0.9055)	(0.9047)
Piston rings		
Number per piston		
Compression	2	
Oil control	1	
Ring groove width		
Top	1.230-1.250	–
	(0.0484-0.0492)	
Second	1.510-1.530	–
	(0.0594-0.0602)	
Third (oil control ring)	2.810-2.830	–
	(0.1106-0.1114)	
Piston rings side clearance		
Top	0.040-0.075	0.180
	(0.0016-0.0030)	(0.0070)
Second	0.025-0.07	0.170
	(0.001-0.0027)	(0.0067)
Piston ring thickness		
Top	1.175-1.190	–
	(0.0463-0.0469)	
Second	1.470-1.485	–
	(0.0579-0.0585)	
End gap (in cylinder bore)		
Top	0.30-0.45 (0.012-0.18)	0.70 (0.028)
Second	0.25-0.40 (0.010-0.016)	0.70 (0.028)

(continued)

4

Table 2 ENGINE TOP END SERVICE SPECIFICATIONS (continued)

Item	New mm (in.)	Service limit mm (in.)
End gap (free)		
Top	Approx. 14.5 (0.57)	11.6 (0.46)
Second	Approx. 11.5 (0.45)	9.2 (0.36)

Table 3 ENGINE TOP END TIGHTENING TORQUE

	N•m	in.-lb.	ft.-lb.
Engine mounting bolts			
Through bolts and nuts	70-80	–	52-59
Mounting bracket Allen bolts	18-28	–	13-20
Sub-frame Allen bolt nuts	40-60	–	29-44
Cylinder head cover bolts			
6 mm	9-13	80-115	–
8 mm	23-27	–	17-20
Cylinder head bolts and nuts			
8 mm bolts			
Initial	10	88	–
Final	23-27	–	17-20
10 mm bolts			
Initial	25	–	18
Final	35-40	–	26-29
Camshaft sprocket bolts	14-16	–	10-11
Camshaft tensioner mounting bolts	12	106	–
Rocker arm shaft (intake)	34-40	–	25-29
Rocker arm shaft plug (exhaust)	25-30	–	18-22
Rear cylinder head cover plut	23-27	–	17-20
Camshaft chain tensioner			
mounting bolt	8-12	71-106	–
Camshaft chain guide			
mounting bolt	8-12	71-106	–

5

ENGINE LOWER END

This chapter describes service procedures for the following lower end components:

 a. Primary drive gear assembly.
 b. Secondary gear assembly.
 c. Crankcase assembly.
 d. Crankshaft.
 e. Connecting rods.
 f. Transmission shaft assemblies (removal and installation only).
 g. Internal shift mechanism (removal and installation only).

Before disassembling the crankcase, clean the entire exterior with a good grade commercial degreaser, like Gunk or Bel-Ray engine degreaser. It is easier to work on a clean engine and you will do a better job.

Make certain that you have all the necessary hand and special tools available. Purchase replacement parts before disassembly. Also make sure you have a clean place to work.

One of the more important aspects of engine overhaul is preparation. Improper preparation before and failing to identify and store parts during removal will make it difficult to reassemble the engine. Before removing the first bolt and to prevent frustration during installation, get a number of boxes, plastic bags and containers and store the parts when removed. Also have on hand a roll of masking tape and a permanent, waterproof marking pen to label parts as required.

The text makes frequent references to the left- and right-hand side of the engine. This refers to the engine as it sits in the vehicle's frame, not as it sits on your workbench.

Table 1 lists engine lower end service specifications.

Table 2 lists engine lower end tightening torques.

Table 3 lists crankshaft side clearance thrust washer thickness.

Tables 4 provides connecting rod bearing selection guidelines and **Table 5** provides connecting rod bearing color codes and insert thickness.

Tables 1-5 are located at the end of this chapter.

OIL COOLER

Removal/Installation

1. Drain the engine oil as described in Chapter Three.

2. Remove the exhaust system as described in Chapter Eight.

3. To remove only the oil cooler hoses, perform the following:

   a. Place a drain pan under the lower fittings where the hoses attach to the crankcase as some residual oil will drain out when the banjo bolt is removed.

   b. On the right-hand side, remove the banjo bolt and sealing washers (**Figure 1**) securing the hose to the crankcase.

   c. On the right-hand side, remove the banjo bolt and sealing washers (A, **Figure 2**) securing the hose to the base of the oil cooler. Remove the right-hand oil hose (B, **Figure 2**).

   d. On the left-hand side, remove the banjo bolt and sealing washers (**Figure 3**) securing the hose to the crankcase.

   e. On the left-hand side, remove the banjo bolt and sealing washers (A, **Figure 4**) securing the hose to the base of the oil cooler. Remove the left-hand oil hose (B, **Figure 4**).

4. To remove the oil cooler and hoses as an assembly, perform the following:

   a. Place a drain pan under the lower fittings where the hoses attach to the crankcase as some residual oil will drain out when the banjo bolt is removed.

   b. On the right-hand side, remove the banjo bolt and sealing washers (**Figure 1**) securing the hose to the crankcase.

   c. On the left-hand side, remove the banjo bolt and sealing washers (**Figure 3**) securing the hose to the crankcase.

   d. Remove the lower bolts and washers (**Figure 5**) securing the oil cooler to the frame bracket.

   e. Remove the upper bolts (A, **Figure 6**) securing the oil cooler to the frame bracket. The cable bracket (B, **Figure 6**) may stay with the oil cooler during removal.

   f. Lower the oil cooler from the frame and remove the assembly. Don't lose the collar in each of the rubber grommets within the mounting bosses.

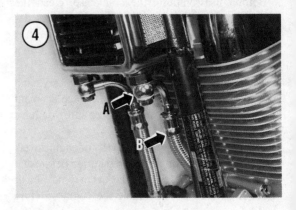

5. Inspect the oil cooler as described in the following procedure.

6. Install by reversing these removal steps while noting the following:

   a. Make sure the banjo bolt holes are clear. Clean out with solvent and compressed air if necessary.

   b. Install new sealing washers at each fitting.

   c. Make sure the collar is in place in each rubber grommet.

   d. Correctly locate the upper hose fitting against the locator (**Figure 7**) on the base of the oil cooler. These locators correctly position the upper end of the hose.

Inspection

1. Check both hoses for damage or leakage, replace if necessary.

2. Inspect the rubber grommets at each mounting point for hardness or deterioration. Replace as necessary.

3. Inspect the cooler fins (**Figure 8**) for damage. Straighten out bent fins with a broad tipped screwdriver or putty knife.

4. If compressed air is available, use short spurts of air directed to the *backside* of the cooler fins to blow out any road dirt and bugs.

5. If the cooler fins are extremely dirty, flush off the exterior of the fins with a garden hose on low pressure. Spray both the front and back sides to remove all road dirt and bugs. Carefully use a wisk broom or stiff brush to remove any stubborn dirt. Dry with compressed air as directed in Step 3.

6. Check for cracks or leaks at the lower fittings.

PRIMARY DRIVE GEAR AND REAR CYLINDER CAMSHAFT CHAIN AND SPROCKET

Removal

1. Remove the clutch assembly as described in Chapter Six.

2. Remove the engine from the frame as described in Chapter Four.

3. Install a clutch holding tool, or equivalent, (A, **Figure 9**) onto the gear to hold it secure while loosening the mounting bolt.

CAUTION
The primary drive gear bolt has
left-hand threads. *Turn the bolt*
clockwise to loosen it.

4. Use a breaker bar and socket (B, **Figure 9**) and loosen the bolt in a *clockwise* direction.

5. Remove the shoulder bolt (A, **Figure 10**) and the primary drive gear (B, **Figure 10**) from the crankshaft.

6. Remove the bolt and washer (A, **Figure 11**) securing the rear cylinder camshaft chain tensioner guide (B, **Figure 11**). Remove the guide and the washer behind it. There is a washer on each side of the tensioner guide. Do not lose the collar in the mounting hole in the tensioner guide (**Figure 12**).

7. Disengage the rear cylinder camshaft chain (C, **Figure 11**) from the camshaft chain sprocket and remove the chain.

8. Remove the rear cylinder camshaft chain sprocket (**Figure 13**) from the crankshaft.

9. Remove the outer thrust washer (**Figure 14**).

10. Inspect all components as described in this chapter.

Installation

1. Position the outer thrust washer with its beveled side (**Figure 15**) toward the crankshaft surface and install the outer thrust washer (**Figure 14**).

2. Position the front cylinder camshaft chain sprocket with its alignment mark facing out. This will position the chain sprocket flange (**Figure 16**) toward the crankcase surface.

3. Align the mark (**Figure 17**) on the rear cylinder camshaft chain sprocket with the mark (**Figure 18**)

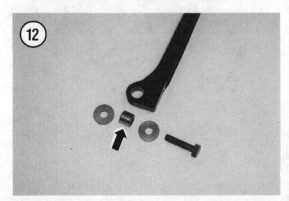

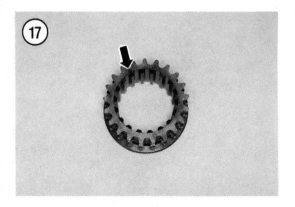

on the end of the crankshaft and install the sprocket onto the crankshaft.

4. Install the rear cylinder camshaft chain (C, **Figure 11**) onto the camshaft chain sprocket and make sure it is properly meshed.

5. Make sure the collar is in place in the tensioner guide mounting hole.

CAUTION
*The collar (**Figure 12**) must be in place and a washer must be installed on each side of the camshaft chain tensioner guide to allow it to pivot freely on the mounting bolt. If these parts are not installed correctly, the guide will not be able to move freely to take the slack out of the camshaft chain.*

6. Install the rear cylinder camshaft chain tensioner guide (B, **Figure 11**). Place a washer between the tensioner guide and the crankcase surface, then install the bolt and washer (A, **Figure 11**). Tighten the bolt securely.

7. Install the primary drive gear (B, **Figure 10**) and bolt (A, **Figure 10**).

8. Use the same tool used in Step 3 of the *Removal* procedure to prevent the crankshaft from rotating while tightening the bolt.

CAUTION
*The primary drive gear bolt has **left-hand threads**. Turn the wrench counterclockwise to tighten it in the following step.*

9. Turn the wrench counterclockwise (**Figure 19**) and tighten the primary drive gear bolt (A, **Figure 10**) to the torque specification listed in **Table 2**.

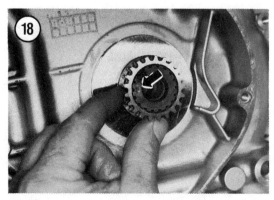

10. Install the clutch assembly as described in Chapter Five.

Inspection

NOTE
If the primary drive gear teeth are damaged, inspect the gear teeth on the clutch outer housing as it may also be damaged and require replacement.

1. Inspect the primary drive gear (A, **Figure 20**) for chipped or missing teeth, wear or damage. Replace the gear if necessary.

2. Check the inner splines (B, **Figure 20**) for wear or damage; replace the gear if necessary.

3. Inspect the front cylinder camshaft chain sprocket (A, **Figure 21**) for chipped or missing teeth, wear or damage. Replace the sprocket if necessary.

4. Check the inner splines (B, **Figure 21**) for wear or damage; replace the sprocket if necessary.

5. Inspect the front cylinder camshaft chain tensioner guide for deterioration, cracks or damage; replace if necessary.

6. Inspect the camshaft chain for wear or damage to the links and pins. Replace if necessary. If the chain is damaged, also inspect the sprocket at each end as they may also be damaged.

7. Measure the camshaft chain for stretching as follows:

   a. Place the chain on a flat surface and pull the chain taut to remove all slack.

   b. Use a vernier caliper and measure the distance between 21 pins (or 20 pitches) as shown in **Figure 22**.

   c. Repeat Steps 7a and 7b several times at various locations around the chain. The chain usually wears unevenly. It is important to identify and

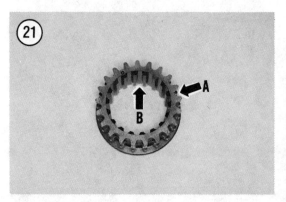

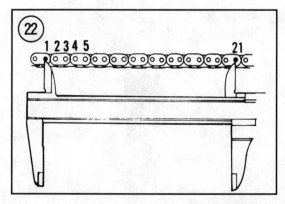

measure the part of the chain that is worn the most.

d. If the length between any 21 pins exceeds 128.9 mm (5.07 in.), replace the chain.

SECONDARY GEAR ASSEMBLY

Removal

1. Remove the engine from the frame as described in Chapter Four.

2. Install the drive shaft's universal joint (A, **Figure 23**) onto the output shaft of the secondary gear housing. This will keep the internal gears from rotating during nut loosening and removal in the following step.

3. Hold onto the universal joint with a large adjustable wrench (B, **Figure 23**).

> *NOTE*
> *Step 4 requires an assistant to hold the crankcase while loosening the secondary gear nut. If your are working by yourself, secure the crankcase to the workbench so it will not move during the next step.*

4. Use a large breaker bar and socket and loosen the flange bolt (A, **Figure 24**) securing the secondary gear.

> *CAUTION*
> *The mainshaft bolt has **left-hand threads**. Turn the bolt clockwise to loosen it.*

5. Use a breaker bar and socket and loosen the mainshaft bolt (B, **Figure 24**)in a *clockwise* direction. Remove the bolt and washer from the mainshaft.

6. Remove the universal joint.

7. Loosen in a crisscross pattern, then remove the secondary gear housing bolts (**Figure 25**).

8. Remove the bolts (**Figure 26**) securing the secondary gear case and remove the case. Do not lose the locating dowels.

9. Remove the secondary bevel gear assembly (A, **Figure 27**) and bearing (B, **Figure 27**).

10. Remove the oil control orifice (**Figure 28**) from the crankcase.

11. Separate the crankcase as described in this chapter.

12. Remove the secondary reduction gear (**Figure 29**) from the secondary bevel drive gear shaft.

13. Remove transmission and internal gearshift mechanism as described in this chapter.

14. Remove the Allen bolts (A, **Figure 30**) securing the secondary bevel drive gear and mounting plate to the crankcase. Remove the mounting plate (B, **Figure 30**).

15. Pull straight up and remove the assembly from the crankcase. Also remove the shims (**Figure 31**) located between the assembly and the crankcase mounting surface. Note the number of shims as the same number must be reinstalled to maintain the correct gear lash between the two bevel gears in the assembly.

16. Inspect the components as described in this chapter.

Installation

1. Apply a light coat of engine oil to the secondary bevel drive gear bore (A, **Figure 32**) in the crankcase.

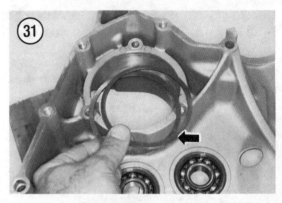

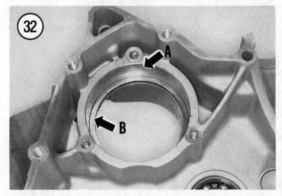

2. Be sure to install the same number of shims (**Figure 31**) between the assembly and the crankcase mounting surface (B, **Figure 32**) as noted during removal.

3. Install the secondary bevel drive gear assembly.

4. Slowly push the secondary bevel drive gear assembly into the receptacle in the crankcase until it is completely seated.

5. Install the mounting plate (B, **Figure 30**) and align the bolt holes.

6. Apply ThreeBond No. TB1342, or Loctite No. 242 threadlocking compound to the Allen bolt threads prior to installation.

7. Install the Allen bolts (A, **Figure 30**) and tighten to the torque specification listed in **Table 2**.

8. Assemble the crankcase as described in this chapter.

9. Make sure the shaft bearing locating pin (A, **Figure 33**) is in place in the crankcase.

10. Install a new O-ring seal (**Figure 34**) onto the secondary bevel gear assembly.

11. Position the secondary bevel gear bearing (B, **Figure 33**) so it will index with the locating pin (A, **Figure 33**) and install the bearing.

12. Make sure the bearing has seated properly onto the locating pin (**Figure 35**).

13. If removed, install the same number of shims (**Figure 36**) prior to installation in the next step.

14. Install the secondary bevel gear assembly into the bearing and the crankcase. Rotate the mounting flange until the relieved area (**Figure 37**) faces toward the crankcase and down.

15. If removed, make sure the small O-ring seal (**Figure 38**) is in place, then install the oil control orifice. Push it in until it seats completely (**Figure 28**).

16. Apply clean engine oil to the bearing.

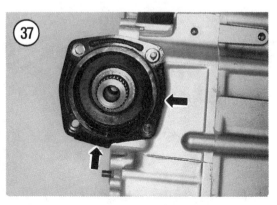

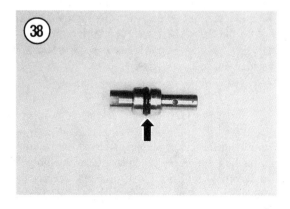

17. If removed, install the case locating dowels (**Figure 39**) in the crankcase.

> *NOTE*
> *Use ThreeBond No. 1104, or equivalent gasket sealer to seal the secondary case. When selecting an equivalent, avoid thick and hard-setting materials.*

> *CAUTION*
> *Do not apply gasket sealer to the oil jet cavity in the cover (A, **Figure 40**). If sealer gets into the cavity the oil flow to the assembly will be reduced or completely blocked.*

18. Apply a light coat of gasket sealer to the secondary case sealing surfaces on the cover (B, **Figure 40**).

19. Check that the mounting flange relieved area (**Figure 37**) is still facing toward the crankcase and down. Reposition if necessary.

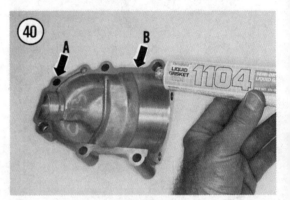

20. Install the case and bolts. Tighten the bolts in 2 stages, initial and final, to the final torque specification listed in **Table 2**.

21. Apply ThreeBond TB1360, or Loctite No. 271 to the secondary gear housing bolts prior to installation.

22. Install the secondary gear housing bolts (**Figure 25**) and tighten to the torque specification listed in **Table 2**.

23. Install the drive shaft's universal joint onto the output shaft of the secondary gear housing. This will keep the internal gears from rotating while tightening the nut in the following step.

24. Install the flange bolt (A, **Figure 41**) onto the end of the shaft.

25. Hold onto the universal joint (A, **Figure 23**) with a large adjustable wrench (B, **Figure 23**) and tighten the bolt (A, **Figure 24**) securing the secondary gear. Tighten the bolt to the torque specification listed in **Table 2**.

> *NOTE*
> *Make sure the transmission is in neutral.*

26. Rotate the universal joint and make sure there is no binding within the secondary gear assembly. If the assembly will not rotate properly, correct the problem at this time. Remove the universal joint.

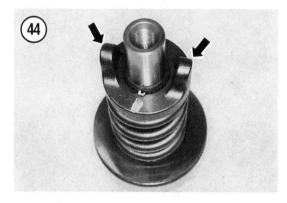

CAUTION:
*The mainshaft bolt has **left-hand threads**. Turn the bolt counterclockwise to tighten it.*

27. Install the mainshaft bolt and washer (B, **Figure 41**).

28. Tighten the mainshaft bolt (B, **Figure 24**) in a *counterclockwise* direction to the torque specification listed in **Table 2**.

29. Install the engine into the frame as described in Chapter Four.

Inspection

1. Inspect for chipped or missing teeth on the drive gear (A, **Figure 42**) and the driven gear (A, **Figure 43**). If either gear is damaged both the drive and driven gears must be replaced as a set.

2. Inspect the driven gear assembly splines for wear or damage. If damaged, both the drive and driven gears must be replaced as a set. Also check the inner splines of the universal joint as they may also be damaged.

3. Inspect driven gear shaft roller bearing. Make sure it rotates freely with no binding. Replace the bearing if necessary. Also check the shaft bearing surface (B, **Figure 43**) for wear or damage.

4. Inspect the spring (B, **Figure 42**) for wear, cracks or damage and replace if necessary.

5. Install the secondary reduction gear onto the drive gear shaft and check for proper engagement. Check the cams (**Figure 44**) and gear ramps for wear, cracks or burrs. Replace if necessary.

6. Inspect the secondary reduction gear (A, **Figure 45**) for chipped or missing teeth. Inspect the inner and outer bearing surfaces of the bushing (B, **Figure 45**) for wear. Insert the bushing into the gear and check for looseness or excessive wear. Replace if necessary.

7. Inspect the drive gear assembly shims for wear or damage. Replace if necessary and replace with shims of the exact same thickness. Take the old shims along to ensure an exact matchup as there are 5 different shim thicknesses available.

8. Check the mounting plate for flatness or damage. Check the bolt holes for elongation.

9. Move the universal joint (**Figure 46**) back and forth and pull in and out on it. Check for looseness or stiffness, replace if necessary.

10. Inspect the universal joint inner splines for wear or damage. If the splines are damaged, also check the outer splines on the drive shaft for damage. Replace the universal joint if necessary.

OIL PUMP

Removal/Installation

The crankcase assembly must be split to service the oil pump.

1. Remove the clutch assembly as described in Chapter Six. During clutch removal, the oil pump drive gear was removed as it is located behind the clutch outer housing.

2. Remove the circlip (A, **Figure 47**) securing the oil pump driven gear to the oil pump drive shaft.

3. Remove the oil pump driven gear (B, **Figure 47**).

4. Remove the dowel pin (**Figure 48**) from the oil pump drive shaft.

5. Disassemble the crankcase as described in the following procedure.

6. Turn the right-hand crankcase half upside down on the workbench.

7. Remove the bolts (**Figure 49**) securing the oil pump to the crankcase and remove the oil pump assembly. Place the oil pump in a reclosable plastic bag to keep it clean and free of debris.

8. Inspect the oil pump mounting surface and oil flow paths (**Figure 50**). Clean with solvent and blow dry with compressed air.

9. Inspect the oil pump as described in this chapter.

NOTE
There are 3 different length bolts used to mount the oil pump to the crankcase. Be sure to install the bolts in the correct location prior to tightening them.

10. Install the oil pump into the crankcase and install the mounting bolts. Tighten the bolts to the torque specification listed in **Table 2**.

11. Assemble the crankcase as described in this chapter.

12. Install the dowel pin **Figure 48** into the oil pump drive shaft.

13. Align the notch (A, **Figure 51**) in the backside of the oil pump driven gear with the dowel pin (B, **Figure 51**) and install the oil pump driven gear (B, **Figure 47**).

14. Push the gear on until it bottoms out, then install the circlip (A, **Figure 47**) securing the oil pump

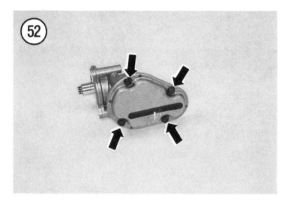

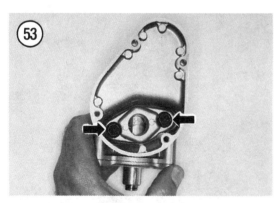

driven gear to the oil pump drive shaft. Make sure the circlip is correctly seated in the drive shaft groove.

15. Install the clutch assembly as described in Chapter Six.

Inspection

There are no replacement parts available for the oil pump. If any part of the oil pump is damaged, replace the oil pump assembly.

1. Remove the screws (**Figure 52**) securing the strainer to the strainer housing and remove the strainer.

2. Remove the bolts (**Figure 53**) securing the strainer housing and separate it from the oil pump body.

3. Wash all parts in solvent and dry with compressed air.

4. Make sure the oil pump mounting screw (A, **Figure 54**) is tight.

5. Inspect the oil pump body (B, **Figure 54**) for wear or cracks.

6. Rotate the drive shaft (C, **Figure 54**) and check for binding, wear or damage.

7. Inspect the strainer housing (A, **Figure 55**) for wear or cracks and replace if necessary. Check the O-ring seal (B, **Figure 55**) for hardness or deterioration and replace if necessary.

8. Check the screen in the strainer (C, **Figure 55**) for damage and breaks. If any area is damaged, replace the strainer.

9. Inspect the oil pump mounting bosses for fractures or damage.

10. Inspect the teeth on the driven gear. Replace the driven gear if the teeth are damaged or any are missing.

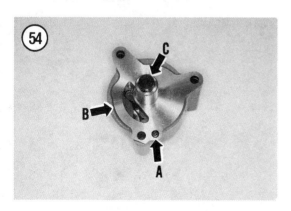

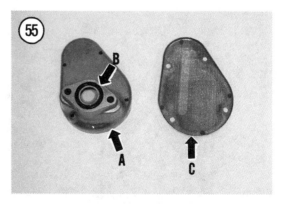

11. Install the strainer housing and tighten the bolts (**Figure 53**) securely.

12. Install the strainer onto the housing and tighten the screws securely (**Figure 52**).

CRANKCASE

Service to the lower end requires that the crankcase assembly be removed from the motorcycle frame and disassembled (split).

Crankcase Disassembly

1. Remove the engine as described in Chapter Four.
2. Remove the following exterior assemblies from the crankcase assembly:
   a. Cylinder head and cylinder assemblies (Chapter Four).
   b. Alternator (Chapter Nine).
   c. Starter clutch assembly (Chapter Nine).
   d. Primary drive gear (this chapter).
   e. Secondary gear assembly (this chapter).
   f. Rear cylinder camshaft chain and tensioner guide (A, **Figure 56**) (this chapter).
   g. Oil pump (this chapter).
   h. External shift mechanism (Chapter Six).
   i. Clutch (Chapter Six).
   j. Starter motor (Chapter Nine).
   k. Neutral switch (Chapter Nine).
   l. Oil pressure switch (Chapter Nine).

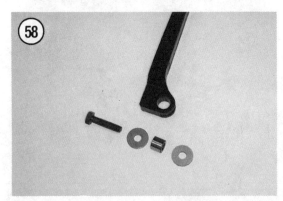

3. If still in place, remove the Woodruff key from the crankshaft taper.

4. Remove the bolt and washer (A, **Figure 57**) securing the front cylinder camshaft chain tensioner guide (B, **Figure 57**). Remove the guide (B, **Figure 56**) and the washer behind it. There is a washer on

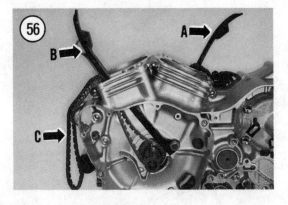

each side of the tensioner guide (**Figure 58**). Do not lose the collar in the mounting hole in the tensioner guide.

5. Disengage the front cylinder camshaft chain (C, **Figure 57**) from the camshaft chain sprocket and remove the chain (C, **Figure 56**).

6. Starting with the left-hand side, loosen all bolts 1/2 turn in a crisscross pattern, then remove the bolts (**Figure 59**). Make sure all bolts are removed.

7. Turn the crankcase over with the right-hand side facing up.

> *NOTE*
> *To help keep track of the crankcase bolts, draw the crankcase outline on a piece of cardboard, then number and punch holes to correspond with each bolt location. After removal, insert the bolts in their appropriate locations. Leave any cable clamps on its respective bolt. This will make installation easier.*

> *NOTE*
> *When the 2 upper bolts (**Figure 60**) are loosened, the crankcase will separate, or may even emit a popping sound. This is not a problem as the spring pressure of the secondary drive gear assembly will push the crankcase halves apart at this time.*

8. On the right-hand side, loosen all bolts 1/2 turn in a crisscross pattern (**Figure 61**). Remove all bolts. Make sure all bolts are removed.

9. Carefully tap around the perimeter of the crankcase with a plastic mallet (do not use a metal hammer) to help separate the case halves. Separate the case halves by pulling the right-hand crankcase up and off the left-hand case half.

10. After removing the right-hand crankcase half, the transmission and crankshaft assemblies should stay with the left-hand crankcase. Check the right-hand crankcase to make sure no transmission shims are stuck to the bearings. If found, reinstall them immediately in their original positions.

11. Remove the 2 small dowel pins from the left-hand crankcase half. Refer to **Figure 62** and **Figure 63**.

12. Remove the small O-ring (**Figure 64**) from the left-hand crankcase half.

13. Remove the thrust bearing from the right-hand side of the crankshaft.

14. Carefully pull the crankshaft assembly (**Figure 65**) straight up and remove from the left-hand crankcase half.

15A. On 1987-1996 models, remove the internal gearshift mechanism as follows:

   a. Hold onto the shift forks and withdraw the shift fork shaft.

   b. Mark the shift forks with L (left-hand) and R (right-hand) so they will be reinstalled in the same location. Remove both shift forks (**Figure 66**).

   c. Remove the shift drum.

15B. On 1997-on models, remove the internal gearshift mechanism as follows:

   a. Hold onto the shift forks and withdraw the shift fork shaft.

   b. Mark the shift forks with L (left-hand) and R (right-hand) so they will be reinstalled in the same location. Remove both shift forks (**Figure 66**).

   c. Remove the cotter pin (**Figure 67**) securing the removable guide pin.

   d. Withdraw the removable guide pin (**Figure 68**) from the shift fork.

   e. Remove the shift drum.

   f. Remove the shift fork.

16. Inspect the internal gearshift mechanism as described in Chapter Seven.

17. Remove the reduction gear (**Figure 69**) and bushing from the secondary bevel drive gear assembly.

> *NOTE*
> *If you are unable to remove the mainshaft assembly from the crankcase, make sure the mainshaft bolt and washer (**Figure 70**) are removed.*

18. Remove the countershaft assembly (A, **Figure 71**) and mainshaft assembly (B, **Figure 71**) from the left crankcase.

19. Remove the secondary bevel drive gear assembly (**Figure 72**) as described under *Secondary Gear Assembly* in this chapter.

20. Inspect the transmission shaft assemblies as described in Chapter Seven.

21. Inspect the secondary bevel gear assembly as described in this chapter.

22. Inspect the crankcase assemblies as described in this chapter.

Inspection

The following procedure may include the use of highly specialized and expensive measuring instruments. If such instruments are not readily available, have the measurements performed by a dealership.

> *NOTE*
> *To help keep track of the crankcase oil jet locations, as soon as they are removed, place them in a reclosable plastic bag and label them. Label a piece of cardboard and indicate the location of the oil jets. This will lessen the possibility of a mixup of oil jet locations and make installation easier.*

1. Remove all old gasket residue material from both crankcase mating surfaces.

2. Soak any old gasket material stuck to the surface with solvent. Use a broad-tipped dull chisel and gently scrape off all gasket residue. Do not gouge the sealing surfaces as oil and air leaks will result.

> *CAUTION*
> *The oil separator plate mounting screws are secured with threadlocking compound and may be difficult to loosen. If necessary, use an impact driver and an appropriate size bit to loosen the screws.*

3. Remove the screws and the oil separator plate (**Figure 73**) from the right-hand crankcase half.

4. Remove the oil pressure switch (A, **Figure 74**) from the exterior of the right-hand crankcase half.

5. Remove the oil plunger retaining bolt (**Figure 75**) from the interior of the right-hand crankcase half. Remove the spring and plunger (**Figure 76**).

6. Remove the oil pressure regulator (B, **Figure 74**) from the exterior of the right-hand crankcase half.

7. Remove all oil gallery plugs and sealing washers from the right-hand crankcase half (**Figure 77**).

8. Remove all oil gallery plugs and sealing washers and bolts from the left-hand crankcase half. Refer to **Figure 78** and **Figure 79**.

9. Remove the screw and bracket (**Figure 80**) securing the right-hand main bearing oil jet and remove the oil jet (**Figure 81**).

10. Remove the screw and bracket (**Figure 82**) securing the left-hand main bearing oil jet and remove the oil jet.

11. Remove the clutch pushrod seal (**Figure 83**) from the left-hand crankcase half.

12. Inspect the oil filter threads. Clean with a wire brush if necessary. Repair damaged threads with an appropriate size metric thread die.

13. Thoroughly clean the inside and outside of both crankcase halves with cleaning solvent. Dry with compressed air. Make sure there is no solvent left in either crankcase as it will contaminate the new engine oil.

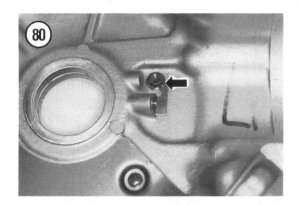

14. Check all bolts and threaded holes for stripping, cross-threading or deposit buildup. Threaded holes should be blown out with compressed air as dirt buildup in the bottom of a hole may prevent the bolt from being torqued properly. Replace damaged bolts and washers.

15. Inspect machined surfaces for burrs, cracks or other damage. Repair minor damage with a fine-cut file or oilstone.

16. Apply compressed air to all oil passages (**Figure 84**) throughout both crankcase halves to make sure they are clean.

17. Check the engine mounting bolt rubber isolators (**Figure 85**).

18. Apply a light coat of engine oil to the bearing surfaces to prevent any rust formation.

19. Inspect the crankcase bearings as described in this chapter.

20. Install the new clutch pushrod oil seal into the left-hand crankcase half. Push it in until it is completely seated.

21. Clean and inspect the oil jets as follows:

    a. Inspect each oil jet for burrs or contamination. Clean with compressed air.

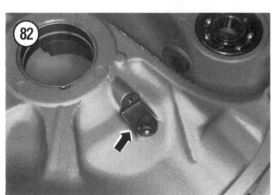

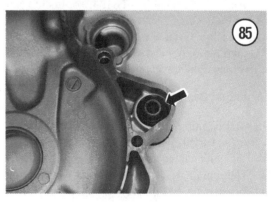

b. Inspect each O-ring and replace if worn or damaged.

c. Lubricate oil jets and their O-rings with engine oil before installing them in the following steps.

22. Install the right-hand main bearing oil jet (**Figure 81**) and push it in until it is completely seated. Install the bracket and screw (**Figure 80**) and tighten securely.

23. Install the left-hand main bearing oil jet and push it in until it is completely seated. Install the bracket and screw (**Figure 82**) and tighten securely.

24. Install all oil gallery plugs and sealing washers into the right-hand crankcase half (**Figure 77**). Tighten securely.

25. Install all oil gallery plugs and sealing washers and bolts into the left-hand crankcase half. Refer to **Figure 78** and **Figure 79**. Tighten securely.

26. Install a new washer onto the oil pressure regulator and install the regulator (B, **Figure 74**) into the exterior of the right-hand crankcase half. Tighten to the torque specification listed in **Table 2**.

27. Install the plunger and spring (**Figure 76**) into the right-hand crankcase half. Push them in until they bottom (A, **Figure 86**), then install the oil plunger retaining bolt (B, **Figure 86**) and tighten securely.

> *NOTE*
> *Clean off all old gasket sealer from the oil pressure switch threads prior to applying any new gasket sealer.*

28. Apply a light coat of gasket sealer to the oil pressure switch threads prior to installation. Install the oil pressure switch (A, **Figure 74**) into the exterior of the right-hand crankcase half. Tighten to the torque specification listed in **Table 2**.

29. Apply ThreeBond No. TB1342, or Loctite No. 242 thread locking agent to the screw threads prior to installation. Install the oil separator plate (**Figure 73**) onto the right-hand crankcase half. Install the screws and tighten securely.

Crankcase Bearing Inspection

1. After cleaning the crankcase halves in cleaning solvent and drying with compressed air, lubricate the bearings with engine oil.

2. With your fingers, rotate the transmission bearing inner races and check for play or roughness. Replace the bearing(s) if it is noisy or if it does not spin smoothly.

3. Rotate the secondary gear shaft bearing inner race slowly and check for play or roughness. Replace the bearing if it is noisy or does not spin smoothly.

4. Rotate the shift drum bearing inner race with your finger and check for play or roughness. Replace the bearing if it is noisy or if it does not spin smoothly.

5. Inspect the crankshaft main bearing (**Figure 87**) in both crankcase halves for wear or damage. Make sure they are locked in place (**Figure 88**). The bearing inside diameter is measured as described under *Crankshaft Bearing and Oil Clearance Measurement* in this chapter. If the bearings are damaged or worn, have them replaced.

Crankcase Bearings Replacement

The crankshaft main bearings are removed and installed from the crankcase halves with a hydraulic press and special tools. After the new bearings are installed, they must be honed.

To avoid damage to a costly set of crankcase halves, refer this procedure to a dealership or ma-

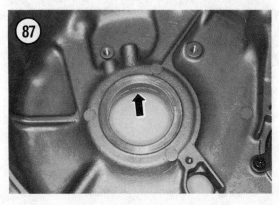

chine shop. Improper removal and installation of the bearings could result in costly crankcase damage.

Crankcase Assembly

1. Prior to installation of all parts, coat all rotating parts with assembly oil or engine oil.
2. Place the left-hand crankcase on wood blocks.
3. Install the secondary bevel drive gear assembly (**Figure 72**) as described under *Secondary Gear Assembly* in this chapter.

4. Apply a light coat of multipurpose grease to the backside of the washer(s) to help hold it in place.
5. Hold onto the washer next to 4th (1987-1996 models) or 5th (1997-on models) gear. Properly mesh both transmission shafts together and install the countershaft (A, **Figure 71**) and mainshaft (B, **Figure 71**) assemblies into the left-hand crankcase half. Push both shafts into the case until they bottom out.
6. Install the bushing into the reduction gear (**Figure 89**). Align the dished receptacles in the reduction gear (A, **Figure 90**) with the raised cams on the secondary bevel drive gear (B, **Figure 90**) and install the gear (**Figure 69**).
7. Apply a light coat of oil to the shift fork shafts, the inside bores of the shift forks, the shift drum bearing surfaces and to the bearings in the crankcase prior to installing any internal gearshift parts.

8A. On 1987-1996 models, install the internal gearshift mechanism as follows:

> *NOTE*
> *After installing the shift drum, make sure it rotates smoothly with no binding.*

   a. Install the shift drum and push it down until it stops.
   b. Install the shift forks (**Figure 66**) into their respective gears. Refer to marks made during removal and disassembly.
   c. Swing the shift forks into place in the shift drum. Make sure the guide pin on each fork is indexed into its respective groove in the shift drum.
   d. Align the shift fork shaft holes in the forks and install the shift fork shaft. Push the shaft down until it stops.

8B. On 1997-on models, install the internal gearshift mechanism as follows:

   a. Position the large shift fork with the manufacturing marks facing up and install the large shift fork into its respective gear (**Figure 91**).

> *NOTE*
> *After installing the shift drum, make sure it rotates smoothly with no binding.*

   b. Install the shift drum through the shift fork (A, **Figure 92**) and into the crankcase bearing (B, **Figure 92**).

5

c. Position the shift drum as shown in A, **Figure 93** to align the groove with the guide pin hole in the large shift fork.

d. Position the removable guide pin as shown in B, **Figure 93** and install the guide pin (**Figure 94**). Align the guide pin cotter pin hole with the shift fork hole. Push the guide pin into the shift drum groove until it stops.

> *CAUTION*
> *Do not use a long cotter pin as the long ends may hang up on another part. If you have to use a long cotter pin, cut off the excess ends.*

e. Install a new cotter pin (**Figure 95**) and bend the ends over completely.

f. Refer to the marks made during removal and disassembly (**Figure 66**). Position the shift fork with the manufacturing marks facing up.

g. Install the left-hand shift fork into its respective gear(**Figure 96**).

h. Install the right-hand shift fork (**Figure 97**) into its respective gear.

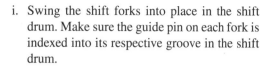

i. Swing the shift forks into place in the shift drum. Make sure the guide pin on each fork is indexed into its respective groove in the shift drum.

j. Align the shift fork shaft holes in the forks and install the shift fork shaft (**Figure 98**). Push the shaft down until it stops.

9. Position the connecting rods within the left-hand crankcase cylinder openings and install the crankshaft (**Figure 99**).

10. Position the thrust bearing with the oil grooves (A, **Figure 100**) and inner chamfer (B, **Figure 100**) facing *down* toward the crankshaft and install the thrust bearing (**Figure 101**).

11. Apply a light coat of oil to the *new* O-ring and install the O-ring seal (**Figure 102**) into the receptacle in the crankcase. Make sure it is seated correctly.

12. Install the 2 small dowel pins into the left-hand crankcase half. Refer to **Figure 103** and **Figure 104**.

13. Apply oil to the transmission shafts and crankshaft bearing surfaces.

14. Clean the crankcase mating surfaces of both halves with an aerosol electrical contact cleaner.

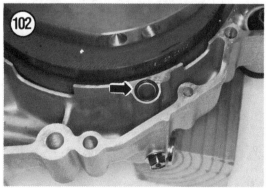

15. Make sure both crankcase half sealing surfaces are perfectly clean, lint-free and dry.

NOTE
Use ThreeBond No. 1104, or equivalent gasket sealerto seal the crankcase. When selecting an equivalent, avoid thick and hard-setting materials.

16. Apply a light coat of gasket sealer to the sealing surfaces of the left-hand crankcase half. Make the coating as thin as possible.

17. Align the right-hand crankcase bearings with the left-hand assembly and install it. Join both halves and tap together lightly with a plastic mallet. Do not use a metal hammer as it will damage the cases.

18. Prior to installing and tightening the crankcase bolts, rotate the transmission shafts and the crankshaft and check for binding. All shafts should rotate smoothly.

NOTE
*After installing the right crankcase half in the following steps, you will note a gap between the cases at the upper right corner of the engine (**Figure 105**). This gap is normal. It is caused by the installed height of the secondary drive gear assembly. This engine is designed to preload the secondary drive gear spring when the crankcase bolts are tightened. When tightening the crankcase bolts in Step 19 and Step 20, the part of the engine shown in **Figure 105** should come together without any excessive force (other than spring pressure). If there is a problem, or if there is a gap at some other point along the crankcase mating surfaces, remove the right crankcase half and inspect the parts.*

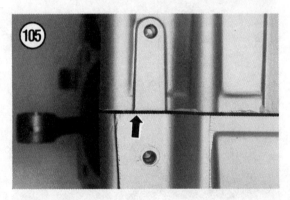

19. Install the bolts in the left-hand crankcase half (**Figure 106**). Tighten in a crisscross pattern in two stages to the torque final listed in **Table 2**.

20. Turn the crankcase assembly over and install the bolts in the right-hand crankcase half (**Figure 107**). Tighten in a crisscross pattern in 2 stages to the torque final listed in **Table 2**.

21. Check that the transmission shifts through all gears as follows:

a. Temporarily install the stopper plate and cam stopper as shown in **Figure 108**. Tighten the mounting bolts finger-tight.

b. Slowly rotate the countershaft (**Figure 109**) by hand while rotating the stopper plate through all gears. This is the time to find that something may be installed incorrectly, not after the crankcase is completely assembled.

c. If the transmission shifts through all gears satisfactorily, remove the stopper plate and cam stopper.

22. Install the front cylinder camshaft chain as follows:

a. Engage the front cylinder camshaft chain (A, **Figure 110**) onto the camshaft chain sprocket.

b. There is a washer on each side of the tensioner guide. Be sure to install the collar in the mounting hole in the tensioner guide.

c. Install the front cylinder camshaft chain tensioner guide (B, **Figure 110**), with a washer on each side, and install the bolt (C, **Figure 110**). Tighten the bolt securely.

23. Install the rear cylinder camshaft chain as follows:

a. Engage the front cylinder camshaft chain (A, **Figure 111**) onto the camshaft chain sprocket.

b. There is a washer on each side of the tensioner guide. Be sure to install the collar in the mounting hole in the tensioner guide.

c. Install the front cylinder camshaft chain tensioner guide (B, **Figure 111**), with a washer on each side, and install the bolt (C, **Figure 111**). Tighten the bolt securely.

24. Install the following exterior assemblies from the crankcase assembly:

a. Oil pressure switch (Chapter Nine).

b. Neutral switch (Chapter Nine).

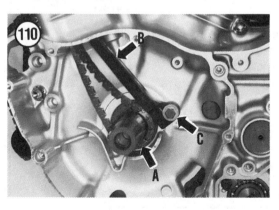

CRANKSHAFT ASSEMBLY

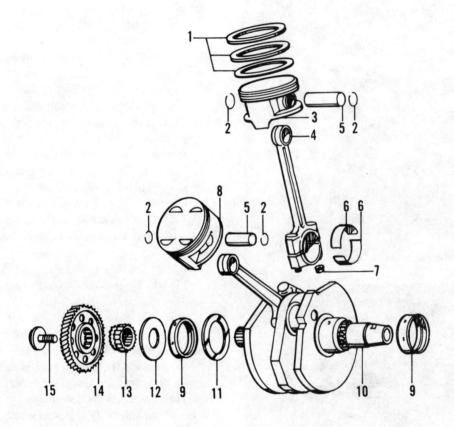

1. Piston ring set
2. Circlip
3. Piston
4. Connecting rod
5. Piston pin
6. Connecting rod
   bearing inserts
7. Connecting rod
   cap nut
8. Piston
9. Crankshaft bearing
   insert
10. Crankshaft
11. Inner thrust washer
12. Outer thrust washer
13. Front cylinder camshaft
    chain drive sprocket
14. Primary drive gear
15. Bolt

c. Starter motor (Chapter Nine).

d. Clutch (Chapter Five).

e. External shift mechanism (Chapter Six).

f. Oil pump (this chapter).

g. Rear cylinder camshaft chain and tensioner guide (this chapter).

h. Secondary gear assembly (this chapter).

i. Primary drive gear (this chapter).

j. Starter clutch assembly (Chapter Eight).

k. Alternator (Chapter Eight).

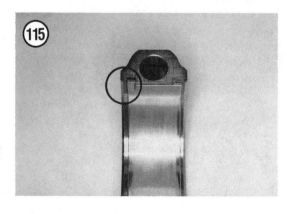

l. Cylinder head and cylinder assemblies (Chapter Four).

25. Install the engine as described in Chapter Four.

CRANKSHAFT AND CONNECTING RODS

Removal/Installation

Refer to **Figure 112** for this procedure.

1. Split the crankcase as described in this chapter.

2. Remove the thrust washer (**Figure 101**) from the right-hand end of the crankshaft.

3. Remove the crankshaft assembly (**Figure 113**) from the left-hand crankcase half.

4. Remove the connecting rod cap bolt nuts (**Figure 114**) and separate the rods from the crankshaft.

> *NOTE*
> *The rear cylinder connecting rod is located nearest the tapered end (alternator rotor location) of the crankshaft.*

5. Mark each rod and cap as a set. Also mark them with F (front) or R (rear) to indicate from what cylinder they were removed.

6. If necessary, remove the bearing inserts from the connecting rod and cap. Identify each insert separately so that it can be reinstalled in its original mounting position.

7. Install the bearing inserts into the connecting rod and cap by aligning the insert tab with the rod or cap groove (**Figure 115**). Make sure each insert is installed in its original mounting position as noted during disassembly.

> *CAUTION*
> *Installing used bearing inserts incorrectly can cause connecting road seizure (too tight) or rod knock (too loose). If the bearing inserts were mixed up, perform the **Connecting Rod Bearing and Oil Clearance Measurement** procedure in this section.*

8. Lubricate the bearings and crankpins with molybdenum disulfide grease.

9. Position the connecting rod and cap with its identification number (**Figure 116**) facing toward the rear of the engine.

10. Install the caps and tighten the caps nuts evenly, in 2 stages, to the torque specification listed in **Table 2**.

11. Position the inner thrust washer with the oil control grooves facing in toward the crankshaft.

12. Install the thrust washer (**Figure 101**) onto the right-hand end of the crankshaft.

> *NOTE*
> *When installing the crankshaft, align the front and rear connecting rods with their respective cylinder position (**Figure 99**). Continue to check this alignment until the crankshaft is completely installed.*

13. Position the crankshaft with the tapered end going into the left-hand crankcase half and install the crankshaft in the left-hand crankcase (**Figure 113**).

14. Inspect the crankshaft side thrust clearance as described in the following procedure.

15. Assemble the crankcase as described in this chapter.

Crankshaft Side Thrust Clearance

Whenever the crankshaft is removed from the crankcase, the side thrust clearance must be checked. Side thrust clearance is adjusted by replacing the thrust washer with one of a different thickness.

1. Position the inner thrust washer with its oil control grooves (A, **Figure 100**) and inner chamfer (B, **Figure 100**) facing in toward the crankshaft.

> *NOTE*
> *When installing the crankshaft, align the front and rear connecting rods with their respective cylinder position in the crankcase (**Figure 99**). Continue to check this alignment until the crankshaft is completely installed.*

2. Install the crankshaft assembly into the right-hand crankcase half

3. Position the outer thrust washer with the beveled side going on first toward the crankshaft surface and install the outer thrust washer (**Figure 117**).

4. Install the front cylinder camshaft chain sprocket with its alignment mark facing out (**Figure 118**). This will locate the chain sprocket flange in toward the crankcase surface.

5. Install the primary drive gear (A, **Figure 119**) and bolt (B, **Figure 119**).

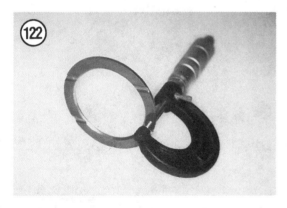

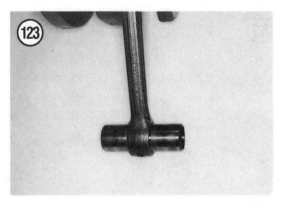

6. Install a clutch holding tool, or equivalent, (**Figure 120**) onto the gear to hold it secure while loosening the mounting bolt.

> *CAUTION*
> *The primary drive gear bolt has **left-hand threads**. Turn the wrench counter clockwise to tighten it.*

7. Tighten the primary drive gear bolt in a *clockwise* direction to the torque specification listed in **Table 2**.

8. Insert a flat feeler gauge (**Figure 121**) between the outer thrust washer and the right-hand crankcase surface. The specified thrust clearance is listed in **Table 1**. If the thrust clearance is incorrect, perform the following:

   a. Reverse Steps 1-7 and remove the crankshaft from the right-hand crankcase half.

   b. Remove and measure the inner thrust washer thickness with a vernier caliper or micrometer (**Figure 122**).

   c. The inner thrust washers are available from a Suzuki dealer in increments of 0.025 mm (0.0010 in.). The thrust washer thickness and part numbers are listed in **Table 3**. Select a new inner thrust washer that will accomplish the specified thrust clearance listed in **Table 1**.

   d. Install the new inner thrust washer and repeat this procedure to make sure the thrust clearance is now within specification.

   e. Remove all components from the right-hand crankcase half, then assemble as described in this chapter.

Connecting Rod Inspection

1. Check each rod and cap for obvious damage such as cracks and burrs.

2. Check the connecting rod small end for wear or scoring.

3. Insert the piston pin into the connecting rod (**Figure 123**) and rotate it. Check for looseness or roughness. Replace the defective part.

4. Measure the inside diameter of the connecting rod small end (**Figure 124**) with an inside micrometer. Compare to the specification listed in **Table 1**. If the small-end bore diameter is greater than specified, replace the connecting rod assembly.

5. Take the connecting rods to a machine shop and have them checked for twisting and bending.

6. Examine the bearing inserts (A, **Figure 125**) for wear, scoring or burning. They may be reused if they are in good condition. Before discarding any bearing insert, check the back and note if it is stamped with a number indicating that it is undersize. A previous owner (or the factory) may have fitted the engine with undersize bearings.

7. Inspect the connecting rod threaded studs (B, **Figure 125**) for wear or damaged threads. If damaged, replace the connecting rod and stud.

8. Check bearing clearance as described in this chapter.

Connecting Rod Bearing and Oil Clearance Measurement

CAUTION
If the old bearings are to be reused, be sure that they are installed in their exact original locations.

1. Wipe bearing inserts and crankpins clean. Install bearing inserts in rod and cap (A, **Figure 125**).

2. Place a piece of Plastigage on one crankpin parallel to the crankshaft.

3. Install rod, cap and nuts, then tighten the nuts to the torque specification listed in **Table 2**.

CAUTION
Do not rotate crankshaft while Plastigage is in place.

4. Remove the nuts and rod cap.

5. Measure width of flattened Plastigage according to the manufacturer's instructions. Measure at both ends of the strip. A difference of 0.001 in. (0.025 mm) or more indicates a tapered crankpin; the crankshaft must be reground or replaced. Use a micrometer and measure the crankpin diameter (**Figure 126**) to get an exact journal dimension.

6. If the crankpin taper is within tolerance, measure the bearing clearance with the same strip of Plastigage. Correct bearing clearance is specified in **Table 1**. Remove Plastigage strips.

7. If the bearing clearance is greater than specified, use the following steps for new bearing selection.

8. The connecting rods and caps are marked with a code number 1, 2 or 3 (**Figure 127**) indicating the inside diameter of the bore in connecting rod.

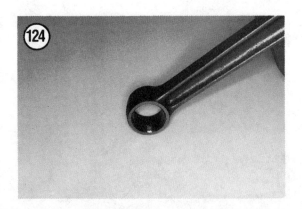

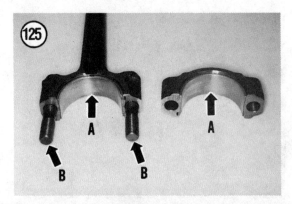

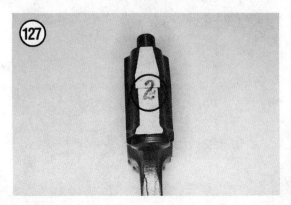

NOTE
The crankshaft has a mark on each counterbalance. Both numbers are stamped on the center counterbalance and look like L 2 2 R.

9. The crankshaft is marked on the counterbalancer with a 1, 2 or 3 (**Figure 128**) indicating the outside diameter of the crankpin journal.

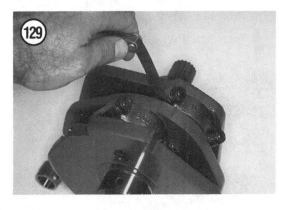

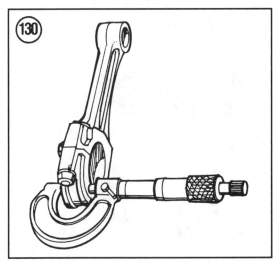

10. Select new bearings by cross-referencing the connecting rod big-end bore diameter code in the vertical column with the crankpin diameter code number in the horizontal column. Where the columns intersect, the new bearing color is indicated. **Table 4** gives the bearing color and **Table 5** gives bearing color and thickness.

11. After new bearings are installed, recheck clearance with Plastigage. If the clearance is out of specification, either the connecting rod or the crankshaft is excessively worn. Refer the engine to a dealership or qualified specialist.

Connecting Rod Side Clearance Measurement

1. With both connecting rods attached to the crankshaft, insert a flat feeler gauge between the counterweight and the connecting rod big end (**Figure 129**).

2. The specified side clearance is listed in **Table 1**.

3. If the clearance is out of specification, perform the following:

    a. Measure the connecting big end width with a micrometer (**Figure 130**) and compare to the dimension listed in **Table 1**. If the width is less than specified, replace the connecting rod assembly.

    b. Measure the crankpin width with a dial caliper (**Figure 131**) and compare to the dimension listed in **Table 1**. If the width is greater than specified, replace the crankshaft.

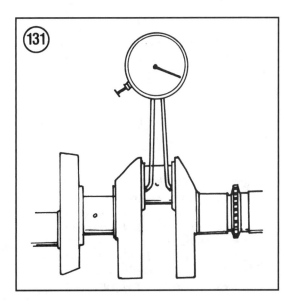

Crankshaft Inspection

1. Clean crankshaft thoroughly with solvent. Clean oil holes with rifle cleaning brushes then flush thoroughly and dry with compressed air. Lightly oil all surfaces immediately to prevent rust.

2. Inspect the connecting rod journals (**Figure 132**) and the main bearing journals (**Figure 133**) for scratches, ridges, scoring, nicks, etc.

3. If the surfaces of all bearing journals are satisfactory, measure the main bearing journals with a micrometer (**Figure 134**) and check for out-of-roundness and taper.

4. Inspect the camshaft chain sprocket (A, **Figure 135**) on the left-hand end. If it is worn or damaged, the crankshaft must be replaced.

5. Inspect the taper (B, **Figure 135**) where the alternator rotor is installed on the left-hand end. If it is worn or damaged, the crankshaft must be replaced.

6. Inspect the splines (**Figure 136**) on the right-hand end for wear or damage. Minor damage can be cleaned up with a fine-cut file, but if damage is excessive the crankshaft must be replaced.

Crankshaft Bearing and Oil Clearance Measurement

1. Wipe bearing inserts in the crankcase and the main bearing journals clean.

2. Use a micrometer and measure the main journal diameter (**Figure 134**) at 2 places. Write these measurements down.

3. Use a bore gauge and measure the main journal insert inner diameter (**Figure 137**) at 2 places. Write these measurements down.

4. To determine oil clearance, subtract the crankshaft journal diameter (Step 2) from the main journal insert inner diameter (Step 3).

5. The oil clearance specification is listed in **Table 1**. If the clearance is out of specifications, either the crankshaft or the bearing insert is worn beyond the service limit.

> *NOTE*
> *The main bearings are removed and installed with a hydraulic press and special tools. After the bearings have been installed, they must be honed to a specific dimension. To avoid damage to a costly set of crankcase halves, this procedure should be entrusted to a*

Suzuki dealership or machine shop. Improper removal and installation of the bearings could result in severe crankcase damage.

ENGINE BREAK-IN

Following cylinder servicing (boring, honing, new rings, etc.) and major lower end work, the engine should be broken-in just as if it were new. The performance and service life of the engine depends

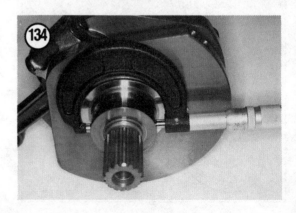

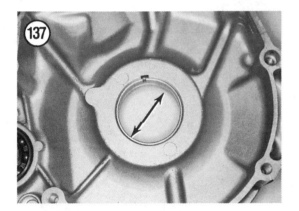

greatly on a careful and sensible break-in. For the first 500 miles, no more than one-third throttle should be used and speed should be varied as much as possible within the one-third throttle limit. Prolonged, steady running at one speed, no matter how moderate, is to be avoided, as is hard acceleration.

Following the 500-mile service, increasingly more throttle can be used but full throttle should not be used until the motorcycle has covered at least 1,000 miles and then it should be limited to short bursts until 1,500 miles have been logged.

The mono-grade oils recommended for break-in and normal use provide a superior bedding pattern for rings and cylinders than multi-grade oils. As a result, piston ring and cylinder bore life are greatly increased. During this period, oil consumption will be higher than normal. It is therefore important to check and correct the oil level frequently. At no time, during break-in or later, should the oil level be allowed to drop below the bottom line on the inspection window; if the oil level is low, the oil will become overheated resulting in insufficient lubrication and increased wear.

500-Mile Service

It is essential that the oil and filter be changed after the first 500 miles. In addition, it is a good idea to change the oil and filter at the completion of break-in (about 1,500 miles) to ensure that all of the particles produced during break-in are removed from the lubrication system. The small added expense may be considered a smart investment that will pay off in increased engine life.

Table 1 ENGINE LOWER END SERVICE SPECIFICATIONS

	New mm (in.)	Service limit mm (in.)
Connecting rod		
Small end inner diameter	23.006-23.014 (0.9057-0.9061)	23.040 (0.9071)
Big end side clearance	0.10-0.20 (0.004-0.008)	0.30 (0.012)
Big end width	21.95-22.0 (0.864-0.866)	–
Crankpin width	22.10-22.15 (0.870-0.872)	–
Connecting rod-to-crankpin oil clearance	0.024-0.042 (0.0009-0.0017)	0.080 (0.0031)
Crankshaft		
Crankpin diameter	49.982-50.000 (1.9678-1.9685)	–
Crankshaft journal oil clearance	0.020-0.050 (0.0008-0.0020)	0.080 (0.0031)
Main journal diameter	51.965-51.980 (2.0459-2.0465)	–
Thrust bearing thickness	1.925-2.175 (0.0758-0.0856)	–
Thrust clearance	0.05-0.10 (0.002-0.004)	–
Runout	–	0.05 (0.0019)
Secondary bevel gear spring free length	–	88.5 (3.48)

Table 2 ENGINE LOWER END TIGHTENING TORQUE

Item	N•m	in.-lb.	ft.-lb.
Oil pressure regulator	25-30	–	18-22
Oil pump mounting bolt	9-13	80-115	–
Oil filter union on crankcase	12-18	106-159	–
Oil separator plate bolt	8-12	71-106	–
Oil pressure switch	12-15	106-132	–
Piston cooling jet retaining plate bolt	8-12	71-106	–
Drain plug	18-23	–	13-17
Oil plug			
6 mm	4-7	35-62	–
8 mm	8-12	71-106	–
12 mm	18-23	–	13-17
14 mm, 16 mm	20-25	–	15-18
Oil pipe union bolt	25-30	–	18-22
Alernator rotor bolt	140-160	–	103-118
Primary drive gear bolt	140-160	–	103-118
Secondary bevel drive gear mounting plate	20-25	–	15-18
Secondary drive gear shaft bolt	90-110	–	66-81
Driveshaft bolt	55-65	–	40-47
Secondar gear housing bolt			
Initial	12-18	106-159	–
Final	20-24	–	15-17
Starter clutch Allen bolts	23-28	–	17-20
(continued)			

Table 2 ENGINE LOWER END TIGHTENING TORQUE (continued)

Item	N•m	in.-lb.	ft.-lb.
Crankcase bolts			
6 mm	0.9-1.3	8-11	–
8 mm			
Initial	12-18	106-159	–
Final	20-24	–	15-17
Connecting rod bolt			
Initial	22-28	–	16-20
Final	49-53	–	36-39

Table 3 CRANKSHAFT SIDE CLEARANCE THRUST WASHER THICKNESS

Part No.	Thrust washer thickness mm (in.)
12228-38B00-0A0	1.925-1.950 (0.0758-0.0768)
12228-38B00--0B0	1.950-1.975 (0.0768-0.0778)
12228-38B00-0C0	1.975-2.000 (0.0778-0.0787)
12228-38B00-0D0	2.000-2.025 (0.0787-0.0797)
12228-38B00-0E0	2.025-2.050 (0.0797-0.0807)
12228-38B00-0F0	2.050-2.075 (0.0807-0.0817)
12228-38B00-0G0	2.075-2.100 (0.0817-0.0827)
12228-38B00-0H0	2.100-2.125 (0.0827-0.0837)
12228-38B00-0I0	2.125-2.150 (0.0837-0.0847)
12228-38B00-0J0	2.150-2.175 (0.0847-0.0856)

Table 4 CONNECTING ROD BEARING SELECTION

Connecting rod identification number	Crankpin journal diameter size code		
	1	2	3
Number 1	Green	Black	Brown
Number 2	Black	Brown	Yellow
Number 3	Brown	Yellow	Blue

Table 5 CONNECTING ROD BEARINGIN INSERT COLOR AND THICKNESS

Color	Thickness
Green	1.485-1.488 mm (0.0585-0.0586 in.)
Black	1.488-1.491 mm (0.0586-0.0587 in.)
Brown	1.491-1.494 mm (0.0587-0.0588 in.)
Yellow	1.494-1.497 mm (0.0588-0.0589 in.)
Blue	1.497-1.500 mm (0.0589-0.0590 in.)

CHAPTER SIX

CLUTCH AND EXTERNAL SHIFT MECHANISM

This chapter provides complete service procedures for the clutch, the clutch release mechanism and the external shift mechanism.

The clutch is a wet multi-plate type which operates immersed in the engine oil. It is mounted on the right-hand end of the transmission mainshaft. The inner clutch hub is splined to the mainshaft and the outer housing can rotate freely on the mainshaft. The outer housing is geared to the crankshaft. The clutch pushrods ride within the channel in the transmission mainshaft.

The clutch release mechanism is hydraulic and requires no adjustment. The mechanism consists of a clutch master cylinder on the left-hand handlebar, a slave cylinder on the left-hand side of the engine and two pushrods that ride within the channel in the transmission mainshaft.

Specifications for the clutch are listed in **Table 1**. **Tables 1-2** are located at the end of this chapter.

EXTERNAL GEARSHIFT MECHANISM

The external gearshift mechanism is located on the same side of the crankcase as the clutch assembly. To remove the internal shift mechanism (shift drum and shift forks), it is necessary to remove the engine, then split the crankcase as described in Chapter Five

Removal

Refer to **Figure 1** for this procedure.

1. Remove the exhaust system as described in Chapter Eight.

2. Remove the front footpeg assembly as described in Chapter Thirteen.

3. Remove the clutch slave cylinder as described in this chapter.

4. Remove the neutral switch, plunger and spring as described in Chapter Nine.

NOTE
A gasket washer is located under the lower 3 bolts. These gasket washers must be reinstalled on the same three bolts to prevent an oil leak.

5. Remove the bolts securing the external gearshift mechanism cover (**Figure 2**) and remove the cover and gasket. Do not lose the 2 locating dowels.

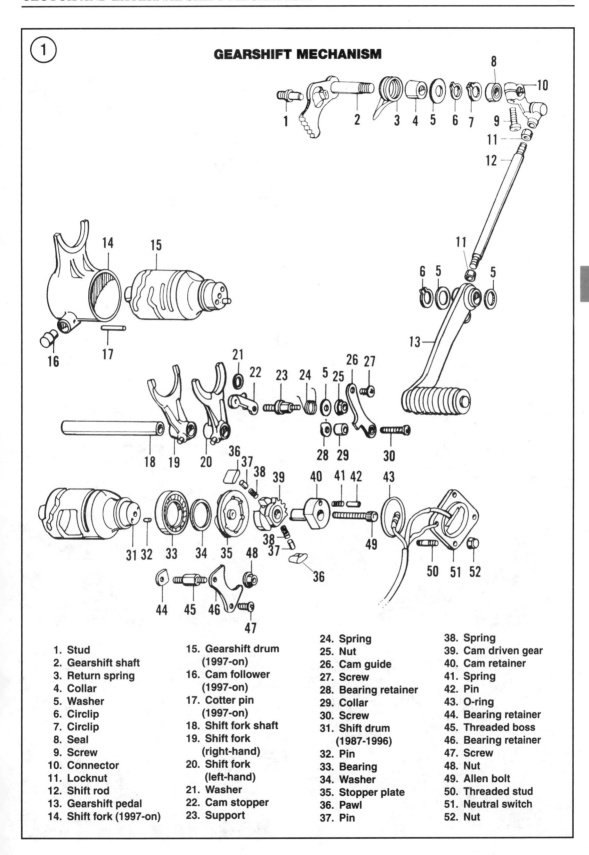

① GEARSHIFT MECHANISM

6

1. Stud
2. Gearshift shaft
3. Return spring
4. Collar
5. Washer
6. Circlip
7. Circlip
8. Seal
9. Screw
10. Connector
11. Locknut
12. Shift rod
13. Gearshift pedal
14. Shift fork (1997-on)

15. Gearshift drum
    (1997-on)
16. Cam follower
    (1997-on)
17. Cotter pin
    (1997-on)
18. Shift fork shaft
19. Shift fork
    (right-hand)
20. Shift fork
    (left-hand)
21. Washer
22. Cam stopper
23. Support

24. Spring
25. Nut
26. Cam guide
27. Screw
28. Bearing retainer
29. Collar
30. Screw
31. Shift drum
    (1987-1996)
32. Pin
33. Bearing
34. Washer
35. Stopper plate
36. Pawl
37. Pin

38. Spring
39. Cam driven gear
40. Cam retainer
41. Spring
42. Pin
43. O-ring
44. Bearing retainer
45. Threaded boss
46. Bearing retainer
47. Screw
48. Nut
49. Allen bolt
50. Threaded stud
51. Neutral switch
52. Nut

6. Withdraw the gearshift shaft (A, **Figure 3**) from the crankcase. Do not lose the washer (B, **Figure 3**) on the outer end of the shaft.

7. Remove the cam stopper assembly (**Figure 4**) from the crankcase. Do not lose the washer on the inner end of the assembly.

> *CAUTION*
> *Some of the following screws had a thread locking agent applied to the threads during installation. If the screws are difficult to loosen, use an impact driver and the correct size bit to loosen the screws. Do not try to loosen a stubborn screw with a screwdriver as the screw head slots may be damaged.*

8. Remove the screws securing the cam guide (**Figure 5**) to the crankcase. Do not lose the collar and bearing retainer located on the lower screw.

9. Remove the nut and screw securing the pawl lifter (A, **Figure 6**) and remove the pawl lifter.

10. Remove the Allen bolt securing the cam retainer (B, **Figure 6**) and remove the cam retainer.

NOTE
Remove the cam gear slowly as the small pawls, pins and springs are loose and will fall out during removal.

11. Slowly remove the cam gear assembly (**Figure 7**) from the stopper plate. As soon as the pawls start to clear the stopper plate hold them in place with your fingers to avoid loosing the small parts. Place the assembly into the small cap from an aerosol spray container (**Figure 8**) then place into a reclosable plastic bag to avoid misplacing any small parts.

12. Remove the stopper plate (**Figure 9**) and washer (**Figure 10**) from the end of the shift drum.

13. If necessary, remove the screw and bearing retainer (**Figure 11**).

14. While the cover is removed, remove the oil jet (**Figure 12**) from the crankcase.

6

Inspection

1. Clean all parts in solvent and dry with compressed air.

2. Inspect the return spring (A, **Figure 13**) on the gearshift shaft assembly. If broken or weak it must be replaced.

3. Inspect the gearshift shaft assembly (B, **Figure 13**) for bending, wear or other damage; replace if necessary.

4. Inspect the gear teeth (**Figure 14**) on the gearshift shaft assembly. If broken or damaged the gearshift shaft must be replaced.

5. Disassemble the cam gear assembly (**Figure 15**) and inspect the pawls, springs and pins for wear or damage. Replace any worn or damaged parts.

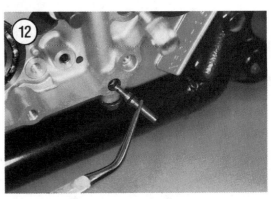

6. Inspect the ramps (**Figure 16**) on the backside of the stopper plate for wear or damage. Replace the stopper plate if necessary.

7. Inspect the cam driven gear receptacle (**Figure 17**) in the stopper plate for wear or damage. Replace the stopper plate if necessary.

8. Inspect the gear teeth (**Figure 18**) on the cam drive gear. If broken or damaged the cam drive gear must be replaced.

9. Assemble the cam gear assembly as follows:

   a. Install the springs into the cam gear body.

   b. Position the pawl pins with the rounded end facing out and install them onto the springs.

   c. Install the pawls onto the pins and into the cam gear body (**Figure 19**).

   d. The pin grooves in the pawls are offset. When the pawls are installed correctly the wider shoulder must face toward the outside (**Figure 20**).

   e. Hold the pawls in place and put the assembly into an aerosol can top (**Figure 21**).

10. Inspect the gearshift cover (A, **Figure 22**) for wear or damage.

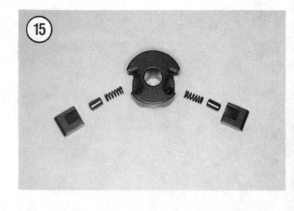

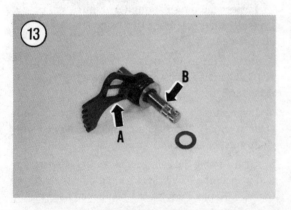

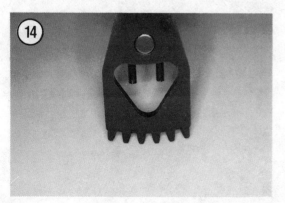

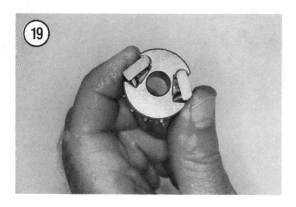

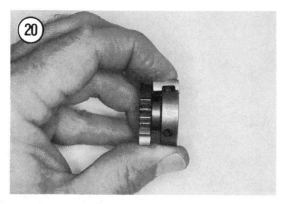

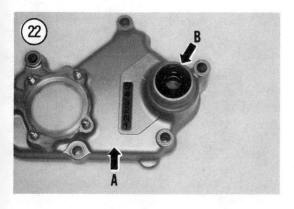

11. Check the gearshift shaft seal (B, **Figure 22**) for deterioration or signs of leakage. Replace if necessary.

12. Inspect the O-ring seal (A, **Figure 23**) for hardness or deterioration, replace as necessary. Make sure the oil control orifice (B, **Figure 23**) is clear. Clean out with solvent and compressed air.

13. Inspect the oil jet O-Ring and replace if damaged.

Installation

> *CAUTION*
> *To prevent the following screws from working loose, apply a small amount of red ThreeBond TB1360 or Loctite No. 271 to the screw threads prior to installation.*

1. Position the oil jet as shown in **Figure 12** and install the jet in the crankcase receptacle.

2. If removed, install the bearing retainer and screw (**Figure 11**). Tighten the screw securely.

3. Install the washer (**Figure 10**) onto the end of the shift drum.

4. The locating pins on the end of the shift drum are offset. Correctly align the locating pin receptacles in the backside of the stopper plate (**Figure 24**) with the shift drum pins and install the stopper plate (**Figure 9**). Push it in until it stops.

5. Remove the cam gear assembly from the cap. Compress the spring-loaded shift storage pawls with your fingers (**Figure 25**). Install the cam gear assembly into the receptacle of the cam driven gear (**Figure 7**).

6. Align the cam retainer locating tab (**Figure 26**) with the notch in the shift drum and temporarily install the cam retainer and Allen bolt and tighten finger-tight at this time.

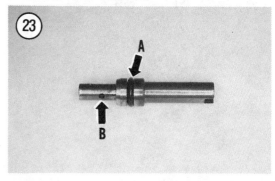

7. Install the pawl lifter, nut and screw and tighten the screw and nut securely.

8. Install the bearing retainer (**Figure 27**) in place on the lower bolt hole.

9. Install the lower screw and collar on the upper screw (**Figure 28**) and install the cam guide (**Figure 29**) onto the crankcase. Tighten the screws securely.

10. Assemble the cam stopper assembly in the order shown in **Figure 30**. Do not forget the small inner screw (**Figure 31**).

11. Install the cam stopper assembly (**Figure 32**) into the crankcase and tighten securely.

12. Use narrow nose Locking pliers to pull the spring up and over the top of the cam stopper arm. Hook the spring end onto the locator (A, **Figure 33**) on the cam stopper and make sure the other end of the spring is against the crankcase wall (B, **Figure 33**). The spring must be in this position for the cam stopper arm to operate correctly.

13. Remove the Allen bolt and cam retainer.

14. Remove the cam stopper assembly (**Figure 32**).

15. Make sure the washer (**Figure 34**) is in place on the gearshift shaft.

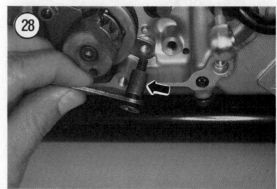

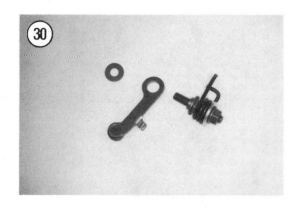

16. Apply clean engine oil to the gearshift shaft and install the gearshift shaft (**Figure 35**) part way into the crankcase. Align the center of the cam driven gear with the center of the gearshift shaft gear (**Figure 36**), then push the shaft assembly all the way in making sure the return spring is meshed correctly with the locator pin (**Figure 37**).

NOTE
*The alignment of the 2 gears (**Figure 38**) is essential for proper gearshift operation. If alignment is incorrect, the*

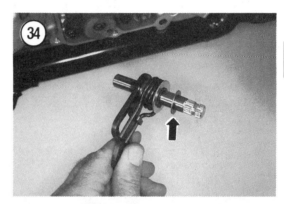

6

*shift mechanism will operate poorly or
not at all.*

17. Recheck the alignment of the center of the cam
driven gear to the center of the gearshift shaft gear
(**Figure 39**). This alignment is necessary for proper
gear shift operation. If necessary, realign the two
gears at this time.

18. Align the cam retainer locating tab (**Figure 40**)
with the notch in the shift drum and temporarily
install the cam retainer and Allen bolt (**Figure 41**)
and tighten securely.

19. Recheck the alignment of the center of the cam
driven gear to the center of the gearshift shaft gear
(**Figure 42**). This alignment is necessary for proper
gear shift operation. If necessary, realign the 2 gears
at this time.

20. If removed, install the locating dowels (A, **Figure 43**) and a new gasket (B, **Figure 43**).

> *NOTE*
> *A gasket washer is located under the
> lower three bolts. These gasket washers
> must be reinstalled on the same three
> bolts to prevent an oil leak.*

21. Install the external gearshift mechanism cover
and bolts. Be sure to install a gasket washer under
the lower three bolts (**Figure 44**). Tighten the bolts
securely

22. Install the neutral switch, plunger and spring as
described in Chapter Nine.

23. Install the clutch slave cylinder as described in
this chapter.

24. Install the front footpeg assembly as described
in Chapter Thirteen.

25. Install the exhaust system as described in Chapter
Eight.

CLUTCH

Removal/Disassembly

Refer to **Figure 45** for this procedure.

1. Drain the engine oil as described in Chapter
Three.

2. Shift the transmission into gear.

3. Remove the front footpeg assembly as described
in Chapter Thirteen.

NOTE
Note the location of the wiring harness clamps and the sealing washers under two of the bolts securing the clutch cover. During assembly these sealing washers must be reinstalled in their original position to prevent an oil leak.

4. Remove the bolts securing the clutch cover (**Figure 46**). Remove the clutch cover and gasket. Don't lose the locating dowels.

5. Place a shop rag between the primary drive gear and the clutch outer housing to keep the clutch assembly from rotating.

6. Using a crisscross pattern loosen the clutch bolts securing the pressure plate. Remove the shop rag.

NOTE
The pressure plate is held in place by 2 different spring sets. Each spring set consists of 4 bolts, spacers and springs. The spring set threaded into the clutch hub is longer than the spring set threaded into the clutch spring slider. Do not intermix the 2 spring sets when removing them in Step 7.

7. Remove the bolts, spacers and springs loosened in Step 6.

8. Remove the pressure plate.

9. Remove the friction discs, clutch plates, wave washer and wave washer seat.

10. Remove the thrust washer, bearing and clutch push piece.

11. If necessary, remove the clutch left-hand pushrod from the transmission shaft.

CAUTION
Do not overtighten the clutch holding tool in Step 12 or it may damage the clutch hub grooves.

12. Secure the clutch hub with a clutch holding tool (A, **Figure 47**).

13. Loosen, then remove the clutch locknut (B, **Figure 47**) and wave washer.

14. Remove the clutch tool from the clutch hub.

15. Slide off and remove the clutch cam No. 1 (A, **Figure 48**).

16. Slide off and remove the clutch cam No. 2 (B, **Figure 48**).

17. Remove the thrust washer (A, **Figure 49**) and the clutch spring slider (B, **Figure 49**).

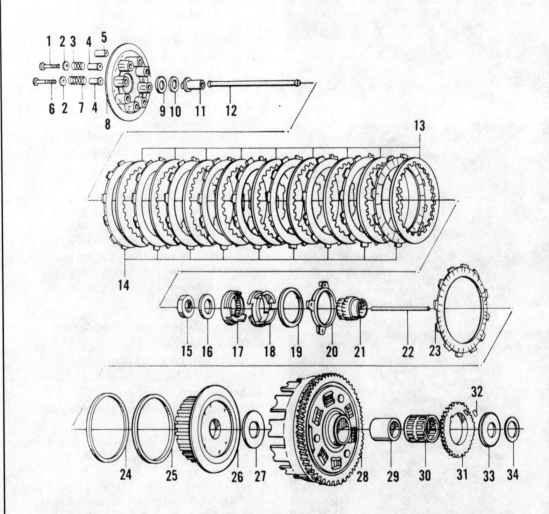

CLUTCH ASSEMBLY

1. Bolt (short)
2. Washer
3. Spring
4. Spacer
5. Spacer
6. Bolt (long)
7. Spring
8. Pressure plate
9. Washer
10. Needle bearing
11. Clutch lifter
12. Push rod (right hand)
13. Clutch plates
14. Friction discs (No. 1)
15. Clutch locknut
16. Wave washer
17. Clutch cam (No. 1)
18. Clutch cam (No. 2)
19. Thrust washer
20. Clutch spring slider
21. Spacer
22. Push rod (left-hand)
23. Friction discs (No. 2)
24. Spring washer
25. Spring washer seat
26. Clutch center
27. Washer
28. Outer housing
29. Bushing
30. Needle bearing
31. Oil pump drive gear
32. Pin
33. Outer washer
34. Inner washer

18. Hold the clutch center and slide the spacer (A, **Figure 50**) off the transmission shaft.

19. Remove the clutch center (B, **Figure 50**).

20. Remove the washer (A, **Figure 51**).

21. Carefully remove the outer housing (B, **Figure 51**). Be careful not to drop the oil pump driven gear (A, **Figure 52**) and locating pin (B, **Figure 52**) located on the backside of the outer housing.

22. Remove the needle bearing (A, **Figure 53**), bushing (B, **Figure 53**), outer washer (A, **Figure 54**)

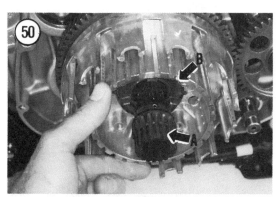

and inner washer (B, **Figure 54**) from the transmission shaft.

23. Inspect all components as described in this chapter.

Inspection

Refer to **Table 1** for clutch specifications.

1. Clean all clutch parts in petroleum-based solvent such as kerosene and thoroughly dry with compressed air.

2. Measure the free length of each clutch spring as shown in **Figure 55**. Compare to the specifiation listed in **Table 1**.

> *NOTE*
> *The thickness of the No. 2 inner narrow friction disc (23, **Figure 45**) is different from all other No. 1 friction discs. Be sure to measure and record its thickness separately.*

3. Measure the thickness of each friction disc at several places around the disc as shown in **Figure 56**. Compare to the specification listed in **Table 1**.

4. Measure the width of all claws on each friction disc as shown in **Figure 57**. Compare to the specification listed in **Table 1**.

5. Check the clutch plates (**Figure 58**) for surface damage from heat or lack of oil.

6. Check the clutch plates for warpage with a flat feeler gauge on a surface plate such as a piece of plate glass (**Figure 59**). If any plate is warped more than specified in **Table 1**, replace the *entire set* of clutch plates.

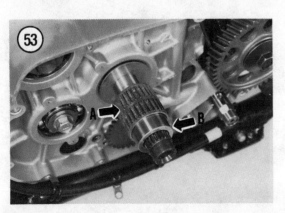

> *NOTE*
> *If any of the friction discs, clutch plates or clutch springs require replacement, replace them in sets to retain maximum clutch performance.*

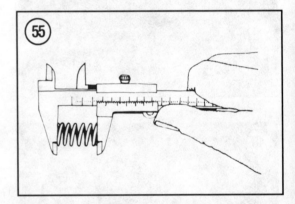

7. Inspect the clutch outer housing slots (A, **Figure 60**) for cracks, nicks or galling. If any severe damage is evident, the housing must be replaced.

8. Inspect the driven gear teeth (A, **Figure 61**) on the clutch outer housing for damage. Remove any small nicks with an oilstone. If damage is severe, the clutch outer housing must be replaced.

9. Inspect the damper springs (B, **Figure 61**). If they are sagged or broken the housing must be replaced.

10. Check the inner surface (C, **Figure 61**) of the clutch outer housing, where the needle bearing rides, for signs of wear or damage. Replace the clutch outer housing if necessary.

11. Inspect the oil pump drive gear teeth (A, **Figure 52**) for damage. Remove any small nicks with a fine-cut file.

12. Inspect the outer grooves (B, **Figure 60**) and studs (C, **Figure 60**) in the clutch hub. If either show signs of wear or galling the clutch hub should be replaced.

13. Inspect the spring receptacles (**Figure 62**) in the clutch pressure plate for wear or damage. Replace the clutch pressure plate if necessary.

14. Check the needle bearing (A, **Figure 63**). Make sure it rotates smoothly with no signs of wear or damage. Replace if necessary.

15. Check the bushing (B, **Figure 63**) for wear or damage. Replace if necessary.

16. Install the bushing into the needle bearing. Rotate the bushing and check for wear. Replace either/or both parts if necessary.

17. Check the clutch cam No. 1 (A, **Figure 64**), clutch cam No. 2 (B, **Figure 64**), the clutch spring

6

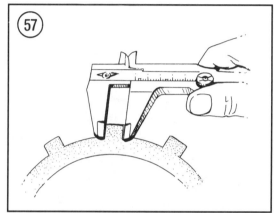

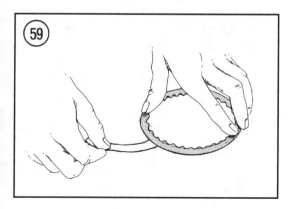

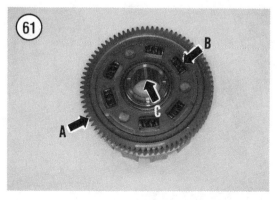

slider (C, **Figure 64**) and the spacer (D, **Figure 64**) for wear or damage. Replace as necessary.

18. Check the clutch lifter (A, **Figure 65**) for wear or damage. Inspect the end (A, **Figure 66**) that rides against the right-hand push rod (B, **Figure 66**). Replace if necessary.

19. Check the clutch springs, bolts, spacers and washers (**Figure 67**) for wear or damage. Replace as sets if necessary.

20. Check the clutch lifter bearing (B, **Figure 65**). Make sure it rotates smoothly with wear or damage. Replace if necessary.

21. Install the bearing and washer onto the lifter rack and rotate them by hand. Make sure all parts rotate smoothly. Replace any worn part.

22. Roll each pushrod on a surface plate or piece of flat glass and check for bending or other damage. Replace if necessary.

CAUTION
Do not attempt to straighten a bent pushrod. Doing so may weaken the pushrod and cause it to break during engine operation.

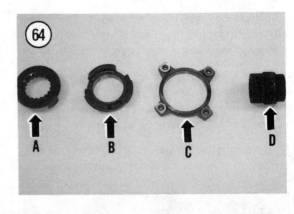

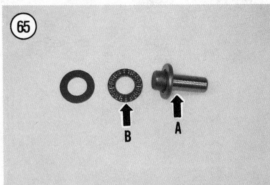

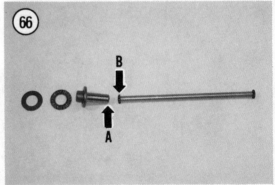

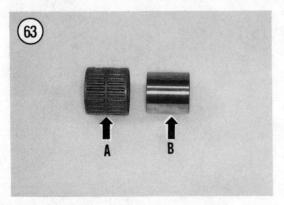

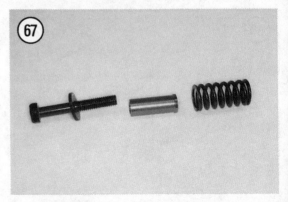

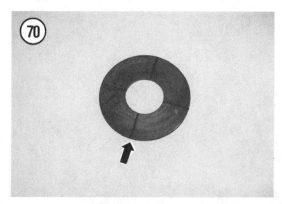

Assembly/Installation

Refer to **Figure 45** for this procedure.

1. Install the inner washer (A, **Figure 68**) and outer washer (B, **Figure 68**) onto the transmission shaft.

2. Install the bushing (B, **Figure 53**) onto the transmission shaft.

3. Apply a good coat of clean engine oil to the needle bearing and install the needle bearing (A, **Figure 53**).

4. Align the notch (A, **Figure 69**) in the oil pump drive gear with the locating pin (B, **Figure 69**) and install it onto the backside of the outer housing. Make sure the gear is completely seated on the outer housing.

5. Install the outer housing onto the transmission shaft. If necessary, rotate the housing to mesh it with the oil pump driven gear. Push the outer housing on until it stops.

6. Position the washer with its grooved side (**Figure 70**) facing out. See **Figure 71**.

7. Install the clutch hub (A, **Figure 72**) onto the transmission shaft.

NOTE
*(**Figure 73**) is shown with the clutch center removed to show the oil hole in the shaft.*

CAUTION
*In Step 8, the spacer must be installed correctly for proper oil flow. Align the oil hole in the spacer (A, **Figure 73**) with the shaft punch mark (B, **Figure 73**). This will align the spacer with the oil hole on the shaft (C, **Figure 73**).*

8. Align the oil hole in the spacer (B, **Figure 72**) with the shaft punch mark (C, **Figure 72**).

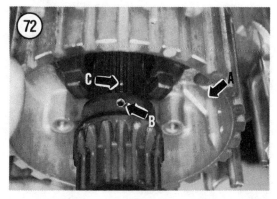

9. Push the spacer into the outer housing until it stops.

10. Position the clutch spring slider with its raised bolt bosses (**Figure 74**) facing out and install it onto the clutch hub (A, **Figure 75**).

11. Install the thrust washer (B, **Figure 75**).

12. Install the clutch cam No. 2 as follows:

   a. Align the clutch cam No. 2 notches (A, **Figure 76**) with the raised bosses (B, **Figure 76**) on the clutch center.

   b. Position the clutch cam No. 2 as shown in **Figure 77** and install the cam onto the clutch center.

   c. Push the clutch cam No. 2 on until it stops. Push in on the cam and try to rotate it back and forth to make sure the notches and bosses are properly engaged.

13. Install the clutch cam No. 1 as follows:

   a. Align the clutch cam No. 1 tabs (A, **Figure 78**) with the notches (B, **Figure 78**) on the clutch cam No. 2.

   b. Position the clutch cam No. 1 as shown in **Figure 79** and install the cam onto the clutch cam No. 2.

   c. Push the clutch cam No. 1 on until it stops. Push in on the cam and try to rotate it back and forth to make sure the tabs and notches are properly engaged.

14. Install the wave washer (A, **Figure 80**) with its concave side facing out (away from clutch).

15. Install the locknut with its chamfered side (B, **Figure 80**) facing out.

> *CAUTION*
> *Do not overtighten the clutch hub tool in Step 16 or it may damage the clutch hub splines.*

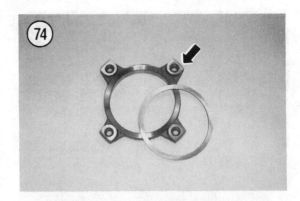

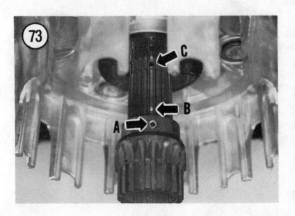

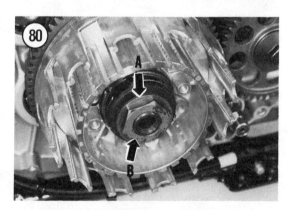

16. Secure the clutch hub with a clutch holding tool.
17. Tighten the clutch locknut to the torque specification listed in **Table 2**.
18. Remove the clutch tool from the clutch hub.

NOTE
The clutch right-hand pushrod is symmetrical so either end can be inserted into the transmission shaft first.

19. Install the clutch right-hand pushrod into the transmission shaft.
20. Install the clutch lifter (A, **Figure 81**) into the transmission shaft.
21. Apply a good coat of clean engine oil to the needle bearing and install the needle bearing (B, **Figure 81**) and washer (C, **Figure 81**) onto the clutch push piece.
22. The push piece will not travel all the way into the transmission shaft because of hydraulic pressure within the clutch slave cylinder. Push on the end of the push piece and press the clutch push rods back into the slave cylinder. Push in until the push piece bottoms out on the end of the transmission shaft.
23. Install the spring washer seat (**Figure 82**) onto the clutch hub.
24. Position the spring washer with the dished side going on first and install the spring washer (**Figure 83**) onto the clutch hub. Push the spring washer seat and the spring washer all the way on until they stop.

NOTE
If new friction discs and clutch plates are being installed, apply new engine oil to all surfaces to avoid having the clutch lock up when used for the first time.

25. Install the No. 2 narrow friction disc onto the clutch hub. Make sure it seats correctly next to the spring washer (**Figure 83**).

26. Install a clutch plate then a friction disc. Continue to install the clutch plates and friction discs, alternating them until all are installed. The last item installed is a friction disc.

27. Prior to installing the pressure plate, note the location of the spring bolt holes in the two different parts. Position the clutch outer housing so one of the bolt holes on the spring slider is at the 12 o'clock position.

28. Install the pressure plate (A, **Figure 84**).

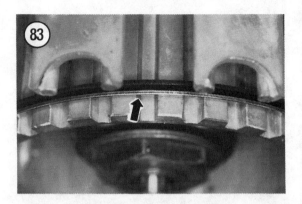

NOTE
*The longer bolts, spacers and springs (A, **Figure 85**) secure the pressure plate to the clutch hub.(A, **Figure 86**) The shorter bolts, spacers and springs (B, **Figure 85**) secure the pressure plate to the clutch spring slider (B, **Figure 86**).*

29. Install the washer (A, **Figure 87**) onto the short bolt, followed by the spacer and spring (B, **Figure 87**). Assemble all 4 of these sets.

30. Install one of the spring and bolt sets in the pressure plate receptacle located at the 12 o'clock position (B, **Figure 84**). Tighten the bolt securely to make sure it is located correctly in the clutch spring slider bolt hole. If the location is correct, install the 3 remaining spring and bolt sets in every other hole.

31. Install the washer onto the long bolt. Position the spacer with the shoulder facing away from the bolt head and install the spacer and spring. Assemble all 4 of these sets.

32. Install the 4 longer bolt spring sets in the reaming receptacles in the pressure plate (**Figure 88**).

33. Place a shop rag between the primary drive gear and the clutch outer housing to keep the clutch assembly from rotating.

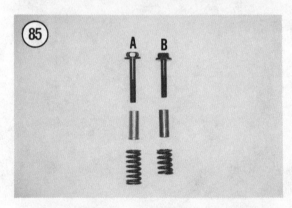

34. Tighten the clutch bolts in a crisscross pattern to the torque specification listed in **Table 2**. Remove the shop rag.

35. Make sure the locating dowels (A, **Figure 89**) are in place.

36. Install a new clutch cover gasket (B, **Figure 89**).

NOTE
There are 4 different length bolts securing the clutch cover, make sure the bolts are installed in the correct location.

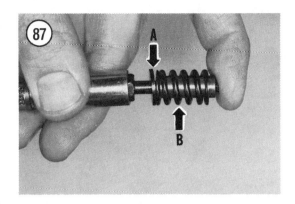

6

NOTE
Be sure to install a sealing washer under the 2 bolts in the next step. If not installed, an oil leak will result.

37. Install the clutch cover and bolts. Install the 2 bolts with the sealing washer as shown in **Figure 90**. Tighten the bolts securely.
38. Install the front footpeg assembly as described in Chapter Thirteen.
39. Refill the engine oil as described in Chapter Three.

CLUTCH HYDRAULIC SYSTEM

The clutch is actuated by hydraulic fluid pressure and is controlled by the hand lever on the clutch master cylinder located on the left-hand handlebar. As clutch components wear, the fluid level in the reservoir will be lower as it automatically adjusts for wear. There is no routine adjustment necessary nor possible.

When working on the clutch hydraulic system, it is necessary that the work area and all tools be absolutely clean. Any tiny particles or foreign matter and grit in the clutch slave cylinder or the master cylinder can damage the components. Also, sharp tools must not be used inside the slave cylinder or on the piston. If there is any doubt about your ability to correctly and safely carry out major service on the clutch hydraulic components, take the job to a dealership or other qualified specialist.

WARNING
Throughout the text, reference is made to hydraulic fluid. Hydraulic fluid is the same as DOT 3 or DOT 4 brake fluid. Use only DOT 3 or DOT 4 brake fluid. Do not use other types of fluids as they are not compatible. Do not intermix silicone based (DOT 5) brake fluid as it can cause clutch component damage leading to clutch system failure.

MASTER CYLINDER

Removal/Installation

CAUTION
Cover the fuel tank, front fender and instrument cluster with a heavy cloth or plastic tarp to protect them from

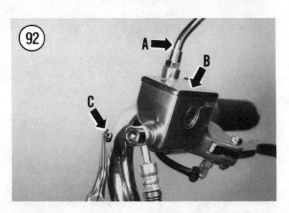

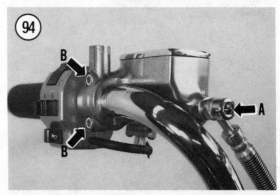

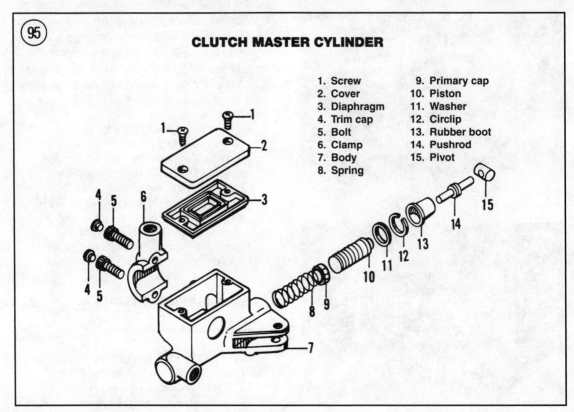

CLUTCH MASTER CYLINDER

1. Screw
2. Cover
3. Diaphragm
4. Trim cap
5. Bolt
6. Clamp
7. Body
8. Spring
9. Primary cap
10. Piston
11. Washer
12. Circlip
13. Rubber boot
14. Pushrod
15. Pivot

accidental hydraulic fluid spills. Wash hydraulic fluid from any painted or plated surfaces or plastic parts immediately, as it will destroy the finish. Use soapy water and rinse completely.

1. Disconnect the electrical connector (**Figure 91**) from the clutch interlock switch.

2. Unscrew and remove the rear view mirror (A, **Figure 92**).

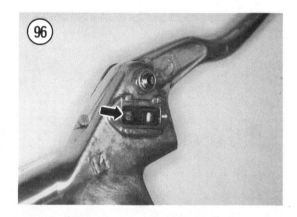

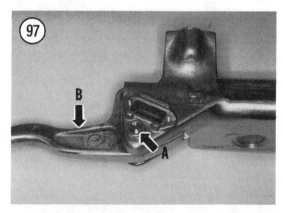

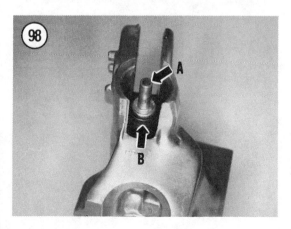

3. Remove the screws, washers and lockwashers securing the clutch interlock switch (**Figure 93**) and remove the switch.

4. Remove the screws and remove the reservoir cover (B, **Figure 92**).

5. If you have a shop syringe, draw all of the hydraulic fluid out of the master cylinder reservoir. Reinstall the cover and screws.

6. Remove the trim cap (C, **Figure 92**) from the banjo bolt.

7. Place a shop cloth under the banjo bolt to catch any spilled hydraulic fluid that will leak out.

8. Unscrew the banjo bolt (A, **Figure 94**) securing the clutch hose to the master cylinder. Do not lose the sealing washer on each side of the hose fitting. Tie the loose end of the hose up to the handlebar and place the loose end in a reclosable bag to prevent the entry of moisture and foreign matter.

9. Remove the caps, clamping bolts (B, **Figure 94**) and the clamp securing the master cylinder to the handlebar and remove the master cylinder.

10. Install by reversing these removal steps while noting the following:

   a. Tighten the upper clamp bolt first, then the lower to the torque specification listed in **Table 2**.

   b. Place a sealing washer on each side of the clutch hose fitting and install the banjo bolt.

   c. Tighten the banjo bolt to the torque specification listed in **Table 2**.

   d. Bleed the clutch as described under *Bleeding The System* in this chapter.

Disassembly

Refer to **Figure 95** for this procedure.

1. Remove the master cylinder as described in this chapter.

2. Remove the starter interlock switch plunger (**Figure 96**) from the master cylinder.

3. Remove the screws securing the top cover and remove the top cover and the diaphragm.

4. Pour out any residual hydraulic fluid and discard it. *Never* reuse hydraulic fluid.

5. Remove the bolt and nut (A, **Figure 97**) securing the hand lever and remove the lever (B, **Figure 97**).

6. Remove the pushrod (A, **Figure 98**) and rubber boot (B, **Figure 98**) from the area where the hand lever actuates the piston assembly.

7. Using circlip pliers, remove the internal circlip (**Figure 99**) from the body. Remove the washer behind the circlip

8. Remove the piston assembly and the spring.

Inspection

1. Clean all parts in denatured alcohol or fresh hydraulic fluid.

2. Inspect the body cylinder bore (**Figure 100**) surface for wear and damage. If less than perfect, replace the master cylinder assembly. The body cannot be replaced separately.

3. Inspect the primary (A, **Figure 101**) and the secondary cup (B, **Figure 101**) for wear.

4. Replace the piston assembly if either the primary or secondary cup and/or spring requires replacement.

5. Inspect the piston contact surfaces (C, **Figure 101**) for signs of wear and damage.

6. Check the end of the piston (A, **Figure 102**) for wear caused by the pushrod. Replace if severely worn or damaged.

7. Check the end of the pushrod (B, **Figure 102**) for wear caused by the piston. Replace the pushrod if severely worn or damaged.

8. Measure the cylinder bore (**Figure 100**) with a bore gauge. Replace the master cylinder if the inside diameter exceeds the service limit. See **Table 1**.

9. Measure the outside diameter of the piston with a micrometer (**Figure 103**). Replace the piston assembly if the outside diameter is less than the service limit in **Table 1**.

10. Make sure the passage (**Figure 104**) in the bottom of the master cylinder body is clear. Clean out if necessary.

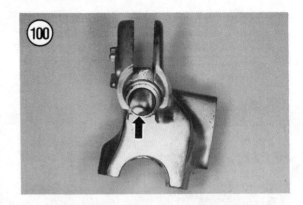
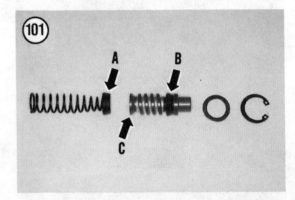
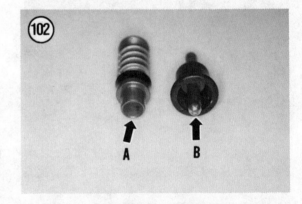
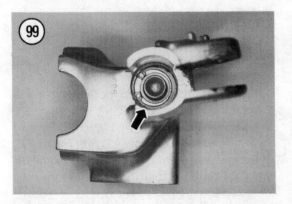

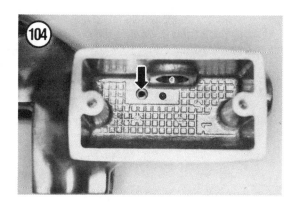

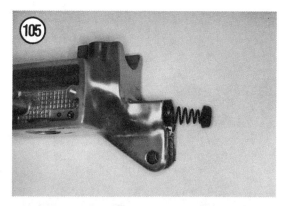

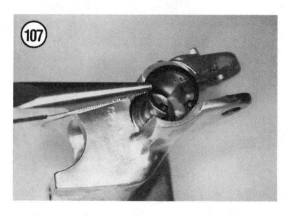

11. Inspect the pivot hole on the hand lever. If worn or elongated the lever must be replaced.

12. Check the top cover and diaphragm for damage and deterioration and replace as necessary.

13. Inspect the threads in the bore for the banjo bolt. If worn or damaged, clean out with a thread tap or replace the master cylinder assembly.

14. Check the hand lever pivot lugs on the master cylinder body for cracks. If damaged, replace the master cylinder assembly.

Assembly

1. Soak the new cups in fresh hydraulic fluid for at least 15 minutes to make them pliable. Coat the inside of the cylinder bore with fresh hydraulic fluid prior to the assembly of parts.

CAUTION
When installing the piston assembly, do not allow the cups to turn inside out as they will be damaged and allow hydraulic fluid leakage within the cylinder bore.

2. Install the spring and primary cup assembly into the cylinder together. Install the spring with its tapered end (**Figure 105**) facing toward the primary cup.

3. Install the piston assembly into the cylinder (**Figure 106**).

4. Install the washer and the circlip (**Figure 107**). Make sure the circlip is correctly seated in the groove (**Figure 99**).

5. Slide in the rubber boot (B, **Figure 98**) and install the pushrod (A, **Figure 98**).

6. Install the diaphragm and top cover. Do not tighten the cover screws at this time as hydraulic fluid will have to be added later when the system is bled.

7. Install the starter interlock switch plunger (**Figure 108**) into the receptacle in the master cylinder body.

8. Install the master cylinder as described in this chapter.

Clutch Hose Assembly
Removal/Installation

There is no factory-recommended replacement interval but it is a good idea to replace the clutch hose assembly every 4 years or if either flexible section is cracked or damaged.

The clutch hose assembly is made up of flexible hose that is attached to each end of a metal line. This assembly cannot be serviced and if any portion is defective the entire hose assembly must be replaced.

> *CAUTION*
> *Cover the front fender and instrument cluster with a heavy cloth or plastic tarp to protect them from accidental hydraulic fluid spills. Wash hydraulic fluid off any painted or plated surfaces or plastic parts immediately, as it will destroy the finish. Use soapy water and rinse completely.*

1. Remove the fuel tank as described in Chapter Eight.

2. Remove the bolts securing the secondary drive cover (**Figure 109**) and remove the cover and bolt spacers.

3. Remove the cap and attach a hose to the bleed valve (**Figure 110**) on the slave cylinder and place the loose end in a container.

4. Open the bleed valve and apply the lever on the clutch master cylinder to pump the hydraulic fluid out of the master cylinder and the clutch hose assembly. Continue to operate the lever until the fluid is pumped out of the hose assembly. Close the bleed valve and remove the hose. Dispose of this hydraulic fluid - *never* re-use hydraulic fluid.

5. Clean the top of the master cylinder of all dirt and foreign matter.

6. Loosen the screws securing the master cylinder top cover (A, **Figure 111**). Pull up and loosen the cover and the diaphragm. This will allow air to enter the reservoir and allow any residual hydraulic fluid to drain out more quickly in the next steps.

7. Place a container under the clutch hose at the slave cylinder.

8. Remove the banjo bolt and sealing washers (A, **Figure 112**) securing the clutch hose to the slave cylinder.

9. Remove the clutch hose and let any residual hydraulic fluid drain out into the container. Dispose of this hydraulic fluid - never re-use hydraulic fluid. To prevent the entry of moisture and dirt, tape over the threaded bore in the slave cylinder.

> *WARNING*
> *Dispose of this hydraulic fluid. Never reuse hydraulic fluid. Contaminated hydraulic fluid can cause clutch problems.*

10. Place a shop cloth under the banjo bolt to catch any spilled hydraulic fluid that will leak out.

11. Unscrew the banjo bolt (B, **Figure 111**) securing the clutch hose to the master cylinder. Do not lose the sealing washer on each side of the hose fitting.

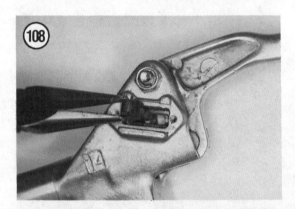

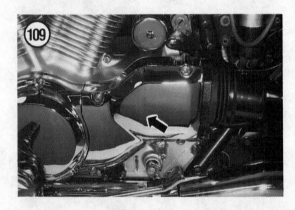

12. Remove any tie wraps or hose clamps securing the hose assembly to the frame.

NOTE
Prior to removing the clutch hose make a drawing of the hose routing through the frame. It is easy to forget how it was, once it has been removed. Replace the hose exactly as it was, avoiding any sharp turns.

13. Pull the clutch hose out from the front fork area and along the top of the frame.

14. Install a new hose, sealing washers and banjo bolts in the reverse order of removal, noting the following:

a. Be sure to install new sealing washers.

b. Tighten the fittings and banjo bolts to the torque specifications listed in **Table 2**.

c. Bleed the clutch system as described under *Bleeding the System* in this chapter.

d. Test ride the bike slowly at first to make sure the clutch is operating correctly.

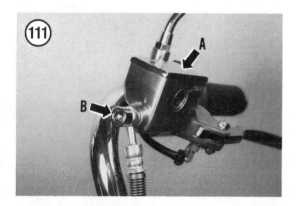

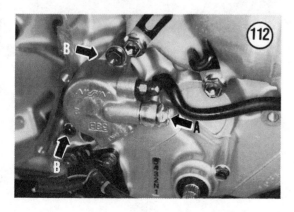

SLAVE CYLINDER

Removal

CAUTION
Cover the fuel tank, front fender and instrument cluster with a heavy cloth or plastic tarp to protect them from accidental hydraulic fluid spills. Wash hydraulic fluid from any painted or plated surfaces or plastic parts immediately as it will destroy the finish. Use soapy water and rinse completely.

1. Remove the bolts securing the secondary drive cover (**Figure 109**) and remove the cover and bolt spacers.

2. Remove the cap and attach a hose to the bleed valve (**Figure 110**) on the slave cylinder, then place the loose end in a container.

3. Open the bleed valve and apply the lever on the clutch master cylinder to pump the hydraulic fluid out of the master cylinder and the clutch hose assembly. Continue to operate the lever until the fluid is pumped out of the hose assembly. Close the bleed valve and remove the hose. Dispose of this hydraulic fluid never re-use hydraulic fluid.

4. Clean the top of the master cylinder of all dirt and foreign matter.

5. Loosen the screws (A, **Figure 111**) securing the master cylinder top cover. Pull up and loosen the cover and the diaphragm. This will allow air to enter the reservoir and allow any residual hydraulic fluid to drain out more quickly in the next steps.

6. Place a container under the clutch hose at the slave cylinder.

7. Remove the banjo bolt and sealing washers (A, **Figure 112**) securing the clutch hose to the slave cylinder.

8. Remove the clutch hose and let any residual hydraulic fluid drain out into the container. Dispose of this hydraulic fluid; never re-use hydraulic fluid. To prevent the entry of moisture and dirt, tape over the threaded bore in the slave cylinder.

WARNING
Never reuse hydraulic fluid. Contaminated hydraulic fluid can cause clutch problems.

9. Remove the bolts (B, **Figure 112**) securing the slave cylinder to the crankcase and remove the slave cylinder assembly.

Disassembly/Inspection/Assembly

Refer to **Figure 113** for this procedure.

1. Remove the retainer (**Figure 114**) from the top of the piston.

2. Place a shop cloth or piece of soft wood at the end of the slave cylinder against the piston.

3. Support the slave cylinder on wooden blocks with the piston side facing *down*. Space the cylinder so that there is room for piston removal. Also, place a wooden block and thick rags directly underneath the piston to stop it when it is forced out of the slave cylinder.

WARNING
Removing the piston with compressed air forces it out of its bore like a bullet. In the next step, keep your hands and fingers out of the way. Wear shop gloves and safety goggles when using compressed air to remove the piston.

4. Hold the top of the slave cylinder securely with one hand (fingers out of the way) and apply compressed air pressure through the hydraulic line fitting to remove the piston and spring. Make sure the bleed valve fitting is tight.

5. Remove the piston and spring from the workbench.

CAUTION
In the following step, do not use a sharp tool to remove the piston seal from the piston. Do not damage the piston surface.

6. Carefully remove the piston seal from the piston. Discard the piston seal as it must be replaced.

7. Inspect the slave cylinder body (**Figure 115**) for damage. If damaged, replace the slave cylinder as an assembly. The body cannot be replaced separately.

8. Inspect the hydraulic fluid passageway (A, **Figure 116**) at base of the piston bore. Make sure it is clean and open. Clean with compressed air.

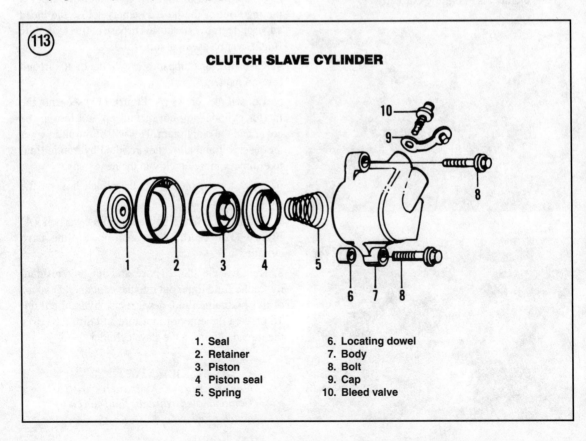

(113)

CLUTCH SLAVE CYLINDER

1. Seal
2. Retainer
3. Piston
4 Piston seal
5. Spring
6. Locating dowel
7. Body
8. Bolt
9. Cap
10. Bleed valve

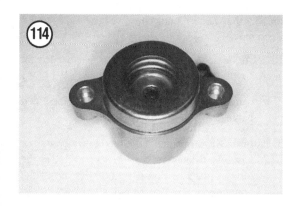

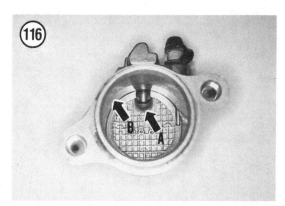

9. Inspect the cylinder wall (B, **Figure 116**) for scratches, scoring or other damage. If rusty or corroded, replace the slave cylinder as an assembly.

10. Measure the cylinder bore with a bore gauge. Replace the slave cylinder if the bore diameter exceeds the service limit dimension listed in **Table 1**.

11. Inspect the piston (A, **Figure 117**) for scratches, scoring or other damage. If damaged, replace the slave cylinder as an assembly. The piston cannot be replaced separately.

12. Measure the outside diameter of the piston (B, **Figure 117**) with a micrometer. Replace the slave cylinder if the outside diameter is worn to the service limit dimension listed in **Table 1**.

13. Inspect the caliper mounting bolt holes on the body. If worn or damaged, replace the slave cylinder assembly.

14. Remove the bleed screw (A, **Figure 118**). Make sure it is clean and open. Apply compressed air to the opening and make sure it is clear.

15. Inspect the threads in the bore (B, **Figure 118**) for the banjo bolt. If worn or damaged, clean out with a metric thread tap or replace the slave cylinder assembly.

16. Inspect the spring for damage or sagging. Replace if necessary. Suzuki does not provide service information for spring free length.

17. If serviceable, clean the slave cylinder with rubbing alcohol and rinse with clean hydraulic fluid.

NOTE
Never reuse the old piston seal. Very minor damage or age deterioration can make the seal useless.

18. Coat the new piston seal (**Figure 119**) with fresh hydraulic fluid.

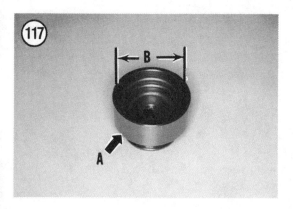

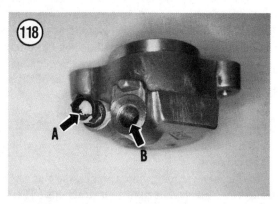

19. Carefully install the new piston seal in the groove in piston (**Figure 120**). Make sure the seal is properly seated in the groove.

20. Coat the piston, cylinder wall and piston seal with fresh hydraulic fluid.

21. Position the spring with the tapered end toward the piston and install the spring into the backside of the piston.

22. Carefully install the piston into the slave cylinder (**Figure 121**). Push the piston in until it bottoms (**Figure 122**).

23. Install the retainer (**Figure 114**) over the piston.

Installation

1. Make sure the clutch left-hand push rod seal (**Figure 123**) is in place and is not leaking.

2. Push the clutch left-hand push rod (A, **Figure 124**) all the way in until it bottoms.

3. If removed, install the locating dowels (B, **Figure 124**).

4. Install the slave cylinder assembly onto the crankcase.

5. Install the bolts (B, **Figure 112**) securing the slave cylinder to the crankcase. Tighten the bolts securely.

6. Install a new sealing washer on each side of the hose fitting. Install the banjo bolt (A, **Figure 112**) securing the clutch hose to the slave cylinder. Tighten the banjo bolt to the torque specification listed in **Table 2**.

7. Install the secondary drive cover, bolt spacers and mounting bolts. Tighten the bolts securely.

BLEEDING THE SYSTEM

Bleed the clutch system when the clutch lever feels spongy, there is a leak in the system, a component was replaced or the system was drained.

This section describes two methods on bleeding the clutch system. The first is with a vacuum pump, and the second is with a container and a piece of clear tubing.

1. Unbolt and remove the secondary drive cover (**Figure 109**) and its bolt spacers.

2. Remove the dust cap from the bleed valve on the slave cylinder.

3A. If using a vacuum pump, assemble the pump by following the manufacturer's instructions. Then connect the vacuum pump hose (**Figure 110**) to the bleed valve.

3B. If a vacuum pump is not being used, perform the following:

   a. Connect a piece of clear tubing onto the bleed valve.

   b. Insert the other end of the tube into a container partially filled with new brake fluid. Tie the tube in place so that it cannot slip out of the container.

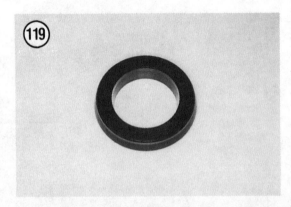

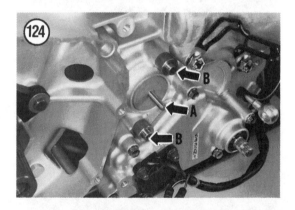

4. Clean the clutch master cylinder cover of all dirt and foreign matter.

5. Turn the front wheel so that the clutch master cylinder is level. On models with riser handlebars, loosen the clutch master cylinder mounting bolts and reposition the master cylinder on the handlebar so that the reservoir is level, then tighten the mounting bolts.

6. Cover the are underneath the clutch master cylinder (wheel, fenderand forks) witha heavy cloth to protect the parts from the accidental spilling of hydraulic fluid.

CAUTION
Wash spilled hydraulic fluid from any plastic, painted or plated surface immediately as it will destroy the finish. Clean with soapy water and rinse completely.

7. Unscrew and remove the clutch master cylinder top cover (A, **Figure 111**) and diaphragm.

8. Fill the master cylinder with hydraulic fluid.

WARNING
Use DOT 3 or DOT 4 hydraulic fluid from a sealed container. Do not intermix different brands of fluid. Do not use a silicone base DOT 5 brake fluid as it can damage the clutch components leading to clutch system failure.

NOTE
When bleeding the clutch, check the fluid level in the clutch master cylinder often. If the reservoir runs dry, air will enter the system. If this occurs, the entire procedure must be repeated.

9A. If using a vacuum pump, perform the following:

   a. Operate the vacuum pump (**Figure 125**) several times to create a vacuum in the attached hose.

   b. Open the bleed valve 1/4 turn to allow air and fluid to be extracted through the line. When the flow of air and fluid starts to slow down, close the bleed valve.

   c. Operate the clutch lever several times and release it.

   d. Refill the master cylinder reservoir as necessary.

e. Repeat these steps until there is a solid feel when operating the clutch lever and there are no bubbles being released from the system.

9B. If a vacuum pump is not being used, perform the following:

a. Operate the clutch lever several times until resistance is felt, then hold it in its applied position. If the system was opened or drained completely, there will be no initial resistance at the clutch lever.

b. Open the bleed valve 1/4 and allow the lever to travel to its limit, then close the bleed valve and release the clutch lever.

c. Operate the clutch lever several times and release it.

d. Refill the master cylinder reservoir as necessary.

e. Repeat these steps until there is a solid feel when operating the clutch lever and there are no bubbles being released from the system.

NOTE
If you are flushing the system, continue with Step 9 until the fluid being drawn from the system is clean.

10. Remove the vacuum pump or container and hose from the system. Snap the bleed valve dust cap onto the bleed valve.

11. If necessary, add fluid to correct the level in the reservoir. It should be to the upper level line (**Figure 126**).

12. Install the diaphragm and cover. Tighten the screws securely.

13. If the master cylinder was repositioned on the handlebar, reinstall it onto its original mounting position. Then tighten the upper clamp bolt first, then the lower bolt to the torque specification listed in **Table 2**.

14. Recheck the feel of the clutch lever. It should be firm and offer the same resistance each time it's operated. If the lever feels spongy, check all of the hoses for leaks and bleed the system again.

15. Test the clutch by starting the engine with the transmission in NEUTRAL. Pull the clutch in and then shift the transmission into first gear. If the bike jumps forward and the engine dies, the clutch has not been bled correctly. When the bike is stopped with the engine running and the transmission in first gear, the bike should move smoothly as the clutch lever is being released. Bleed the clutch assembly again, if necessary.

Table 1 GENERAL CLUTCH SPECIFICATIONS

Item	New mm (in.)	Service limit mm (in.)
Clutch plate warp	–	0.10 (0.004)
Clutch spring free length		
No. A	–	27.6 (1.09)
No. B	–	20.0 (0.79)
Number of clutch plates		
Steel clutch plates	9	–
Friction plates		
No. 1	9	
No. 2	1	
Friction plate thickness		
No. 1 (quantity 9)	2.72-2.88 (0.107-0.113)	2.42 (0.095)
No. 2 (quantity 1)	3.45-3.55 (0.136-0.140)	3.15 (0.124)
Friction plate claw width		
No. 1 (quantity 9)	15.8-16.0 (0.622-0.630)	15.2 (0.600)
No. 2 (quantity 1)	15.9-16.0 (0.626-0.630)	15.2 (0.600)
Clutch master cylinder		
Bore inside diameter	14.000-14.043 (0.5512-0.5529)	– –
Piston outer diameter	13.957-13.984 (0.5495-0.5506)	– –
Clutch slave cylinder		
Bore inside diameter	35.700-35.762 (1.4055-1.4079)	– –
Piston outer diameter	35.650-35.675 (1.4035-1.4045)	– –

6

Table 2 CLUTCH TIGHTENING TORQUES

Item	N·m	in.-lb.	ft.-lb.
Clutch hub nut	90-110	—	66-81
Clutch spring bolts	8-12	71-106	—
Clutch master cylinder clamp bolts	8-12	71-106	—
Clutch hose banjo bolts	20-25	—	15-18

CHAPTER SEVEN

TRANSMISSION AND
INTERNAL SHIFT MECHANISM

To gain access to the transmission and internal gearshift components, it is necessary to remove the engine and separate the crankcase as described in Chapter Four and Chapter Five. Once the crankcase has been disassembled, the transmission, shift drum and shift fork assemblies can be removed from the crankcase.

These overhaul procedures refer to the transmission countershaft and mainshaft. The mainshaft is connected to the clutch and the countershaft is connected to the secondary bevel gear assembly attached to the left-hand side of the crankcase.

Transmission ratios are listed in **Table 1** and service specifications for the internal shift mechanism are listed in **Table 2**. **Table 1** and **Table 2** are found at the end of this chapter.

TRANSMISSION

Removal/Installation

Removal and installation of the transmission mainshaft and countershaft are described under *Crankcase Disassembly* and *Crankcase Assembly* in Chapter Five.

Preliminary Inspection

After the transmission shaft assemblies have been removed from the crankcase, clean and inspect the assemblies prior to disassembling them. Place the assembled shaft into a large can or plastic bucket and thoroughly clean with a petroleum based solvent such as kerosene and a stiff brush. Dry with compressed air or let it sit on rags to drip dry. Repeat for the other shaft assembly.

1. After they have been cleaned, visually inspect the components of the assemblies for excessive wear. Any burrs, pitting or roughness on the teeth of a gear will cause wear on the mating gear. Minor roughness can be cleaned up with an oilstone but there's little point in attempting to remove deep scars.

NOTE
Defective gears should be replaced. It is
a good idea to replace the mating gear

on the other shaft even though it may not show as much wear or damage.

2. Carefully check the engagement dogs. If any are chipped, worn, rounded or missing, the affected gear must be replaced.

3. Rotate the transmission bearings in both crankcase halves by hand. Check for roughness, noise and radial play. Any bearing that is suspect should be replaced as described in this chapter.

4. If the transmission shafts are satisfactory and are not going to be disassembled, apply assembly oil or engine oil to all components and reinstall them in the crankcase as described in Chapter Five.

NOTE
When disassembling the transmission, pay attention to any additional shims that may have been added by a previous owner. These may have been added to take up the tolerance of worn components and must be reinstalled in the same position since the shims have developed a wear pattern. If new parts are going to be installed these shims

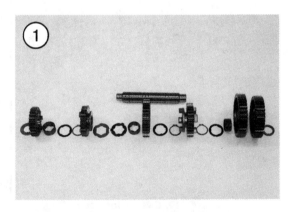

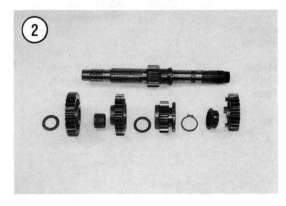

may be eliminated. This is something you must determine upon reassembly.

Transmission Service Notes

1. As you remove a part from the shaft set it in the exact order of removal and in the same position from which it was removed. Refer to **Figure 1** for the mainshaft and **Figure 2** for the countershaft. This is an easy way to remember the correct relationship of all parts.

2. The circlips are a tight fit on the transmission shafts. Replace all circlips during reassembly.

3. Circlips will turn and fold over making removal and installation difficult. To ease replacement, open the circlips with a pair of circlip pliers while at the same time holding the back of the circlip with a pair of pliers and remove them. Repeat for installation.

7

1987-1996 Models
Four-Speed Transmission

Mainshaft disassembly

Refer to **Figure 3** for this procedure.

1. If not cleaned in the *Preliminary Inspection* sequence, place the assembled shaft into a large can or plastic bucket and thoroughly clean with solvent and a stiff brush. Dry with compressed air or let it sit on rags to dry.

2. Slide off the washer and the reduction gear.

3. Slide off the first gear and first gear bushing.

4. Slide off the splined washer and remove the circlip.

5. Slide off the sliding dog No. 1.

6. Remove the circlip and slide off the splined washer.

7. Slide off the second gear and second gear bushing.

8. From the other end of the shaft, remove the washer.

9. Slide off the Fourth gear and Fourth gear bushing.

10. Slide off the splined washer and remove the circlip.

11. Slide off the sliding dog No. 2.

12. Remove the circlip and slide off the splined washer.

13. Slide off the third gear and third gear bushing.

14. Slide the No.1 lockwasher off the shaft.

③

TRANSMISSION (4-SPEED 1987-1996)

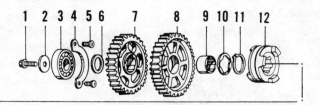

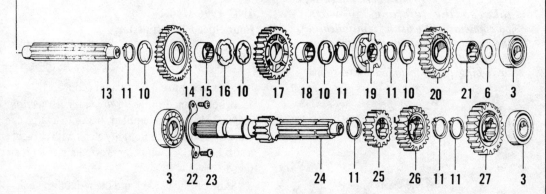

1. Bolt (short)	11. Circlip	19. Sliding dog No. 2
2. Washer	12. Sliding dog No. 1	20. Mainshaft 4th gear
3. Bearing	13. Mainshaft	21. Mainshaft 4th gear
4. Bearing retainer	14. Mainshaft 2nd gear	bushing
5. Screw	15. Mainshaft 2nd gear	22. Bearing retainer
6. Washer	bushing	23. Screw
7. Reduction gear	16. Tanged lockwasher	24. Countershaft/ 1st gear
8. Mainshaft 1st gear	17. Mainshaft 3rd gear	25. Countershaft 2nd gear
9. Mainshaft 1st gear	18. Mainshaft 3rd gear	26. Countershaft 3rd gear
bushing	bushing	27. Countershaft 4th gear
10. Splined washer		

15. Rotate the No.2 lockwasher in either direction to disengage its splines from the grooves on the transmission shaft. Slide off the No. 2 lockwasher.

16. Inspect the mainshaft components as described under *Inspection (All Models)* in this chapter

Mainshaft assembly

Refer to **Figure 3** for this procedure.

1. Apply a light coat of clean engine oil to all sliding surfaces.

NOTE
Perform Steps 2-13 by installing the parts from the mainshaft's left-hand side (except for the No. 1 lockwasher installed in Step 3).

NOTE
The No. 2 lockwasher is a splined lockwasher with 3 slots cut into its outer edge. The No. 1 lockwasher is a splined lockwasher with 3 offset arms that lock into the No. 2 lockwasher slots.

2. Install the No. 2 lockwasher into the middle transmission shaft groove. Then turn the lockwasher and align its raised splines with the transmission splines. This alignment locks the washer in place so that it cannot slide off the shaft.

3. Install the No. 1 lockwasher from the shaft's right-hand side (threaded hole side). Slide the No. 1 lockwasher in place so that its offset arms lock into the slots in the No. 2 lockwasher.

4. Slide on the third gear bushing and push it against the splined lockwasher.

5. Position the third gear with the sliding dog No. 2 receptacles going on last and slide on the third gear.

6. Slide on the splined washer and install the circlip. Make sure the circlip is correctly seated in the shaft groove.

7. Position the sliding dog No. 2 with the shift dogs side going on first and slide on the shift dog.

8. Install the circlip and make sure it is correctly seated in the shaft groove.

9. Slide on the splined washer.

10. Slide on the fourth gear bushing and push it up against the splined washer.

11. Position the fourth gear with the shift dog receptacles going on first and slide on the 4th gear.

12. Apply a light coat of multipurpose grease to the backside of the washer to hold it in place. Install the washer against the fourth gear.

13. Hold onto the assembled gear components and turn the mainshaft around.

NOTE
Perform Steps 14-24 by installing the parts from the mainshaft's right-hand side.

14. Slide on the second gear bushing and push it up against the splined lockwasher.

15. Position the second gear with the shift dog receptacles going on last and slide on the second gear.

16. Slide on the splined washer.

17. Install the circlip and make sure it is correctly seated in the shaft groove.

18. Position the sliding dog No. 1 with the smaller size dogs side going on first and slide on the shift dog.

19. Install the circlip and make sure it is correctly seated in the shaft groove.

20. Slide on the splined washer.

21. Slide on the first gear bushing and push it up against the splined washer.

22. Position the first gear with the shift dog receptacles going on first and slide on the first gear.

23. Position the reduction gear with the flush side going on last and install the gear.

24. Apply a light coat of multipurpose grease to the backside of the washer to hold it in place. Install the washer up against the fourth gear.

25. Make sure all circlips are correctly seated in the countershaft grooves.

26. Make sure each gear engages the adjoining gear properly, where applicable.

Countershaft disassembly

Refer to **Figure 3** for this procedure.

1. If not cleaned in the *Preliminary Inspection* sequence, place the assembled shaft into a large can or plastic bucket and thoroughly clean with solvent and a stiff brush. Dry with compressed air or let it sit on rags to dry.

2. Slide off the fourth gear.

3. Remove the circlip.

4. Remove the next circlip adjacent to the third gear.

5. Slide off third gear and the second gear.

6. Remove the circlip.

7. Inspect the countershaft components as described under *Inspection (All Models)* in this chapter

Countershaft assembly

1. Apply a light coat of clean engine oil to all sliding surfaces prior to installing any parts.
2. Install the circlip in the third groove in the shaft. Make sure the circlip is correctly seated in the countershaft groove.
3. Position the second gear with the flush side going on last and slide the second gear on.
4. Position the third gear with the flush side going on first and slide the third gear on.
5. Install the circlip in the second groove in the shaft. Make sure the circlip is correctly seated in the countershaft groove.
6. Install the circlip in the first groove in the shaft. Make sure the circlip is correctly seated in the countershaft groove.
7. Position the fourth gear with the flush side going on last and slide the fourth gear on.
8. Make sure all circlips are correctly seated in the countershaft grooves.
9. After both transmission shafts have been assembled, mesh the 2 assemblies together in the correct position. Check that each gear engages properly with the adjoining gear. This is your last check prior to installing the shaft assemblies into the crankcase; make sure they are correctly assembled.

1997-on Models
Five-Speed Transmission

Mainshaft disassembly

Refer to **Figure 4** for this procedure.
1. If not cleaned in the *Preliminary Inspection* sequence, place the assembled shaft into a large can or plastic bucket and thoroughly clean with solvent and a stiff brush. Dry with compressed air or let it sit on rags to dry.
2. Slide off the washer and the reduction gear.
3. Slide off the first gear and first gear bushing.
4. Slide off the splined washer and remove the circlip.
5. Slide off the third gear.
6. Remove the circlip and slide off the splined washer.

7. Slide off the second gear and second gear bushing.
8. From the other end of the shaft, remove the washer.
9. Slide off the fifth gear and fifth gear bushing.
10. Slide off the splined washer and remove the circlip.
11. Slide off the fourth gear.
12. Slide off the No. 1 lockwasher.
13. Rotate the No. 2 lockwasher in either direction to disengage its splines from the grooves on the transmission shaft. Slide off the No.2 lockwasher.
14. Keep the parts in the exact order of removal and in the same position from which it was removed as shown in **Figure 1**.
15. Inspect the mainshaft components as described under *Inspection (All Models)* in this chapter

Mainshaft assembly

1. Apply a light coat of clean engine oil to all sliding surfaces.

> *NOTE*
> *Perform Steps 2-8 by installing the parts from the mainshaft's left-hand side (except for the No. 1 lockwasher installed in Step 3).*

> *NOTE*
> *The No. 2 lockwasher is a splined lockwasher with 3 slots cut into its outer edge. The No. 1 lockwasher is a splined lockwasher with 3 offset arms that lock into the No. 2 lockwasher slots.*

2. Install the No. 2 lockwasher into the second groove (**Figure 5**) from the shaft's left-hand side. Then turn the lockwasher and align its raised splines with the transmission splines. This alignment locks the washer in place so that it cannot slide off the shaft.
3. Install the No. 1 lockwasher from the shaft's right-hand side (threaded hole side). Slide the No. 1 lockwasher in place so that its offset arms lock into the slots in the No. 2 lockwasher (**Figure 6**).
4. Position the fourth gear with the shift fork groove (A, **Figure 7**) going on first and install the fourth gear (**Figure 8**).
5. Install the circlip (B, **Figure 7**). Make sure the circlip is seated correctly in the mainshaft groove.
6. Slide on the splined washer (C, **Figure 7**).

④

TRANSMISSION (5-SPEED 1997-ON)

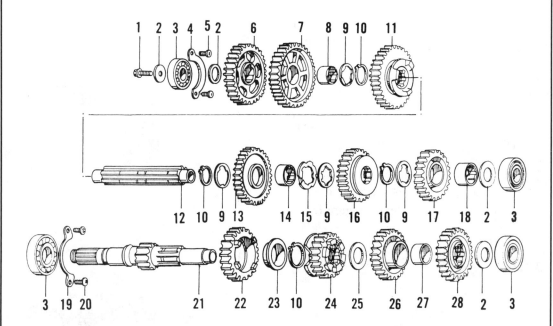

1. Bolt (short)
2. Washer
3. Bearing
4. Bearing retainer
5. Screw
6. Reduction gear
7. Mainshaft 1st gear
8. Mainshaft 1st gear bushing
9. Splined washer
10. Circlip
11. Mainshaft 3rd gear
12. Mainshaft
13. Mainshaft 2nd gear
14. Mainshaft 2nd gear bushing
15. Tanged lockwasher
16. Mainshaft 3rd gear
17. Mainshaft 5th gear
18. Mainshaft 5th gear bushing
19. Bearing retainer
20. Screw
21. Countershaft/ 1st gear
22. Countershaft 3rd gear
23 Countershaft 3rd gear bushing
24. Countershaft 2nd gear
25. Washer
26. Countershaft 4th gear
27. Countershaft 4th gear bushing
28. Countershaft 5th gear

7

7. Align the oil hole in the fifth gear bushing (A, **Figure 9**) with the transmission shaft oil hole (B, **Figure 9**) and slide on the bushing. This alignment is necessary for proper gear lubrication.

8. Slide the fifth gear (**Figure 10**) onto the bushing.

NOTE
Perform Steps 9-17 by installing the parts from the mainshaft's right-hand side.

9. Align the oil hole in the second gear bushing (A, **Figure 11**) with the transmission shaft oil hole (B, **Figure 11**) and slide on the bushing. This alignment is necessary for proper gear lubrication.

10. Position the second gear with the shift dog receptacle side going on last and slide on the gear (**Figure 12**).

11. Position the third gear with the shift fork groove (A, **Figure 13**) going on first and install the third gear (**Figure 14**).

12. Install the circlip (B, **Figure 13**). Make sure the circlip is seated correctly in the mainshaft groove.

13. Slide on the splined washer (C, **Figure 13**).

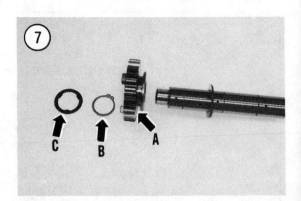

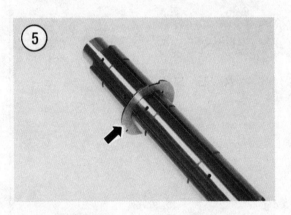

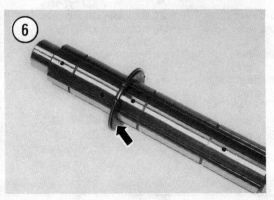

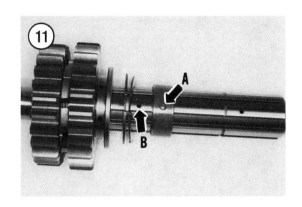

14. Align the oil hole in the first gear bushing (A, **Figure 15**) with the transmission shaft oil hole (B, **Figure 15**) and slide on the bushing. This alignment is necessary for proper gear lubrication.

15. Position the second gear with the shift dog receptacle side going on first and slide on the gear (**Figure 16**).

16. Position the reduction gear with the larger shoulder side (A, **Figure 17**) going on last and install the reduction gear (**Figure 18**).

7

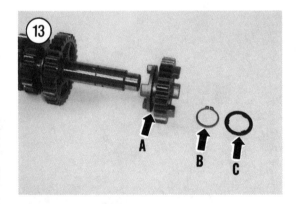

17. Apply a light coat of multipurpose grease to the backside of the washer to hold it in place. Install the washer (B, **Figure 17**).

18. Refer to **Figure 19** for correct placement of all gears. Make sure all circlips are correctly seated in the mainshaft grooves.

19. Make sure each gear engages the adjoining gear properly, where applicable.

Countershaft disassembly

Refer to **Figure 4** for this procedure.

1. If not cleaned in the *Preliminary Inspection* sequence, place the assembled shaft into a large can or plastic bucket and thoroughly clean with solvent and a stiff brush. Dry with compressed air or let it sit on rags to dry.

2. Slide off the washer.

3. Slide off the fifth gear.

4. Slide off the fourth gear and the fourth gear bushing.

5. Slide off the washer.

6. Slide off the second gear.

7. Remove the circlip.

8. Slide off the third gear and third gear bushing.

9. Keep the parts in the exact order of removal and in the same position from which it was removed as shown in **Figure 2**.

10. Inspect the countershaft components as described under *Inspection (All Models)* in this chapter

Countershaft assembly

1. Apply a light coat of clean engine oil to all sliding surfaces prior to installing any parts.

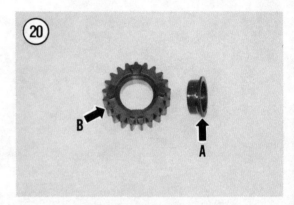

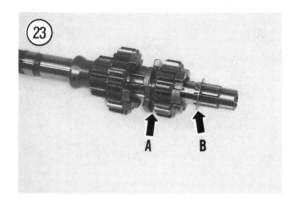

2. Position the third gear bushing with the flange side (A, **Figure 20**) going on last. Insert the third gear bushing (**Figure 21**) into the third gear.

3. Position the third gear with the shift dog side (B, **Figure 20**) side going on last and slide on the third gear and third gear bushing assembly (A, **Figure 22**).

4. Install the circlip and make sure it is correctly seated in the countershaft groove (B, **Figure 22**).

5. Position the second gear with the shift fork groove side (A, **Figure 23**) going on first and slide the second gear on the countershaft.

6. Slide on the washer (B, **Figure 23**).

7. Insert the fourth gear bushing (A, **Figure 24**) into the fourth gear (B, **Figure 24**).

8. Position the fourth gear with the long shoulder (**Figure 25**) going on last.

9. Slide on the fourth gear and fourth gear bushing assembly onto the shaft.

10. Position the fifth gear with the long shoulder (**Figure 26**) going on last and slide on the fifth gear (A, **Figure 27**).

11. Apply a light coat of multipurpose grease to the backside of the washer to hold it in place. Install the washer (B, **Figure 27**).

12. Refer to **Figure 28** for correct placement of all gears. Make sure all circlips are correctly seated in the countershaft grooves.

13. After both transmission shafts have been assembled, mesh the 2 assemblies together in the correct position (**Figure 29**). Check that each gear engages properly with the adjoining gear. This is your last check prior to installing the shaft assemblies into the crankcase; make sure they are correctly assembled.

7

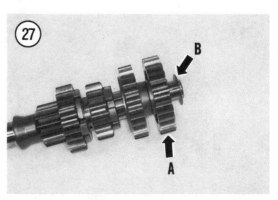

Transmission Inspection
(All Models)

1. Check each gear for excessive wear, burrs, pitting or chipped or missing teeth (**Figure 30**). Make sure the shift dogs (**Figure 31**) on the gears are in good condition. Check the shift dog receptacles (**Figure 32**) for wear or damage.

2. Check the inner splines of each gear bushing (A, **Figure 33**) for excessive wear, pitting or damage. Replace if necessary.

3. Check each gear bushing inner splines for excessive wear or damage. Replace if necessary.

4. On gears with bushings, inspect the inner surface of the gear (B, **Figure 33**) where the bushing rides for wear, pitting or damage.

5. Inspect the lockwashers (A, **Figure 34**) for wear, cracks or damage. Replace if necessary.

6. Inspect the circlips and splined washers for bending wear or damage. Replace if necessary.

7. Inspect the shift fork-to-gear clearance as described under *Internal Gearshift Mechanism* in this chapter.

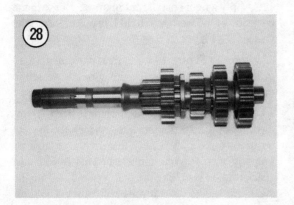

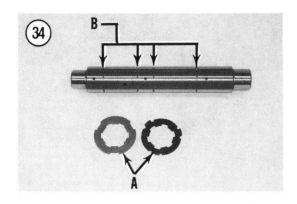

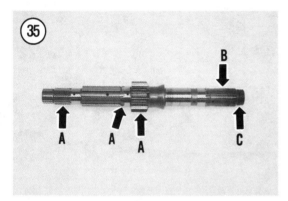

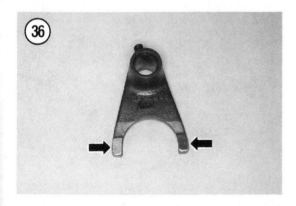

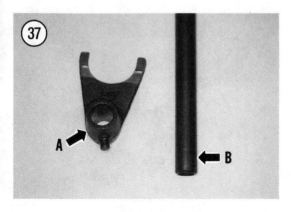

NOTE
Defective gears should be replaced. It is a good idea to replace the mating gear on the countershaft even though it may not show as much wear or damage.

8. Make sure all gears and bushings slide smoothly on their respective shaft splines.

NOTE
Install new circlips when reassembling the transmission shafts. Do not expand a circlip more than necessary to slide it over the shaft.

9. Inspect the splines and circlip grooves (B, **Figure 34**) of the mainshaft. If any are damaged, the shaft must be replaced.
10. Inspect the splines, the circlip grooves and the first gear portion (A, **Figure 35**) of the countershaft. If any are damaged, the shaft must be replaced.
11. Inspect the clutch hub splines (B, **Figure 35**) and clutch nut threads (C, **Figure 35**) of the countershaft. If any splines are damaged, the shaft must be replaced. If the threads have burrs or minor damage, clean with a proper size metric thread die.

INTERNAL GEARSHIFT MECHANISM

Removal/Installation

Removal and installation of the internal gearshift mechanism is described under *Crankcase Disassembly* and *Crankcase Assembly* in Chapter Five.

Inspection

1. Clean all parts in solvent and thoroughly dry with compressed air.
2. Inspect each shift fork for signs of wear or cracking. Check for any arc-shaped wear or burned marks on the fingers of the shift forks (**Figure 36**). This indicates that the shift fork has come in contact with the gear. The fork fingers have become excessively worn and the fork must be replaced.
3. Check the bore of each shift fork (A, **Figure 37**) and the shift fork shaft (B, **Figure 37**) for burrs, wear or pitting. Replace any worn parts.
4. Install each shift fork onto the shaft and make sure it moves freely on the shaft with no binding.

5. Check the cam follower pins (**Figure 38**) on each shift fork for wear or damage. Replace the shift fork(s) as necessary.

6. Roll the shift fork shaft on a flat surface, such as a piece of plate glass, and check for any bends. If the shaft is bent, it must be replaced.

7. Check the grooves in the shift drum (A, **Figure 39**) for wear or roughness. If any of the groove profiles have excessive wear or damage, replace the shift drum.

8. On 1997-on models, check the large shift fork (B, **Figure 39**) for wear or damage. Install it on the shift drum and move it in its normal rotational direction and check for binding.

9. Inspect the cam gear locating pins and threaded hole (**Figure 40**) in the end of the shift drum for wear or damage. Replace the shift drum if necessary.

10. Check the neutral switch contact plunger and spring for wear or damage. If the spring has sagged, replace it.

11. Check the shift drum bearings (**Figure 41**). Make sure they operate smoothly with no wear or damage. If damaged, replace as described under

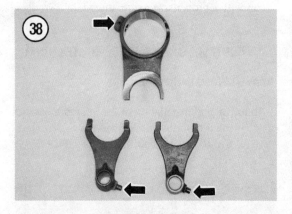

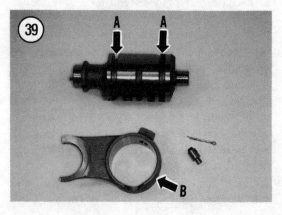

Crankcase Bearings Removal/Installation in Chapter Five.

CAUTION
It is recommended that marginally worn shift forks be replaced. Worn forks can cause the transmission to slip out of gear, leading to more serious and expensive damage.

12. Inspect the shift fork-to-gear clearance as follows:
   a. Install each shift fork into its respective gear. Use a flat feeler gauge and measure the clearance between the fork and the gear as shown in **Figure 42**. Compare to the specifications listed in **Table 2**.
   b. If the clearance is greater than specified in **Table 1**, measure the width of the gearshift fork fingers with a micrometer (**Figure 43**). Replace the shift fork(s) if worn to the service limit listed in **Table 2**.
   c. If the shift fork finger width is within tolerance, measure the shift fork groove width in the gears. Compare to the specification listed in **Table 2**. Replace the gear(s) if the groove is worn to the service limit or more.

Table 1 TRANSMISSION RATIOS AND SPECIFICATIONS

Transmission	
Type	
1987-1996	4-speed, constant mesh
1997-on	5-speed, constant mesh
Gear ratio (1987-1996)	
1st	3.000 (36/12)
2nd	1.823 (31/17)
3rd	1.333 (28/21)
4th (1987-1990)	1.041 (25/24)
4th (1991-1996)	
U.S., Canada and General	1.041 (25/24)
France, Sweden, Belgiun, Germany and Italy	1.086 (25/23)
5th	
France, Sweden, Belgium, Germany and Italy	0.969 (24/25)
Gear ratio (1997-on)	
1st	3.000 (36/12)
2nd	1.823 (31/17)
3rd	1.333 (28/21)
4th	1.086 (25/23)
5th	0.960 (24/25)

Table 2 INTERNAL SHIFT MECHANISM SERVICE SPECIFICATIONS

New	Specification mm (in.)	Service limit mm (in.)
Shift fork-to-groove clearance (in gear)	0.1-0.3 ((0.004-0.012)	0.5 (0.020)
Shift fork groove width (in gear)	5.50-5.60 (0.217-0.0220)	–
Shift fork finger thickness at gear contact point	5.30-5.40 (0.209-0.213)	–

CHAPTER EIGHT

FUEL, EMISSION CONTROL AND EXHAUST SYSTEMS

The fuel system consists of the fuel tank, main shutoff valve, sub shutoff valve, fuel pump, fuel pump relay, 2 carburetors and a separate air filter assembly for each carburetor. The exhaust system consists of 2 exhaust pipes and 2 mufflers.

The emission controls consist of crankcase emission system and on California models the Evaporative Emission Control System.

This chapter includes service procedures for all parts of the fuel system and exhaust system. Air filter service is covered in Chapter Three.

Carburetor specifications are listed in **Table 1** at the end of this chapter.

> *WARNING*
> *Gasoline is a known carcinogen, as well as extremely flammable, and must be handled carefully. Wear latex gloves when working on components when you may come in contact with gasoline. If your skin comes in contact with gasoline, rinse it off immediately and thoroughly wash with soap and warm water.*

CARBURETOR OPERATION

For proper operation, a gasoline engine must be supplied with fuel and air mixed in proper proportions by weight. A mixture in which there is an excess of fuel is said to be rich. A lean mixture is one which contains insufficient fuel. A properly adjusted carburetor supplies the proper mixture to the engine under all operating conditions.

Each carburetor consists of several major systems. A float and float valve mechanism maintains a constant fuel level in the float bowl. The pilot system supplies fuel at low speeds. The main fuel system supplies fuel at medium and high speeds.

The choke circuit is a bystarter system in which the choke lever on the left-hand side, below the fuel tank opens an enrichment valve rather than closing a butterfly valve in the venturi area as on some carburetors. In the open position, the pilot jet discharges a stream of fuel into the starter circuit from the float chamber through the starter jet, to enrichen the mixture when the engine is cold.

CARBURETOR SERVICE

Major carburetor service (removal and cleaning) should be performed if the engine performs poorly, hesitates and there is little or no response to mixture adjustment. Alterations in jet size, throttle slide cutaway and changes in jet needle position, should be attempted only if you're experienced in this type of tuning work; a bad guess could result in poor performance or costly engine damage. If, after servicing the carburetor and making the adjustments described

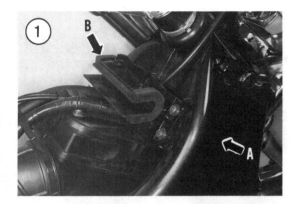

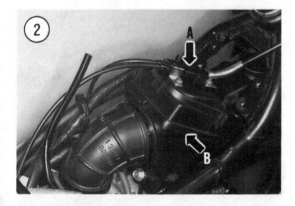

in this chapter, the bike does not perform correctly (and assuming that other factors affecting performance are correct, such as ignition component condition), the bike should be checked by a dealer or a qualified performance tuning specialist.

CARBURETOR ASSEMBLY

Removal/Installation

Remove each carburetor and its throttle cable as an assembled unit. Leaving the cables attached to both will save time during the installation procedure and make the synchronization procedure a lot easier.

1. Remove both seats as described in Chapter Thirteen.
2. Remove the fuel tank as described in this chapter.
3. Remove both frame head side covers (A, **Figure 1**) as described in Chapter Thirteen.
4. Disconnect the battery negative lead as described in Chapter Nine.
5. Remove the bolts securing the fuel tank front mounting bracket (B, **Figure 1**) and remove the bracket.
6. Remove the right-hand side cover on the front cylinder head and the left-hand side cover on the rear cylinder head.
7. Loosen the throttle cable adjuster locknut at both carburetors.
8. Remove the screws (A, **Figure 2**) securing the throttle cable joint to the air filter housing and remove the joint from the clip on the air filter housing.
9. Remove the front air filter air box assembly (B, **Figure 2**).
10. Separate the throttle cable joint and disconnect the 2 carburetor throttle cables from the plastic fitting of the throttle grip throttle cable, then move the throttle grip throttle cable out of the way.
11. Remove the choke bystarter control lever assembly from the frame (**Figure 3**), then move the assembly out of the way. Do not try to disconnect the choke cable from the carburetor at this time.
12. At the front carburetor, perform the following:
    a. Loosen the clamp screw (A, **Figure 4**) on the air inlet pipe and remove the pipe (B, **Figure 4**).
    b. Loosen the clamp screws (**Figure 5**) at the cylinder head inlet pipe.
    c. Slide the clamp onto the inlet pipe.

d. Partially remove the front carburetor from the front cylinder head.

13. At the rear carburetor, perform the following:

a. Remove the screws (A, **Figure 6**) securing the wiring harness electrical connector panel. Unhook the connectors from the panel (B, **Figure 6**) and remove the panel.

b. Remove the front ignition coil (A, **Figure 7**) as described in Chapter Nine.

c. Disconnect the fuel pump outlet hose (B, **Figure 7**). Plug the end of the hose to prevent the entry of foreign matter and prevent any loss of any residual fuel in the line.

d. Loosen the screws on the clamp (A, **Figure 8**) securing the air inlet pipe and remove the pipe (B, **Figure 8**).

e. Loosen the clamping screw (**Figure 9**) on the intake pipe and move the band away from the carburetor.

14. On California models, disconnect the evaporation hose from each carburetor.

15. Move the rear carburetor assembly partially up and out of the frame area, then unscrew and disconnect the choke bystarter cable (**Figure 10**) from the rear carburetor. Move the cable out of the way.

16. Carefully remove both the carburetor assembly and their attached cables. Make sure all cables and hoses necessary for carburetor removal are disconnected. Take the assembly to a workbench for disassembly and cleaning.

17. Install by reversing these removal steps, noting the following:

a. Make sure the carburetors are fully seated in the rubber holders attached to the cylinder head. You should feel a solid bottoming out when they are correctly seated.

b. Make sure the screws on the clamping bands are tight to avoid a vacuum loss and possible engine damage from a lean fuel mixture.

c. Adjust the throttle cables as described in Chapter Three.

CARBURETOR SERVICE

Carburetor disassembly and assembly is separated into 3 different procedures. The piston valve assembly and coasting valve are basically the same on both the front and rear carburetors and are covered in one procedure. The components in the float chamber area, floats and jets, vary considerably between the

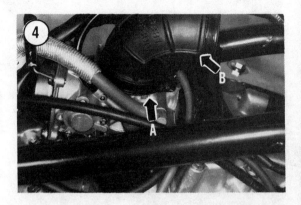

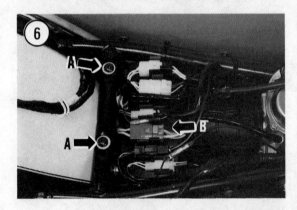

front and rear carburetors and are covered separately to avoid confusion.

Piston Valve Assembly and Coasting Valve

Refer to the following illustrations for this procedure:
 a. **Figure 11**–front carburetor.
 b. **Figure 12**–rear carburetor.
Disassemble only one carburetor at a time to prevent accidental interchange of parts.

Disassembly

1. Remove the screws (A, **Figure 13**) securing the top cover and remove the cover (B, **Figure 13**). Note the location of any hose clamps, that must be reinstalled in the same location.
2. Remove the spring and the piston valve/diaphragm from the carburetor.
3. Loosen the screws (**Figure 14**) securing the jet needle stopper plate.
4. Use needlenose pliers and remove the stopper plate from the piston valve.
5. Turn the assembly over and remove the jet needle and spring.
6. Remove the screws securing the coasting valve cover and remove the cover (**Figure 15**).
7. Remove the spring (**Figure 16**) and the diaphragm (A, **Figure 17**) from the carburetor.

Assembly

1. Install the coasting valve diaphragm (A, **Figure 17**) onto the carburetor. Align the hole in the diaphragm with the hole in the carburetor body (B, **Figure 17**).
2. Install the spring (**Figure 16**) onto the diaphragm.
3. Install the coasting valve cover (**Figure 15**) and screws. Tighten the screws securely.
4. Install the spring into the piston valve.
5. Install the jet needle (**Figure 18**) through the spring and into the hole in the bottom of the piston valve.
6. Use needlenose pliers and install the stopper plate and screws into the piston valve (**Figure 19**). Align the screw holes and tighten the screws securely.
7. Install the piston valve/diaphragm into the carburetor (**Figure 20**). Be sure to align the tab hole in the diaphragm with the hole in the carburetor body (**Figure 21**).
8. Insert your finger into the carburetor venturi and hold the piston valve up so the diaphragm is in the raised position. This will lessen the chances of it getting pinched when the top cover is installed.
9. Install the spring (A, **Figure 22**) into the piston valve and install the top cover (B, **Figure 22**). Make sure the diaphragm tab hole is still aligned with the hole in the body.
10. Push the cover down while guiding the jet needle into the needle jet (**Figure 23**). Push the cover all

⑪

FRONT CARBURETOR ASSEMBLY

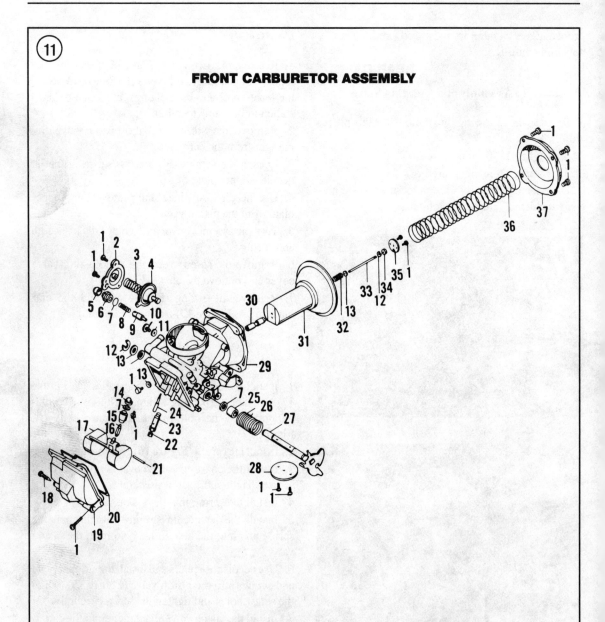

1. Screw	14. Filter screen	26. Spring
2. Cover	15. Needle valve seat	27. Throttle valve shaft
3. Spring	16. Needle valve	28. Throttle valve
4. Coasting valve	17. Float	29. Body
5. Boot	18. Drain screw	30. Needle jet
6. Nut	19. Float bowl	31. Piston valve/diaphragm
7. O-ring	20. O-ring gasket	32. Spring
8. Spring	21. Float pivot pin	33. Jet needle
9. Choke plunger	22. Main jet	34. Spacer
10. Balance screw	23. Main jet holder	35. Stopper plate
11. Washer	24. Pilot jet	36. Spring
12. E-clip	25. Bushing	37. Cover
13. Washer		

REAR CARBURETOR ASSEMBLY

1. Screw
2. Clip
3. Cover
4. Spring
5. Screw
6. Stopper plate
7. Spacer
8. Jet needle
9. Washer
10. Spring
11. Piston valve/diaphragm
12. Needle jet
13. Boot
14. Nut
15. O-ring
16. Spring
17. Choke plunger
18. Pilot screw
19. Spring
20. O-ring
21. Washer
22. Throttle valve shaft
23. Throttle stop screw
24. Throttle valve
25. Pilot jet
26. Balance screw
27. Needle valve
    stopper screw
28. Main jet
29. Drain screw
30. Float bowl
31. Gasket
32. Float pivot pin
33. Float
34. Needle valve assembly
35. Filter screen
36. Cover
37. Spring
38. Coasting valve
39. Body

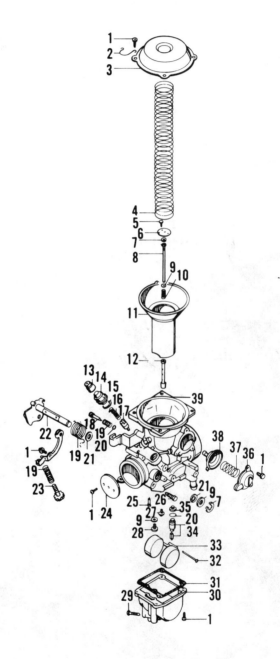

8

the way down and install the screws and any hose clamps in the correct location.

11. Tighten the screws (A, **Figure 13**) securely.

Front Carburetor Float Chamber and Carburetor Body Disassembly/Assembly

Refer to **Figure 11** for this procedure.

1. Remove the screws securing the float bowl and remove the float bowl and O-ring seal.

2. Push the float pin (A, **Figure 24**) out of the mounting boss and remove it.

3. Remove the float (B, **Figure 24**) and needle valve assembly.

4. Remove the screw (A, **Figure 25**) securing the needle valve seat and filter assembly. Remove the needle valve seat and filter assembly (B, **Figure 25**).

5. Unscrew the main jet (A, **Figure 26**) and the main jet holder (B, **Figure 26**).

6. Unscrew the pilot jet (**Figure 27**).

7. Remove the needle jet (**Figure 28**).

8. Remove the O-ring seal (**Figure 29**) from the float bowl.

9. Remove the drain screw from the float bowl.

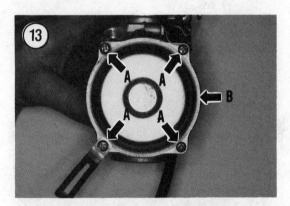

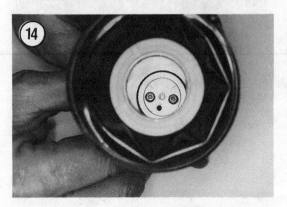

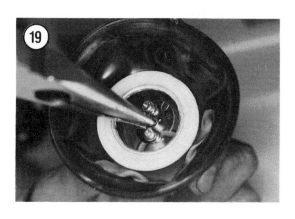

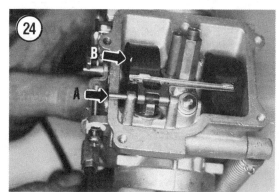

8

NOTE
*Further disassembly is neither necessary nor recommended. If throttle shaft or butterfly valve (**Figure 30**) are damaged, take the carburetor body to a dealer for replacement.*

10. Clean and inspect all parts as described under *Cleaning and Inspection* in this chapter.

11. Reverse these steps to assemble the carburetor while noting the following:

   a. Make sure to install the O-ring seal onto the needle valve. Then install the needle valve seat and filter assembly (B, **Figure 25**) into the carburetor. Push the assembly down until it bottoms out.

   b. Adjust the idle speed and synchronize the carburetors as described in Chapter Three.

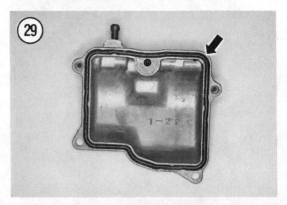

Rear Carburetor Float Chamber and Carburetor Body Disassembly/Assembly

Refer to **Figure 12** for this procedure.

1. Remove the screws securing the float bowl and remove the float bowl and gasket.

2. Unscrew the main jet (**Figure 31**).

3. To remove the needle jet (**Figure 32**), turn the carburetor body on it side and tap on the other side of the carburetor body. Once the needle jet is loose, withdraw it through the piston valve portion of the carburetor body with needle nose pliers (**Figure 33**).

4. Unscrew the pilot jet (**Figure 34**).

5. Push the float pin out of the mounting boss and remove it.

6. Remove the float and needle valve assembly (A, **Figure 35**).

7. Remove the screw (B, **Figure 35**) securing the needle valve seat and filter assembly.

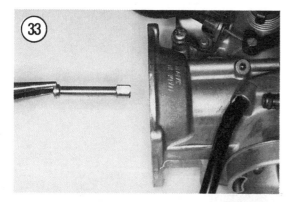

8. Remove the gasket from the float bowl.

9. Remove the drain screw from the float bowl.

NOTE
*Further disassembly is neither necessary nor recommended. If the throttle or butterfly valve (**Figure 30**) are damaged, take the carburetor body to a dealer for replacement.*

10. Clean and inspect all parts as described under Cleaning and Inspection in this chapter.

11. Reverse these steps to assemble the carburetor while noting the following:

CAUTION
In the next step, make sure that the flat portion on the needle jet is correctly aligned with the protrusion in the main jet stantion. If alignment is not correct, you will be unable to screw the main jet into the needle jet.

a. Position the needle jet so the flat portion (A, **Figure 36**) aligns with the protrusion (B, **Figure 36**) in the main jet stantion of the carburetor body.

b. Using needle nose pliers, install the needle jet through the piston valve portion of the carburetor body (**Figure 33**).

c. Observe the float bowl end of the needle jet to make sure the alignment is correct, then carefully push the needle jet in until it bottoms.

d. Adjust the idle speed and synchronize the carburetors as described in Chapter Three.

8

Cleaning and Inspection
(Front and Rear Carburetors)

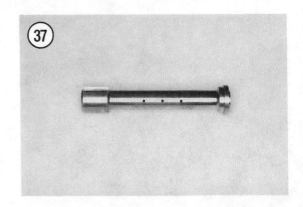

> *NOTE*
> *Figures accompanying these procedures show components for both the front and rear carburetor assemblies.*

1. Thoroughly clean and dry all parts. Suzuki does not recommend the use of a caustic carburetor cleaning solvent. Instead, clean carburetor parts in a petroleum based solvent. Then rinse in clean water.

2. Allow the carburetor to dry thoroughly before assembly and blow dry with compressed air. Blow out the jets and needle jet holder with compressed air.

3. Inspect all O-ring seals. O-ring seals tend to become hardened after prolonged use and heat and therefore lose their ability to seal properly.

> *CAUTION*
> *If compressed air is not available, allow the parts to air dry or use a clean lint-free cloth. Do not use a paper towel to dry carburetor parts, as small paper particles may plug openings in the carburetor body or jets.*

> *CAUTION*
> *Do not use a piece of wire to clean openings or jets, because minor gouges can alter flow rate and upset the fuel/air mixture.*

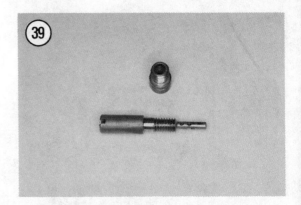

4. Make sure the holes in the needle jet (**Figure 37**) are clear. Clean out if they are plugged in any way. Replace the needle jet if you cannot unplug the holes.

5. Make sure the holes in the main jet and pilot jet are clear. Refer to **Figure 38** and **Figure 39**. Clean out if they are plugged in any way. Replace the main jet or pilot jet if you cannot unplug the holes.

6. Examine the jet needle parts (**Figure 40**) of the piston valve/diaphragm assembly for wear or damage. Make sure the diaphragm (A, **Figure 41**) is not torn or cracked. Replace any damaged or worn parts.

7. Inspect the piston valve (B, **Figure 41**) portion of the piston valve/diaphragm assembly for wear or damage. Replace the assembly if necessary.

8. Clean and inspect the filter screen (**Figure 42**) of the needle valve. Replace if any area is broken or starting to deteriorate.

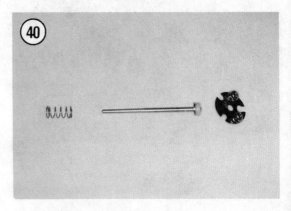

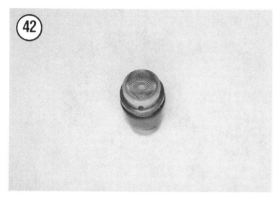

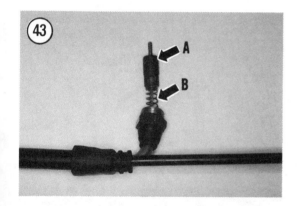

9. Inspect the float for deterioration, damage or leakage. If the float is suspected of leakage, place it in a container of water and push it down. If the float sinks or if bubbles appear (indicating a leak), replace the float assembly.

10. Make sure all openings in the carburetor body are clear. Clean out if they are plugged in any way.

11. Inspect the choke plunger (A, **Figure 43**) and spring (B, **Figure 43**) for wear or damage. Replace if necessary.

Carburetor Separation

The carburetors can be removed, disassembled, cleaned, assembled and reinstalled without disconnecting any of the cables or lines from either carburetor. If necessary, they can be separated, but first tag each cable and connector prior to removal for ease of re-assembly.

Refer to **Figure 44** for the identification of the cables and fuel and vent lines:

    a. Synchronizing cable (A).
    b. No. 2 throttle cable (front carburetor) (B).
    c. No. 1 Throttle cable (rear carburetor) (C).
    d. Fuel line (D).
    e. Vent lines (E).

1. To disconnect the carburetor synchronizing cable, perform the following:

    a. At the front carburetor, loosen the locknut (A, **Figure 45**) and disconnect the cable end from the throttle wheel (B, **Figure 45**).
    b. Disconnect the cable from the bracket on the front carburetor (C, **Figure 45**).
    c. At the rear carburetor, disconnect the cable end from the throttle wheel (A, **Figure 46**) and disconnect the cable from the bracket on the carburetor (B, **Figure 46**).

8

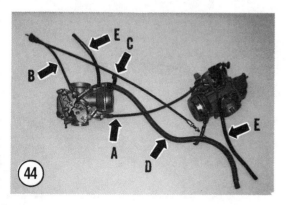

d. Remove the cable.

2. To disconnect the No. 2 throttle cable, perform the following:

   a. Loosen the locknut (A, **Figure 47**) and disconnect the cable end from the throttle wheel (B, **Figure 47**).

   b. Remove the No. 2 throttle cable (C, **Figure 47**) along with the No. 1 throttle cable (D, **Figure 47**) that was disconnected during carburetor removal.

   c. Remove the throttle cable assembly.

3. To remove the choke cable, perform the following:

   a. Unscrew the nut (A, **Figure 48**) securing the choke cable to the front carburetor.

   b. Remove the choke cable assembly (B, **Figure 48**) from the front carburetor.

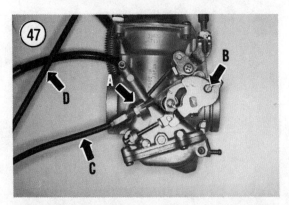

4. If necessary, remove the fuel line (**Figure 49**) from the fitting on the front carburetor.

5. If necessary, remove the vent line (**Figure 50**) from the fitting on the front carburetor.

6. Install all vent lines, the fuel line, choke and throttle cable assemblies by reversing these removal steps. Synchronize the carburetors as described in Chapter Three.

CARBURETOR ADJUSTMENTS

Float Adjustment

The carburetor assembly has to be removed and partially disassembled for this adjustment.

1. Remove the carburetor assembly as described in this chapter.

2. Remove the screws securing the float bowl and remove the float bowl and O-ring seal (front carburetor) or gasket (rear carburetor).

3. Hold the carburetor assembly with the carburetor inclined until the float arm is just touching the float needle but not pushing it down. Use a float level gauge, vernier caliper or small ruler and measure the distance from the carburetor body to the bottom surface of the float body. Refer to **Figure 51** for the front carburetor and **Figure 52** for the rear carburetor. The correct height is listed in **Table 1**.

4. Adjust by carefully bending the tang (**Figure 53**) on the float arm. If the float level is too high, the result will be a rich fuel/air mixture. If it is too low, the mixture will be too lean.

5. Reassemble and install the carburetors.

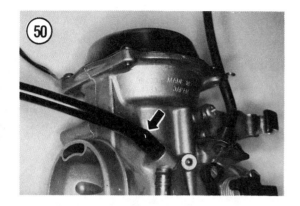

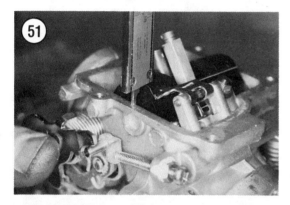

Rejetting The Carburetors

Do not try to solve a poor running engine problem by rejetting the carburetors if all of the following conditions hold true:

a. The engine runs properly with the standard jetting.

b. The engine is not modified.

c. The motorcycle is being operated in the same geographical region under the same general climatic conditions as in the past.

d. The motorcycle is being ridden at average highway speeds.

If these conditions all hold true, the chances are that the problem is due to a malfunction in the carburetor or in another component that needs repair. Changing carburetor jet size probably won't solve the problem. Rejetting the carburetors may be necessary if any of the following conditions hold true:

a. Non-standard type of air filter elements are being used.

b. A non-standard exhaust system is installed on the motorcycle.

c. Any of the top end components in the engine (pistons, camshafts, valves, compression ratio, etc.) have been modified.

d. The motorcycle is in use at considerably higher or lower altitudes or in a considerably hotter or colder climate than in the past.

e. The motorcycle is being operated at considerably higher speeds than before and changing to colder spark plugs does not solve the problem.

f. Someone has previously changed the carburetor jetting.

g. The motorcycle has never held a satisfactory engine tune.

If it is necessary to re-jet the carburetors, check with a dealer or motorcycle performance tuner for recommendations as to the size of jets to install for your specific situation.

If you do change the jets do so only one size at a time. After rejetting, test ride the bike and perform a spark plug test; refer to *Reading Spark Plugs in Chapter Three*.

THROTTLE CABLE REPLACEMENT

This procedure describes the replacement of the throttle cable from the throttle grip to the throttle

8

cable connector at the carburetor assembly. Replacement of the throttle cables attached to both carburetors is covered under *Carburetor Separation* in this chapter.

1. Remove the seats as described in Chapter Thirteen.

2. Remove the fuel tank as described in this chapter.

3. Disconnect the battery negative lead as described in Chapter Nine.

4. Loosen the throttle cable locknut (A, **Figure 54**) at the throttle grip. Turn the adjuster (B, **Figure 54**) to achieve the maximum amount of slack in the throttle cable.

5. Remove the screws securing the right-hand switch assembly together and separate the switch halves (A, **Figure 55**).

6. Disengage the throttle cable (B, **Figure 55**) from the throttle grip.

7. Remove the screw and disconnect the throttle cable from the switch assembly.

8. Remove the bolts securing the fuel tank front mounting bracket and remove the bracket.

9. Remove the screw securing the throttle cable joint to the air filter housing and remove the joint from the clip on the air filter housing.

10. Separate the throttle cable joint (**Figure 56**) and disconnect the 2 carburetor throttle cables (**Figure 57**) from the plastic fitting on the throttle grip throttle cable.

> *NOTE*
> *The piece of string attached in the next step will be used to pull the new throttle cable back through the frame so it will be routed in exactly the same position as the old one was.*

11. Tie a piece of heavy string or cord (approximately 3 ft. [1 m long]) to the throttle cable joint end of the throttle cable. Wrap this end with masking or duct tape. Tie the other end of the string to the frame in the adjacent area.

12. At the throttle grip end of the cable, carefully pull the cable (and attached string) out through the frame. Make sure the attached string follows the same path as the cable through the frame.

13. Remove the tape and untie the string from the old cable.

14. Lubricate the new cable as described in Chapter Three.

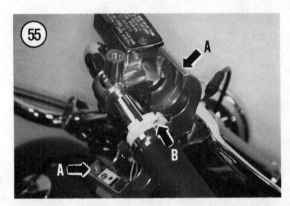

15. Tie the string to the new throttle cable and wrap it with tape.

16. Carefully pull the string back through the frame routing the new cable through the same path as the old cable.

17. Remove the tape and untie the string from the cable and the frame.

18. Connect the 2 carburetor throttle cables (**Figure 57**) onto the plastic fitting on the throttle grip throttle cable.

19. Connect the throttle cable joint and make sure both halves are securely attached together (**Figure 56**).

20. Install the throttle cable joint into the clip on the air filter housing and install the screws securing the throttle cable joint. Tighten the screw securely.

21. Install the fuel tank mounting bracket and bolts. Tighten the bolts securely.

22. Insert the throttle cable into the upper half of the right-hand switch assembly.

23. Engage the throttle cable with the receptacle of the throttle grip.

24. Install the upper half and install the screws securing the right-hand switch assembly together.

25. Connect the battery negative lead as described in Chapter Nine.

26. Install the fuel tank as described in this chapter.

27. Install the seats as described in Chapter Thirteen.

28. Adjust the throttle cable as described in Chapter Three.

29. Synchronize the throttle cables as described in Chapter Three.

30. Test ride the bike slowly at first and make sure the throttle is operating correctly.

FUEL TANK

Removal/Installation

Refer to **Figure 58** for this procedure.

1. Remove the rider's seat as described in Chapter Thirteen.

2. Disconnect the battery negative lead as described in Chapter Nine.

8

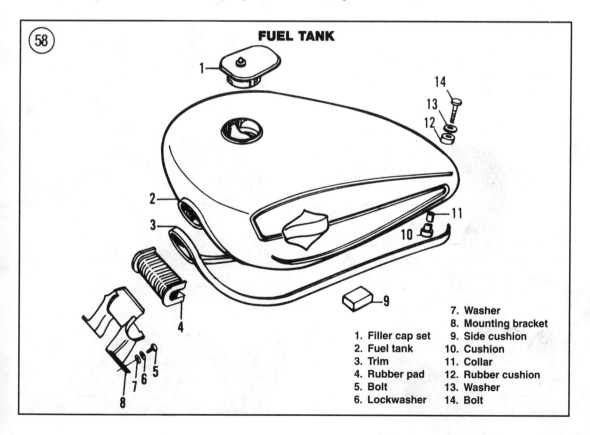

FUEL TANK

1. Filler cap set
2. Fuel tank
3. Trim
4. Rubber pad
5. Bolt
6. Lockwasher
7. Washer
8. Mounting bracket
9. Side cushion
10. Cushion
11. Collar
12. Rubber cushion
13. Washer
14. Bolt

WARNING
Some fuel may spill in the following procedure. Work in a well-ventilated area at least 50 ft. (15 m) from any sparks or flames, including gas appliance pilot lights. Do not allow anyone to smoke in the area. Keep a BC rated fire extinguisher handy.

3. Turn the main fuel shutoff valve to the OFF position (A, **Figure 59**).

CAUTION
If the fuel tank is more than one-half full of gasoline, drain the fuel into a can approved for gasoline storage. Place the container in a safe place. This will reduce the weight of the tank to help eliminate the possibility of damage to the fuel tank during the remainder of the removal procedure.

4. If it is necessary to drain the fuel tank, perform the following:
   a. Turn the main shutoff valve to the OFF position.
   b. Disconnect the single fuel hose from the base of the valve going to the fuel pump.
   c. Connect a long length of fuel hose to the outlet on the main valve and place the other end of the can approved for gasoline storage.
   d. Turn the main shutoff valve to the RES position and drain the fuel into the can. Store the can in a safe location.
   e. Turn the main shutoff valve to the OFF position and disconnect the fuel hose.
   f. Reconnect the single fuel hose onto the base of the valve going to the fuel pump.

NOTE
Prior to disconnecting the fuel lines from the main fuel shutoff valve, mark them with tape to identify them as the front RES hose and rear ON hose. This will help to avoid connecting the hose to the wrong fitting during installation.

5. Disconnect the fuel hoses (B, **Figure 59**) from the main fuel shutoff valve. Plug the end of the hoses to prevent the entry of foreign matter and prevent the loss of any residual fuel in the line.
6. Remove the bolts and washers (**Figure 60**) securing the rear of the fuel tank.

7. Place several shop cloths between the front of the fuel tank and the steering head area to protect the fuel tank in the following steps.
8. Pull the fuel tank partially up at the rear and toward the rear to disengage the front of the tank from the frame mounting bracket. Block up the rear of the fuel tank to gain access to the sub-fuel tank shutoff valve and hoses.
9. Turn the sub-fuel shutoff valve (A, **Figure 61**) to the OFF position.

NOTE
*Prior to disconnecting the fuel lines from the sub-fuel shutoff valve, mark them with tape to identify them as the right RES hose (B, **Figure 61**) and left ON hose (C, **Figure 61**). This will help to avoid connecting the hose to the wrong fitting during installation.*

10. Disconnect the fuel hoses (B and C, **Figure 61**) from the sub-fuel shutoff valve. Plug the end of the hoses to prevent the entry of foreign matter and prevent the loss of any residual fuel in the line.

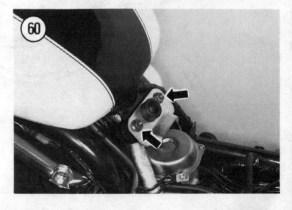

11. On California models, disconnect the evaporative emission system vent lines (D, **Figure 61**) from the fuel tank.

12. Carefully lift the fuel tank up the rest of the way and remove the fuel tank from the frame. Store it in an area where it will not be damaged.

13. Inspect the rubber cushion in the front mounting bracket where the fuel tank attaches to the frame. Replace the cushion if it is damaged or starting to deteriorate.

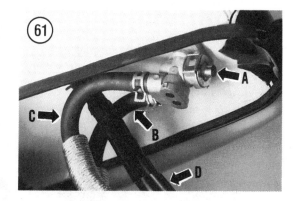

14. Inspect the front mounting bracket for cracks or damage. If necessary, remove the bolts on each side and remove the bracket.

15. Check the rear mounting bracket, collars and rubber cushions (**Figure 62**) for wear or damage.

16. Install by reversing these removal steps, noting the following:
   a. Refill the fuel tank if it was drained.
   b. Make sure the rubber cushion is in place in the frame mounting bracket.
   c. Be sure to reconnect the fuel hoses onto the correct fittings.
   d. Turn the fuel tank shutoff valve to the ON position.
   e. Tighten the fuel tank mounting bolts securely.
   f. Turn the fuel valve on and check for fuel leaks.

FUEL SHUTOFF VALVES

Removal/Installation (Main Valve)

> *WARNING*
> *Some fuel may spill in the following procedure. Work in a well-ventilated area at least 50 ft. (15 m) from any sparks or flames, including gas appliance pilot lights. Do not allow anyone to smoke in the area. Keep a BC rated fire extinguisher handy.*

1. Remove the rider's seat as described in Chapter Thirteen.
2. Remove the bolt securing the frame left-hand side cover and remove the cover.
3. Remove the fuel tank and drain it of all fuel as described in this chapter.
4. Disconnect the single fuel hose from the base of the main valve going to the fuel pump.
5. Remove the bolt and lockwasher (A, **Figure 63**) securing the main shutoff valve (B, **Figure 63**) to the frame and remove it.
6. Install by reversing the removal steps.

Removal/Installation (Sub-Valve)

> *WARNING*
> *Some fuel may spill in the following procedure. Work in a well-ventilated area at least 50 ft. (15 m) from any*

8

sparks or flames, including gas appliance pilot lights. Do not allow anyone to smoke in the area. Keep a BC rated fire extinguisher handy.

1. Remove the fuel tank and drain it of all fuel as described in this chapter.
2. Place some cardboard on the workbench to protect the surface of the fuel tank.
3. Turn the fuel tank on its side with the fuel shutoff valve side up.
4. Remove the bolts and gaskets (**Figure 64**) securing the shutoff valve to the fuel tank.
5. Remove the valve and O-ring gasket.
6. After removing the valve, insert the corner of a lint-free cloth into the opening in the tank to prevent the entry of foreign matter or tape it closed.
7. Inspect the shutoff valve mounting O-ring; replace if necessary.
8. Clean the filter portion of the valve with a soft toothbrush and blow out with compressed air. Replace the filter if it is broken in any area or starting to deteriorate.
9. Install by reversing the removal steps. Pour a small amount of gasoline in the tank after installing the valve and check for leaks. If a leak is present, solve the problem immediately; do not reinstall the fuel tank with a leaking valve.

FUEL PUMP

The electromagnetic fuel pump is located on the left-hand side of the bike above the swing arm pivot point. Fuel pump and fuel pump relay testing procedures are located in Chapter Nine.

Removal/Installation

WARNING
Some fuel may spill in the following procedure. Work in a well-ventilated area at least 50 ft. (15 m) from any sparks or flames, including gas appliance pilot lights. Do not allow anyone to smoke in the area. Keep a BC rated fire extinguisher handy.

1. Remove the rider's seat as described in Chapter Thirteen.
2. Disconnect the battery negative lead as described in Chapter Nine.

3. Turn the main fuel shutoff valve to the OFF position.
4. Remove the bolts securing the frame left-hand side cover and remove the cover.
5. On models so equipped, disconnect the hose (A, **Figure 65**) from the ignition timing advance boost solenoid and move the hose out of the way.
6. Loosen the bolts and washers (B, **Figure 65**) securing the mounting bracket to the frame.
7. Pull the fuel pump (C, **Figure 65**) and mounting bracket part way out of the frame and disconnect the 2-pin electrical connector from the pump.

NOTE
Prior to disconnecting the fuel lines from the fuel pump, mark them with tape to identify them as the inlet IN hose (from the fuel tank) and outlet OUT hose (going to the rear carburetor). This will help to avoid connecting the hose to the wrong fitting during installation.

8. Disconnect both fuel lines from the base of the fuel pump. Plug the end of the lines to prevent the

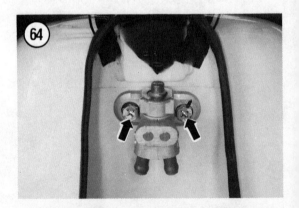

entry of foreign matter and to prevent the loss of residual fuel in the lines.

9. Install by reversing these removal steps, noting the following:

   a. Make sure the electrical connector is free of corrosion and is tight.

   b. Prior to installing the frame side cover, reconnect the battery negative lead and start the engine to check for a fuel leak. If a leak is present, solve the problem immediately.

CRANKCASE BREATHER SYSTEM (U.S. ONLY)

To comply with air pollution standards, all models are equipped with a closed crankcase breather system. The system routes the engine combustion gases into the air filter air boxes where they are burned in the engine.

Inspection/Cleaning

Make sure that all hose clamps are tight. Check hoses for deterioration and replace if necessary.

Open the end of each drain tube attached to each air filter air case and drain out all residue. This cleaning procedure should be done more frequently if a considerable amount of riding is done at full throttle or in the rain.

EVAPORATIVE EMISSION CONTROL SYSTEM (CALIFORNIA MODELS ONLY)

To comply with the California Air Resources Board, an evaporative emission control system is installed on all models sold in California.

Fuel vapor from the fuel tank is routed into a charcoal canister. This vapor is stored when the engine is not running. When the engine is running these vapors are drawn through a purge control valve and into the carburetors to be burned. **Figure 66** show the hose routing and components of the system.

Make sure all hose clamps are tight. Check all hoses for deterioration and replace as necessary.

Prior to removing the hoses from any of the parts of this system, mark each hose and fitting with a piece of masking tape to identify where the hose goes. There are so many vacuum hoses on these

models it can be very confusing where each one is supposed to be attached.

The charcoal canister is located behind the rear cylinder block.

Charcoal Canister Removal/Installation

1. Remove the rider's seat as described in Chapter Thirteen.

2. Disconnect the battery negative lead as described in Chapter Nine.

3. Remove the screw and cover from both ends of the canister.

4. Remove the bolts securing the frame right-hand side cover and remove the cover.

5. Remove the bolt and washer (A, **Figure 67**) securing the charcoal canister to the crankcase.

NOTE
Prior to removing the hoses from the purge control valve and the charcoal canister, mark each hose and fitting with a piece of masking tape to identify where each hose goes.

6. Disconnect the hose from the right-hand side (B, **Figure 67**) and the hose on the left-hand side.

7. Remove the charcoal canister from the mounting bracket and remove it from the engine and frame.

8. Check the canister and its fittings for cracks or damage; replace if necessary.

9. Install by reversing these removal steps, noting the following:

   a. Be sure to attach the hoses to the correct fittings on the charcoal canister.

   b. Make sure the hoses are not kinked, twisted or in contact with any sharp surfaces.

EXHAUST SYSTEM

The exhaust system is a vital performance component. Check the exhaust system for deep dents and fractures and repair or replace them immediately. Check the muffler frame mounting flanges for fractures and loose bolts. Check the cylinder head mounting flanges for tightness. A loose exhaust pipe connection can cause a decrease in engine performance.

8

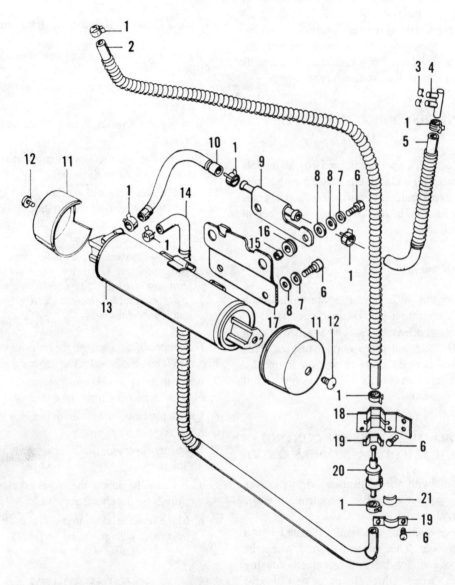

**EVAPORATIVE EMISSION CONTROL SYSTEM
(CALIFORNIA ONLY)**

1. Hose clamp
2. Hose (fuel tank)
3. Hose clamp
4. Connector
5. Hose (connector)
6. Bolt
7. Lockwasher
8. Washer
9. Canister pipe
10. Hose
(canister pipe joint)
11. End cap
12. Screw
13. Canister
14. Hose
(canister/valve joint)
15. Collar
16. Rubber cushion
17. Mounting bracket
18. Hose bracket
19. Clip
20. Breather valve
21. Cushion

Removal/Installation

Refer to **Figure 68** for the following procedure.
1. Loosen the clamping bolt where both mufflers attach at the common connector just forward of the rear wheel.

2. Loosen the clamping bolt (**Figure 69**) where the exhaust pipe connects to the muffler.
3. Remove the bolt, washer and nut (**Figure 70**) securing the muffler to the frame mounting bracket.
4. Disengage the muffler from the common connector of the other muffler, then remove the muffler.
5. Repeat Steps 3 and 4 for the other muffler.
6. On the rear cylinder, perform the following:
   a. Remove the bolts (**Figure 71**) securing the exhaust pipe clamp to the cylinder head.
   b. Install a tie-wrap just below the clamp to keep it in place.
   c. Pull the exhaust pipe off the cylinder head and remove it from the engine and frame.
7. On the front cylinder, perform the following:
   a. Remove the bolts (A, **Figure 72**) securing the exhaust pipe clamp (B, **Figure 72**) to the cylinder head.

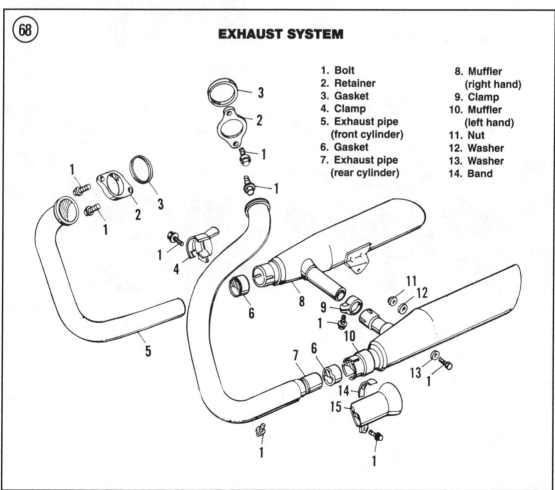

EXHAUST SYSTEM

8

1. Bolt
2. Retainer
3. Gasket
4. Clamp
5. Exhaust pipe (front cylinder)
6. Gasket
7. Exhaust pipe (rear cylinder)
8. Muffler (right hand)
9. Clamp
10. Muffler (left hand)
11. Nut
12. Washer
13. Washer
14. Band

b. Install a tie-wrap just below the clamp to keep it in place.

c. Pull the exhaust pipe off the cylinder head and remove it from the engine and frame.

8. Inspect the gaskets at all joints; replace as necessary.

9. Install a new gasket in each exhaust port.

10. Attach the exhaust pipes to the engine.

11. Install the exhaust pipe cylinder head bolts and tighten finger-tight.

12. Install both mufflers and mounting bolts, washers and nuts and tighten finger-tight. Make sure the exhaust pipes are correctly seated in the exhaust ports.

13. Tighten the exhaust pipe cylinder head bolts first to minimize exhaust leaks at the cylinder head. Tighten the bolts securely.

14. Tighten the rest of the exhaust system bolts securely.

15. After installation is complete, start the engine and check for exhaust leaks.

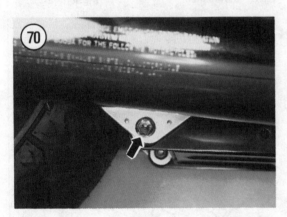

Table 1 CARBURETOR SPECIFICATIONS

	1987-1995 U.S. and Canada	
	Rear cylinder	Front cylinder
Manufacturer/type	Mikuni BS36SS	Mikini BDS36SS
Model No.	38B00	38B00
Bore size	36 mm	36 mm
Main jet	140	125
Main air jet	1.8 mm (0.07 in.)	1.8 mm (0.07 in.)
Jet needle	5D35-1	5D21-1
Needle jet	6	
Throttle valve		
1987-1989	110	110
1990-1995	120	110
Needle jet	P-2	P-0
Pilot outlet		
1987-1989	0.8 mm (0.03 in.)	0.8 mm (0.03 in.)
1990-1995	0.7 mm (0.027 in.)	0.8 mm (0.03 in.)
Valve seat	1.5 mm (0.06 in.)	1.5 mm (0.06 in.)
Starter jet	25	25
Pilot screw		
1987-1990	Fixed (not adjustable)	Fixed (not adjustable)
1991-1995	Preset (1 3/4 turns back)	Preset (1 3/4 turns back)
Pilot air jet No. 1		
1987-1989	60	55
1990-1995	70	40
Pilot air jet No. 2		
1987-1989	2.0 mm (0.08 in.)	2.0 (0.08 in.)
1990	1.55 mm (0.61 in.)	1.4 mm (0.55 in.)
Fuel level below the mark		
1987	9-10 mm (0.35-0.39 in.)	17-18 mm (0.67-0.71 in.)
1988-1990	9-10 mm (0.35-0.39 in.)	16.5-17.5 mm (0.65-0.69 in.)
Float height	27.2-28.2 mm (1.07-1.11 in.)	8.6-9.6 mm (0.34-0.38 in.)
	1996-on U.S. and Canada	
	Rear cylinder	Front cylinder
Manufacturer/type	Mikuni BS36SS	Mikini BDS36SS
Model No.		
U.S. (49-sate), Canada		
1996	35B40	38B40
1997-on	38BE	38BE
U.S. (California)		
1996	38B50	35B50
1997-on	38BF	38BF
Bore size	36 mm	36 mm
Main jet	140	125
Main air jet	1.8 mm (0.07 in.)	1.8 mm (0.07 in.)
Jet needle	5D35-1st	5D51-1st
Needle jet	P-2	P-0
Throttle valve	120	110
Pilot jet	55	50
Pilot outlet	0.7 mm (0.0027 in.)	1.0 (0.04 in.)
Valve seat	1.5 mm (0.06 in.)	1.5 mm (0.06 in.)
Starter jet	25	25
Pilot screw	Preset (1 3/4 turns back)	Preset (1 3/4 turns back)
Fuel level below mark	9-10 mm (0.35-0.39 in.)	16.5-17.5 mm (0.65-0.69 in.)
Float height	27.2-28.2 mm (1.07-1.11 in.)	8.6-9.6 mm (0.34-0.38 in.)

(continued)

8

Table 1 CARBURETOR SPECIFICATIONS (continued)

| | 1996-on England, France, Italy, Germany | |
	Rear cylinder	Front cylinder
Manufacturer/type	Mikuni BS36SS	Mikuni BDS36SS
Model No.		
England, France, Italy	38BB	38BB
Germany	38BC	38BC
Bore size	36 mm	36 mm
Main jet	130	112.5
Main air jet	1.8 mm (0.07 in.)	1.8 mm (0.07 in.)
Jet needle	5D38-3rd	5D39-3rd
Needle jet	P-3	P-0
Throttle valve	120	110
Pilot jet	55	50
Pilot outlet	0.8 mm (0.031 in.)	1.0 mm (0.04 in.)
Valve seat	1.5 mm (0.06 in.)	1.5 mm (0.06 in.)
Starter jet	25	25
Pilot screw	Preset (1 turn back)	Preset (2 turns back)
Fuel level below the mark	9-10 mm (0.35-0.39 in.)	16.5-17.5 mm (0.65-0.69 in.)
Float height	27.2-28.2 mm (1.07-1.11 in.)	8.6-9.6 mm (0.34-0.38 in.)

| | 1996-on Australia and Canada | |
	Rear cylinder	Front Cylinder
Manufacturer/type	Mikuni BS36SS	Mikuni BS36SS
Model No.		
Australia	38B90	38B90
Canada	38B70	38B70
Bore size	36 mm	36 mm
Main jet	140	125
Main air jet	1.8 mm (0.07 in.)	1.8 mm (0.07 in.)
Jet needle	5D38-3rd	5D39-3rd
Needle jet	P-3	P-0
Throttle valve	120	110
Pilot jet	57.5	50
Pilot outlet	0.8 mm (0.031 in.)	1.0 mm (0.04 in.)
Valve seat	1.5 mm (0.06 in.)	1.5 mm (0.06 in.)
Starter jet	25	25
Pilot screw	Preset (1 3/4 turns back)	Preset (1 3/4 turns back)
Pilot air jet No. 1	60	55
Pilot air jet No. 2	1.9 mm (0.074 in.)	1.7 mm (0.067 in.)
Fuel level below the mark	9-10 mm (0.35-0.39 in.)	16.5-17.5 in. (0.65-0.69 in.)
Float height	27.2-28.2 mm (1.07-1.11 in.)	8.6-9.6 mm (0.34-038 in.)

CHAPTER NINE

ELECTRICAL SYSTEMS

This chapter contains operating principles, service procedures and test procedures for all electrical system components. Information regarding the battery and spark plugs are covered in Chapter Three.

The electrical system includes the following systems:

a. Charging system.

b. Ignition system.

c. Starting system.

d. Lighting system.

e. Directional signal system.

f. Switches.

g. Various electrical components.

Tables 1-3 are located at the end of this chapter.

> *NOTE*
> *Where differences occur relating to the United Kingdom (U.K.) models they are identified. If there is no (U.K.) designation relating to a procedure, photo or illustration, it is identical to the United States (U.S.) model.*

BASIC INFORMATION

Electrical Component Resistance Testing

To get accurate resistance measurements for an electrical component, the component, or the specific coil portion of a component, must be at approximately 20° C (68° F). Manufacturer's perform their tests at this controlled temperature and base their resistance specifications on tests performed at this specific temperature.

Any temperature variation other that that specified will change the resistance reading of the component—increase when hot or decrease when cold.

Resistance tests performed at a temperature other than specified, may result in the unnecessary replacement of a good component.

> *NOTE*
> *When using an analog ohmmeter, always touch the test leads, then zero the needle to ensure correct readings.*

Suzuki specifies the use of a specific multimeter for accurate resistance readings. The specified meter is the Suzuki Pocket Tester (part No. 09900-25002). Because of the different resistance characteristics of the semiconductors used in this meter, the use of another meter may give you a different reading. This meter can be purchased through a Suzuki dealership or you can remove the electronic component and have it tested at a dealership.

Electrical Component Replacement

Most motorcycle dealerships and parts suppliers will not accept the return of any electrical part. If you have been unable to determine the exact cause of any electrical system malfunction, have a Suzuki dealership retest that specific system to verify your test results. If you purchase a new electrical component(s), install it, and then find that the system still does not work properly, you will, in most cases, be unable to return the unit for a refund.

Electrical Connection Location

The location of electrical connectors varies with the different years. Also, if the bike has been worked on by someone else, they may have positioned the connector differently than the factory location. The photographs shown in this chapter are based on the 1997 VS1400 Intruder model, but electrical connector location on the bike you are working on may vary. Always check the connectors wire colors called out in the procedures to make sure you are working with the correct electrical connector. To double check, follow the electrical cable from the specific component to where it connects to the wiring harness or to an other electrical component within that system.

ELECTRICAL CONNECTORS

The 1400 Intruder is equipped with many electrical components, connectors and wires. Corrosion-causing moisture can enter these electrical connectors and cause poor electrical connections leading to component failure. Troubleshooting an electrical circuit with one or more corroded electrical connectors can be time consuming and frustrating.

When reconnecting electrical connectors, pack them with a dielectric grease compound. Dielectric grease is especially formulated for sealing and waterproofing electrical connectors and will not interfere with the current flow through the electrical

connectors. Use only this compound or an equivalent designed for this specific purpose. Do not use a substitute that may interfere with the current flow within the electrical connector. Do not use silicone sealant.

After cleaning both the male and female connectors, make sure they are thoroughly dry. Pack one of the connector halves with dielectric grease compound before joining the 2 connector halves. On multi-pin connectors, pack the male side and on single-wire connectors, pack the female side. Use a good-size glob so that it will squish out when the two halves are pushed together. For best results, the compound should fill the entire inner area of the connector. On multi-pin connectors, also pack the backside of both the male and female side with the compound to prevent moisture from entering the backside of the connector. After the connector is fully packed, wipe the exterior of all excess compound.

Get into the practice of cleaning and sealing all electrical connectors every time they are unplugged. This may prevent a breakdown on the road and also save you time when troubleshooting a circuit.

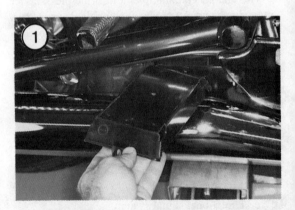

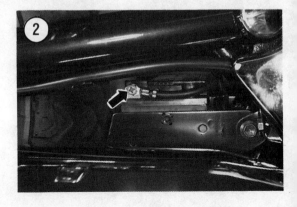

Always make sure the ground connections are tight and free of corrosion.

BATTERY NEGATIVE TERMINAL

Some of the component replacement procedures and some of the test procedures in this chapter re-

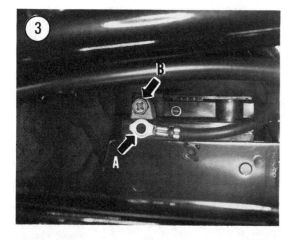

quire disconnecting the battery negative (–) lead as a safety precaution.

1. Remove the screw on each side securing the battery cover and remove the cover (**Figure 1**).

2. Remove the bolt and disconnect the battery negative (**Figure 2**) lead.

3. Reach into the battery case and move the negative lead (A, **Figure 3**) out of the way so it will not accidentally make contact with the battery negative terminal (B, **Figure 3**).

4. Connect the battery negative lead to the terminal and tighten the bolt securely.

5. Install the cover and screws and tighten securely.

CHARGING SYSTEM

The charging system consists of the battery, alternator and a solid-state voltage regulator/rectifier (**Figure 4**).

Alternating current generated by the alternator is rectified to direct current. The voltage regulator maintains constant voltage to the battery and electri-

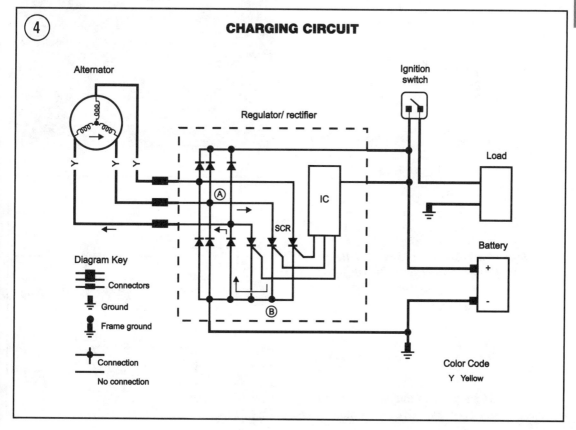

CHARGING CIRCUIT

Alternator

Ignition switch

Regulator/ rectifier

Load

IC

SCR

Battery
+
–

Diagram Key

Connectors

Ground

Frame ground

Connection

No connection

Color Code
Y Yellow

9

cal loads, like the lights and ignition system, regardless of engine speed and load.

A malfunction in the charging system generally causes the battery to remain undercharged. To prevent damage to the alternator and the regulator/rectifier when testing and repairing the charging system, note the following precautions:

1. Always disconnect the negative battery cable, as described in this chapter, before removing a component from the charging system.
2. When it is necessary to charge the battery, remove the battery from the motorcycle and recharge it as described in Chapter Three.
3. Inspect the physical condition of the battery. Look for bulges or cracks in the case, leaking electrolyte or corrosion buildup.
4. Check the wiring in the charging system for signs of chafing, deterioration or other damage.
5. Check the wiring for corroded or loose connections. Clean, tighten or reconnect as required.

Battery Drain

Perform this test prior to performing the output test to determine if some electrical component is remaining on and draining the battery.

NOTE
Due to the location of the battery and its leads it is necessary to remove the battery from the motorcycle to perform this test.

1. Remove the battery as described in Chapter Three.
2. Turn the ignition switch OFF.

CAUTION
Before connecting the ammeter into the circuit in Step 4, set the meter to its highest amperage scale. This will prevent a possible large current flow from damaging the meter or blowing the meter's fuse, if so equipped.

NOTE
Make sure there is a good electrical connection at both ends of the jumper wire. Otherwise the test results may be faulty.

3. Connect a jumper wire from the battery positive (+) lead and the battery positive (+) terminal.

4. Connect an ammeter between the battery negative (–) lead and the negative (–) terminal of the battery.
5. The ammeter should read less than 0.1 mA. If the amperage is greater, this indicates there is a voltage drain in the system that will discharge the battery.
6. If the current drain is excessive, the probable causes are:
   a. Damaged battery.
   b. Short circuit in the system.
   c. Loose, dirty or faulty electrical system connectors in the charging system wiring harness system.
7. Install the battery as described in Chapter Three.

Charging System Output Test

Whenever a charging system malfunction is suspected, make sure the battery is fully charged and in good condition before going any further. Clean and

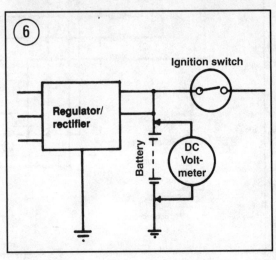

test the battery as described in Chapter Three. Make sure all electrical connectors are tight and free of corrosion.

NOTE
This procedure requires the use of an assistant due to the location of the battery. Have an assistant attach the positive test lead on the left-hand side of the bike while you work on the right-hand side along with the meter while having access to the throttle grip. This will lessen the possibility of getting burned on one of the HOT mufflers.

1. Start the engine and let it reach normal operating temperature. Shut off the engine.

2. Connect a portable tachometer following the manufacturer's instructions.

3. Remove the screw on each side securing the battery cover and remove the cover (**Figure 1**).

4. Remove the screw (**Figure 5**) securing the battery positive (+) cable terminal.

5. Restart the engine and let it idle.

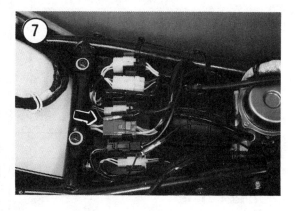

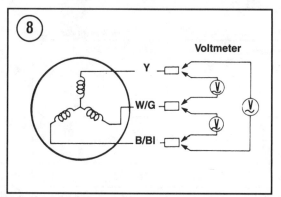

WARNING
The exhaust system is HOT. Protect your hands while connecting the test leads to the battery terminals.

6. Have the assistant connect a 0-20 DC voltmeter positive test lead to the positive (+) test lead to the battery positive terminal (**Figure 5**) on the left-hand side of the bike.

7. Attach the voltmeter negative (–) test lead to the negative terminal (**Figure 2**) on the left-hand side of the bike (**Figure 6**).

8. Increase engine speed to 5,000 rpm. The voltage reading should be 14-15 volts. If the voltage reading is less than 14 volts or more than 15 volts, perform the *Charging System No-load Test* and the *Voltage Regulator/Rectifier Testing* procedures in this chapter.

9. After the test is completed, shut off the engine and disconnect the voltmeter and portable tachometer.

10. Install the battery positive (+) cable and tighten the screw securely.

11. Install the battery cover and tighten the screws securely.

Charging System No-load Test

1. Remove the rider's seat and the frame side covers as described in Chapter Thirteen.

2. Start the engine and let it reach normal operating temperature. Shut off the engine.

3. Connect a portable tachometer following the manufacturer's instructions.

4. Locate the alternator's 3-pin electrical connector containing 3 yellow wires (**Figure 7**) and disconnect the connector.

5. Restart the engine and let it idle.

6. Increase engine speed to 5,000 rpm.

NOTE
In Step 7 connect the voltmeter test leads to the alternator side of the electrical connectors disconnected in Step 4.

7. Connect a 0-150 AC voltmeter between 2 of the yellow wire connector terminals as shown in **Figure 8**. Voltage should be more than 80 volts (AC). Move one of the voltmeter probes to the other yellow wire terminal connector and check voltage again. Voltage should again be more than 80 volts (AC).

8. If any test indicates less than the specified voltage, the alternator is faulty and must be replaced.

9. Shut off the engine.

10. After completing the test, disconnect the voltmeter and portable tachometer.

11. Reconnect the alternator's 3-pin electrical connector going to the voltage regulator/rectifier. Make sure connectors are corrosion free and tight.

12. Install the frame side covers and the rider's seat as described in Chapter Thirteen.

VOLTAGE REGULATOR/RECTIFIER

Testing

Suzuki specifies the use of the Suzuki Pocket Tester (part No. 09900-25002) for accurate resistance reading for testing of the regulator/rectifier unit. Refer to the *Basic Information* section at the beginning of this chapter regarding this tester.

> *NOTE*
> *Prior to making this test, check the condition of the pocket tester battery. If necessary, install a new battery.*

> *NOTE*
> *Refer to the **Basic Information** section at the beginning of this chapter regarding the specified test temperature of 20° C (68° F). If the component is not at the specified temperature, the resulting resistance readings will be inaccurate.*

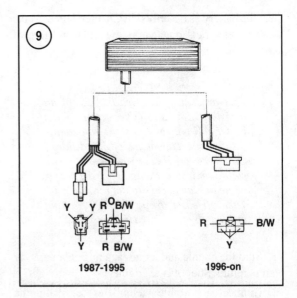

1987-1995   1996-on

VOLTAGE REGULATOR/RECTIFIER (1987-1995)

Unit: Approx. kΩ

(-) Probe of tester to:	(+) Probe of tester to:			
		R	O	B/W	Y
R			∞	∞	∞
O		70		34	45
B/W		6.5	4.2		2.5
Y		2.5	∞	∞	

VOLTAGE REGULATOR/RECTIFIER (1996-ON)

Unit: Approx. kΩ

(-) Probe of tester to:	(+) Probe of tester to:				
		R	B/W	Y_1	Y_2	Y_3
R			∞	∞	∞	∞
B/W		1-20		1-10	1-10	1-10
Y_1		1-10	∞		∞	∞
Y_2		1-10	∞	∞		∞
Y_3		1-10	∞	∞	∞	

1. Remove the rider's seat and the frame side covers as described in Chapter Thirteen.

2A. On 1987-1995 models, disconnect the two regulator/rectifier unit electrical connectors (Figure 7) as follows:

    a. Locate the alternator's 3-pin electrical connector containing 3 yellow wires and disconnect the connector.

    b. Locate the alternator's 5-pin electrical connector containing 5 wires (1 orange, 2 red, 2 black/white) and disconnect the connector.

    c. Set the pocket tester to the R × 1,000 (K) ohms scale.

    d. Refer to **Figure 9** for wire colors within the electrical connectors.

    e. Refer to **Figure 10** for the pocket tester lead connections and values.

2B. On 1996-on models, disconnect the single regulator/rectifier unit electrical connector (**Figure 7**) as follows:

    a. Locate the alternator's 5-pin electrical connector containing 5 wires (1 red, 1 black/white, 3 yellow and disconnect the connector.

    b. Set the pocket tester to the R × 1000 (K) ohms scale.

    c. Refer to **Figure 9** for wire colors within the electrical connectors.

    d. Refer to **Figure 11** for the tester connections and values.

3. If any of the meter readings differ from the stated values, replace the regulator/rectifier unit as described in this chapter.

4. If the voltage regulator/rectifier checked out okay, install the frame side covers and the rider's seat and as described in Chapter Thirteen.

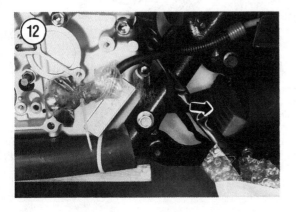

Voltage Regulator/Rectifier Removal/Installation

1. Remove the rider's seat and the frame side covers as described in Chapter Thirteen.

2. Disconnect the battery negative (–) lead as described in this chapter.

3. Remove both mufflers as described in Chapter Eight.

4A. On 1987-1995 models, disconnect the two regulator/rectifier unit electrical connectors as follows:

    a. Locate the alternator's 3-pin electrical connector containing 3 yellow wires and disconnect the connector.

    b. Locate the alternator's 5-pin electrical connector containing 5 wires (1 orange, 2 red, 2 black/white) and disconnect the connector.

4B. On 1996-on models, disconnect the single regulator/rectifier unit electrical connector (**Figure 7**). Locate the alternator's 5-pin electrical connector containing 5 wires (1 red, 1 black/white, 3 yellow and disconnect the connector.

5. Remove the bolts located under the voltage regulator/rectifier (**Figure 12**) that attach the regulator/rectifier to the front of the battery box.

6. Carefully pull the electrical wiring harness out through the frame, noting its path and remove the voltage regulator/rectifier assembly from the frame.

7. Install by reversing these removal steps while noting the following:

    a. Tighten the mounting bolts securely.

    b. Make sure all electrical connections are tight and free of corrosion.

    c. Connect the battery negative (–) lead.

ALTERNATOR

The alternator is a form of electrical generator in which a magnetized field called a rotor revolves around a set of stationary coils called a stator assembly. As the rotor revolves, alternating current is induced in the stator coils. The current is then rectified to direct current and is used to operate the electrical system and to keep the battery charged. The rotor is permanently magnetized.

9

Rotor Testing

The rotor is permanently magnetized and cannot be tested except by replacing it with a known good one. The rotor can lose magnetism from old age or a sharp hit. If defective, the rotor must be replaced; it cannot be remagnetized.

Stator Testing

Suzuki specifies the use of the Suzuki Pocket Tester (part No. 09900-25002) for accurate resistance reading for testing of the regulator/rectifier unit. Refer to the *Basic Information* section at the beginning of this chapter regarding this tester.

NOTE
Prior to making this test, check the condition of the pocket tester battery. If necessary, install a new battery.

NOTE
*Refer to the **Basic Information** section at the beginning of this chapter regarding the specified test temperature of 20° C (68° F). If the component is not at the specified temperature, the resulting resistance readings will be inaccurate.*

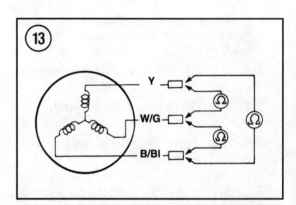

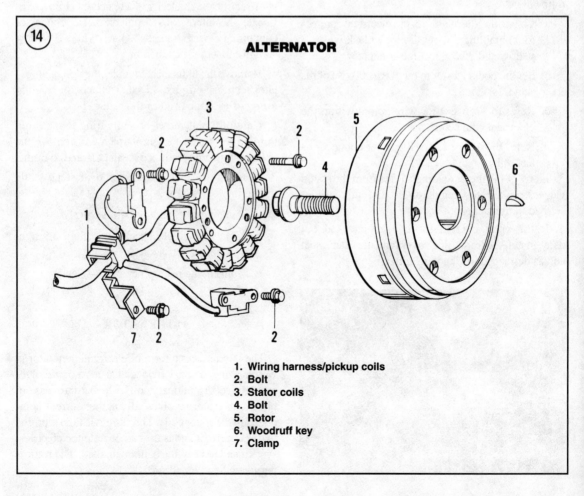

ALTERNATOR

1. Wiring harness/pickup coils
2. Bolt
3. Stator coils
4. Bolt
5. Rotor
6. Woodruff key
7. Clamp

1. Remove the rider's seat and the frame side covers as described in Chapter Thirteen.

2. Start the engine and let it reach normal operating temperature. Shut off the engine.

3. Locate the alternator's 3-pin electrical connector containing 3 yellow wires (**Figure 7**) and disconnect the connector.

4. Connect an ohmmeter set at R × 1 (to check continuity) between two of the yellow terminals on the alternator stator side of the connector (**Figure 13**). Move one of the probes to the third yellow terminal.

5. Replace the stator assembly if any yellow terminal indicates no continuity (infinite resistance) to the other two yellow terminals. This would indicate an open in the stator coil winding.

6. Use an ohmmeter set at R × 1 to check continuity between ground and each yellow terminal on the alternator stator side of the connector.

7. Replace the stator assembly if any yellow terminal shows continuity (indicated resistance) to ground. This would indicate a short within the stator coil winding.

NOTE
Prior to replacing the stator assembly, check the electrical wires to and within the electrical connector for any open or poor connections.

8. If the stator assembly fails either of these tests, it must be replaced as described in this chapter.

9. Reconnect the alternator's 3-pin electrical connector.

10. Install the frame side covers and the rider's seat as described in Chapter Thirteen.

Stator Assembly Removal/Installation

The stator assembly and the ignition pulse generators are attached to the back side of the alternator cover.

Refer to **Figure 14** for this procedure.

1. Remove the rider's seat and the frame side covers as described in Chapter Thirteen.

NOTE
The 4-pin electrical connector (1 green, 1 blue, 1 yellow, 1 black) for the ignition pickup coils was disconnected from the ignitor unit when the seat was removed.

2. Locate the alternator stator 3-pin electrical connector containing 3 yellow wires (**Figure 7**) and disconnect the connector.

3. Remove the bolts securing the secondary drive cover (**A, Figure 15**) and remove the cover. Do not lose the spacer at each bolt location.

NOTE
The following figures are shown with the front footpeg assembly completely removed for clarity. It is not necessary to remove the assembly completely for this procedure.

4. Remove the mounting bolts and lower the front footpeg assembly (**B, Figure 15**) as described in Chapter Thirteen. Rest the assembly on wooden blocks or lower the footpeg assembly to the ground.

5. Remove the bolts securing the alternator cover (A, **Figure 16**) and remove the cover and gasket. Note the location of the wiring harness clamps (B, **Figure 16**) under the cover bolts. Do not lose the locating dowel pins.

6. Carefully withdraw the wiring harness from the frame, while noting its path. Remove the alternator stator assembly and wiring harness from the frame.

7. Place several shop cloths on the workbench to protect the chrome finish of the alternator cover. Turn the alternator cover upside down on these cloths.

8. Remove the screws and small metal clamps (A, **Figure 17**) securing the stator assembly wiring harness to the alternator cover. Note the location of each of these metal clamps because they must all be reinstalled in the same location.

9

9. Remove the other screws securing the ignition signal generators, (B, **Figure 17**) to the alternator cover.

10. Remove the bolts securing the stator assembly (C, **Figure 17**) to the cover. Carefully pull the rubber grommet (D, **Figure 17**) loose from the cover and remove the stator and ignition signal generator assembly from the cover.

11. Install by reversing these removal steps, noting the following:

a. Apply a light coat of ThreeBond TB1342, Loctite No. 242, or equivalent, to the mounting bolt threads prior to installation. Tighten the bolts securely.

b. The small metal clamp (**A, Figure 17**) securing the stator assembly and ignition signal generators wiring harness to the cover must be installed in the correct location. These clamps secure the wiring harness to the cover and away from the spinning rotor. If these wires come in contact with the rotor they will be damaged.

c. Make sure the electrical connectors are free of corrosion and are tight.

d. If removed, install the locating dowels (**A, Figure 18**) and a new gasket (**B, Figure 18**).

e. Be sure to install the wiring harness clamps (**B, Figure 16**) under the cover bolts in the correct location.

Rotor Removal/Installation

Refer to **Figure 14** for this procedure.

1. Remove the alternator stator assembly as described in this chapter.

2. Remove the starter drive gear and its shaft (**A, Figure 19**).

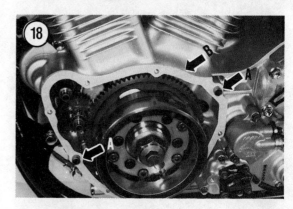

3. Withdraw the idler gear shaft (**B, Figure 19**) and remove the No. 1 idler gear (**C, Figure 19**).

4A. If you have access to an adjustable holding tool, install it onto the outer surface of the alternator rotor and tighten securely (**Figure 20**). This will prevent the alternator rotor from turning in the next step.

4B. Place a 36 mm offset box wrench onto the hex fitting (**A, Figure 21**) on the rotor to prevent the alternator rotor from turning in the next step.

NOTE
In Step 5, do not remove the rotor bolt. Break it loose, then loosen it several

*turns and leave it in place (A, **Figure 21**). The bolt must remain installed because it is used in conjunction with the rotor remover tool in Step 6.*

5. Loosen, but do not remove, the alternator rotor bolt (**B, Figure 21**). Loosen it several turns and leave it in place. The inner bolt on the rotor removal tool seats against the alternator bolt head.

CAUTION
Do not try to remove the rotor without a puller. Any attempt to do so will

ultimately lead to some form of damage to the engine and/or rotor. Aftermarket pullers are available from motorcycle dealerships or mail order houses. If you can't buy or borrow one, have the dealership remove the rotor.

6. Install the rotor removal tool, Suzuki special tool (part No. 09930-30720) onto the threads of the rotor.
7. Hold the rotor removal tool (**A, Figure 22**) with a 36 mm open-end wrench and turn the center bolt (**B, Figure 22**). Turn the center bolt until the rotor disengages from the crankshaft taper.

NOTE
If the rotor is difficult to remove, strike the end of the puller (not the rotor as it will be damaged) firmly with a hammer. This will usually break it loose.

CAUTION
If normal rotor removal attempts fail, do not force the puller as the threads may be stripped from the rotor causing expensive damage. Take the bike to a Suzuki dealership and have the rotor removed.

8. Unscrew and remove the rotor puller from the rotor.
9. Unscrew the bolt, then remove the rotor from the crankshaft.
10. Remove the Woodruff key (**A, Figure 23**) from the crankshaft and place it on the inner magnetic surface of the rotor.
11. Remove the starter clutch gear (**B, Figure 23**) assembly from the crankshaft.
12. Inspect the inside of the rotor (**Figure 24**) for small bolts, washers or other metal debris that may have been picked up by the magnets. These small metal bits can cause severe damage to the alternator stator assembly.
13. Inspect the rotor keyway (**Figure 25**) for wear or damage. If damage is excessive, replace the rotor.
14. Install by reversing these removal steps while noting the following:
    a. Use an aerosol electrical contact cleaner and clean all oil residue from the crankshaft taper where the rotor slides onto it and the matching tapered surface in the rotor. This is to assure a good tight fit of the rotor onto the crankshaft.
    b. Install the Woodruff key (**Figure 23**) in the crankshaft groove.

c. Apply a light coat of ThreeBond TB3060, Loctite No. 271, or equivalent, to the mounting bolt threads prior to installation. Tighten the bolts securely.

d. Tighten the rotor bolt (**Figure 21**) to the torque specification listed in **Table 3**.

TRANSISTORIZED IGNITION SYSTEM

The 1400 Intruder is equipped with a solid-state transistorized ignition system that uses no breaker points. The signal generator portion of the system consists of a raised tab on the alternator rotor and two signal generators that are attached to the alternator cover next to the alternator stator coil assembly. The ignition circuit is shown in **Figure 26**.

As the alternator rotor is turned by the crankshaft, the raised tab passes the pickup coils and a signal is sent to the ignition unit. This signal turns the ignitor unit transistor alternately ON and OFF. As the transistor is turned ON and OFF, the current passing through the primary windings of the ignition coil, is also turned ON and OFF. Thus it induces the secondary current in the ignition coil secondary windings to fire the spark plugs.

The ignitor unit has a built-in rpm limiter as well as a reverse rotation protection. If the engine is run past the 7000 rpm limit or the engine somehow tries to rotate in the reverse direction, the ignitor unit will cut off the primary current to the ignition coils.

Two additional safety features of the ignition system are the sidestand and neutral relays. These relays allow the ignition system to operate only when the sidestand is in the raised position and the transmission is shifted into neutral.

Ignition System Precautions

Certain measures must be taken to protect the ignition system. Damage to the semiconductors in the system may occur if any of the electrical connections are broken while the engine is running.

Troubleshooting

Refer to *Ignition System* in Chapter Two.

Ignition Pickup Coil Resistance Test

Suzuki specifies the use of the Suzuki Pocket Tester (part No. 09900-25002) for accurate resistance readings of the regulator/rectifier unit. Refer to the *Basic Information* section at the beginning of this chapter regarding this tester.

NOTE
Prior to making this test, check the condition of the pocket tester batteries. If necessary, install a new battery.

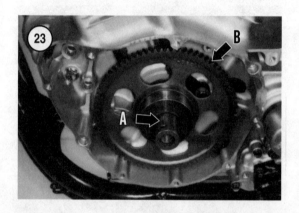

*Refer to the **Basic Information** section at the beginning of this chapter regarding the specified test temperature of 20° C (68° F). If the component is not at the specified temperature, the resulting resistance readings will be inaccurate.*

1. Remove the rider's seat and the frame side covers as described in Chapter Thirteen.

NOTE
*The 4-pin electrical connector (1 green, 1 blue, 1 yellow, 1 black) (**Figure 27**) for the ignition pickup coils is disconnected*

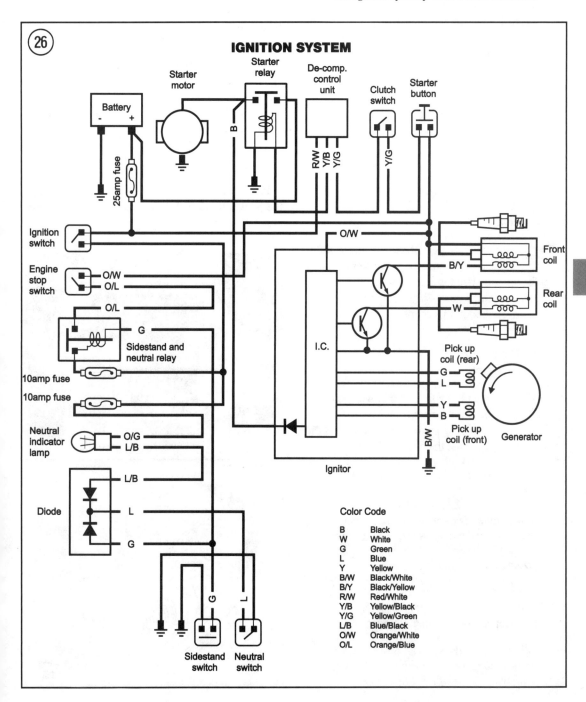

IGNITION SYSTEM

Color Code

B	Black
W	White
G	Green
L	Blue
Y	Yellow
B/W	Black/White
B/Y	Black/Yellow
R/W	Red/White
Y/B	Yellow/Black
Y/G	Yellow/Green
L/B	Blue/Black
O/W	Orange/White
O/L	Orange/Blue

from the ignitor unit when the seat is removed.

2. Use an ohmmeter set at R × 1,000 and check the resistance between the following wires in the pickup coil side of the electrical connector. Check between the green and blue terminals and the black and yellow terminals. The specified resistance is listed in Table 1.

3. If the resistance shown is less than specified or there is no indicated resistance (infinite resistance) between the 2 wires, the pickup coils are damaged and must be replaced as described under *Alternator Stator* in this chapter.

4. If the pickup coils check out okay, reconnect the electrical connector during seat installation. Make sure the electrical connector is free of corrosion and is tight.

5. Install the frame covers and the rider's seat.

Pickup Coil Replacement

The pickup coils are part of the alternator stator assembly harness and cannot be replaced separately from the alternator stator assembly.

If replacement is necessary, refer to *Alternator Stator* as described in this chapter.

Ignition Coil Performance Test

1. Disconnect the plug wire and remove one of the spark plugs as described in Chapter Three.

2. Insert the spark plug into its cap and touch the spark plug base against the cylinder head to ground it. Position the spark plug so you can see the electrode (**Figure 28**).

> **WARNING**
> *If the engine is flooded, do not perform this test. Fuel that is ejected through the spark plug holes can be ignited by the firing of the spark plug.*

3. Turn the engine over with the electric starter. A fat blue spark should be evident across the spark plug electrode. Repeat for the other cylinder.

> **WARNING**
> *If necessary, hold onto the spark plug wire with a pair of insulated pliers. Do*

not hold the spark plug, wire or connector with your hand or a serious electrical shock may result.

4. If a fat blue spark occurs, the ignition coil is good. If not, perform the following resistance test.

Ignition Coil Resistance Test

Suzuki specifies the use of the Suzuki Pocket Tester (part No. 09900-25002) for accurate resistance readings of the regulator/rectifier unit. Refer to the *Basic Information* section at the beginning of this chapter regarding this tester.

> *NOTE*
> Prior to making this test, check the condition of the pocket tester battery. *If necessary, install a new battery.*

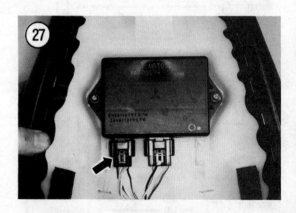

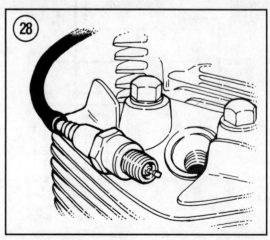

NOTE
*Refer to the **Basic Information** section at the beginning of this chapter regarding the specified test temperature of 20° C (68° F). If the component is not at the specified temperature, the resulting resistance readings will be inaccurate.*

The ignition coil is a form of transformer which develops the high voltage required to jump the spark plug gap. The only maintenance required is that of keeping the electrical connections clean and tight and occasionally checking to see that the coils are mounted securely.

If the condition of the coil(s) is doubtful, there are several checks which may be made.

1. Remove the rider's seat as described in Chapter Thirteen.

2. Disconnect the battery negative lead as described in this chapter.

3. Remove the frame left-hand side cover as described in Chapter Thirteen.

4. Disconnect all ignition coil wires (including the spark plug leads from the spark plugs) before testing.

NOTE
In Step 5 and Step 6, the resistance specification is not as important as the fact that there is continuity between the terminals. If the ignition coil windings are in good condition the resistance values will be approximate to those specified in Table 1.

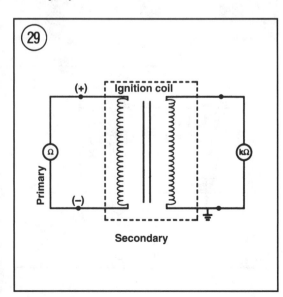

5. Use an ohmmeter set at R × 1 and measure the primary coil resistance between the ignition coil positive (+) and negative (–) terminals **(Figure 29)**. The specified resistance value is listed in Table 1.

6. Use an ohmmeter set at R × 1000 and measure the secondary coil resistance between the spark plug lead and one of the primary coil terminals **(Figure 29)**. The specified resistance value is listed in Table 1.

7. Repeat Step 5 and Step 6 for the other ignition coil.

8. If the coil resistance does not meet (or come close to) either of these specifications, the coil must be replaced. If the coil exhibits visible damage, replace it as described in this chapter.

9. Reconnect all ignition coil wires to the ignition coil.

10. Install the left-hand frame side cover and the rider's seat as described in Chapter Thirteen.

Ignition Coil Removal/Installation

1. Remove the rider's seat as described in Chapter Thirteen.

2. Disconnect the battery negative lead as described in this chapter.

3. Remove the frame left-hand side cover as described in Chapter Thirteen.

4. Disconnect the primary leads (A, **Figure 30**) from the ignition coil.

5. Disconnect the high voltage lead (B, **Figure 30**) from the spark plug.

6. Remove the bolts and spacers (C, **Figure 30**) securing the ignition coil to the frame.

7. Carefully withdraw the high voltage lead through the frame, noting its path, and remove the coil.

8. If necessary, repeat Steps 4-7 for the other ignition coil.

9. Install by reversing these removal steps. Make sure all electrical connections are free of corrosion and are tight.

Ignitor Unit
Resistance Test
(1987 Models Only)

Suzuki specifies the use of the Suzuki Pocket Tester (part No. 09900-25002) for accurate resistance reading for testing of the regulator/rectifier unit. Refer to the *Basic Information* section at the beginning of this chapter regarding this tester.

> **NOTE**
> *Prior to making this test, check the condition of the pocket tester battery. If necessary, install a new battery.*

> **NOTE**
> *Refer to the **Basic Information** section at the beginning of this chapter regarding the specified test temperature of 20° C (68° F). If the component is not at the specified temperature, the resulting resistance readings will be inaccurate.*

1. Remove the rider's seat as described in Chapter Thirteen.

> **NOTE**
> *The 4-pin and 6-pin electrical connectors are disconnected from the ignitor unit when the seat is removed.*

2. If necessary, remove the ignitor unit from the seat (**Figure 31**).

3. Set the pocket tester to the R x 1000 (K) ohms scale.

4. Refer to **Figure 32** for wire colors.

5. Refer to **Figure 33** for the pocket tester lead connections and values.

6. If any of the meter readings differ from the stated values, replace the ignitor unit as described in this chapter.

7. Install the ignitor unit onto the seat if removed. Install the rider's seat as described in Chapter Thirteen.

Ignitor Unit Test
(1988-on Models Only)

Complete testing of the ignition unit on these models requires the Suzuki Digital Ignitor Checker (part No. 09931-64410). Refer ignitor unit testing to a Suzuki dealership as this tool is very expensive. If the pickup coil and both ignition coils are working properly, then this simple check can be performed by the dealership to confirm the ignitor unit is faulty.

Ignitor Unit Replacement

1. Remove the rider's seat as described in Chapter Thirteen.

> **NOTE**
> *The 4-pin and 6-pin electrical connectors are disconnected from the ignitor unit when the seat is removed.*

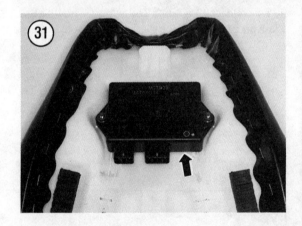

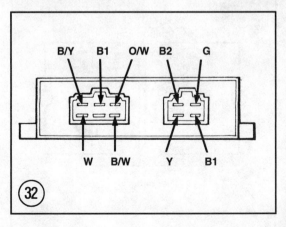

2. Remove the mounting nuts securing the ignitor unit (**Figure 31**) to the seat and remove it.

3. Reinstall the ignitor unit and tighten the mounting nuts securely.

4. Install the rider's seat as described in Chapter Thirteen.

Ignition Timing Control Boost Sensor (1992 and later Models) Test

1. Remove the rider's seat as described in Chapter Thirteen.

2. Remove the frame left-hand side cover as described in Chapter Thirteen.

3. Make sure the bike's battery is fully charged, otherwise the test results will not be accurate. Check the battery as described under *Battery* in Chapter Three.

NOTE
Do not disconnect the electrical connector (A, Figure 34) from the boost sensor for the following test.

4. Disconnect the boot sensor hose (B, **Figure 34**) from the fitting on the front cylinder intake port (**Figure 35**).

5. Set the pocket tester to the 10 volt DC scale.

6. Refer to **Figure 36** and connect the positive (+) test probe to terminal No. 3 and the negative (–) test probe to terminal 2 as shown in **Figure 37**.

7. Turn the ignition switch ON and observe the meter reading. The voltage reading should be approximately 3.0 volts.

8. Connect a hand held vacuum pump to the boost sensor hose (**Figure 38**) disconnected in Step 4.

9. Apply 250 mmHg (333.25 mbar) of vacuum to the sensor hose and observe the meter reading. The voltage reading should be approximately 2.0 volts.

10. If the boost sensor fails either of these tests, the boost sensor is faulty and must be replaced.

11. Disconnect the vacuum pump and pocket tester.

12. Connect the boot sensor hose onto the fitting on the front cylinder intake port. Push it on until it is correctly seated to avoid an air leak.

13. Install the frame left-hand side cover and rider's seat as described in Chapter Thirteen.

Control Boost Sensor Removal/Installation

1. Remove the rider's seat as described in Chapter Thirteen.

---

(33)

IGNITOR UNIT TEST

Unit: Approx. kΩ

		B/Y	B₁	O/W	W	B/W	B₂	Y	G	B₁
					(-) Probe of tester to:					
(+) Probe of tester to:	B/Y		30	3.6	OFF	2.6	14	14	14	14
	B₁	OFF		18	OFF	17	40	40	40	40
		OFF	18		OFF	1	7	7	7	7
		OFF	30	3.5		2.5	14	14	14	14
		OFF	19	1	OFF		5	5	5	5
		OFF	90	60	OFF	60		0.5	100	100
		OFF	90	60	OFF	60	0.5		106	100
		OFF	90	60	OFF	60	200	100		0.5
		OFF	90	60	OFF	60	100	100	0.5	

9

2. Remove the frame left-hand side cover as described in Chapter Thirteen.

3. Disconnect the vacuum hose (A, **Figure 34**) from the boost sensor.

4. Disconnect the electrical connector (B, Figure 34) from the boost sensor.

5. Remove the nuts securing the boost sensor (C, **Figure 34**) to the mounting bracket and remove the sensor from the frame.

6. If necessary, disconnect the boot sensor hose from the fitting on the front cylinder intake port. Carefully remove the hose from the frame, noting its path through the frame and the clips holding the hose in place.

7. Install by reversing these removal steps. Make sure the hose is pushed on until it is correctly seated at both ends to avoid an air leak (**Figure 35**).

AUTOMATIC COMPRESSION RELEASE CONTROL AND STARTER SYSTEM

The Automatic Compression Release Control portion of the starter system operates the compression release solenoid and the mechanism contained within both cylinder heads. When the starter button is pressed, the control unit activates the solenoid, lifting the compression release lever on each cylinder head. The lever opens the exhaust valves a slight amount to relieve compression. This allows the relatively small starter motor to turn over the large 1,400 cc displacement engine with the least amount of stress on the motor.

The starter system includes an ignition switch, a starter button, clutch interlock switch, sidestand interlock switch, starter relay, battery and starter motor as shown in **Figure 39**. Each component of this system is covered separately in this chapter except the battery, which is covered in Chapter Three.

ELECTRIC STARTER

Removal/Installation

1. Disconnect the battery negative (–) lead as described in this chapter.

2. Slide back the rubber boot from the electrical cable connector.

3. Remove the nut and disconnect the starter electrical motor cable (A, **Figure 40**) from the starter motor.

4. Remove the 2 bolts (B, **Figure 40**) securing the starter motor to the crankcase.

5. Partially lift up and pull the starter motor toward the right-hand side to disengage it from the idler gears. Remove the starter motor from the crankcase.

6. Install by reversing these removal steps. Apply a light coat of engine oil to the O-ring seal (A, **Figure 41**).

Preliminary Inspection

The overhaul of a starter motor is best left to an expert. This procedure shows how to detect a defective starter.

Inspect the O-ring seal (A, **Figure 41**). O-ring seals tend to harden after prolonged use and heat and

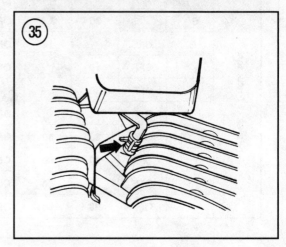

therefore lose their ability to seal properly. Replace as necessary.

Inspect the starter shaft (B, **Figure 41**) for chipped or missing teeth. If damaged, the starter assembly must be replaced.

Disassembly

Refer to **Figure 42** for this procedure.

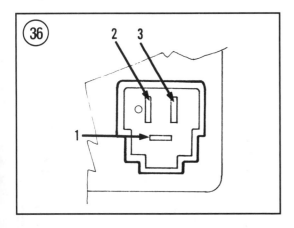

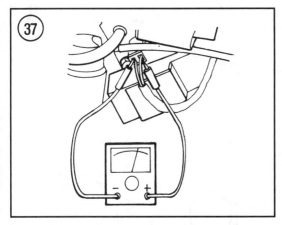

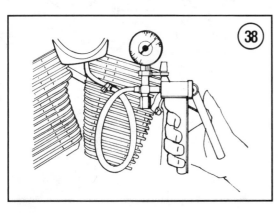

1. Remove the through-bolts and washers (A, **Figure 43**), then separate the right-hand end cap (B, **Figure 43**) from the case.
2. Remove the washers (**Figure 44**) from the ball bearing.
3. Remove the left-hand end cap (C, **Figure 43**).
4. Withdraw the armature from the case (**Figure 45**).
5. Remove the nut, washers and insulators (A, **Figure 46**) securing the brush holder assembly to the case. Keep all of these parts in order (**Figure 47**) as they must be reassembled in the same sequence to insulate the positive brush set.
6. Withdraw the threaded stud of the brush holder from the case and carefully pull the brush holder assembly (B, **Figure 46**) from the armature.

> *CAUTION*
> *Do not immerse the wire windings in the case or the armature coil in solvent as the insulation may be damaged. Wipe the windings with a cloth lightly moistened with solvent and thoroughly dry.*

7. Clean all grease, dirt and carbon from all components.
8. Inspect the starter motor components as described in this chapter.

Assembly

1. If removed, install the O-ring seal into both ends of the case.
2. Push all 4 brushes into their holders.
3. Make sure the O-ring (**Figure 48**) is still in place on the brush holder stud.
4. Install the threaded stud into the case, then carefully install the brush holder assembly (**Figure 49**) into the case.
5. Align the tab on the negative brush holder with the notch in the case (**Figure 50**) and push the holder down until it stops.
6. Install the insulators, washers and nut (**Figure 47**) securing the brush holder assembly to the case. Tighten the nut securely.
7. Partially install the armature coil assembly into the case (**Figure 45**). Carefully push the brushes back into their holders, then slowly push the armature coil assembly past the brushes. Make sure the

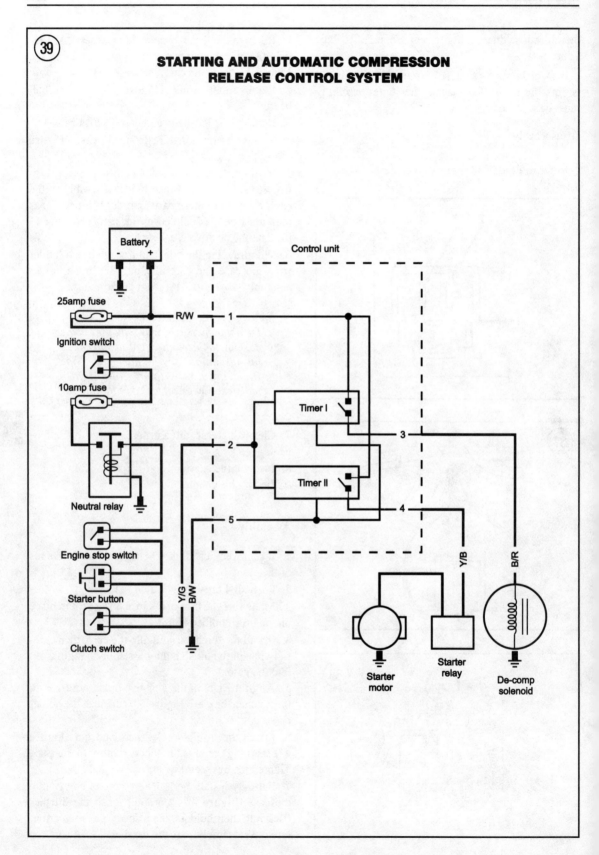

STARTING AND AUTOMATIC COMPRESSION RELEASE CONTROL SYSTEM

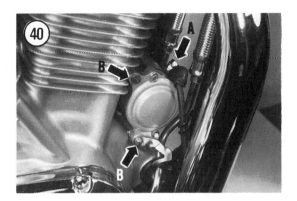

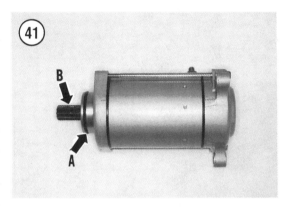

brushes are properly seated against the armature (**Figure 51**).

8. Install the washers (**Figure 44**) onto the end of the armature.

9. Install the left-hand end cap (A, **Figure 52**) and the right-hand end cap (B, **Figure 52**) onto the case.

10. Correctly align the case screw holes in both end caps and push the caps onto the case until they bottom out.

11. Apply a small amount of Loctite (No. 242) to the through-bolt threads prior to installation.

12. Install the through-bolts and washers (C, **Figure 52**) and tighten securely.

Inspection

1. Measure the length of each brush (**Figure 53**) with a vernier caliper. If the length is 9.0 mm (0.35 in.) or less for any one of the brushes, replace the brush sets. The brushes cannot be replaced individually.

2. Inspect the commutator (A, **Figure 54**). The mica should be just below the surface of the copper bars. On a worn commutator the mica and copper bars

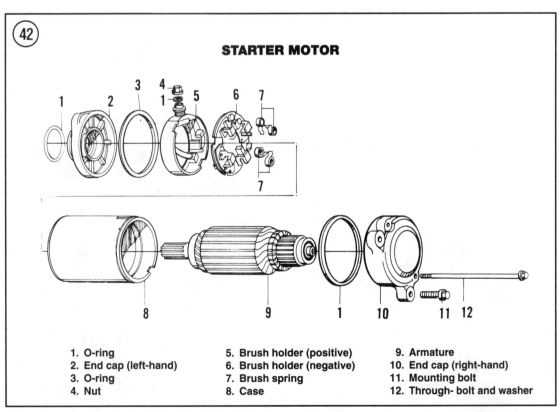

STARTER MOTOR

1. O-ring
2. End cap (left-hand)
3. O-ring
4. Nut
5. Brush holder (positive)
6. Brush holder (negative)
7. Brush spring
8. Case
9. Armature
10. End cap (right-hand)
11. Mounting bolt
12. Through- bolt and washer

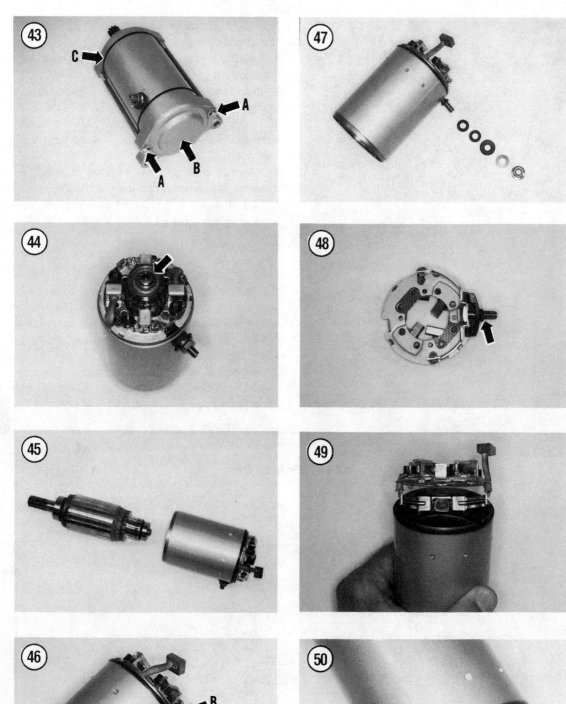

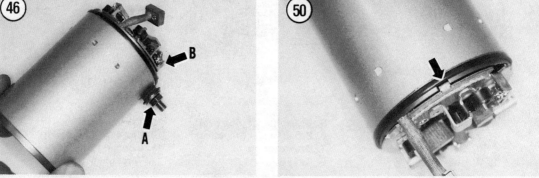

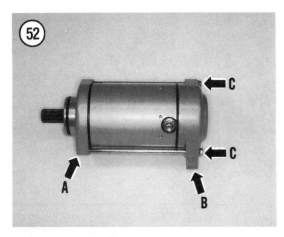

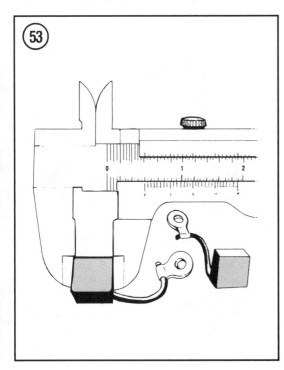

may be worn to the same level (**Figure 55**). If necessary, have the commutator serviced by a dealership or electrical repair shop.

3. Inspect the commutator copper bars for discoloration. If a pair of bars are discolored, grounded armature coils are indicated.

4. Use an ohmmeter and perform the following:

  a. Check for continuity between the commutator bars (**Figure 56**); there should be continuity between any 2 of the bars.

  b. Check for continuity between the commutator bars and the shaft (**Figure 57**); there should be no continuity (infinite resistance).

  c. If the unit fails either of these tests, the starter assembly must be replaced. The armature cannot be replaced individually.

5. Use an ohmmeter and perform the following:

  a. Check for continuity between the starter cable terminal and the starter case; there should be continuity.

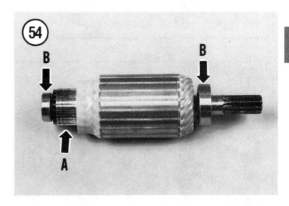

9

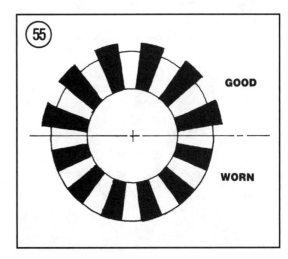

b. Check for continuity between the starter cable terminal and the brush wire terminal; there should be no continuity (infinite resistance).

c. If the unit fails either of these tests, the starter assembly must be replaced. The case/field coil assembly cannot be replaced individually.

6. Inspect the bearings (B, **Figure 54**) for the armature coil assembly. They must rotate freely with no evidence of wear. If the bearing(s) is worn, replace the armature coil assembly. The bearings cannot be replaced individually.

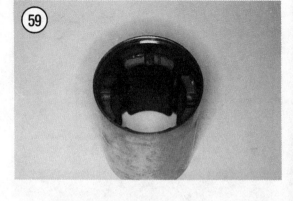

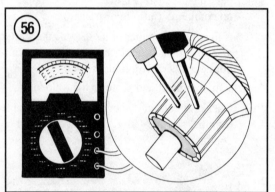

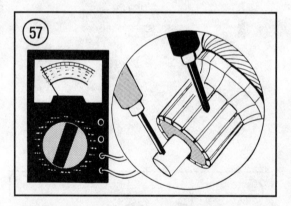

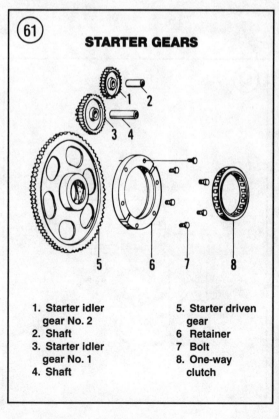

STARTER GEARS

1. Starter idler gear No. 2
2. Shaft
3. Starter idler gear No. 1
4. Shaft
5. Starter driven gear
6. Retainer
7. Bolt
8. One-way clutch

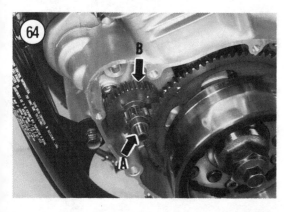

7. Inspect the seal (**Figure 58**) in the left-hand end cap for wear, damage or deterioration. The seal cannot be replaced. If damaged, replace the left-hand end cap.

8. Inspect the right-hand end cap for wear or damage, replace if necessary.

9. Inspect the case assembly for wear or damage. Make sure the field coils (**Figure 59**) are bonded securely in place. If damaged or any field coils are loose, replace the case assembly.

10. Inspect the brush holder assembly (**Figure 60**) for wear or damage, if damaged; replace the assembly.

11. Inspect the positive (+) brush holder and brush springs assembly for wear or damage; replace any damaged parts.

12. Inspect the negative (–) brush holder and brush springs assembly for wear or damage.

STARTER CLUTCH AND GEARS

The starter gears can be removed with the engine in the frame. This procedure is shown with the engine removed for clarity.

Refer to **Figure 61** for this procedure.

9

Removal

1. Remove the alternator stator assembly as described in this chapter.

2. Remove the collar (**Figure 62**) from the starter drive gear shaft.

3. Remove the drive gear shaft (A, **Figure 63**) and drive gear (B, **Figure 63**).

4. Remove the idle gear shaft (A, **Figure 64**) and idle gear (B, **Figure 64**).

5. Remove the alternator rotor as described in this chapter.

6. Remove the Woodruff key (A, **Figure 65**) from the crankshaft and place it on the inner magnetic surface of the rotor.

7. Remove the starter clutch gear (B, **Figure 65**) assembly from the crankshaft.

8. If removed, install the starter driven gear (**Figure 66**) into the backside of the alternator rotor.

9. Try to rotate the starter driven gear (**Figure 67**). It should rotate freely in one direction and lock up in the other direction.

10. If the starter driven gear rotates in both directions or locks up in both directions, replace the starter clutch as described in this chapter.

Inspection

1. Inspect the starter idler gears for wear or damage. Replace if necessary. Insert the shaft into its respective gear and rotate the gear. Suzuki does not provide specifications for the shafts nor the inside diameter of the gears. If there is a noticeable amount of play, replace the gear(s) and shaft(s) as a set.

2. Inspect the starter driven gear (**Figure 68**) for wear, chipped or missing teeth. Replace if necessary.

3. Inspect the starter driven gear inner bushing surface (**Figure 69**) where it rides on the crankshaft and the outer surface (**Figure 70**) where it engages the one-way clutch. If either surface is damaged, replace the gear.

4. Inspect the rollers (**Figure 71**) of the one-way clutch for burrs, wear or damage. Replace if necessary.

5. Inspect the shaft receptacles in the left-hand crankcase for wear or damage.

Installation

1. Install the starter clutch gear (B, **Figure 65**) assembly onto the crankshaft.

2. Install the Woodruff key (A, **Figure 65**) onto the crankshaft and make sure it is seated correctly.

3. Install the alternator rotor as described in this chapter.

4. Position the idle gear with the larger diameter gear (**Figure 72**) going in first and move the gear into position.

5. Install the idle gear shaft (**Figure 73**) through the gear and into the crankcase receptacle. Push the shaft in until it stops.

6. Position the drive gear with the long shoulder (**Figure 74**) facing out and move the gear into position.

7. Install the drive gear shaft (A, **Figure 63**) through the gear (B, **Figure 63**) and into the crankcase receptacle. Push the shaft in until it stops.

8. Install the collar (**Figure 62**) onto the starter drive gear shaft.

9. Install the alternator stator assembly as described in this chapter.

Starter Clutch Replacement

1. If still installed, remove the starter driven gear from the backside of the alternator rotor.

2. Hold onto the center of the rotor with a 36 mm offset wrench.

3. Remove the 6mm Allen bolts (**Figure 75**) securing the starter clutch assembly to the backside of the rotor.

4. Separate the starter one-way clutch and retainer (**Figure 76**) from backside of the rotor.

5. Install a new one-way clutch with the flange side going on first.

6. Install the retainer, align the bolt holes and turn the assembly over.

7. Apply a light coat of ThreeBond TB1360 or Loctite No. 271 to the 6 mm Allen bolt threads prior to installation.

8. Use the same tool set-up used for removal to hold the alternator rotor stationary while tightening the bolts. Tighten the Allen bolts in a crisscross pattern to the torque specification listed in Table 3.

STARTER RELAY

Testing

1. Remove the rider's seat and frame left-hand side cover as described in Chapter Thirteen.

> *CAUTION*
> *When disconnecting the starter wire at the starter relay in Step 2, do not touch or ground the wrench against the other starter relay terminal. Doing so will short the terminals together.*

> *NOTE*
> *Refer to the **Basic Information** section at the beginning of this chapter regarding the specified test temperature of 20° C (68° F). If the component is not at the specified temperature, the resulting resistance readings will be inaccurate.*

2. Disconnect the black electrical wire going from the starter relay to the starter. Leave the other electrical wire connected to the relay.
3. Shift the transmission into NEUTRAL.
4. Set the ohmmeter to R × 1 and connect the test leads across the 2 large terminals (**Figure 77**).
5. Turn the ignition switch ON.
6. Pull the clutch lever in until it stops. Hold the lever in this position against the grip with a plastic tie.
7. Press the START button while reading the resistance scale on the ohmmeter. When the start button is pressed, the starter relay should "click" once and the ohmmeter should read continuity (low resistance). If there is continuity the relay is good. If there is no continuity (infinite resistance), the relay may be faulty, proceed to Step 8.
8. Disconnect the battery (+) wire and the ground (–) wire from the large terminals on the relay.
9. Disconnect the relay coil wire 2-pin electrical connectors (1 yellow/black, 1 black/white) from the relay.
10. Set the ohmmeter to R × 1 and connect the test leads across the 2 small terminals (**Figure 78**) on the relay and check the resistance. The specified resistance is 2-6 ohms. If the resistance is not within specified range, the relay coil is faulty and the relay must be replaced.
11. If the relay checks out okay, install all electrical wires to the relay and the large terminals tighten the

nuts securely. Make sure the electrical connectors are on tight and the rubber boot is properly installed to keep out moisture.

12. Install the left-hand side cover and seat.

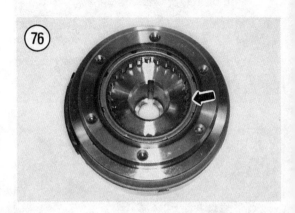

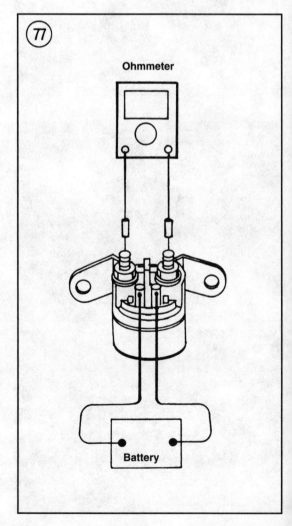

Removal/Installation

1. Remove the rider's seat and frame left-hand side cover as described in Chapter Thirteen.

2. Slide off the rubber protective boots and disconnect the large electrical wires from the top terminals of the relay.

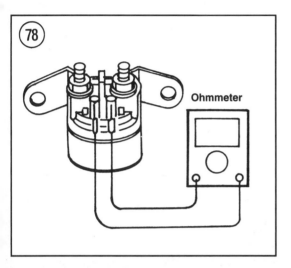

Ohmmeter

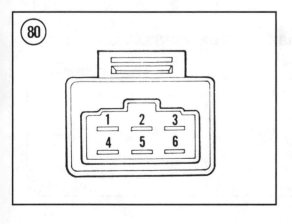

3. Disconnect the relay coil wire 2-pin electrical connector containing 2 wires (1 yellow/black, 1 black/white) from the relay.

4. Remove the bolts securing the relay to the frame and remove the relay and coil wiring and connector from the frame.

5. Replace by reversing these removal steps while noting the following:

    a. Install all electrical wires to the solenoid and on the large terminals tighten the nuts securely.

    b. Make sure the electrical connectors are on tight and that the rubber boot is properly installed to keep out moisture.

Compression Release Control Unit
Timer Test

There are 2 timers built into the control unit and each is tested separately.

1. Remove both seats as described in Chapter Thirteen.

2. Disconnect the battery negative lead as described in this chapter.

3. Disconnect the 6-pin electrical connector from the compression release control unit, then remove the control unit (**Figure 79**) from the rear fender mount.

4. To test the No. 1 timer portion of the control unit, refer to **Figure 80** and **Figure 81** and perform the following:

    a. Set the pocket tester to the 25 volt DC range.

    b. Connect the positive (+) test probe to the No. 3 terminal.

    c. Connect the negative (–) test probe to the No. 5 terminal.

    d. Connect the positive (+) battery jumper lead to the No. 1 and No. 2 terminals.

    e. Connect the negative (–) battery jumper lead to the No. 5 terminal and observe the tester.

    f. The volt meter should read 12 volts for 0.7 seconds, then return to 0 volts.

    g. If the voltage is correct the No. 1 timer portion is operating correctly.

5. To test the No. 2 timer portion of the control unit, refer to **Figure 80** and **Figure 82** and perform the following:

    a. Set the pocket tester to 25 volt DC range.

    b. Connect the positive (+) test probe to the No. 4 terminal.

c. Connect the negative (–) test probe to the No. 5 terminal.

d. Connect the positive (+) battery jumper lead to the No. 1 and No. 2 terminals.

e. Connect the negative (–) battery jumper lead to the No. 5 terminal and observe the tester.

f. The volt meter should read 0 volts for the first 0.2 seconds, then increase to 12 volts.

g. If the voltage is correct the No. 2 timer portion is operating correctly.

6. If the control unit fails either test in Step 4 and Step 5, replace the control unit.

7. If the control unit is okay, reinstall it onto the rear fender and reconnect the electrical connector.

8. Install both seats as described in Chapter Thirteen.

Compression Release Control Unit
Resistance Test

Suzuki specifies the use of the Suzuki Pocket Tester (part No. 09900-25002) for accurate resistance testing of the regulator/rectifier unit. Refer to the *Basic Information* section at the beginning of this chapter regarding this tester.

> *NOTE*
> *Prior to making this test, check the condition of the pocket tester battery. If necessary, install a new battery.*

> *NOTE*
> *Refer to the **Basic Information** section at the beginning of this chapter regarding a component specified test temperature of 20° C (68° F). If the component is not at the specified*

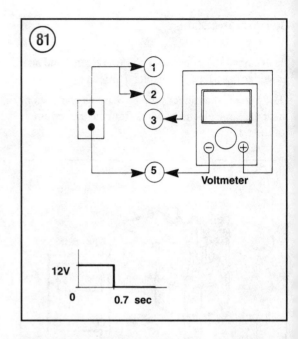

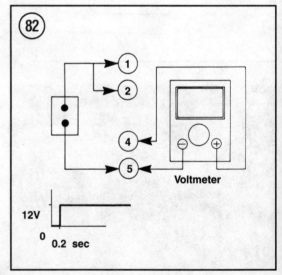

AUTOMATIC COMPRESSION RELEASE SOLENOID CONTROL UNIT TEST

Unit: Approx. kΩ

(–) Probe of tester to:	(+) Probe of tester to:				
	B/W	Y/B	B/R	Y/G	R/W
B/W		OFF	2.2	3	OFF
Y/B	2.8		5.5	7	OFF
B/R	2	OFF		5	OFF
Y/G	3	OFF	5		OFF
R/W	OFF	OFF	OFF	OFF	

temperature, the resulting resistance readings will be inaccurate.

1. Remove both seats as described in Chapter Thirteen.

2. Disconnect the battery negative lead as described in this chapter.

3. Disconnect the 6-pin electrical connector from the compression release control unit, then remove the control unit (**Figure 79**) from the rear fender mount.

4. Set the pocket tester to the Rx 1,000 (K) ohms scale.

5. Refer to **Figure 80** for wire colors within the electrical connectors.

6. Refer to **Figure 83** for pocket tester lead connections and values.

7. If any of the meter readings differ from the stated values, replace the control unit as described in this chapter.

8. If the control unit is good, reinstall it onto the rear fender and reconnect the electrical connector.

9. Install both seats as described in Chapter Thirteen.

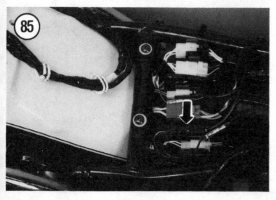

Control Unit Replacement

1. Remove both seats as described in Chapter Thirteen.

2. Disconnect the battery negative lead as described in this chapter.

3. Disconnect the 6-pin electrical connector from the compression release control unit, then remove the control unit (**Figure 79**) from the rear fender mount.

4. Reinstall the control unit onto the rear fender and reconnect the electrical connector.

5. Install both seats as described in Chapter Thirteen.

Compression Release Solenoid Test

1. Remove the fuel tank as described in Chapter Eight.

2. Shift the transmission into neutral.

3. Remove the bolts securing the right-hand front cylinder head side cover and the left-hand rear cylinder head side cover. Remove both covers.

4. Turn the ignition switch ON.

5. Press the start button and momentarily start the engine.

6. Observe that the solenoid pulls on the compression release cable (**Figure 84**) to open the exhaust valves.

7. If the cable is operating correctly, the solenoid is good.

8. If the cable is not pulled, proceed with the following steps.

9. Disconnect the compression release solenoid 2-pin electrical connector (**Figure 85**). The main wiring harness wire colors are 1 black/white and 1 black/red. The 2 wires going to the solenoid are white.

> **CAUTION**
> *In Step 10, do not apply 12 volts to the solenoid for more than 5 seconds or the solenoid coil will be damaged.*

> **NOTE**
> *Polarity is not important when connecting the 12 volts to the solenoid terminals.*

10. Momentarily apply 12 volts to the solenoid side of the electrical connector (**Figure 86**). Disconnect the 12 volts from the solenoid immediately.

11. Observe that the solenoid pulls on the compression release cable to open the exhaust valves.

12. If the cable is not pulled, the solenoid is faulty and must be replaced as described in this chapter.

13. If the cable is now being pulled, check for a loose or broken wire in the circuit. Refer to **Figure 87** and the wiring diagrams at the end of this manual.

14. Install the right-hand front cylinder head side cover and the left-hand rear cylinder head side cover and tighten the bolts securely.

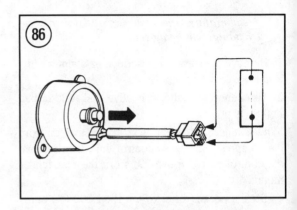

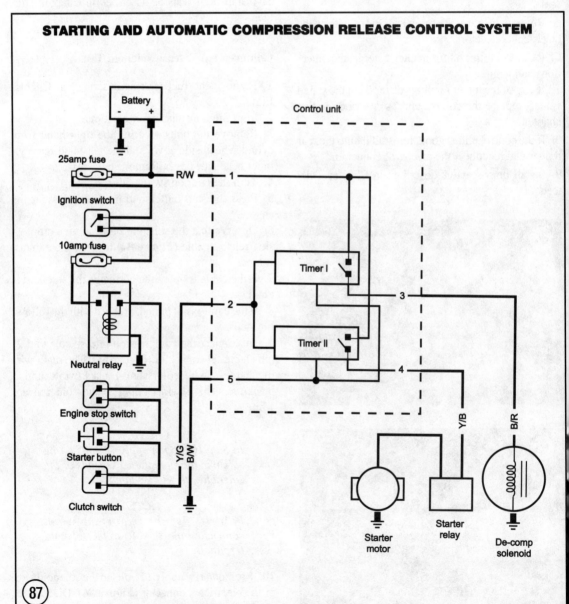

STARTING AND AUTOMATIC COMPRESSION RELEASE CONTROL SYSTEM

15. Install the fuel tank as described in Chapter Eight.

Compression Release Solenoid Removal/Installation

1. Remove the fuel tank as described in Chapter Eight.
2. Remove the frame left-hand side cover as described in Chapter Thirteen.
3. Remove the No. 1 rear cylinder's ignition coil as described in this chapter. The No. 1 coil is mounted at the front of the two coils.
4. Remove the rear air filter case and rear carburetor as described in Chapter Eight.
5. Remove the intake pipe from the rear cylinder.
6. Remove the engine rear upper through bolt and nut.

> *NOTE*
> *The Allen bolts screw into the nuts welded to the solenoid mounting bracket assembly.*

7. Remove the Allen bolts and lockwashers securing both the right- and left-hand upper engine mounting brackets. Remove both mounting brackets.
8. Remove the E-clip and clevis pin securing the compression release cable to the top of the solenoid shaft. Pull the cable up and out of the solenoid mounting bracket. Reinstall the clevis pin and E-clip onto the cable to avoid misplacing these small parts.
9. If the solenoid is going to be replaced, remove the screws and the cable mounting bracket from the solenoid and transfer the bracket to the new solenoid. Tighten the screws securely.
10. Install by reversing these removal steps while noting the following:
   a. Position the solenoid assembly into the frame with the electrical wires facing toward the rear of the bike.
   b. Install the mounting brackets onto the frame and solenoid assembly. Install the Allen bolts and lockwasher and tighten finger-tight at this time.
   c. Install the engine rear upper through bolt from the left-hand side and install the nut.
   d. Tighten the Allen bolts and though bolt to the torque specification listed in Table 3.

LIGHTING SYSTEM

The lighting system consists of a headlight, taillight/brakelight, directional lights, indicator lights and a speedometer illumination light. Table 2 lists replacement bulbs for these components.

Always use the correct wattage bulb as indicated in Table 2. The use of a larger wattage bulb will give a dim light and a smaller wattage bulb will burn out prematurely.

Headlight Bulb and Lens Replacement

Refer to **Figure 88** for this procedure.
1. Remove the screws (**Figure 89**) at the bottom of the headlight case.
2. Pull on the bottom of the headlight trim ring and disengage it from the headlight case. Remove the trim ring and headlight lens unit assembly from the case and pivot it down to gain access to the backside of the assembly.
3. Disconnect the electrical connector (A, **Figure 90**) from the backside of the bulb, then remove the headlight lens assembly.
4. Remove the rubber cover (B, **Figure 90**) from the back of the headlight lens unit.

> *CAUTION*
> *Carefully read all instructions shipped with the replacement quartz bulb. Do not touch the bulb glass with your fingers because any traces of skin oil on the quartz halogen bulb will drastically reduce bulb life. Clean any traces of oil from the bulb with a cloth moistened in alcohol or lacquer thinner.*

5. Unhook the clip (A, **Figure 91**) and remove the light bulb (B, **Figure 91**). Replace with a new bulb.
6. To remove the headlight lens unit, perform the following:
   a. Remove the adjustment screws (**Figure 92**).
   b. Remove the screws, washers and spacers (**Figure 93**) securing the lens unit to the mounting ring and remove the mounting ring and trim ring from the lens unit.
7. Install by reversing these removal steps, noting the following.
   a. Install the rubber cover with the TOP arrow (A, **Figure 94**) facing upward.

9

b. Make sure the electrical connector (B, **Figure 94**) is on tight and that the rubber cover is properly installed to keep out moisture.

c. Adjust the headlight as described in this chapter.

Front Position Light Bulb Replacement (U.K. Models)

1. Reach up under the headlight case and remove the socket/bulb and electrical connector from the headlight case.

2. Remove the bulb from the socket.

3. Replace the bulb and install the socket assembly.

Headlight Case Removal/Installation

1. Remove the headlight bulb and lens assembly from the headlight case as described in this chapter.

2. Release the electrical wires from the clamps holding the wiring to the case.

3. Straighten all individual wiring and harness assemblies out in front.

4. Remove the bolts (**Figure 95**) securing the headlight case to the mounting bracket.

5. Carefully withdraw the case off of the wiring and remove the case.

6. If the steering stem is going to be removed, perform the following:

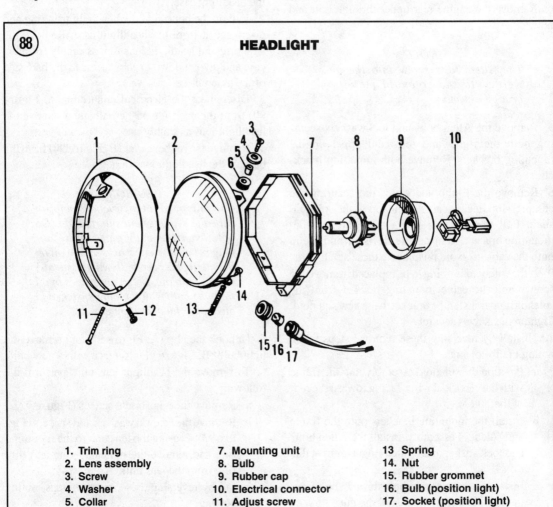

HEADLIGHT

1. Trim ring	7. Mounting unit	13 Spring
2. Lens assembly	8. Bulb	14. Nut
3. Screw	9. Rubber cap	15. Rubber grommet
4. Washer	10. Electrical connector	16. Bulb (position light)
5. Collar	11. Adjust screw	17. Socket (position light)
6. Rubber grommet	12. Screw	

a. Remove the nuts securing the headlight case mounting bracket to the lower fork bridge.

b. Carefully withdraw the bracket off of the wiring and remove the bracket.

7. Install by reversing these removal steps while noting the following:

a. Make sure the large rubber grommet is in place on the mounting bracket prior to installation.

b. Adjust the headlight as described in this chapter.

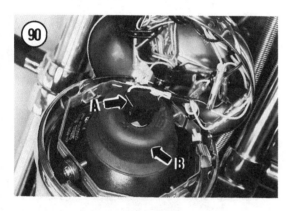

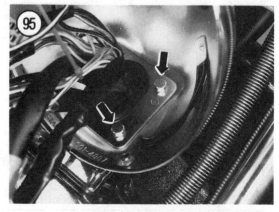

9

Headlight Adjustment

Adjust the headlight horizontally and vertically according to the Department of Motor Vehicle regulations in your area.

Turn the screws on the bottom of the trim ring until the aim is correct. Turn the left-hand adjust screw to adjust the headlight horizontally (**Figure 96**). Turn the right-hand adjust screw to adjust the headlight vertically. (**Figure 97**).

Taillight/Brakelight Bulb Replacement

Refer to **Figure 98** for this procedure.
1. Remove the screws securing the lens (A, **Figure 99**) and remove the lens and gasket.
2. Wash the lens with a mild detergent and wipe dry.
3. Inspect the lens gasket and replace if damaged.
4. Push in and turn the bulb counterclockwise and remove the bulb.
5. Carefully wipe off the reflector surface behind the bulb with a soft cloth.
6. Replace the bulb and install the lens and gasket. Do not over-tighten the screws as the lens may crack.

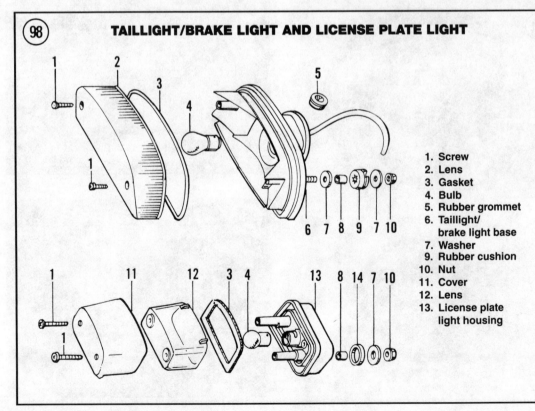

TAILLIGHT/BRAKE LIGHT AND LICENSE PLATE LIGHT

1. Screw
2. Lens
3. Gasket
4. Bulb
5. Rubber grommet
6. Taillight/brake light base
7. Washer
8.
9. Rubber cushion
10. Nut
11. Cover
12. Lens
13. License plate light housing

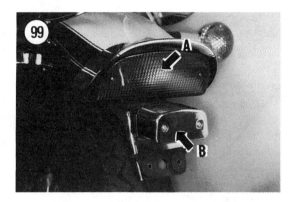

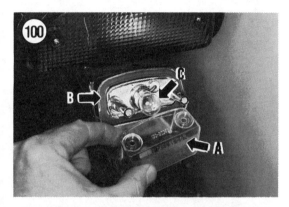

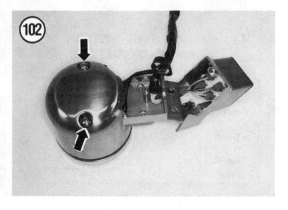

License Plate Light Bulb Replacement

Refer to **Figure 98** for this procedure.

1. Remove the screws securing the cover (B, **Figure 99**) and remove the cover.
2. Remove the lens (A, **Figure 100**) from the housing on the license plate bracket.
3. Wash out the inside and outside of the lens with a mild detergent and wipe dry.
4. Inspect the lens gasket (B, **Figure 100**) and replace if damaged.
5. Push in and turn the bulb (C, **Figure 100**) counterclockwise to remove it.
6. If removed, install the gasket onto the housing.
7. Replace the bulb, then install the lens and cover.
8. Make sure mounting hole collars are in place in the bracket.
9. Install the screws securing the assembly and tighten securely.

Directional Signal Light Bulb Replacement

1. Remove the screws securing the lens and remove the lens.
2. Push in and turn the bulb (A, **Figure 101**) counterclockwise to remove it.
3. Wash the lens with a mild detergent and wipe dry.
4. Carefully wipe off the reflector surface (B, **Figure 101**) behind the bulb with a soft cloth.
5. Replace the bulb and install the lens and gasket. Do not over-tighten the screws as the lens may crack.

Speedometer Illumination Light and Indicator Light Replacement

1. Remove the speedometer assembly as described in this chapter.
2. Remove the screw securing the lower cover and remove the lower cover.
3. To replace the speedometer illumination bulbs, perform the following:
   a. Remove the screws, washers and rubber grommets (**Figure 102**) securing the speedometer housing to the case.
   b. Carefully pull the speedometer housing up and out of the case.
   c. Carefully pull the defective speedometer illumination lamp holder/electrical wire assembly (**Figure 103**) from the backside of the speedometer housing.

9

d. Pull the bulb straight out of the holder and replace the defective bulb.

4. To replace the indicator light bulbs, perform the following:

    a. Remove the screws and washers (**Figure 104**) securing the meter case together. Separate the case assembly.

    b. Carefully remove the indicator light base assembly from the meter case.

    c. Carefully pull the defective indicator lamp holder/electrical wire assembly (**Figure 105**) from the backside of the indicator light base.

    d. Pull the bulb straight out of the holder and replace the defective bulb.

    e. Install the indicator light base assembly onto the meter case.

NOTE
If a new bulb will not work, check the wire connections for loose or broken wires. Also check the bulb socket for corrosion. Replace as necessary.

5. Push the lamp socket/electrical wire assembly back into the housing. Make sure it is completely seated to prevent the entry of water and moisture.

6. Make sure the rubber cushion is in place and install the speedometer housing into the case.

7. Be sure to install the rubber grommets under the washers when securing the speedometer housing to the case. This is necessary to keep out moisture.

8. Install the screws and washers (**Figure 104**) securing the meter case together. Tighten the screws securely.

106	IGNITION SWITCH			
	Red/ white	Orange	Gray	Brown
Off				
On	•——————•		•——————•	
Park	•——————————————•			

107	ENGINE STOP SWITCH AND START BUTTON		
	O/BL	O/W	Y/G
OFF			
RUN	•——————•		
START (Push)		•——————•	

SIDESTAND SWITCH

	Green	Black/White
ON (Upright position)	•———————•	
OFF (Down position)		

(109)

CLUTCH SWITCH

	Yellow/Green	Yellow/Green
ON (Squeeze lever)	•———————•	
OFF		

(110)

FRONT BRAKE SWITCH

	Orange/Green	White/Black
ON (Squeeze lever)	•———————•	
OFF		

9. Install the lower cover and tighten the screw securely.

SWITCHES

Check and Testing

Switches can be tested for continuity with an ohmmeter (see Chapter One) or a test light at the switch connector plug by operating the switch in each of its operating positions and comparing results with the switch operation. For example, **Figure 106** shows a continuity diagram for the ignition switch. It shows which terminals should show continuity when the ignition switch is in a given position.

When the ignition switch is in the PARK position, there should be continuity between terminals red/white and brown. This is indicated by the line on the continuity diagram. An ohmmeter connected between these 2 terminals should indicate little or no resistance and a test lamp should light. When the ignition switch is OFF, there should be no continuity between any of the terminals.

If the switch or button doesn't perform properly, replace it. Refer to the following figures when testing the switches:

a. Ignition switch: **Figure 106**.
b. Engine stop switch and start button: **Figure 107**.
c. Sidestand switch: **Figure 108**.
d. Clutch switch: **Figure 109**.
e. Front brake switch: **Figure 110**.
f. Rear brake switch: **Figure 111**.
g. Dimmer switch: **Figure 112**.

9

(111)

REAR BRAKE SWITCH

	Orange	White/Black
ON (Depress pedal)	•———————•	
OFF		

h. Directional signal switch: **Figure 113**.
i. Neutral indicator switch: **Figure 114**.
j. Horn switch: **Figure 115**.

When testing switches, note the following:

a. First check the fuses as described under (ital)Fuses(ital) in this chapter.

b. Check the battery as described under *Battery* in Chapter Three; charge the battery to the correct state of charge, if required.

c. Disconnect the negative (–) cable from the battery, as described in this chapter, if the switch connectors are not disconnected in the circuit.

> *CAUTION*
> *Do not attempt to start the engine with the battery negative (–) cable disconnected or you may damage the wiring harness.*

d. When separating 2 electrical connectors, depress the retaining clip and pull on the electrical connector housings and not the wires.

> *NOTE*
> *Electrical connectors can be serviced by disconnecting them and cleaning with electrical contact cleaner. Multiple pin connectors should be packed with a dielectric compound (available at most automotive and motorcycle supply stores).*

e. After locating a defective circuit, check the electrical connectors to make sure they are clean and properly connected. Make sure there are no bent metal pins on the male side of the connector (**Figure 116**) and that all wires going into electrical connector housing are properly positioned without loose wire ends (**Figure 117**).

(113)

DIRECTIONAL SIGNAL SWITCH

	Blue	Light blue	Light green
Right		•———————•	
Off			
Left	•————•		

(114)

NEUTRAL INDICATOR SWITCH

	Black	Ground
Neutral	•—————————•	
The others		

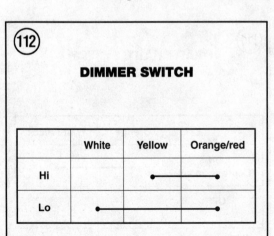

DIMMER SWITCH

	White	Yellow	Orange/red
Hi		•————————•	
Lo	•—————————•		

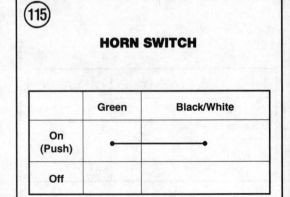

HORN SWITCH

	Green	Black/White
On (Push)	•—————————•	
Off		

f. To connect electrical connectors properly, push them together until they click and are locked into place (**Figure 118**).

g. When replacing handlebar switch assemblies, on models with electrical wiring external of the handlebar, make sure the wiring is routed correctly so that it is not crimped when the handlebar is turned from side to side. Also

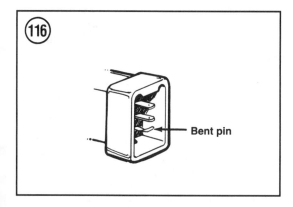

Bent pin

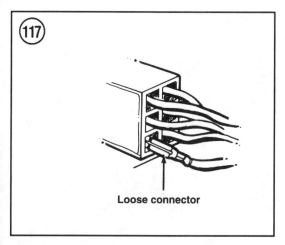

Loose connector

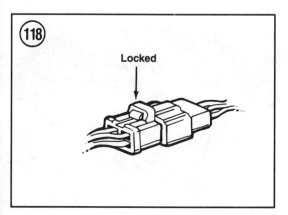

Locked

secure the wiring to the handlebar with plastic tie wraps.

NOTE
On all models, the switch electrical wires run through the interior of the handlebar. The wiring enters a opening in the handlebar adjacent to the switch and exits at the base of the upper fork bridge. If the electrical wiring cannot be disconnected at the switch assembly, the electrical wiring must be pulled through the handlebar during removal and again during installation.

Ignition Switch
Removal/Installation

1. Remove the rider's seat and frame left-hand side cover as described in Chapter Thirteen.
2. Disconnect the battery negative (–) lead as described in this chapter.
3. Follow the wiring harness from the ignition switch to the wiring harness.
4. Disconnect the ignition switch 4-pin electrical connector containing 4 wires (1 red/white, 1 orange, 1 gray and 1 brown).
5. Remove the mounting screw and washer securing the ignition switch to the frame on the left-hand side.
6. Remove the switch assembly (**Figure 119**) from the frame.
7. Install the new ignition switch onto the frame and tighten the screw securely.
8. Reconnect the 4-pin electrical connector. Make sure the electrical connector is free of corrosion and is tight.
9. Connect the battery negative (–) lead as described in this chapter.

9

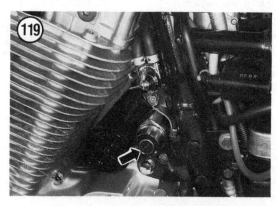

10. Install the side cover and seat.

Right-hand Combination Switch and Front Brake Light Switch Removal/Installation

The right-hand combination switch assembly contains both the engine start and engine stop switches. If any portion of the switch is faulty the entire switch assembly must be replaced.

> *NOTE*
> *Removal and installation of the switch wiring harness is a complicated and difficult task. The wiring harness runs through the handlebar tubing, down through the handlebar holders and the upper fork bridge and then into the backside of the headlight case. Pulling the old wire harness out through this complicated path can be accomplished with the handlebar in place—but pulling the new wiring harness back through is difficult even when done carefully. There is the possibility of stripping some of the insulation off the wiring as the harness travels past some sharp metal corners of this path. If this happens it this will result in a short. It is therefore suggested that the handlebar assembly be removed for this procedure.*

1. Remove the handlebar as described in Chapter Ten.

2A. If the switch is faulty and is going to be replaced, cut off the ends of the individual wires and connectors (A, **Figure 120**). This will make removal much easier.

2B. If the switch is in good condition and is just being removed for handlebar replacement, tape the ends of the wiring together with electrical tape to protect the connectors.

> *NOTE*
> *The flexible wire attached in Step 3 will be used to pull the new switch wire back through the handlebar.*

3. Securely attach a length of flexible wire to the end of the old wiring harness and tape the wire ends together with electrical tape.

4. Remove the screws securing the right-hand combination switch together and remove the switch assembly (B, **Figure 120**).

5. Slowly pull the wiring harness and wire out through the handlebar opening (C and D, **Figure 120**). Leave the wire in place in the handlebar as it will be used to pull the new switch wires back through.

6. Disconnect the wire from the old switch wires and reconnect it to the new switch wiring harness. Securely attach a length of wire to the end of the new wiring harness and tape the wire ends together.

7. Slowly pull the wire and new wiring harness into the handlebar opening (D and C, **Figure 120**). Disconnect the wire.

8. Install the new switch and tighten the screws securely. Do not overtighten the screws or the plastic switch housing may crack.

9. Install the handlebar as described in Chapter Ten.

10. Make sure the electrical connector(s) are free of corrosion and are tight.

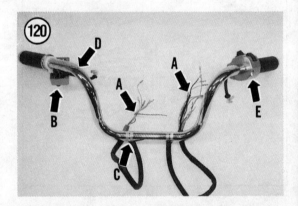

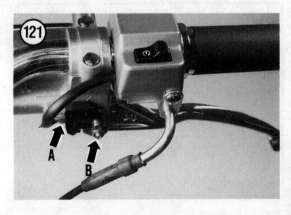

Left-hand Combination Switch and Starter Interlock Switch, Headlight Dimmer Switch, Directional Signal Switch, Horn Switch Removal/Installation

The left-hand combination switch assembly contains the headlight dimmer switch, turn signal switch and horn switch. If any portion of the switch is faulty the entire switch assembly must be replaced.

Removal and installation of the left-hand combination switch is the same as for the right-hand combination switch. Refer to the previous procedure and remove the left-hand combination switch (D, **Figure 120**) instead of the right-hand switch from the handlebar.

Front Brake Light Switch Removal/Installation

1. Disconnect the electrical connector (A, **Figure 121**) from the switch.
2. Remove the screws securing the front brake light switch to the front brake lever housing and remove the switch assembly (B, **Figure 121**).

3. Install a new switch and tighten the screws securely.
4. Reconnect the electrical connector.
5. Make sure the electrical connector is free of corrosion and is tight.

Rear Brake Light Switch Removal/Installation

1. Remove the rider's seat and frame right-hand side cover as described in Chapter Thirteen.
2. Remove the mounting bolts and lower the front footpeg assembly as described in Chapter Thirteen. Rest the assembly on wooden blocks or lower the footpeg assembly to the ground.
3. Remove the screws securing the brake light switch (**Figure 122**) to the master cylinder.
4. Carefully move the switch away and remove the spring and washer (**Figure 123**).
5. Remove any tie wraps securing the wiring to the frame.
6. Follow the 2 electrical wires (1 white/black, 1 orange/green) from the switch to where it connects to the harness.
7. Locate and disconnect the individual electrical connectors.
8. Remove the switch and electrical wires from the frame.
9. Install by reversing these removal steps, noting the following:
a. Make sure the brake light switch is contacting the brake lever arm correctly (A, **Figure 121**).
b. Make sure the electrical connectors are free of corrosion and are tight.
    c. Adjust the switch as described in Chapter Three.

Neutral Switch Removal/Installation

The neutral switch is located on the left-hand side of the bike below the clutch slave cylinder.
1. Remove the left-hand muffler as described in Chapter Eight.
2. Remove the bolts securing the secondary drive cover and remove the cover.
3. Disconnect the sidestand switch electrical connectors from the neutral switch electrical harness.
4. Remove any tie-wraps securing the electrical harness to the frame.
5. From the neutral switch, follow the electrical harness to the electrical connector in the upper por-

CHAPTER NINE

tion of the frame and disconnect the electrical connector.

NOTE
Steps 6-12 are shown with the alternator and clutch slave cylinder removed for clarity.

It is not necessary to remove these components for this procedure.

6. Remove the screws securing the neutral switch (**Figure 124**) and separate the neutral switch assembly from the crankcase.

7. Remove the O-ring seal (**Figure 125**) from the switch.

8. To avoid the loss of small parts, remove the switch contact plunger (**Figure 126**) and spring from the end of the gearshift drum.

9. Carefully remove the electrical harness from the frame noting its path through the frame. The harness for the new switch must follow the same path.

10. Install the switch contact spring and plunger (**Figure 126**) into the end of the gearshift drum. Make sure they are completely seated (**Figure 127**).

11. Apply a light coat of oil to the O-ring and install the O-ring seal (**Figure 128**) onto the switch. Make sure it is seated correctly.

12. Install the neutral switch (**Figure 124**) and screws. Tighten the screws securely.

13. Continue the installation by reversing these removal steps, noting the following:

    a. Be sure to reconnect the electrical connectors to the sidestand check switch.

    b. Make sure all electrical connectors are free of corrosion and are tight.

    c. Attach any tie-wraps securing the electrical wire to the frame.

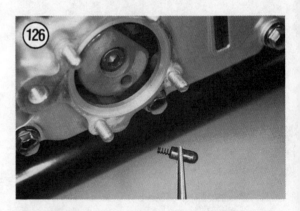

Sidestand Check Switch
Removal/Installation

1. Remove the mounting bolts and lower the front footpeg assembly as described in Chapter Thirteen. Rest the assembly on wooden blocks or lower the footpeg assembly to the ground.

NOTE
The sidestand check switch is attached to the front footpeg bracket assembly and the electrical connector is disconnected during footpeg removal.

2. Remove the screws and lockwashers securing the switch (**Figure 129**) to the footpeg assembly and remove the switch.

3. Install by reversing these removal steps, noting the following:

    a. Make sure all electrical connectors are free of corrosion and are tight.

    b. Secure the electrical harness under the wire strap.

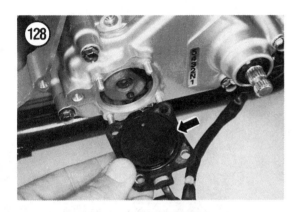

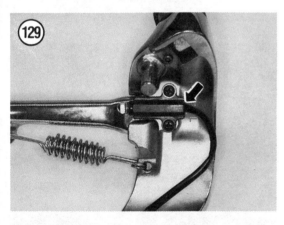

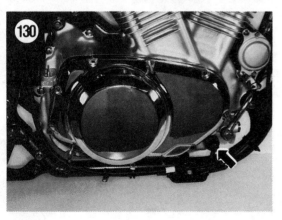

Oil Pressure Switch
Removal/Installation

The oil pressure switch is located on the front right-hand corner of the crankcase in front of the clutch cover.

1. Remove the right-hand muffler as described in Chapter Eight.

2. Remove the mounting bolts and lower the front footpeg assembly as described in Chapter Thirteen. Rest the assembly on wooden blocks or lower the footpeg assembly to the ground.

3. Drain the engine oil as described in Chapter Three.

4. Pull the rubber boot (**Figure 130**) off the switch.

5. Disconnect the oil pressure sending switch wire.

6. Unscrew the oil pressure switch from the crankcase.

7. Apply a light coat of gasket sealer to the switch threads prior to installation. Install the switch and tighten to the torque specification listed in Table 3.

8. Connect the oil pressure sending switch wire and tighten the screw securely.

9. Move the rubber boot back into place on the switch. Make sure it is installed correctly to protect the switch from moisture and corrosion.

10. Refill the engine with the specified type and quantity engine oil.

11. Install the front footpeg assembly as described in Chapter Thirteen.

12. Install the right-hand muffler as described in Chapter Eight.

ELECTRICAL COMPONENTS

This section contains information on electrical components other than switches. Some of the test procedures covered in this section instruct taking a meter reading within the electrical connector while it is still attached to a specific part. Under these conditions make sure that the meter test lead has penetrated the connector and is touching the bare metal wire not the insulation on the wire. If the test lead does not touch the bare metal wire the reading will be false and may lead to the unnecessary purchase of an expensive electrical part that cannot be returned for a refund. Most dealerships and parts houses will not accept any returns on electrical parts.

If you are having trouble with some of these components, perform the following preliminary checks and they may save you a lot of time.

    a. Disconnect each electrical connector and check that there are no bent metal pins on the male side of the electrical connector. A bent pin will not connect to its mating receptacle in the female end of the connector causing an open circuit.

    b. Check each female end of the connector. Make sure that the metal connector on the end of each wire is pushed in all the way into the plastic connector. If not, carefully push them in with a narrow bladed screwdriver.

    c. Check all electrical wires where they enter the individual metal connector in both the male and female plastic connector.

    d. After all is checked out, push the connectors together and make sure they are fully engaged and locked together.

Battery Case
Removal/Installation

1. Remove the battery as described in Chapter Three.

2. Remove the trim panel (A, **Figure 131**) at the rear of the rear brake pedal.

3. Remove both mufflers (B, **Figure 131**) or the exhaust system as described in Chapter Eight.

4. Remove the voltage regulator/rectifier as described in this chapter.

5. Remove the bottom bolt (**Figure 132**) from each side that secures the battery case to the frame.

6. Remove the top bolt (**Figure 133**) from each side that secures the battery case to the frame.

7. Lower the battery case down and out of the frame.

8. If the battery case is corroded by electrolyte spillage, thoroughly clean with baking soda and water and rinse thoroughly. Then clean with solvent and dry completely. Clean the metal and repaint any areas of bare or corroded metal.

9. Install by reversing these removal steps.

Speedometer and
Indicator Lamp Housing
Removal/Installation

Refer to **Figure 134** for this procedure.

1. Disconnect the battery negative lead as described in this chapter.

2. Unscrew the speedometer drive cable from the base of the speedometer case.

3. Remove the headlight bulb and lens assembly from the headlight case as described in this chapter.

> *NOTE*
> *The following wire colors are connected to the speedometer and indicator lamp housing side of the connector. The wire color on the harness side of the*

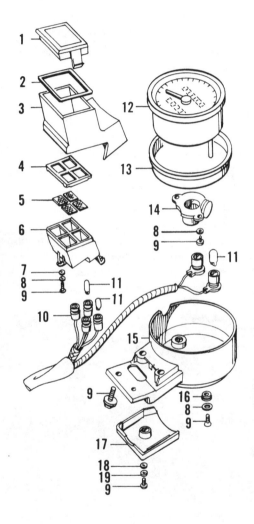

(134)
INSTRUMENT CLUSTER

1. Lens
2. Rubber gasket
3. Indicator light base
4. Trim plate
5. Lens set
6. Indicator light base
7. Washer
8. Lockwasher
9. Screw
10. Wiring harness/
    lamp sockets
11. Bulb
12. Speedometer
13. Rubber cushion
14. Speedometer
    gear box
15. Meter case
16. Rubber cushion
17. Lower cover
18. Washer
19. Lockwasher

connector vary slightly due to different model years and the country in which the bike was sold.

4. Release the electrical wires from the clamps holding the wiring to the case. Disconnect the 6-pin connector containing 6 wires (1 gray, 1 light green, 1 black, 1 blue, 1 orange, 1 green/yellow).

5. Straighten all individual wiring and harness assemblies.

6. Remove the bolts (**Figure 135**) securing the headlight case to the mounting bracket.

7. Carefully pull the headlight case forward until you can gain access to the speedometer and indicator lamp housing mounting bolts above the case.

8. Remove the bolts securing the speedometer and indicator lamp housing to the upper fork bridge.

9. Carefully pull the wiring harness out through the backside of the headlight case.

10. Remove the speedometer and indicator lamp assembly and wiring harnesses from the frame.

11. Install by reversing these removal steps. Make sure the electrical connectors are free of corrosion and are tight.

Fuel Pump
Resistance Check

NOTE
*Refer to the **Basic Information** section at the beginning of this chapter regarding the specified test temperature of 20° C (68° F). If the component is not at the specified temperature, the resulting resistance readings will be inaccurate.*

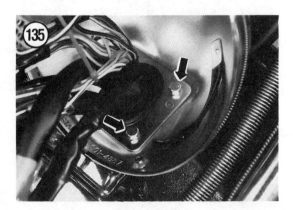

(135)

1. Remove the rider's seat as described in Chapter Thirteen.

2. Disconnect the battery negative lead as described in this chapter.

3. Remove the bolts securing the frame left-hand side cover and remove the cover.

4. From the fuel pump, follow the electrical harness to the electrical connector in the upper portion of the frame and disconnect the 2-pin electrical connector (1 black/white, 1 brown/black).

5. Connect an ohmmeter between both terminals of the fuel pump electrical connector. The specified resistance is 1-2 ohms. If the resistance shown is infinity or lower than specified, replace the fuel pump.

6. Install all items removed by reversing these removal steps. Make sure the electrical connector is free of corrosion and is tight.

Fuel Pump Flow Test

The electromagnetic fuel pump pumps fuel from the fuel tank to the carburetors. When the ignition switch is turned ON the electromagnet is energized, pulling the armature and the diaphragm up. This causes a vacuum and pulls fuel through the inlet check valve. As the armature reaches the limit of its upward travel, the contact points are opened in the switch and the circuit is broken. The electromagnet is pushed down by the return spring which in turn pushes the fuel through the outlet check valve and to the carburetor assembly. This continuing up and down movement moves or pumps the fuel from the fuel tank into the carburetors.

1. Remove the fuel pump as described in Chapter Eight.

WARNING
*Perform this test with **kerosene**. Do not use gasoline due to the extreme fire hazard.*

NOTE
The fuel pump should pump over 600 ml (1.27 U.S. pt.) of fuel in 1 minute. Have a sufficient amount of kerosene in the container and use a graduated beaker large enough to contain it. If you have a smaller graduated beaker, run the test for only 30 seconds and multiply the amount of fuel delivered by 2 to achieve the same results.

2. Connect a short section of fuel line to the fuel pump fitting that goes to the carburetors. Place the loose end of the fuel line into a graduated beaker.

3. Connect another piece of hose to the fuel pump fitting that goes to the fuel tank. Place the loose end of the fuel line into the container of kerosene.

4. Connect jumper wires from a 12V battery to the fuel pump electrical connector as follows:

    a. Connect the battery positive (+) lead to the black/brown terminal.

    b. Connect the battery negative (−) lead to the black/white terminal.

5. Allow the kerosene to run out of the fuel line and into the graduated beaker for 1 minute.

6. Disconnect the battery from the fuel pump.

7. The fuel pump specified flow capacity is over 600 ml (1.27 U.S. pt.) of fuel in 1 minute.

8. If the fuel pump does not flow to the specified capacity, install a new pump.

9. Disconnect the fuel hoses from the fuel pump and drain out any residual kerosene from the fuel pump. Any kerosene remaining within the fuel pump will not harm the carburetor or the engine.

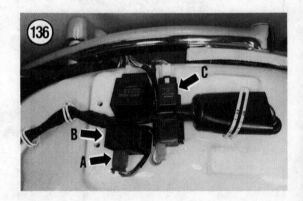

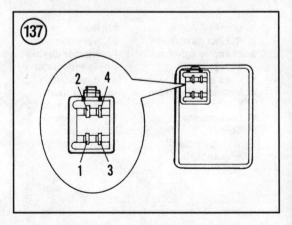

10. Install by reversing these removal steps.

11. Make sure the electrical connector is free of corrosion and is tight.

Fuel Pump Relay
Resistance Check

Suzuki specifies the use of the Suzuki Pocket Tester (part No. 09900-25002) for accurate resistance reading for testing of the regulator/rectifier unit. Refer to the *Basic Information* section at the beginning of this chapter regarding this tester.

NOTE
Prior to making this test, check the condition of the pocket tester battery. If necessary, install a new battery.

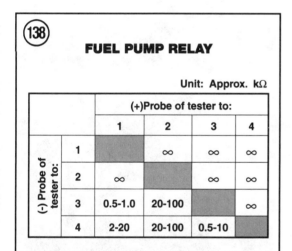

FUEL PUMP RELAY

Unit: Approx. kΩ

		(+)Probe of tester to:			
		1	2	3	4
(-) Probe of tester to:	1		∞	∞	∞
	2	∞		∞	∞
	3	0.5-1.0	20-100		∞
	4	2-20	20-100	0.5-10	

FUEL PUMP RELAY

Unit: Approx. kΩ

		(+)Probe of tester to:			
		1	2	3	4
(-) Probe of tester to:	1		∞	∞	∞
	2	∞		∞	∞
	3	∞	10-100		∞
	4	∞	20-200	1-5	

NOTE
*Refer to the **Basic Information** section at the beginning of this chapter regarding the specified test temperature of 20° C (68° F). If the component is not at the specified temperature, the resulting resistance readings will be inaccurate.*

1. Remove both seats as described in Chapter Thirteen.

2. Disconnect the battery negative lead as described in this chapter.

3. Disconnect the 4-pin electrical connector (A, **Figure 136**) from the fuel pump relay, then remove the relay (B, **Figure 136**) from the rear fender mount.

4. Set the pocket tester to the R × 1,000 (K) ohms scale.

5. Refer to **Figure 137** for pin numbers within the electrical connector on the relay.

6A. On models with relay Part No. 05A00 (white electrical coupler), refer to **Figure 138** for the pocket tester lead connections and values.

6B. On models with relay Part No. 38B00 (red electrical coupler), refer to **Figure 139** for the pocket tester lead connections and values.

7. If any of the meter readings differ from the stated values, replace the fuel pump relay as described in this chapter.

8. If the relay is okay, reinstall it onto the rear fender and reconnect the electrical connector.

9. Install both seats as described in Chapter Thirteen.

Sidestand and Neutral Relay
Resistance Check

Suzuki specifies the use of the Suzuki Pocket Tester (part No. 09900-25002) for accurate resistance reading for testing of the regulator/rectifier unit. Refer to the *Basic Information* section at the beginning of this chapter regarding this tester.

NOTE
Prior to making this test, check the condition of the pocket tester battery. If necessary, install a new battery.

NOTE
*Refer to the **Basic Information** section at the beginning of this chapter*

9

regarding the specified test temperature of 20° C (68° F). If the component is not at the specified temperature, the resulting resistance readings will be inaccurate.

1. Remove both seats as described in Chapter Thirteen.

2. Disconnect the battery negative lead as described in this chapter.

3. Disconnect the 4-pin electrical connector from the sidestand and neutral relay, then remove the relay (C, **Figure 136**) from the rear fender mount.

4. Set the pocket tester to the R × 1,000 (K) ohms scale.

5. Refer to **Figure 140** and perform the following:

   a. Connect an ohmmeter between terminals No. 3 and No. 4. There should be no continuity (infinite resistance).

   b. Connect a 12 volt battery positive (+) cable to the No. 1 terminal and the battery negative (–) cable to the No. 2 terminal.

   c. With battery voltage applied to the No. 3 and No. 4 terminals, reconnect an ohmmeter between terminals No. 1 and No. 2. This time the ohmmeter should indicate the resistance listed in **Table 1**.

6. If the relay fails either one of these tests it is defective and must be replaced.

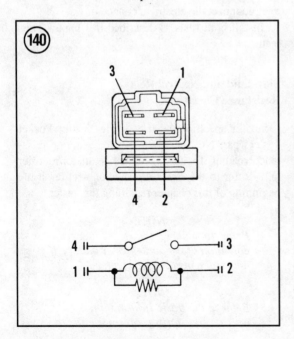

7. If the relay is good, reinstall it onto the rear fender and reconnect the electrical connector.

8. Install both seats as described in Chapter Thirteen.

Horn Testing

1. Disconnect horn wires from harness.

2. Connect a 12 volt battery to the horn.

3. If the horn is good it will sound. If not, replace it.

Horn Removal/Installation

1. Remove the fuel tank as described in Chapter Eight.

2. Disconnect the electrical connectors from the horn.

3. Remove the bolts, washers and nuts securing the horn (**Figure 141**) to the frame and remove the horn.

4. Install by reversing these removal steps. Make sure the electrical connectors are free of corrosion and are tight.

FUSES

The fuse panel is located under the frame left-hand side cover.

Whenever the fuse blows, find out the reason for the failure before replacing the fuse. Usually, the trouble is a short circuit in the wiring. This may be

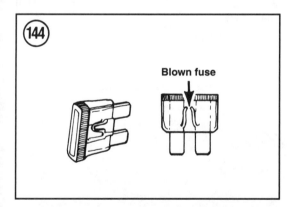

Blown fuse

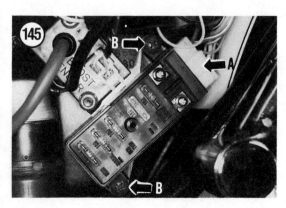

caused by worn-through insulation or a disconnected wire shorted to ground.

CAUTION
Never substitute metal foil or wire for a fuse. Never use a higher amperage fuse than specified. An overload could result in a fire and complete loss of the bike.

CAUTION
When replacing a fuse, make sure the ignition switch is in the OFF position. This will lessen the chance of a short circuit.

Fuse Replacement

1. Remove the rider's seat as described in Chapter Thirteen.

2. Remove the bolts securing the frame left-hand side cover and remove the cover.

3. Remove the screw (A, **Figure 142**) attaching the fuse panel cover and remove the cover (B, **Figure 142**).

4. Remove the fuse (**Figure 143**) with your fingers and inspect it. If the fuse is blown there will be a break in the element (**Figure 144**). A spare fuse was originally installed inside the cover.

5. Install the new fuse and push it all the way down until it seats completely, then install the cover and screw. Tighten the screw securely but don't over-tighten it as the cover may fracture.

6. Install the seat.

Fuse Panel Removal/Installation

1. Remove the rider's seat as described under *Seat Removal/Installation*) in Chapter Thirteen.

2. Remove the frame left-hand side cover.

3. Disconnect the electrical connector (A, **Figure 145**) from the base of the fuse panel.

4. Remove the screws (B, **Figure 145**) securing the fuse panel to the frame and remove it.

5. Install by reversing these removal steps.

6. Make sure the electrical connector is free of corrosion and is tight.

WIRING DIAGRAMS

Wiring diagrams for all models are located at the end of this book.

9

Table 1 ELECTRICAL SYSTEM SPECIFICATIONS

Item	Specification
Battery capacity*	12 volt, 14 amp hour
Alternator	Three-phase AC
Rated output	14-15.5 volts @ 5,000 rpm
Minimum starter motor brush length	9.0 mm (0.35 in.)
Starter relay resistance	2-6 ohms
Pickup coil resistance	220-260 ohms
Ignition coil resistance	
Primary windings	1-7 ohms
Secondary windings	10,000-25,000 ohms
Compression release solenoid resistance	0.1-1.0 ohms
Sidestand and neutral relay resistance	96-144 ohms
Fuel pump resistance	1-2 ohms
Fuel pump discharge rate	More than 600 ml (1.27 U.S. pt.)/min.
Fuses	
Main	25 amp
All other	10 amp

* All models are equipped with a maintenance free sealed battery. Never replace the battery with any type other than a sealed battery.

Table 2 REPLACEMENT BULBS

Item	Specification
Headlight	
Type	Semi-sealed beam
Bulb (quartz-halogen)	12 volt, 60/55 watt (2)
Running light	
1987	12 volt, 8 watt
1988-on	12 volt, 5 watt
City or parking light (1991-on U.K.)	12 volt, 3.4 watt
Taillight/brakelight	
U.K.	12 volt, 5/21 watt
All others	12 volt, 8/27 watt (2)
License plate light	
U.S., Canadian	12 volt, 7.5 watt
All others	12 volt, 5 watt
Turn signal	
U.S., Canadian	12 volt, 23 watt (4)
All others	12 volt, 21 watt (4)
Indicator lights	
High beam	12 volt, 1.7 watt
Neutral indicator, turn signal,	
Oil pressure warning	12 volt, 3 watt
Illumination light	
Speedometer	12 volt, 3 watt

Table 3 ELECTRICAL SYSTEM TIGHTENING TORQUES

Item	N·m	in.-lb.	ft.-lb.
Alternator rotor mounting bolt	140-160	—	103-118
Oil pressure switch	12-15	106-132	—
Starter clutch 6mm Allen bolts	23-28	—	17-20
Engine mounting bolts			
Through bolts and nuts	70-80	—	51-59
Mounting bracket Allen bolts	18-28	—	13-20
Subframe Allen bolt nuts	40-60	—	29-44

CHAPTER TEN

FRONT SUSPENSION AND STEERING

This chapter describes repair and maintenance procedures for the front wheel, front forks and steering components.

Front suspension torque specifications are covered in **Table 1**. **Tables 1-4** are located at the end of this chapter.

FRONT WHEEL

Removal

CAUTION
Care must be taken when removing, handling and installing a wheel with a disc brake rotor. The rotor is relatively thin in order to dissipate heat and to minimize unsprung weight. The rotor is designed to withstand tremendous rotational loads, but can be damaged when subjected to side impact loads. If the rotor is knocked out of true by a side impact, a pulsation will be felt in the front brake lever when braking. The rotor is too thin to be trued and must be replaced with a new one. Protect the rotor when transporting a wheel to a dealership for tire service. Do not place

a wheel in a car trunk or pickup bed without protecting the rotor.

1. Remove the front axle trim cap from each fork leg.
2. Loosen the front axle pinch bolt (**Figure 1**).
3. Loosen the front axle (**Figure 2**) from the right-hand fork leg.
4. Place a suitable size jack, or wooden blocks, under the footpeg assembly to support the bike securely with the front wheel off the ground.
5. Remove the speedometer cable from the speedometer gear box.
6. Completely unscrew the axle from the right-hand fork leg and remove the axle.
7. Pull the wheel down and forward and remove the wheel from the front fork and the brake caliper.

NOTE
Insert a piece of vinyl tubing or wood in the caliper in place of the brake disc. Then, if the brake lever is inadvertently squeezed, the piston will not be forced out of the cylinder. If this does happen, the caliper must be disassembled to reseat the piston and the system will have to be bled.

8. Remove the spacer (**Figure 3**) from the brake disc side of the hub.

9. Remove the speedometer gear box from the left-hand side of the hub.

10. Reinstall the spacer and speedometer gear box onto the axle to keep from misplacing them.

> *CAUTION*
> *Do not set the wheel down on the disc surface as it may get scratched or warped. Set the sidewalls on 2 wooden blocks.*

11. Inspect the wheel as described in this chapter.

Inspection

1. Remove any corrosion from the front axle with a piece of fine emery cloth. Clean axle with solvent, then wipe the axle clean with a lint-free cloth.

2. Check axle runout. Place the axle on V-blocks and place the tip of a dial indicator in the middle of the axle (**Figure 4**). Rotate the axle and measure runout. If the runout exceeds 0.25 mm (0.010 in.), replace the axle; do not attempt to straighten it.

3. Check rim runout as follows:

   a. Measure the radial (up and down) runout of the wheel rim with a dial indicator as shown at A, **Figure 5**. If runout exceeds 2.0 mm (0.08 in.), check the wheel bearings.

   b. Measure the axial (side to side) runout of the wheel rim with a dial indicator as shown at B, **Figure 5**. If runout exceeds 2.0 mm (0.08 in.), check the wheel bearings.

   c. If the wheel bearings are good, wire wheels can be trued as described under *Wire Wheel Spoke Adjustment* in this chapter.

   d. Replace the front wheel bearings as described under *Front Hub* in this chapter.

4. Inspect the rim for dents, bending or cracks. Check the rim and rim sealing surface for scratches deeper than 0.5 mm (0.01 in.). If any of these conditions are present, replace the rim.

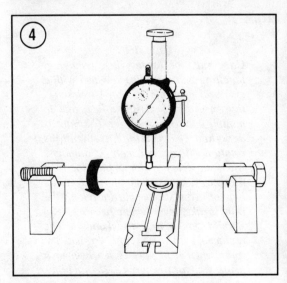

Installation

1. Make sure the axle bearing surfaces of the fork sliders and axle are free from burrs and nicks.

2. Install the spacer (**Figure 3**) into the brake disc side of the hub.

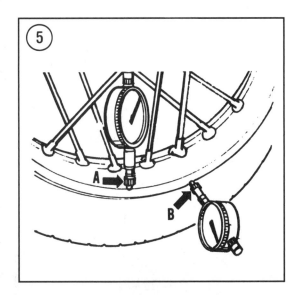

3. Align the tangs of the speedometer drive gear (A, **Figure 6**) with the notches (B, **Figure 6**) in the front hub and install the speedometer gear box. Make sure the gear box seats completely. If the speedometer components do not mesh properly, the wheel hub components will be too wide for installation.

4. Position the wheel, inserting the brake disc into the caliper carefully to prevent damage to the brake pads.

5. Apply a light coat of grease to the front axle. Insert the front axle through the fork leg, speedometer gear box and the wheel hub.

6. Make sure the spacer (**Figure 7**) is still in place on the brake disc side of the wheel.

7. Screw the axle into the right-hand fork leg, but do not tighten it.

8. Slowly rotate the wheel and install the speedometer cable into the speedometer housing. Position the speedometer housing and cable so that the cable does not have a sharp bend in it.

9. Tighten the front axle (A, **Figure 8**) to the torque specification listed in **Table 1**.

10. Remove the jack or wooden block(s) from under the foot peg assembly.

11. With the front brake applied, push down hard on the handlebars and pump the forks several times to seat the front axle.

12. Tighten the front axle pinch bolt (B, **Figure 8**) to the torque specification listed in **Table 1**.

13. Roll the bike back and forth several times. Apply the front brake as many times as necessary to seat the brake pads against the brake disc correctly.

14. Install the front axle trim cap into each fork leg.

10

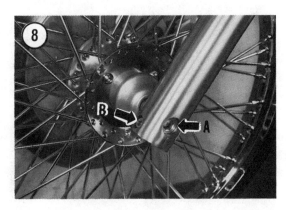

**Speedometer Gear Box
Inspection and Lubrication**

> *NOTE*
> *The speedometer gear box is a sealed
> assembly and no replacement parts are
> available. If any part of the gear box is
> defective the entire assembly must be
> replaced.*

1. Remove the front wheel as described in this chapter.

2. Inspect the seal (A, **Figure 9**) for leakage.

3. Inspect the tangs (B, **Figure 9**) of the speedometer drive gear for wear or damage.

4. Inspect the notches (**Figure 10**) in the front hub for wear or damage. Repair the hub or replace the wheel.

5. Install the front wheel as described in this chapter.

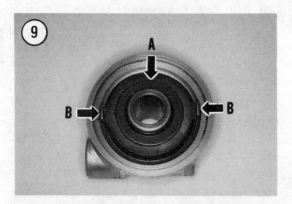

FRONT HUB

Inspection

Inspect each wheel bearing prior to removing it from the wheel hub.

> *CAUTION*
> *Do not remove the wheel bearings for
> inspection purposes as they will be
> damaged during the removal process.
> Remove wheel bearings only if they are
> to be replaced.*

1. Perform Steps 1-4 of Disassembly in the following procedure.

2. Turn each bearing by hand. Make sure bearings turn smoothly.

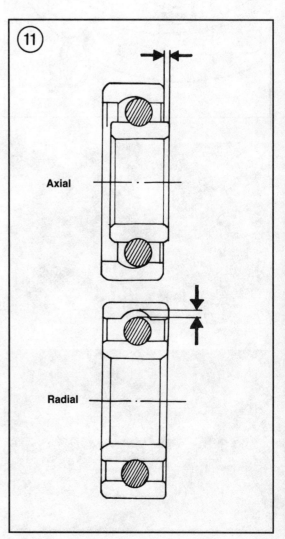

3. Inspect the play of the inner race of each wheel bearing. Check for excessive axial play and radial play (**Figure 11**). Replace the bearing if it has an excess amount of free play.

4. On unsealed bearings, check the balls for evidence of wear, pitting or excessive heat (bluish tint). Replace the bearings if necessary; always replace as a complete set. When replacing the bearings, be sure to take your old bearings along to ensure a perfect matchup.

NOTE
Fully sealed bearings are available from bearing specialty shops. Fully sealed bearings provide better protection from dirt and moisture that may get into the hub.

Disassembly

Refer to **Figure 12** for this procedure.

1. Remove the front wheel as described in this chapter.

2. If still in place, remove the spacer (**Figure 3**) from the brake disc side of the hub.

3. If still in place, remove the speedometer gear box from the left-hand side of the hub.

4. If necessary, remove the bolts securing the brake disc and remove the disc.

5. Before proceeding further, inspect the wheel bearings as described in this chapter. If they must be replaced, proceed as follows.

6A. If the special tools are not used, perform the following:

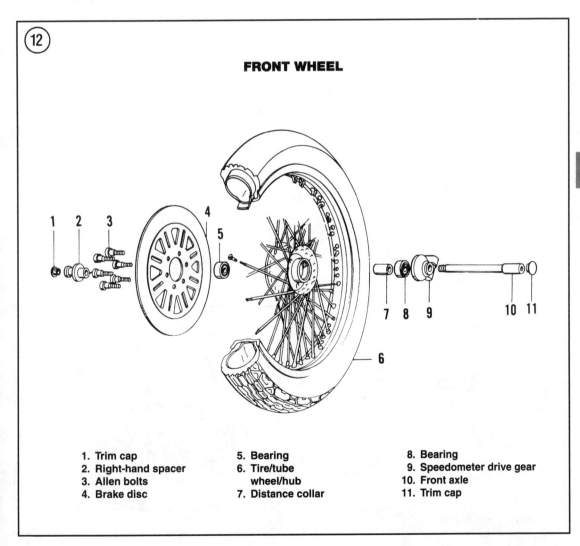

FRONT WHEEL

10

1. Trim cap
2. Right-hand spacer
3. Allen bolts
4. Brake disc
5. Bearing
6. Tire/tube wheel/hub
7. Distance collar
8. Bearing
9. Speedometer drive gear
10. Front axle
11. Trim cap

a. To remove the right- and left-hand bearings and distance collar, insert a soft aluminum or brass drift into one side of the hub.

b. Push the inner spacer over to one side and place the drift on the inner race of the lower bearing.

c. Tap the bearing out of the hub with a hammer, working around the perimeter of the inner race. Remove the bearing and distance collar.

d. Repeat for the bearing on the other side.

NOTE
The Kowa Seiki Wheel Bearing Remover set can be ordered by a Suzuki dealership through K & L Supply Co. in Santa Clara, CA.

WARNING
Be sure to wear safety glasses while using the wheel bearing remover set.

6B. To remove the bearings with the Kowa Seiki Wheel Bearing Remover set, perform the following:

a. Select the correct size remover head and insert it into the bearing.

b. Turn the wheel over and insert the remover shaft into the backside of the remover head. Tap the shaft and force it into the slit in the adapter (**Figure 13**). This will force the adapter against the bearing inner race.

c. Tap on the end of the remover shaft with a hammer and drive the bearing out of the hub. Remove the bearing and the distance collar.

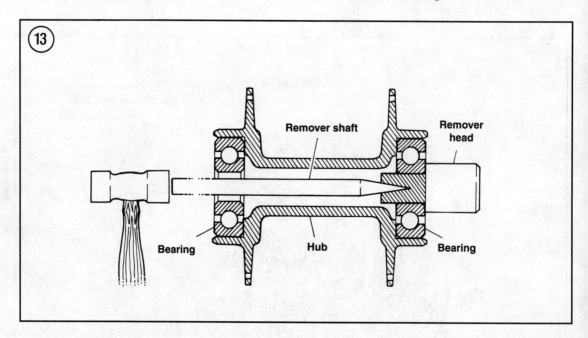

(13)

Remover shaft   Remover head

Bearing   Hub   Bearing

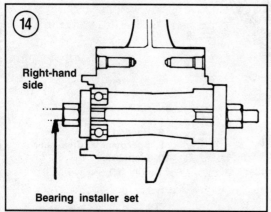

(14)

Right-hand side

Bearing installer set

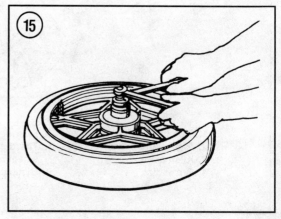

(15)

d. Repeat for the bearing on the other side.

7. Clean the inside and the outside of the hub with solvent. Dry with compressed air.

Assembly

1. On unsealed bearings, pack the bearings with a good quality bearing grease. Work the grease in between the balls thoroughly. Turn the bearing by hand a couple of times to make sure the grease is distributed evenly inside the bearing.

2. Blow any dirt or foreign matter out of the hub prior to installing the bearings.

> *CAUTION*
> *Install unsealed bearings with the single sealed side facing outward. Tap the bearings squarely into place and tap on the outer race only. Do not tap on the inner race or the bearing might be damaged. Be sure that the bearings are completely seated.*

3A. The Suzuki bearing installer (Suzuki part No. 09924-84510) can be used to install the wheel bearings as follows:

 a. Install the right-hand bearing into the hub first.

 b. Set the bearing with the sealed side facing out and install the bearing installer as shown in **Figure 14**.

 c. Tighten the bearing installer (**Figure 15**) and pull the right-hand bearing into the hub until it is completely seated. Remove the bearing installer.

 d. Turn the wheel over (right-hand side up) on the workbench and install the distance collar.

 e. Set the left-hand bearing with the sealed side facing out and install the bearing installer as shown in **Figure 16**.

 f. Tighten the bearing installer and pull the left-hand bearing into the hub until there is a slight clearance between the inner race and the distance collar.

 g. Remove the bearing installer.

3B. If special tools are not used, perform the following:

 a. Tap the right-hand bearing squarely into place and tap on the outer race only. Use a driver (**Figure 17**) that matches the outer race diameter. Do not tap on the inner race or the bearing might be damaged. Be sure that the bearing is completely seated.

 b. Turn the wheel over (right-hand side up) on the workbench and install the distance collar.

 c. Use the same tool set-up and drive in the left-hand bearing until there is a slight clearance between the inner race and the distance collar.

4. If the brake disc was removed, perform the following:

 a. Use a small amount of a locking compound such as ThreeBond No. TB1360 or Loctite No. 271 to the brake disc bolt threads prior to installation.

 b. Install the brake disc and bolts. Tighten to the torque specification listed in **Table 1**.

5. Install the spacer into the brake disc side of the hub.

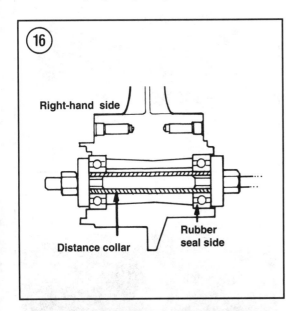

16

Right-hand side

Distance collar

Rubber seal side

17

10

6. Align the tangs of the speedometer drive gear with the notches in the front hub and install the speedometer gear box. Make sure the gear box seats completely. If the speedometer components do not mesh properly the hub components of the wheel will be too wide for installation.

7. Install the front wheel as described in this chapter.

WHEELS

Wheel Balance

An unbalanced wheel is unsafe. Depending on the degree of imbalance and the speed of the motorcycle, the rider may experience anything from a mild vibration to a violent shimmy which may even result in loss of control.

The weights are attached to the wheel spokes. Weight kits are available from a motorcycle dealership. Before you attempt to balance the wheel, make sure the wheel bearings are in good condition and properly lubricated. The wheel must rotate freely.

> *NOTE*
> *When balancing the wheels do so with the brake disc attached. The brake disc rotates with the wheel and will affect the balance.*

1. Remove the wheel as described in this chapter or Chapter Eleven.

2. Mount the wheel on a fixture such as the one shown in **Figure 18** so it can rotate freely.

3. Give the wheel a spin and let it coast to a stop. Mark the tire at the lowest point (**Figure 19**).

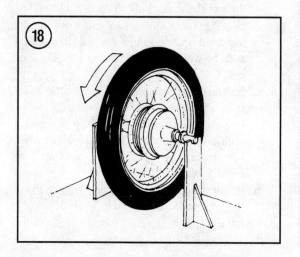

4. Spin the wheel several more times. If the wheel keeps coming to rest at the same point, it is out of balance.

5. Attach a test weight to the upper (or light) side of the wheel at the spoke or tape a test weight (**Figure 20**) to the rim.

6. Experiment with different weights until the wheel, when spun, comes to a rest at a different position each time.

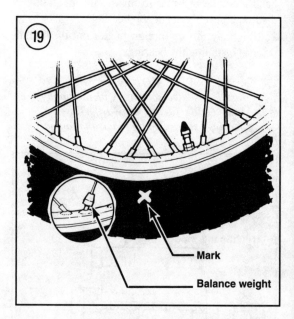

Mark

Balance weight

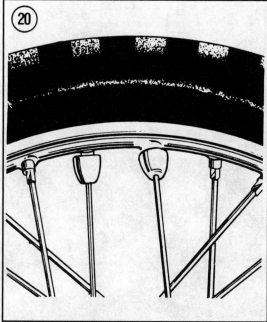

7. Remove the test weight and install the correct size weight and crimp it in place on the spoke.

Wire Wheel Spoke Adjustment

Spokes loosen with use and should be checked periodically. If all appear loose, tighten all of the spokes evenly.

After tightening the spokes, check the rim runout to make sure you haven't pulled the rim out of shape. One way to check rim runout is to mount a dial indicator to the front fork or swing arm so that it bears on the rim.

If you don't have a dial indicator, fabricate the tester shown in **Figure 21**. Adjust the position of the bolt until it just clears the wheel rim. Rotate the wheel and note whether the clearance between the bolt and the rim increases or decreases. Mark the tire with chalk or crayon in areas that produce signifi-

cantly large or small clearances. Clearance must not change by more than 2 mm (0.08 in.).

To pull the rim out, tighten the spokes which terminate on the same side of the hub (**Figure 22**). In most cases, only a small amount of adjustment is necessary to true a rim. After adjustment, rotate the wheel and make sure another area has not been pulled out of true. Continue adjusting and checking until the runout does not exceed 2 mm (0.08 in.).

TIRES

Tire Safety

After installing new tires on the bike, break them in correctly. Remember that a new tire has relatively poor adhesion to the road surface until it is broken in properly. Don't subject a new tire to any high speed riding for at least the first 60 miles (100 km).

Even after the tires are broken in properly, always warm them up prior to the first ride of the day. This

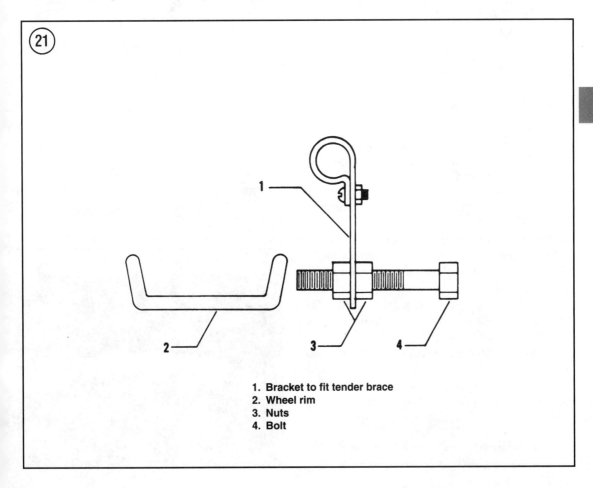

1. Bracket to fit tender brace
2. Wheel rim
3. Nuts
4. Bolt

will lessen the possibility of loss of control of the bike. If you have purchased a tire brand other than those originally installed by the factory, maintain the correct tire inflation pressure recommended by that tire manufacturer and not those listed in **Table 2**. **Table 2** is for original equipment tires only.

TIRE CHANGING

The wheels can easily be damaged during tire removal. Special care must be taken with tire irons when changing a tire to avoid scratches and gouges to the outer rim surface. Insert scraps of leather or rim protectors between the tire iron and the rim to protect the rim from damage. The stock wire wheels are designed for use with tube type tires.

Removal

> *CAUTION*
> *To avoid damage when removing the tire, support the wheel on 2 blocks of wood, so the brake disc does not contact the floor.*

> *NOTE*
> *To make tire removal easier, warming the tire will make it softer and more pliable. Place the wheel and tire assembly in the sun. If possible, place the wheel assembly in a completely closed vehicle. At the same time, place the new tire in the same location.*

1. Remove the wheel as described in this chapter or Chapter Eleven.
2. If you are going to reinstall the existing tire, mark the valve stem location on the tire (**Figure 23**) so the tire can be installed in the same position for easier balancing.
3. Remove the valve stem core to deflate the tire. On models so equipped, unscrew the locknut (**Figure 24**) from the valve stem.
4. Press the entire bead on both sides of the tire into the center of the rim. Make sure the tire is broken loose around the entire perimeter of the wheel.
5. Lubricate the beads with soapy water.

> *CAUTION*
> *Use rim protectors (**Figure 25**) or insert scraps of leather between the tire irons*

and the rim to protect the rim from damage.

> *NOTE*
> *Use only quality tire irons without sharp edges (**Figure 26**). If necessary, file the ends of the tire irons to remove rough edges.*

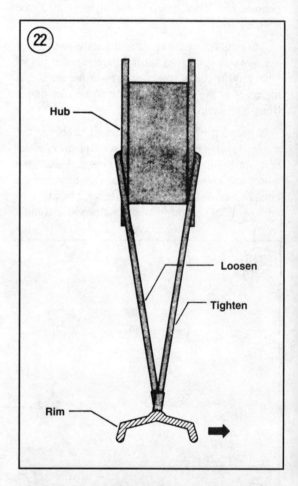

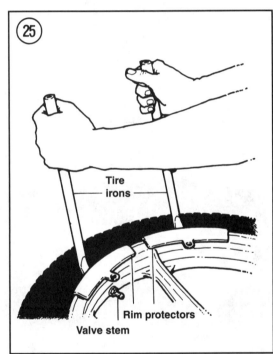

Tire irons

Rim protectors

Valve stem

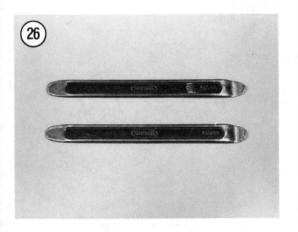

6. Insert the tire iron under the bead next to the valve (**Figure 27**). Force the bead on the opposite side of the tire into the center of the rim and pry the bead over the rim with the tire iron.

7. Insert a second tire iron next to the first to hold the bead over the rim. Then work around the tire with the first tire iron, prying the bead over the rim. Be careful not to pinch the inner tube with the tire irons.

8. Remove the valve from the hole in the rim and remove the inner tube from the tire.

NOTE
Step 9 is only necessary to remove the tire from the rim completely, as in tire replacement.

9. Stand the tire on end or turn it over. Insert the tire iron between the second bead and the side of the rim that the first bead was pried over (**Figure 28**). Force the bead on the opposite side from the tire iron into the center of the rim. Pry the second bead off the rim, working around as with the first. Remove the tire from the rim.

10. Inspect the rim as described in this chapter.

Tire and Rim Inspection

1. Wipe off the inner surfaces of the wheel rim. Clean off any rubber residue or oxidation.

WARNING
Carefully consider whether a tire should be replaced. If there is any doubt about the condition of the existing tire, replace it with a new one. Do not take a chance on a tire failure at any speed.

10

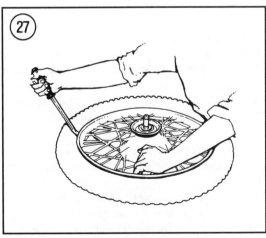

2. If any one of the following is observed; replace it with a new one:

   a. A puncture or split whose total length or diameter exceeds 6 mm (0.24 in.).

   b. A scratch or split on the side wall.

   c. Any type of ply separation.

   d. Tread separation or excessive abnormal wear pattern.

   e. Tread depth of less than 1.6 mm (0.06 in.) in the front tire or less than 2.0 mm (0.08 in.) in the rear tire on original equipment tires. Aftermarket tires tread depth minimum may vary.

   f. Scratches on either sealing bead.

   g. The cord is cut in any place.

   h. Flat spots in the tread from skidding.

   i. Any abnormality in the inner liner.

3. Inspect the valve stem hole in the rim. Remove any dirt or corrosion from the hole and wipe dry with a clean cloth.

Installation

1. A new tire may have balancing rubbers inside. These are not patches and should not be disturbed or removed.

2. If the wheel was serviced, check that the spoke ends do not protrude through the nipples into the center of the rim. If they do they will puncture the inner tube. File off any protruding spoke ends.

3. Make sure the rubber rim tape is in place with the rough side toward the rim.

4. Install the tube valve stem core into the valve stem. Place the tube into the tire and inflate it just enough to round it out. Too much air will make installing the tire difficult and too little air will increase the chances of pinching the tube with the tire irons.

5. Lubricate both beads of the tire with soapy water.

6. When installing the tire onto the rim make sure the correct tire, either front or rear is installed onto the correct wheel and that the tire's direction arrow (**Figure 29**) faces the direction of wheel rotation.

7. If remounting the old tire, align the mark made in Step 1 under *Removal* with the valve stem. If a new tire is being installed, align the colored spot near the bead (indicating a lighter point on the tire) with the valve stem.

8. If the tire was completely removed from the rim, place the backside of the tire into the center of the rim (**Figure 30**). The lower bead should go into the

center of the rim and the upper bead outside. Work around the tire in both directions (**Figure 31**). Use a tire iron for the last few inches of bead (**Figure 32**).

9. Wiggle the valve stem to be sure the tube is not trapped under the tire bead. Set the valve squarely in the rim hole before screwing on the valve stem nut.

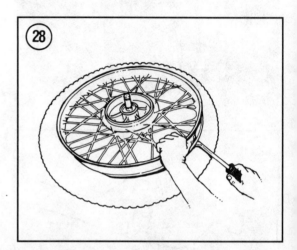

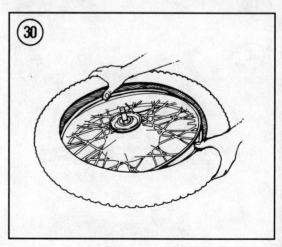

10. Check the bead on both sides of the tire for an even fit around the rim.

11. Bounce the wheel several times, rotating it each time. This will force the tire beads against the rim flanges. After the tire beads are in contact with the rim, inflate the tire to seat the beads.

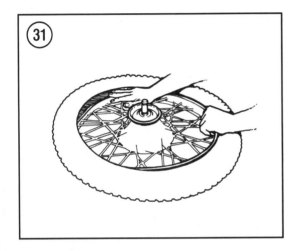

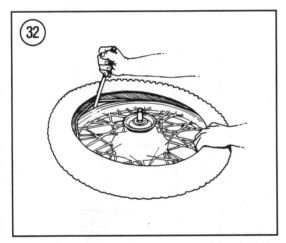

WARNING
In the next step inflate the tire to approximately 10-15% over the recommended inflation pressure. Do not exceed this pressure as the tire could burst causing severe injury. Never stand directly over a tire while inflating it.

12. After inflating the tire, check to see that the beads are fully seated and that the tire rim lines are the same distance from the rim all the way around the tire. If the beads won't seat, deflate the tire and re-lubricate the rim and beads with soapy water.

13. Reinflate the tire to the required pressure listed in **Table 2**. Install the valve stem cap. Always make sure to install the cap (**Figure 33**) as it prevents small pebbles and dirt from collecting in the valve stem. This could allow air leakage or result in incorrect tire pressure readings.

14. Balance the wheel as described in this chapter.

15. Install the wheel as described in this chapter or Chapter Eleven.

TIRE REPAIRS

Patching a tube on the road is very difficult. A can of pressurized tire sealant may inflate the tire and seal the hole, although this is only a temporary fix.

Due to the variations of material supplied with different tire repair kits, follow the instructions and recommendations supplied with the repair kit.

HANDLEBAR

There are two different types of handlebars used among the various models. One is the straight bar while the other is a riser type. Removal and installation of the handlebar is the same for both design configurations.

On all models, the handlebar switch wiring harnesses are routed through the handlebar tubing and down through the hollow handlebar holders. The harness then enters the backside of the headlight housing where all of the handlebar switch electrical connectors are located.

Removal

Refer to **Figure 34** for this procedure.

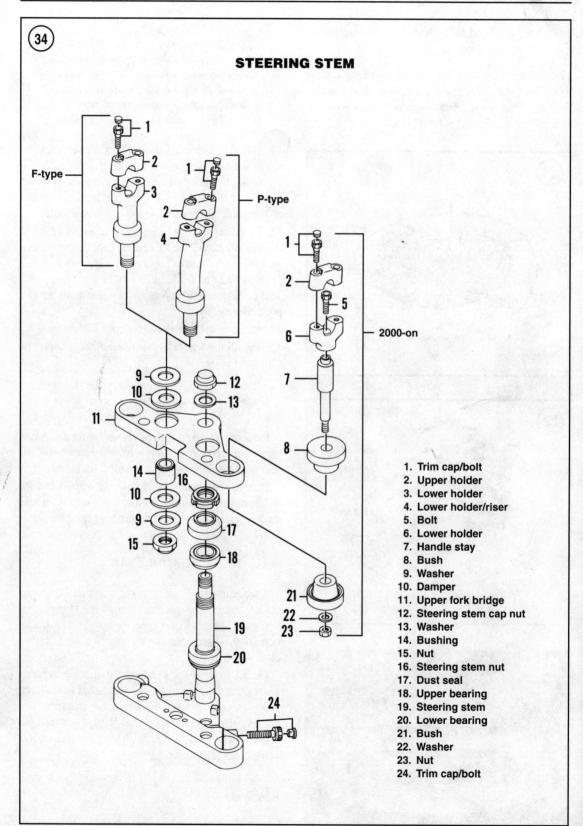

STEERING STEM

1. Trim cap/bolt
2. Upper holder
3. Lower holder
4. Lower holder/riser
5. Bolt
6. Lower holder
7. Handle stay
8. Bush
9. Washer
10. Damper
11. Upper fork bridge
12. Steering stem cap nut
13. Washer
14. Bushing
15. Nut
16. Steering stem nut
17. Dust seal
18. Upper bearing
19. Steering stem
20. Lower bearing
21. Bush
22. Washer
23. Nut
24. Trim cap/bolt

1. Remove the fuel tank as described in Chapter Eight.

2. Remove the headlight lens assembly to gain access to the switch electrical connectors. Refer to Chapter Nine.

3. Follow the wiring harness from the base of the handlebar holders into the headlight case. Locate and disconnect all connectors (**Figure 35**) relating to both handlebar switch assemblies. Carefully withdraw both wiring harnesses out through the backside of the headlight case rubber grommets.

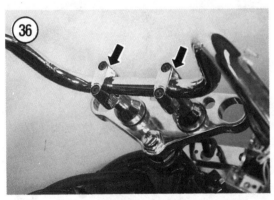

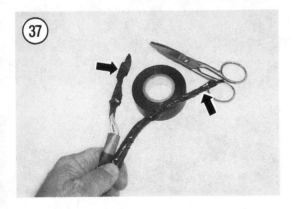

NOTE
The following steps of this procedure are shown with the headlight case assembly, the speedometer and meter assembly and front forks removed for clarity. It is not necessary to remove these components for handlebar removal and installation.

4. Remove the front brake master cylinder as described in Chapter Twelve.

5. Remove the clutch master cylinder as described in Chapter Six.

6. Disconnect the throttle cable from the throttle grip as described in Chapter Eight.

7. Remove the trim caps from the Allen bolts securing the handlebar upper holders.

8. Remove the Allen bolts securing the handlebar upper holders (**Figure 36**) and remove the upper holders.

9. Carefully and slowly pull the handlebar assembly up and off the handlebar lower holders while guiding the wiring harness up through the upper fork bridge.

10. Continue to pull the handlebar assembly up until both switch harnesses are free from the lower holders. Remove the handlebar assembly.

Installation

1. Clean the lower and upper handlebar holders to maintain a good grip on the handlebar.

2. Carefully clean both ribbed portions of the handlebar where they contact the holders. Do not use a wire brush as the chrome plated surface on each side of the ribbed portions will be damaged.

3. Apply several layers of black electrical tape to the ends of the wiring harness (**Figure 37**). This will make installation easier when the harness is inserted down through handlebar lower holder and upper fork bridge

4. Insert the harness ends into the handlebar lower holders (**Figure 38**). Carefully push the harness down through the holders while moving the handlebar into position.

5. Align the handlebar punch mark with the top surface of the handlebar lower holder (**Figure 39**).

6. Hold the handlebar in this position, then install the upper holders and Allen bolts (**Figure 36**).

7. Tighten the Allen bolts to the torque specification listed in **Table 1**. Tighten the bolts so the space between the handlebar upper and lower holders is

10

equal at the front and back. Install the trim caps into
the Allen bolts.

8. Connect the throttle cable onto the throttle grip
as described in Chapter Eight.

9. Install the clutch master cylinder as described in
Chapter Six.

10. Install the front brake master cylinder as described in Chapter Twelve.

> *WARNING*
> *After installation is completed, make
> sure the brake lever does not come in
> contact with the throttle grip assembly
> when it is pulled on fully. If it does the
> brake fluid may be low in the reservoir;
> refill as necessary. Refer to **Front Disc
> Brakes** in Chapter Twelve.*

11. Insert the wiring harnesses into the backside of
the headlight case and reconnect all connectors.

12. Check the operation of the switch functions on
both switch assemblies.

13. Install the headlight lens assembly as described
in Chapter Nine.

14. Install the fuel tank as described in Chapter
Eight.

15. Adjust the throttle operation as described in
Chapter Three.

STEERING HEAD AND STEM

Removal

Refer to **Figure 34** for this procedure.

1. Remove the front wheel as described in this chapter.

2. Remove the handlebar assembly as described in
this chapter.

3. Remove the front forks as described in this chapter.

4. Remove the headlight lens and housing assembly
as described in Chapter Nine.

5. Remove the speedometer and meter assembly as
described in Chapter Nine.

6. Remove the nuts (**Figure 40**) securing the headlight case mounting bracket to the lower fork bridge.
Carefully remove the bracket off the wiring harnesses and remove it.

7. Carefully withdraw the front brake and clutch
hydraulic hoses through the holes in both the upper
and lower fork bridges. Cover the end of the hoses

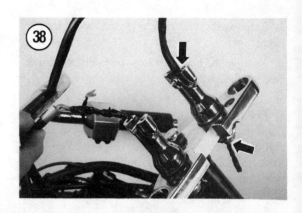
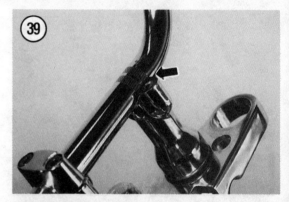

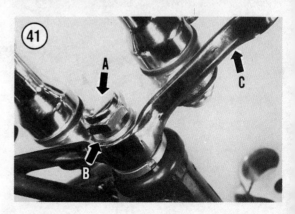

with a reclosable plastic bag and tie the loose end up to the frame.

8. Remove the steering stem cap nut (A, **Figure 41**) and washer (B, **Figure 41**).

9. Remove the upper fork bridge (C, **Figure 41**).

10. Loosen the steering stem nut (**Figure 42**). To loosen the nut, use a large drift and hammer or use the easily improvised tool shown in **Figure 43**.

11. Hold onto the lower end of the steering stem assembly and remove the steering stem nut.

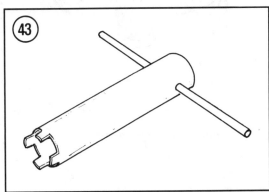

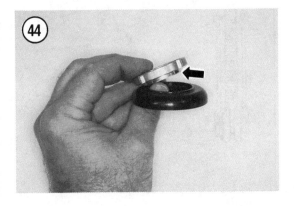

12. Remove the dust seal from the top of the headset.

13. Lower the steering stem assembly down and out of the steering head.

14. Remove the upper bearing from the top of the headset area of the steering head portion of the frame.

15. If necessary, remove the nut, washer and damper and remove the handlebar lower holders.

Inspection

1. Clean the bearing races in the steering head and the bearings with solvent.

2. Check the welds around the steering head for cracks and fractures. If any are found, have them checked by a Suzuki dealership or a competent frame shop.

3. Check the balls for pitting, scratches or discoloration indicating wear or corrosion. Replace them in sets if any are bad.

4. Check the races for pitting, galling and corrosion. If any of these conditions exist, replace the races as described in this chapter.

5. Check the steering stem for cracks, damage or wear. If damaged in any way replace the steering stem.

6. Inspect the cap nut, washer, steering stem nut and upper bearing for wear or damage. Replace as necessary.

Installation

Refer to **Figure 34** for this procedure.

1. Make sure the steering head outer races are properly seated.

2. Apply an even complete coat of wheel bearing grease to the steering head outer races, to both bearings and to the dust seal and cap nut.

3. Install the upper bearing into the steering head.

4. Install the steering stem into the head tube and hold it firmly in place.

5. Install the dust seal onto the top of the headset.

NOTE
*Position the steering stem nut with its shoulder side (**Figure 44**) facing the dust seal.*

10

6. Install the steering stem nut (**Figure 42**) and tighten it to the torque specification listed in **Table 1**.

7. Turn the steering stem from lock-to-lock 5-6 times to seat the bearings.

8. Loosen the steering stem nut 1/4 turn (**Figure 45**), then retighten so that no play can be detected in the steering stem.

9. Move the steering stem from side-to-side (**Figure 46**). The steering stem should move freely with no looseness or stiffness. If necessary, repeat Steps 6-8 and readjust the steering stem nut.

10. Install the upper fork bridge.

11. Install the washer and the steering stem cap nut. Tighten the cap nut finger-tight at this time.

NOTE
Steps 12-15 must be performed in this order to assure proper upper and lower fork bridge to fork alignment.

12. Temporarily slide the fork tubes into position until they bottom out in the stops in the upper fork bridge. Tighten the cap bolt to the torque specification listed in **Table 1**.

13. Temporarily install the front axle into the fork legs and tighten securely.

14. Tighten the lower fork bridge bolts to the torque specification listed in **Table 1**.

15. Tighten the steering stem cap nut to the torque specification listed in **Table 1**.

16. Remove the front axle and fork cap bolt. Loosen the lower fork bridge bolts and slide the front fork tubes down and out.

17. Install the handlebar assembly as described in this chapter.

18. Install the headlight case mounting bracket to the lower fork bridge. Tighten the nuts securely.

19. Remove the reclosable plastic bag from the loose end of the front brake and clutch hoses.

20. Carefully insert the hydraulic hoses through the holes and rubber grommets in both the upper and lower fork bridges. Attach the hydraulic hoses to the respective master cylinders as described in Chapter Six and Chapter Twelve.

21. Install the speedometer and meter assembly as described in Chapter Nine.

22. Install the headlight lens and housing assembly as described in Chapter Nine.

23. Reconnect the electrical connectors within the headlight housing.

24. Install the front forks as described in this chapter.

25. Install the front wheel as described in this chapter.

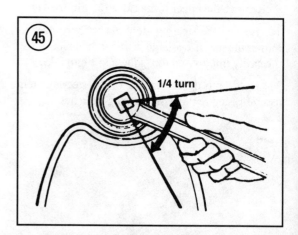

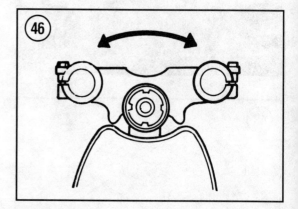

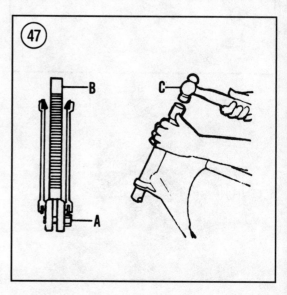

STEERING HEAD BEARING RACES

The headset and steering stem bearing races are pressed into the headset portion of the frame. Because the races are easily bent, do not remove them unless they require replacement.

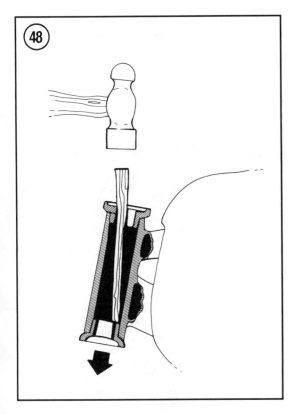

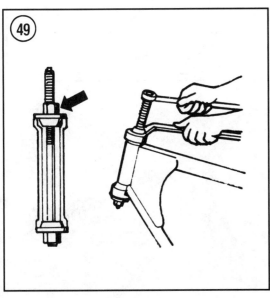

Headset Bearing Race Removal/Installation

1. Remove the steering stem as described in this chapter.

2A. Use the Suzuki bearing outer race remover (part No. 09941-54911), and the steering bearing remover/installer (part No. 09941-74910) to remove the headset bearing race as follows:

    a. Install the outer race remover (A, **Figure 47**) into one of the outer races.

    b. Insert the bearing remover (B, **Figure 47**) into the backside of the outer race remover.

    c. Tap on the end of the bearing remover with a hammer (C, **Figure 47**) and drive the bearing outer race out of the steering head. Remove the special tool from the outer race.

    d. Repeat for the bearing outer race at the other end of the headset.

2B. If the special tools are not used, perform the following:

    a. Insert a hardwood stick or soft punch into the head tube and carefully tap the outer race out from the inside (**Figure 48**).

    b. After it is started, work around the outer race in a crisscross pattern so that neither the race nor the head tube is damaged.

3A. Use the Suzuki bearing installer (part No. 09941-34513) to install the headset bearing race as follows:

    a. Position the outer races into the headset and just start them into position lightly with a soft-faced mallet. Just tap them in enough to hold them in place.

    b. Position the bearing installer (**Figure 49**) into both of the outer races.

    c. Tighten the nuts on the bearing installer and pull the outer races into place in the headset. Tighten the nuts until both bearing outer races are completely seated in the head set and is flush with the steering head surface.

    d. Remove the special tool.

3B. If the special tools are not used, perform the following:

    a. Position one of the outer races into the headset and just start it into position lightly with a soft-faced mallet. Just tap it in enough to hold it in place.

    b. Tap the outer race in slowly with a block of wood or a suitable size socket or pipe (**Figure**

10

50). Make sure that the race is squarely seated in the headset race bore before tapping it into place. Tap the race in until it is flush with the steering head surface.

c. Repeat for the other outer race.

Steering Stem Lower Bearing Removal/Installation

Do not remove the steering stem lower bearing and seal (**Figure 51**) unless it is going to be replaced. The lower bearing can be difficult to remove. If you cannot remove it as described in this procedure, take the steering stem to a dealership service department and have them replace the bearing.

Never reinstall a lower bearing that has been removed as it is no longer true and will damage the rest of the bearing assembly if reused.

1A. If special tools are used, perform the following:

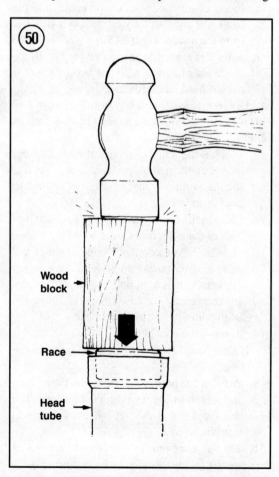

a. Install the Suzuki bearing remover (part No. 09941-84510) (A, **Figure 52**) onto the steering stem assembly (B, **Figure 52**).

b. Tighten the upper bolt (C, **Figure 52**) and withdraw the lower bearing from the steering stem.

c. Remove the special tool, lower bearing and grease seal from the steering stem.

1B. If special tools are not used, perform the following:

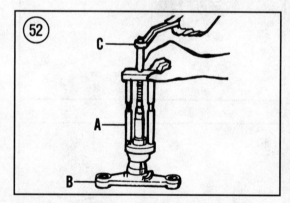

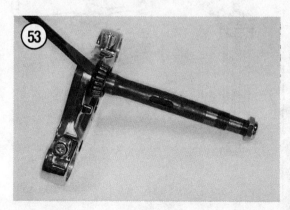

a. Install the steering stem bolt onto the top of the steering stem to protect the threads.

b. Loosen the lower bearing from the shoulder at the base of the steering stem with a chisel as shown in **Figure 53**. Slide the lower bearing and grease seal off the steering stem. Discard the lower bearing and the grease seal.

2. Clean the steering stem with solvent and dry thoroughly.

3. Position the new grease seal so the seal outer lips are facing down.

4. Slide the new grease seal and the lower bearing onto the steering stem until they stop on the raised shoulder.

5. Install the Suzuki steering stem bearing installer (part No. 09941-74910) (A, **Figure 54**) on top of the lower bearing (B, **Figure 54**).

6. Using a hammer (C. **Figure 54**), carefully tap on the bearing installer and drive the lower bearing into place.

7. Remove the bearing installer.

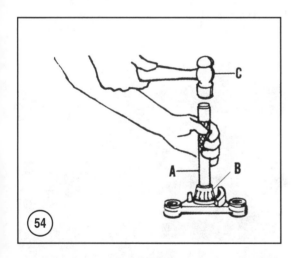

8. Make sure it is seated squarely and is all the way down.

9. Pack the bearing rollers with wheel bearing grease.

FRONT FORK

Front Fork Service

Before suspecting major trouble, drain the front fork oil and refill with the proper type and quantity fork oil as described in this chapter. If you still have trouble, such as poor damping, a tendency to bottom or top out or leakage around the oil seals, follow the service procedures in this section.

To simplify fork service and to prevent the mixing of parts, service the fork tubes separately.

Removal

1. Remove the fork cap bolt (**Figure 55**).

2. Remove the brake caliper as described in Chapter Twelve.

3. Remove the front wheel as described in this chapter.

4. Remove the front fender as described in Chapter Thirteen.

5. If the fork tube is going to be disassembled, perform the following:

a. Loosen (just break it loose) the Allen bolt at the base of the slider, using an Allen wrench. If the bolt is loosened too much, fork oil may start to drain from the slider.

> *NOTE*
> *If you cannot loosen the Allen bolt using this technique, special tools will be required to hold the damper rod. These are described under the fork tube **Disassembly and Reassembly** procedures.*

b. Use a 14 mm Allen wrench and breaker bar (**Figure 56**) and loosen the spring stopper at the top of the fork tube.

6. Disconnect the front turn signal electrical connector.

7. Loosen the Allen bolt (A, **Figure 57**) securing the front turn signal mounting bracket to the front fork tube.

10

8. Loosen the lower fork bridge bolt (B, **Figure 57**).

NOTE:
The fork leg also goes through the directional signal mounting bracket as well as the upper and lower fork bridges.

9. Slide the fork tube from the upper fork bridge, then tighten the lower fork bridge bolt.

10. Carefully slide the directional signal assembly up and off the fork tube and remove it.

11. Loosen the lower fork bridge bolt and carefully lower the fork assembly out of the lower fork bridge. It may be necessary to rotate the fork tube slightly while pulling it down and out. Remove the fork assembly and take to a workbench for service. If the fork is not going to be serviced, wrap it in a bath towel or blanket to protect the surface from damage.

Installation

NOTE
The right-hand fork assembly has the brake caliper mounting bosses. If both fork assemblies were removed, be sure to install them correctly.

1. Install the fork assembly into the lower fork bridge, push it mid-way between the bridge assemblies, and temporarily tighten the lower fork bridge bolt.

2. Wrap the wiring harness around the locating pin (**Figure 58**) on the front directional signal assembly.

3. Install the front directional assembly (A, **Figure 59**) onto the fork tube. Keep the wiring harness correctly positioned behind the pin (B, **Figure 59**).

4. Loosen the lower fork bridge bolt and push the fork tube up until it bottoms out against the stop in the upper fork bridge. Tighten the lower fork bridge bolt to the torque specification listed in **Table 1**.

5. Keep the front directional assembly wiring harness correctly positioned behind the pin (B, **Figure 59**) and push it all the way down onto the lower fork bridge. Position it correctly and tighten the clamp bolt securely.

6. Reconnect the electrical connector.

7. Install the front fender as described in Chapter Thirteen.

8. Install the front wheel as described in this chapter.

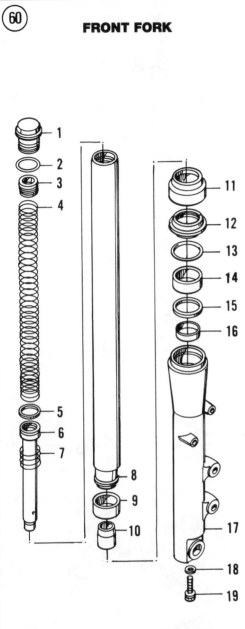

FRONT FORK (60)

1. Cap bolt
2. O-ring
3. Spring stopper
4. Spring
5. Piston ring
6. Damper rod
7. Rebound spring
8. Fork tube
9. Fork tube bushing
10. Oil lock piece
11. Trim cap
12. Dust seal
13. Stopper ring
14. Fork seal
15. Retainer
16. Slider bushing
17. Slider
18. Gasket
19. Allen bolt

9. Install the brake caliper as described in Chapter Twelve.

10. If the fork was disassembled for service, use a 14 mm Allen wrench and tighten the spring stopper to the torque specification listed in **Table 1**.

11. Inspect the O-ring seal on the fork cap bolt for hardness or deterioration, replace if necessary.

12. Install the fork cap bolt (**Figure 55**) and tighten to the torque specification listed in **Table 1**.

Disassembly

Refer to **Figure 60** during the disassembly and assembly procedures.

1. If not loosened during the fork removal sequence, perform the following:

   a. Hold the fork slider in a vise with soft jaws in a horizontal position.

   b. Have an assistant compress the fork tube into the slider. This will place additional pressure on the damper rod to keep it from rotating while loosening the Allen bolt.

   c. Use an Allen wrench and impact wrench and loosen the Allen bolt (**Figure 61**) on the bottom of the slider. Do not remove the Allen bolt and gasket from the slider as the fork is still full of fork oil.

NOTE
If you cannot loosen the Allen bolt by this method, Step 11 in this procedure describes how to hold the damper rod and loosen the Allen bolt using special tools.

2. Reposition the fork slider in a vise with soft jaws in a vertical position.

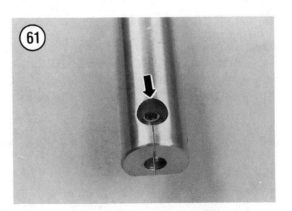

(61)

3. Use a 14 mm Allen wrench and loosen the spring stopper (**Figure 62**).

> *WARNING*
> *Be careful when removing the spring stopper as it is under pressure. Protect your eyes accordingly.*

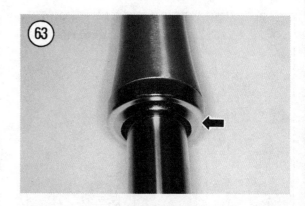

4. Remove the spring stopper (**Figure 62**) from the fork tube.

5. Remove the fork spring.

6. Remove the fork assembly from the vise.

7. Turn the fork assembly upside down and drain the fork oil into a suitable container. Pump the fork several times by hand to expel most of the remaining oil. Dispose of the fork oil properly.

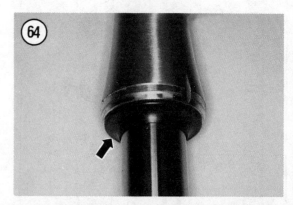

> *NOTE*
> *If you recycle your engine oil, do not add the fork oil to the engine oil because the recycler will probably not accept the mixed oil.*

8. Remove the dust seal trim cap (**Figure 63**) from the slider.

9. Remove the dust seal (**Figure 64**) from the slider.

10. Remove the stopper ring (**Figure 65**) from the slider.

11. If the Allen bolt was not loosened, use the listed Suzuki tools and perform the following:

   a. Install the attachment A (part No. 09940-34530) onto the T handle (part No. 09940-34520).

   b. Insert this special tool setup into the fork tube and index it into the hex receptacle in the top of the damper rod (**Figure 66**) to hold the damper rod in place.

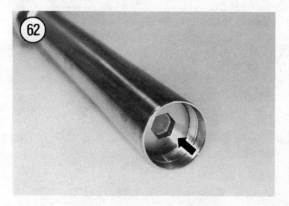

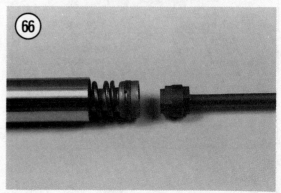

c. Using an Allen wrench, loosen then remove the Allen bolt and washer (**Figure 61**) from the base of the slider.

NOTE
On this type of fork, force is needed to remove the fork tube from the slider.

12. Install the fork tube in a vise with soft jaws.
13. There is an interference fit between the bushing in the fork slider and the bushing on the fork tube. In order to remove the fork tube from the slider, pull hard on the fork tube using quick in-and-out strokes (**Figure 67**). Doing so will withdraw the bushing, washer and the oil seal from the slider.

NOTE
It may be necessary to heat the area on the slider around the oil seal slightly prior to removal. Use a rag soaked in hot water; do not apply a flame directly to the fork slider.

14. Withdraw the fork tube from the slider.

NOTE
Do not remove the fork tube bushing unless it is going to be replaced. Inspect it as described in this chapter.

15. Remove the oil lock piece from the damper rod.
16. Remove the damper rod and rebound spring from the slider.
17. Inspect the components as described in this chapter.

Inspection

1. Thoroughly clean all parts in solvent and dry them. Check the fork tube for signs of wear or scratches.
2. Check the damper rod for straightness. **Figure 68** shows one method. The damper rod should be replaced if the runout is 0.2 mm (0.008 in.) or greater.

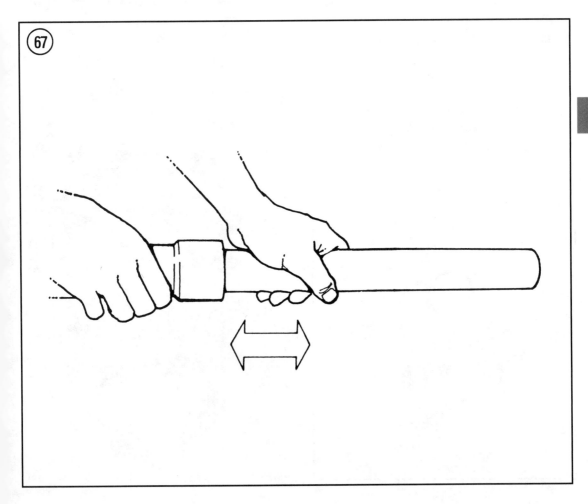

10

3. Make sure the oil holes in the damper rod are clear. Clean out if necessary.

4. Inspect the damper rod and piston ring (**Figure 69**) for wear or damage. Replace as necessary.

5. Check the fork tube for straightness. If bent or severely scratched, it should be replaced.

6. Check the slider for dents or exterior damage that may cause the upper fork tube to stick. Replace if necessary.

7. Inspect the brake caliper mounting bosses on the slider for cracks or other damage. If damaged, replace the slider.

8. Inspect the slider (**Figure 70**) and fork tube bushings (**Figure 71**). If either is scratched or scored they must be replaced. If the Teflon coating is worn off so that the copper base material is showing on approximately 3/4 of the total surface, the bushing must be replaced. Also check for distortion on the washer; replace as necessary.

9. Inspect the fork cap bolt and spring stopper threads in the fork tube for wear or damage.

10. Inspect the fork cap bolt threads for wear or damage.

11. Inspect the spring stopper threads for wear or damage.

12. Inspect the oil seal seating area in the slider for damage or burrs. Clean up if necessary.

13. Inspect the gasket on the Allen bolt; replace if damaged.

14. Clean the threads of the Allen bolt thoroughly with cleaning solvent or spray contact cleaner.

15. Measure the free length of the fork spring (not the rebound spring) as shown in **Figure 72**. If the spring free length is less than the service limit listed in **Table 4**, replace the spring.

16. Any parts that are worn or damaged should be replaced. Simply cleaning and reinstalling unserviceable components will not improve performance of the front suspension.

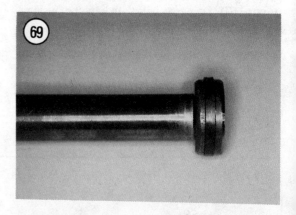

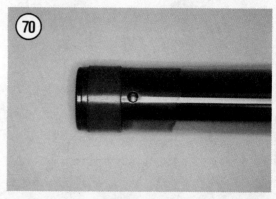

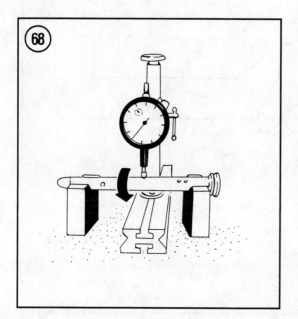

Assembly

1. Coat all parts with fresh SAE 10 fork oil prior to installation.

2. Install the rebound spring onto the damper rod (**Figure 73**) and insert this assembly into the fork tube (**Figure 74**).

3. Temporarily install the fork spring and spring stopper to hold the damper rod in place. Tighten the spring stopper securely.

4. Install the oil lock piece onto the damper rod (**Figure 75**).

5. Install the upper fork assembly into the slider.

6. Make sure the gasket is on the Allen bolt.

7. Use a small amount of a locking compound such as ThreeBond TB1303 or Loctite No. 242 on the Allen bolt threads prior to installation. Install the Allen bolt and tighten to the torque specification listed in **Table 1**.

8. Slide the fork slider bushing (A, **Figure 76**) and the washer (B, **Figure 76**) down the fork tube and rest it on top of the fork slider.

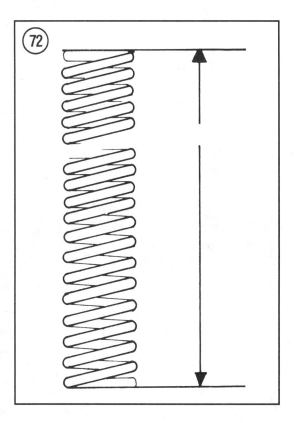

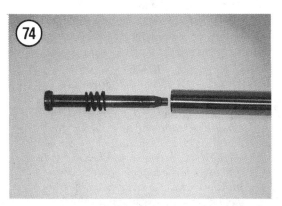

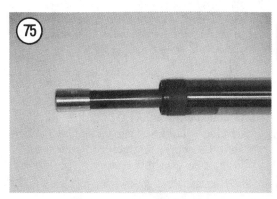

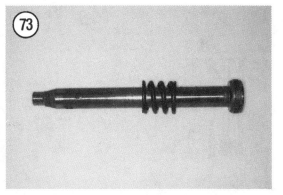

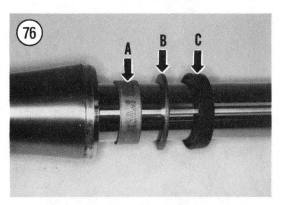

10

NOTE
Place a plastic bag over the end of the slider and coat it with fork oil. This will avoid damage to the dust seal and the oil seal lips when installing them over the top of the slider. You can then slide both seals over the fork slider without damaging them.

9. Install the new oil seal as follows:

   a. Coat the new seal with fresh SAE 10W fork oil.

   b. Position the seal with the open groove facing upward and slide the oil seal (C, **Figure 76**) down onto the fork tube.

NOTE
*A fork seal driver (**Figure 77**) is required to install the fork slider bushing and fork seal into the slider. A number of different aftermarket fork seal drivers are available that can be used for this purpose. Another method is to use a piece of pipe or metal collar with the correct dimensions to slide over the fork tube and seat against the seal. When selecting or fabricating a driver tool, it must be have sufficient weight to drive the bushing and oil seal into the slider.*

   c. Slide the fork seal driver down the fork tube and seat it against the seal.

   d. Operate the driver tool to drive the fork slider bushing and fork seal into the slider. Continue until the stopper ring groove in the slider is visible above the fork seal.

10. Slide the stopper ring down the fork tube.

11. Install the stopper ring and make sure it is completely seated in the groove in the fork slider (**Figure 78**).

12. Install the dust seal (**Figure 64**) into the slider. Press it in until it is completely seated.

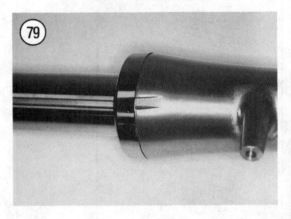

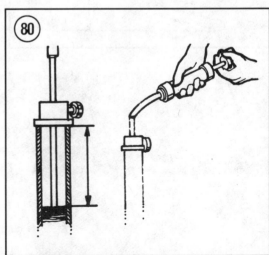

13. Install the dust seal trim cap (**Figure 63**) onto the slider. Index it into the groove in the slider (**Figure 79**).

14. Unscrew the spring stopper and remove the fork spring from the fork tube.

NOTE
Suzuki recommends to measure the fork oil level to ensure a more accurate filling.

NOTE
To measure the correct amount of fluid, use a plastic baby bottle. These bottles have measurements in milliliters (ml) on the side.

15. Compress the fork completely.

16. Add the recommended amount of SAE 10W fork oil to the fork assembly listed in **Table 3**.

17. Hold the fork assembly as close to perfect vertical as possible.

18. Use an accurate ruler or the Suzuki oil level gauge (part No. 09943-74111), or equivalent, to achieve the correct oil level listed in **Table 3**. Refer to **Figure 80**.

NOTE
*An oil level measuring devise can be made as shown in **Figure 81**. Position the lower edge of the hose clamp the specified oil level distance up from the small diameter hole. Overfill the fork with slightly more than the required amount of oil. Position the hose clamp on the top edge of the fork tube and draw out the excess oil until the level reaches the small diameter hole. A precise oil level can be achieved with this simple device.*

19. Allow the oil to settle completely and recheck the oil level measurement. Adjust the oil level if necessary.

20. Install the fork spring with the closer wound coils (**Figure 82**) going in last.

21. Hold the fork assembly upright so the fork oil will not drain out.

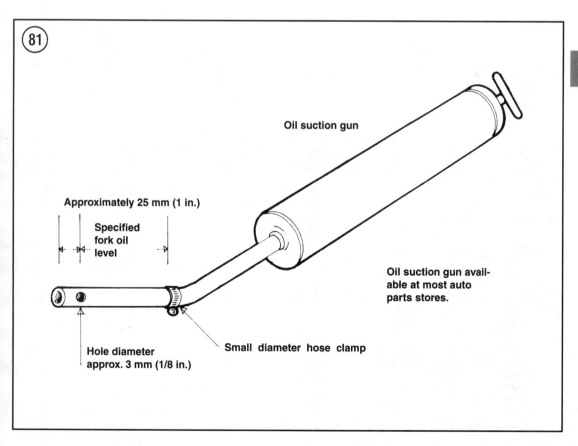

(81)

Oil suction gun

Approximately 25 mm (1 in.)

Specified fork oil level

Oil suction gun available at most auto parts stores.

Hole diameter approx. 3 mm (1/8 in.)

Small diameter hose clamp

10

22. Install the spring stopper and tighten securely. Do not try to tighten to the correct torque at this time.

23. Install the fork assemblies as described in this chapter.

NOTE
If you are unable to tighten the spring stopper to the correct torque specification at this time, tighten it after the fork assembly is reinstalled in the fork bridge assembles.

24. Tighten the spring stopper to the torque specification listed in **Table 1**.

25. Inspect the O-ring seal on the fork cap bolt; replace if necessary.

26. Install the top fork cap bolt and tighten to the torque specification listed in **Table 1**.

27. Repeat this procedure for the other fork assembly.

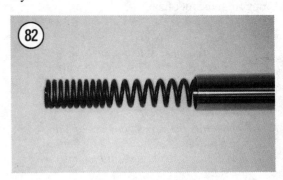

Table 1 FRONT SUSPENSION TIGHTENING TORQUES

item	N·m	in.-lb.	ft.-lb.
Front axle	36-52	—	26-38
Front axle clamp bolt	15-25	—	11-18
Front wheel hub flange bolt	20-30	—	15-22
Brake disc mounting bolt	15-25	—	11-18
Spoke nipple	4-5	35-44	—
Handlebar			
Mounting bolts	15-25	—	11-18
Holder nut	80-100	—	59-74
Steering stem head nut	80-100	—	59-74
Fork bridge lower clamp bolt	25-40	—	18-29
Front fork			
Cap bolt	45-55	—	33-40
Spring stopper	40-50	—	29-36
Damper rod lower Allen bolt	15-25	—	11-18
Front brake master cylinder clamp bolt	8-12	71-106	—
Front caliper mounting bolts	25-40	—	18-29
Clutch master cylinder clamp bolt	8-12	71-106	—
Steering stem nut	80-100	—	59-74

Table 2 TIRE INFLATION PRESSURE (COLD)*

	kPa	psi
Front		
Solo riding	200	29
Dual riding	200	29
Rear		
Solo riding	200	29
Dual riding	228	33

*Tire inflation pressure for factory equipped tires. Aftermarket tires may require different inflation pressure.

Table 3 FORK OIL CAPACITY AND DIMENSIONS

Front fork oil capacity (each fork leg)	
Completely dry	354 ml (12.0 U.S. oz. or 12.5 Imp. oz.)
Front fork oil level dimesnion from top surface (after completely dry)	
1991-1992	203 mm (7.99 in.)
Front fork oil-type	SAE 10

Table 4 FRONT SUSPENSION SPECIFICATIONS

Item	Specification
Front fork stroke	160 mm (6.3 in.)
Minimum front fork spring free length	549 mm (21.16 in.)
Fork oil type and weight	SAE 10
Front wheel rim runout limit	
Axial and radial	0.2 mm (0.008 in.)
Front axle wobble limit	0.25 mm (0.010 in.)

10

CHAPTER ELEVEN

REAR SUSPENSION AND FINAL DRIVE

This chapter includes repair and replacement procedures for the rear wheel and rear suspension components. Tire changing and wheel balancing are covered in Chapter Ten.

Refer to **Table 1** for rear suspension torque specifications. **Table 1** and **Table 2** are located at the end of this chapter.

REAR WHEEL

Removal

1. Remove the trim cap covering the rear axle and rear axle nut.

2. Have an assistant apply the rear brake, then loosen the rear axle nut (**Figure 1**). Do not remove the nut at this time.

3. Remove the right-hand shock absorber as described in this chapter.

4. Remove the rear brake caliper as described in Chapter Twelve.

5. Place a suitable size jack, or wooden blocks, under the frame to support the bike securely with the rear wheel off the ground.

NOTE
The rear axle may have been installed from either side. The correct direction is from the left-hand side with the rear axle nut located on the right-hand side next to the brake torque link.

6. Remove the rear axle nut and washer (**Figure 1**).

7. Use an aluminum or brass drift and carefully tap the axle from the right-hand side. Tap it out sufficiently to clear the brake torque link, then remove the torque link.

8. Remove the right-hand spacer (**Figure 2**) from the rear hub.

9. Withdraw the axle (**Figure 3**), then slide the wheel to the right to disengage the hub spline from the final drive splines.

10. Lower the rear wheel and remove it from the swing arm.

11. Install all of the rear axle components onto the rear axle to prevent misplacing them.

12. Inspect the wheel as described in this chapter.

Inspection

1. Remove any corrosion from the rear axle with a piece of fine emery cloth. Clean axle with solvent, then wipe the axle clean with a lint-free cloth.

2. Check axle runout. Place the axle on V-blocks and place the tip of a dial indicator in the middle of the axle (**Figure 4**). Rotate the axle and measure runout. If the runout exceeds 0.25 mm (0.010 in.), replace the axle; do not attempt to straighten it.

3. Check rim runout as follows:

a. Measure the radial (up and down) runout of the wheel rim with a dial indicator as shown at A, **Figure 5**. If runout exceeds 2.0 mm (0.08 in.), check the wheel bearings.

b. Measure the axial (side to side) runout of the wheel rim with a dial indicator as shown at B, **Figure 5**. If runout exceeds 2.0 mm (0.08 in.), check the wheel bearings.

c. If the wheel bearings are in good condition but the wheel is out of true, retrue the wheel as described under *Wheels* in Chapter Ten.

d. Replace the front wheel bearings as described under *Rear Hub* in this chapter.

4. Inspect the rim for dents, bending or cracks. Check the rim and rim sealing surface for scratches deeper than 0.5 mm (0.01 in.). If any of these conditions are present, replace the rim.

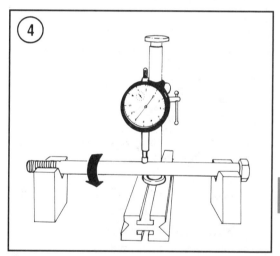

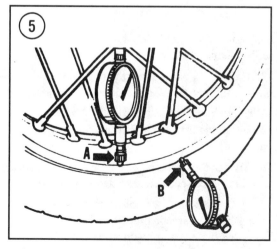

11

Installation

1. Apply a light coat of grease (lithium based NLGI No. 2 grease with molybdenum disulfide) to the final driven flange spline (A, **Figure 6**) and to the rear wheel ring gear (**Figure 7**).

2. Make sure the spacer (B, **Figure 6**) is installed in the final drive unit.

3. Loosen the final drive case mounting nuts (C, **Figure 6**) on the swing arm.

4. Roll the rear wheel forward and into the swing arm.

5. Position the rear wheel so that the splines of the final driven flange and the final drive align.

6. Lift the wheel into position, slowly move the wheel back and forth and push the wheel to the left until it completely seats into the final drive case.

7. Insert the rear axle from the left-hand side (**Figure 3**) and push it through the swing arm and partially through the rear wheel until it starts to come out on the right-hand side.

8. Position the right-hand spacer (**Figure 8**) on the right-hand side of the hub and push the rear axle though it.

9. Correctly position the rear brake caliper torque link as shown in **Figure 9**.

10. Move the torque link into position, make sure the right-hand spacer is still in place, then push the rear axle through the swing arm.

11. Install the axle nut washer and nut. Tighten the nut only finger-tight at this time.

12. Install the rear brake caliper as described in Chapter Twelve.

13. Install the right-hand shock absorber as described in this chapter.

14. Have an assistant apply the rear brake to keep the axle from turning. Then tighten the rear axle nut to the torque specifications listed in **Table 1**.

15. Install the trim caps covering the rear axle and nut.

16. Tighten the final drive gear case nuts (C, **Figure 6**) to the torque specification listed in **Table 1**.

17. After the wheel is installed, rotate it while applying the brake several times to make sure it rotates freely and that the brake works properly.

REAR HUB

Inspection

Inspect each wheel bearing prior to removing it from the wheel hub.

> *CAUTION*
> *Do not remove the wheel bearings for inspection because they will be damaged during removal. Remove wheel bearings only if they are to be replaced.*

1. Perform Step 1 and Step 2 of *Disassembly* in this chapter.

2. Turn each bearing by hand. Make sure bearings turn smoothly.

3. Inspect the play of the inner race of each wheel bearing. Check for excessive axial play and radial play. Replace the bearing if it has an excess amount of free play.

4. On unsealed bearings, check the balls for evidence of wear, pitting or excessive heat (bluish tint). Replace the bearings if necessary; always replace as

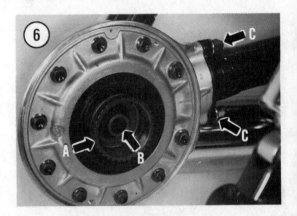

a complete set. When replacing the bearings, be sure to take your old bearings along to ensure a perfect matchup.

NOTE
Fully sealed bearings are available from bearing specialty shops. Fully sealed bearings provide better protection from dirt and moisture that may get into the hub.

5. Inspect the splines of the final driven flange. If any are damaged the flange must be replaced.

Disassembly

Refer to **Figure 10** for this procedure.

1. Remove the rear wheel as described in this chapter.

2. Straighten the locking tabs on the lockwashers, then loosen and remove the bolts (**Figure 11**).

3. Remove the lockwashers and thrust washers. Remove all 3 sets.

4. Pull straight up and remove the final driven flange from the hub.

5. Remove the O-ring seal (**Figure 12**) from the rear hub.

6. Before proceeding further, inspect the wheel bearings as described in this chapter. If they must be replaced, proceed as follows.

7A. If the special tools are not used, perform the following:

   a. To remove the right- and left-hand bearings and distance collar, insert a soft aluminum or brass drift into one side of the hub.

   b. Push the inner spacer over to one side and place the drift on the inner race of the lower bearing.

   c. Tap the bearing out of the hub with a hammer, working around the perimeter of the inner race. Remove the bearing and distance collar.

   d. Repeat for the bearing on the other side.

NOTE
The Kowa Seiki Wheel Bearing Remover set can be ordered by a Suzuki dealership through K & L Supply Co. in Santa Clara, CA.

WARNING
Be sure to wear safety glasses while using the wheel bearing remover set.

7B. To remove the bearings with the Kowa Seiki Wheel Bearing Remover set, perform the following:

   a. Select the correct size remover head and insert it into the bearing.

   b. Turn the wheel over and insert the remover shaft into the backside of the adapter. Tap the wedge and force it into the slit in the remover (**Figure 13**). This will force the head against the bearing inner race.

   c. Tap on the end of the remover shaft with a hammer and drive the bearing out of the hub. Remove the bearing and the distance collar.

   d. Repeat for the bearing on the other side.

8. Clean the inside and the outside of the hub with solvent. Dry with compressed air.

9. Clean the inside and the outside of the final driven flange with solvent. Dry with compressed air.

10. Inspect each rubber cushion (**Figure 14**) for wear or deterioration. Replace if necessary.

11. Inspect the final driven flange as follows:

   a. Inspect the inner splines (**Figure 15**) for wear or missing teeth.

11

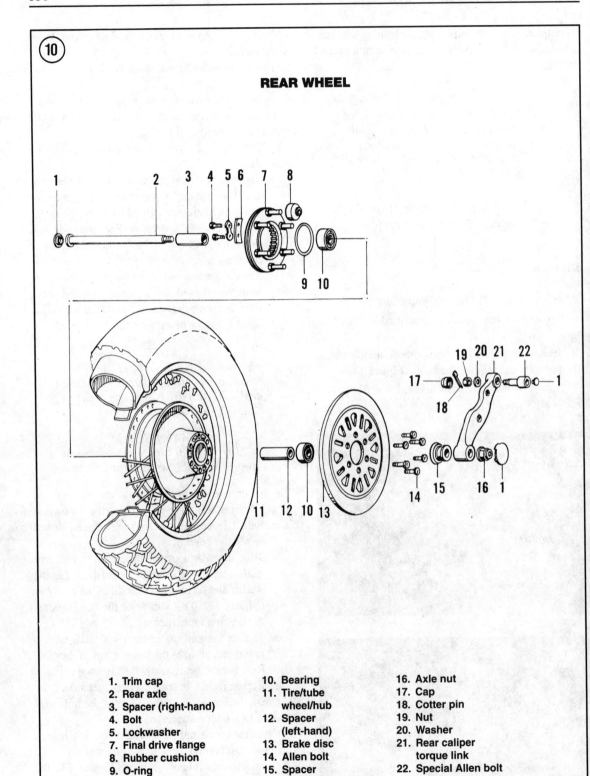

(10)

REAR WHEEL

1. Trim cap
2. Rear axle
3. Spacer (right-hand)
4. Bolt
5. Lockwasher
7. Final drive flange
8. Rubber cushion
9. O-ring
10. Bearing
11. Tire/tube
   wheel/hub
12. Spacer
   (left-hand)
13. Brake disc
14. Allen bolt
15. Spacer
   (right-hand)
16. Axle nut
17. Cap
18. Cotter pin
19. Nut
20. Washer
21. Rear caliper
   torque link
22. Special Allen bolt

b. Inspect the studs (**Figure 16**) for cracks or damage.

c. Inspect the flange for cracks or warpage.

d. Replace the driven flange if any of these areas are damaged.

Assembly

1. On unsealed bearings, pack the bearings with a good quality bearing grease. Work the grease in between the balls thoroughly. Turn the bearing by hand a couple of times to make sure the grease is distributed evenly inside the bearing.

2. Blow any dirt or foreign matter out of the hub prior to installing the bearings.

> *CAUTION*
> *Install non-sealed bearings with the single sealed side facing outward.*

3. Pack the hub with multipurpose grease.

4A. The Suzuki bearing installer (part No. 09924-84510) can be used to install the wheel bearings as follows:

a. Install the right-hand bearing into the hub first.

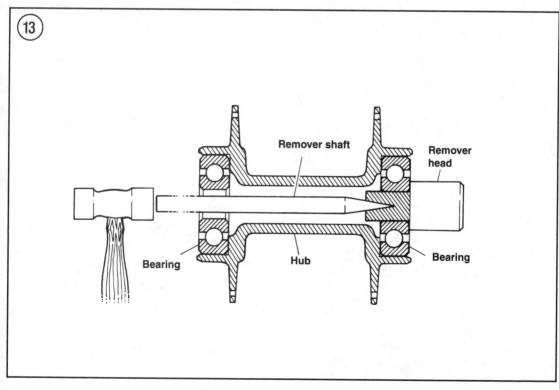

b. Set the bearing with the sealed side facing out and install the bearing installer as shown in **Figure 17**.

c. Tighten the bearing installer and pull the bearing into the hub until it is completely seated. Remove the bearing installer.

d. Turn the wheel over (left-hand side up) on the workbench and install the distance collar.

e. Set the bearing with the sealed side facing out and install the bearing installer as shown in **Figure 18**.

f. Tighten the bearing installer and pull the bearing into the hub until there is a small amount of clearance between the inner race and the distance collar.

g. Remove the bearing installer.

4B. If special tools are not used, perform the following:

a. Tap the left-hand bearing squarely into place and tap on the outer race only. Use a socket that matches the outer race diameter. Do not tap on the inner race or the bearing might be

damaged. Be sure that the bearing is completely seated.

b. Turn the wheel over (right-hand side up) on the workbench and install the distance collar.

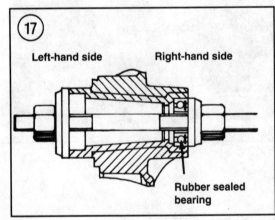

Left-hand side   Right-hand side

Rubber sealed bearing

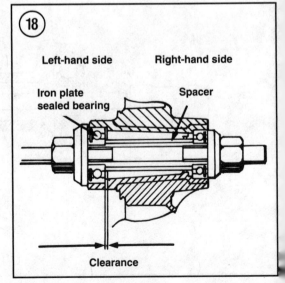

Left-hand side   Right-hand side

Iron plate sealed bearing   Spacer

Clearance

c. Use the same tool setup and drive in the right-hand bearing until there is a slight clearance between the inner race and the distance collar.

5. Install a new O-ring seal into the groove in the hub. Coat the O-ring with multipurpose grease.

6. Install the final driven flange into the rear hub. Push it down until it is completely seated in the rear hub.

7. Install the 3 thrust washers into the locking ring in the final driven flange.

8. Install new lockwashers.

9. Use a small amount of a locking compound such as ThreeBond TB1360 or Loctite No. 271 to the bolt threads prior to installation, then install the bolts.

10. Tighten the bolts to the torque specification listed in **Table 1**.

11. Bend up the locking tab against a flat on each bolt.

12. Install the rear wheel as described in this chapter.

FINAL DRIVE UNIT, DRIVE SHAFT AND UNIVERSAL JOINT

Removal

1. Remove the rear wheel as described in this chapter.

2. Drain the final drive unit oil as described in Chapter Three.

3. Remove the upper and lower mounting nuts and washers (**Figure 19**), then remove the left-hand shock absorber.

NOTE
*In **Figure 20** only 2 of the nuts and washers are shown. Be sure to remove all 3 nuts and washers.*

4. Remove the nuts and washers (**Figure 20**) securing the final drive unit to the swing arm.

5. Pull the final drive unit and drive shaft straight back (**Figure 21**) until it is disengaged from the splines on the universal joint.

6. Loosen the clamp (A, **Figure 22**) securing the rubber boot to the swing arm and move the rubber boot away from the swing arm.

7. Remove the screw securing the swing arm trim panel (B, **Figure 22**) and remove the panel.

11

8. Pull the universal joint toward the rear and disengage it from the bevel gear drive unit.

9. Carefully pull the universal joint out through the swing arm opening and remove it.

Final Drive Unit and Drive Shaft Inspection

The final drive unit requires a considerable number of special tools for disassembly and assembly. The price of all of these tools could be more than the cost of most repairs or seal replacement by a Suzuki dealership.

1. Check that the bearing case flange bolts (**Figure 23**) are in place and are tight.

2. Inspect the splines on the final driven ring gear (**Figure 24**). If they are damaged or worn, the ring gear must be replaced.

> *NOTE*
> *If these splines are damaged, also inspect the splines (**Figure 25**) on the rear wheel final driven flange, which may also need to be replaced.*

3. If removal is necessary, carefully pull the drive shaft from the final drive unit, using a circular motion.

4. Inspect the splines on the universal joint end of drive shaft (**Figure 26**). If they are damaged or worn, the drive shaft must be replaced. If these splines are damaged, also inspect the splines on the universal joint; it may also need to be replaced.

5. Inspect the splines on the final drive unit end of drive shaft. If they are damaged or worn, the drive shaft must be replaced. If these splines are damaged,

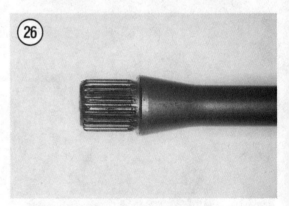

also inspect the splines in the final drive unit; it may also need to be replaced.

6. Check the threads on the studs (**Figure 27**) for wear or thread damage. If necessary, clean the threads with an appropriate size metric die.

7. Check that gear oil is not been leaking from either the ring gear side (**Figure 28**) or pinion joint side (**Figure 29**) of the unit. If there are traces of oil leakage, take the unit to a Suzuki dealership for seal replacement.

Universal Joint Inspection

1. Clean the universal joint in solvent and thoroughly dry with compressed air.

2. Inspect the universal joint pivot points for play (**Figure 30**). Rotate the joint in both directions. If there is noticeable side play the universal joint must be replaced.

3. Inspect the splines at each end of the universal joint. If they are damaged or worn, the universal joint must be replaced.

NOTE
If these splines are damaged, also inspect the splines in the final drive unit and the engine output shaft; they may also need to be replaced.

4. Apply a light coat of molybdenum disulfide grease (NGLI No. 2) to both splined ends.

Installation

1. Apply a light coat of molybdenum disulfide grease (NGLI No. 2) to the splines at each end of the universal joint.

2. Position the universal joint with the short end (**Figure 31**) going in first and toward the drive shaft.

3. Carefully push the universal joint in through the swing arm opening.

4. Align the splines and push the universal joint forward and engage it with the bevel gear drive unit. Push the universal joint in until it seats completely.

5. If removed, install the drive shaft onto the final drive unit. Using a soft-faced mallet, tap on the end of the drive shaft to make sure the drive shaft is completely seated into the final drive unit splines.

6. Apply a light coat of molybdenum disulfide grease (NGLI No. 2) to the splines of the drive shaft.

11

7. Install the final drive unit and drive shaft into the swing arm. Insert your fingers into the opening in the drive shaft to hold the rear end of the universal joint up to accept the drive shaft.

8. Slowly push the final drive unit forward and mesh the drive shaft with the universal joint. It may be necessary to rotate the final driven spline slightly back and forth to align the splines of the drive shaft and the universal joint.

9. Push the final drive unit all the way forward until it is seated correctly.

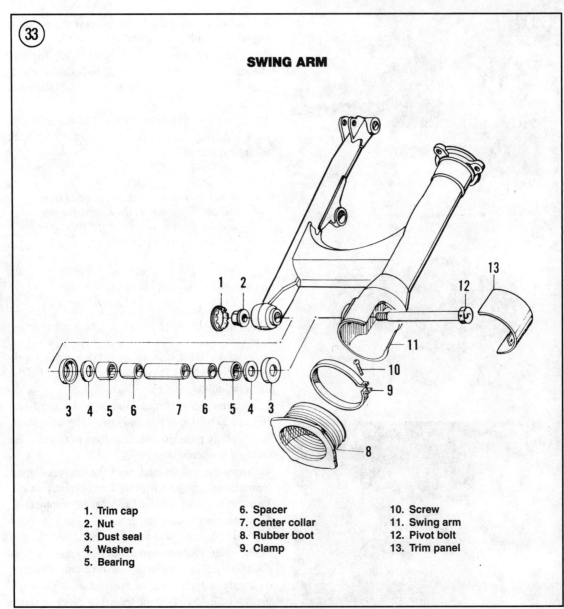

SWING ARM

1. Trim cap
2. Nut
3. Dust seal
4. Washer
5. Bearing
6. Spacer
7. Center collar
8. Rubber boot
9. Clamp
10. Screw
11. Swing arm
12. Pivot bolt
13. Trim panel

10. Install the final drive mounting nuts and washers (**Figure 20**) finger-tight at this time. Do not tighten the nuts until the rear wheel and rear axle are in place.

11. Hook the tab (A, **Figure 32**) on the trim panel on the backside opening of the swing arm (B, **Figure 32**) and install the trim panel (B, **Figure 22**) and screw. Tighten the screw securely.

12. Install the rubber boot onto the swing arm. Make sure it is correctly installed and tighten the clamping

bolt securely. This is necessary to keep out dirt and water.

13. Install the rear wheel as described in this chapter.

14. Tighten the final drive unit nuts (**Figure 20**) to the specification listed in **Table 1**.

15. Install the shock absorber and the upper and lower washers and nuts. Tighten to the torque specification listed in **Table 1**.

16. Refill the final drive unit with the correct amount and type of gear oil. Refer to Chapter Three.

SWING ARM

In time, the needle bearings will wear and will have to be replaced. The condition of the bearings can greatly affect handling performance and if worn parts are not replaced they can produce erratic and dangerous handling. Common symptoms are wheel hop, pulling to one side during acceleration and pulling to the other side during braking.

Refer to **Figure 33** for this procedure.

Removal

1. Remove the rear wheel as described in this chapter.

2. Remove the final drive unit, drive shaft and universal joint as described in this chapter.

3. Remove both shock absorbers as described in this chapter.

4. Protect both mufflers with shop cloths or towels.

5. Place a piece of plywood across both mufflers on top of the shop cloths.

6. Remove the trim cap from the right-hand side covering the pivot bolt nut.

7. Grasp the rear end of the swing arm and try to move it from side to side in a horizontal arc. There should be no noticeable side play. If play is evident and the pivot bolt nut is tightened correctly, the bearings should be replaced.

8. Secure the pivot bolt to keep it from rotating, then loosen and remove the pivot bolt nut (**Figure 34**).

9. Using a long aluminum or brass drift, carefully tap the pivot bolt out toward the left-hand side.

10. Withdraw the pivot bolt (**Figure 35**) from the swing arm and frame.

11. Pull back on the swing arm, free it from the frame, rest it on the plywood (**Figure 36**) and remove it from the frame.

11

12. If necessary, remove the rubber boot.

Inspection

1. Check the welded sections on the swing arm for cracks or fractures.

2. Inspect the final drive unit mounting bolt holes (**Figure 37**) in the swing arm. If the holes are elongated or worn, replace the swing arm.

3. Inspect the right-hand shock absorber mounting bracket and pivot hole on the swing arm. If the hole is elongated or worn, replace the swing arm.

4. Inspect the swing arm pivot points for wear or damage.

5. Inspect the rear axle mounting boss for wear or damage.

Installation

1. If removed, install the rubber boot.

2. Make sure the needle bearing dust cover (**Figure 38**) is in place on each side of the frame.

3. Position the swing arm into the mounting area of the frame. Align the holes in the swing arm with the holes in the frame. Make sure both dust covers are still in place. Reposition if necessary.

4. Apply a light coat of molybdenum disulfide grease to the pivot bolt.

5. Install the pivot bolt (**Figure 35**) from the left-hand side and push it all the way through the swing arm and frame.

6. Install the pivot bolt washer and nut (**Figure 34**). Secure the pivot bolt and tighten the nut to the torque specification listed in **Table 1**.

7. Move the swing arm up and down several times to make sure all components are properly seated.

8. Install the trim cap over the pivot bolt nut.

9. Install the final drive unit, drive shaft, universal joint and shock absorbers as described in this chapter.

10. Install the rubber boot onto the swing arm. Make sure it is correctly installed and tighten the clamping bolt securely. This is necessary to keep out dirt and water.

11. Install the rear wheel as described in this chapter.

Bearing Replacement

The swing arm needle bearings are installed in the frame and must be removed with a blind bearing removal tool. Discard the bearings after removing them.

1. Remove the swing arm as described in this chapter.

2. Remove the dust seal and washer from each side of the frame.

3. Remove the spacer from each bearing.

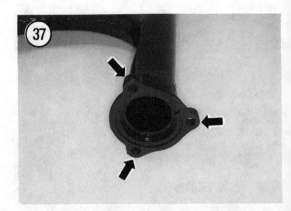

4. Remove the center collar (**Figure 39**).

5. Insert the bearing remover into the needle bearing (**Figure 40**) and attach it to the backside of the bearing. Attach the slide hammer and weight to the bearing remover.

6. Use the slide hammer to slowly withdraw the needle bearing from the frame receptacle. Discard the needle bearing.

7. Repeat Step 5 and Step 6 for the other bearing. Discard this needle bearing also.

8. Remove the center collar from the frame pivot area.

9. Thoroughly clean out the inside of the frame pivot area with solvent and dry with compressed air.

10. Apply a light coat of molybdenum disulfide grease to all parts before installation.

CAUTION
Never reinstall a needle bearing that has been removed. During removal it becomes slightly damaged and will create an unsafe riding condition.

NOTE
Either the right- or left-hand needle bearing can be installed first.

11. To avoid damage to the needle bearing or mounting bore in the frame, assemble an installation tool and install the bearing as follows:

   a. Cut a length of threaded rod so the rod ends protrude out of the frame about 2-3 inches.
   b. On one end of the threaded rod install 2 nuts and tighten them together then place 2 thick washers (larger diameter than the race seat in the frame) against the threaded rod.
   c. Insert the threaded rod through the pivot bolt area of the frame with the washers up against the frame (**Figure 41**).

NOTE
Position the new needle bearing with the markings facing outward.

   d. Place the bearing onto the threaded rod then install a socket that matches the outer diameter of the bearing.
   e. Next to the socket place 2 additional thick washers and another nut (**Figure 42**).
   f. Have an assistant hold onto the nuts on the other side of the rod to prevent the rod from turning in the next step.
   g. Correctly align the needle bearing with the frame mounting bore and slowly tighten the nut (**Figure 43**) to press the needle bearing into the frame. Press the bearing in until it is flush with the outer surface of the frame mounting bore.
   h. Remove the threaded rod tool.

12. Repeat Step 11 for the other bearing.

13. Make sure both bearings are properly seated.

14. Install the center collar.

11

15. Apply molybdenum disulfide grease to the new needle bearings

16. Apply molybdenum disulfide grease to the spacers and install the spacer into the bearing. Push the spacers all the way in until they are seated.

17. Apply molybdenum disulfide grease to the dust seals and washers. Install a washer into each dust seal.

18. Install the washer and dust seal onto each side of the frame.

19. Install the swing arm as described in this chapter.

SHOCK ABSORBERS

Removal/Installation

Removal and installation of the rear shocks is easier if done separately. The remaining unit will support the rear of the bike and maintain the correct relationship between the top and bottom shock mounts.

NOTE
As a precautionary measure, remove the rider's seat to avoid damage to the seat should a tool slip while removing the shock absorber upper nut.

1. Place a suitable size jack, or wooden blocks, under the frame to support the bike securely with the rear wheel off the ground.
2. Adjust both shocks to their softest setting, completely counterclockwise.
3. Remove the trim cap from the upper mount.
4. On the right-hand side, remove the upper nut and washer (A, **Figure 44**) and the lower bolt, nut and

washers (B, **Figure 44**) securing the shock absorber to the frame and to the swing arm.

5. On the left-hand side, remove the upper (A, **Figure 45**) and lower nuts and washers (B, **Figure 45**) securing the shock absorber to the frame and to the final drive unit.
6. Pull the unit straight off the upper mount and remove it.

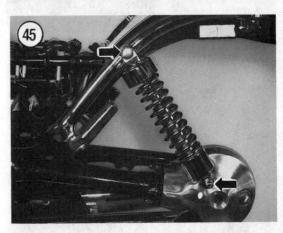

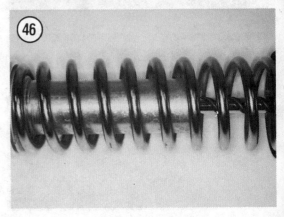

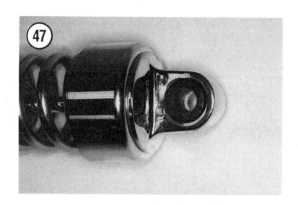

7. Install by reversing these removal steps. Tighten the upper and lower mounting nut or bolt to the torque specification listed in **Table 1**.

Preliminary Inspection

1. Check the damper unit (A, **Figure 46**) for leakage and make sure the damper rod (B, **Figure 46**) is straight.

NOTE
The damper unit cannot be rebuilt; it must be replaced as a unit.

2. Inspect the rubber bushings in the upper (**Figure 47**) and lower (**Figure 48**) joints for wear or deterioration. If damaged, replace the shock absorber as they cannot be replaced.

3. Inspect the spring for wear, damage or sagging. If damaged, replace the shock absorber as the spring cannot be replaced.

Table 1 REAR SUSPENSION TIGHTENING TORQUES

Item	N·m	ft.-lb.
Rear axle nut	60-95	44-70
Rear torque link bolt and nut	40-60	29-44
Brake disc mounting bolt	15-25	11-18
Rear caliper mounting bolt	25-40	18-29
Shock absorber mounting bolt	20-30	15-22
Swing arm pivot shaft nut	50-80	37-59
Final drive unit-to- swing arm nuts	35-45	26-33
Final gear case cover bolts		
8 mm	20-26	15-19
10 mm	40-60	29-44

Table 2 REAR SUSPENSION SPECIFICATIONS

Item	Specification
Rear wheel travel	105 mm (4.1 in.)
Maximum rear wheel rim runout	
Axial	0.5 mm (0.02 in.)
Radial	0.8 mm (0.03 in.)
Maxixmum rear axle wobble limit	0.25 mm (0.010 in.)
Maximum swing arm pivot shaft runout	0.30 (0.012 in.)

CHAPTER TWELVE

BRAKE SYSTEM

The brake system on all models consists of a single disc on the front wheel and a single disc on the rear. This chapter describes repair and replacement procedures for all brake components.

Table 1 contains the brake system torque specifications and **Table 2** contains brake system specifications. **Table 1** and **Table 2** are located at the end of this chapter.

DISC BRAKES

The disc brakes are actuated by hydraulic fluid and are controlled by a hand lever for the front brake or the brake pedal for the rear brake that are attached to the front or rear master cylinder. As the brake pads wear, the brake fluid level drops in the reservoir and automatically adjusts for wear.

When working on hydraulic brake systems, the work area and all tools must be absolutely clean. Any tiny particles of foreign matter and grit in the caliper assembly or the master cylinder can damage the components. Also, sharp tools must not be used inside the master cylinders or calipers or on the piston. If there is any doubt about your ability to correctly and safely carry out major service on the brake components, take the job to a Suzuki dealership or brake specialist.

> *NOTE*
> *If you recycle your old engine oil, **never** add used brake fluid to the old oil. Most oil retailers that accept old oil for recycling may not accept the oil if other fluids (fork oil, brake fluid, or any other type of fluids) have been combined with it.*

Consider the following when servicing the front and rear brake systems.

1. Disc brake components rarely require disassembly, so do not disassemble them unless necessary.

2. When adding brake fluid use only a brake fluid clearly marked DOT3 or DOT 4 from a sealed container. Other types may cause brake failure. Always use the same brand name; do not intermix fluids as many brands are not compatible. Brake fluid will draw moisture which greatly reduces its ability to perform correctly. It is a good idea to purchase brake fluid in small containers and discard any small leftover quantities properly. Do not store a container of brake fluid with less than 1/4 of the fluid remaining as this small amount will draw moisture very rapidly.

CAUTION
Do not intermix silicone based (DOT 5) brake fluid as it can cause brake component damage leading to brake system failure.

CAUTION
Never reuse brake fluid (like fluid expelled during brake bleeding). Contaminated brake fluid can cause brake failure. Dispose of used brake fluid according to local, or EPA toxic waste regulations.

3. Do not allow disc brake fluid to contact any plated, plastic parts or painted surfaces as surface damage will occur.

4. Always keep the master cylinder's reservoir cover installed to prevent dust or moisture from entering.

5. Use only DOT 3 or DOT 4 brake fluid or isopropyl alcohol to wash parts. Never use petroleum-based solvents of any kind on the brake system's internal components. Petroleum-based solvents will cause the seals to swell and require replacement.

6. Whenever *any* component has been removed from the brake system the system is considered opened and must be bled to remove air bubbles. Also if the brake feels spongy, this usually means there are air bubbles in the system and it must be bled. For safe operation, refer to *Bleeding the System* in this chapter.

WARNING
*Whenever working on the brake system, do **not** inhale brake dust. If may contain asbestos, which can cause lung injury and cancer. Wear a face mask that meets OHSA requirements for trapping asbestos particles, and wash your hands and forearms thoroughly after completing the work.*

WARNING
Never *use compressed air to clean any parts of the brake system as this will release the harmful brake pad dust. Use an aerosol brake cleaner to clean parts when servicing any component still installed on the bike.*

FRONT BRAKE PAD REPLACEMENT

There is no recommended mileage interval for changing the friction pads in the disc brakes. Pad wear depends greatly on riding habits and conditions. The pads should be checked for wear every 6 months and replaced when the wear indicator reaches the edge of the brake disc. To maintain an even brake pressure on the disc, always replace both pads in the caliper at the same time.

Disconnecting the hydraulic brake hose from the brake caliper is not necessary for brake pad replacement. Disconnect the hose only if the caliper assembly is going to be removed.

CAUTION
Check the pads more frequently when the wear line approaches the disc. On some pads the wear line is very close to the metal backing plate. If pad wear happens to be uneven for some reason the backing plate may come in contact with the disc and cause damage.

Front Brake Pad Replacement

Refer to **Figure 1** for this procedure.

1. Remove the dust cover (**Figure 2**) from the brake caliper.

2. Remove the clips securing both pad pins.

3. Withdraw both pad pins and remove the pad springs.

4. Withdraw both brake pads and shims from the caliper assembly. Keep them in the order of removal so they can be reinstalled in the same location if they do not require replacement.

5. Check the brake pad friction surface for oil contamination or fraying. Check the pad plates for cracks or other damage. If the brake pads appear okay, measure the pad thickness with a scale or Vernier caliper. Replace the pads as a set if the pad thickness is less than the service limit listed in **Table 2**.

6. Clean the pad recess and the end of the pistons with a soft brush. Do not use solvent, a wire brush or any hard tool which would damage the cylinders or pistons.

7. Carefully remove any rust or corrosion from the disc.

12

8. Lightly coat the end of the pistons, the backs of the new pads (not the friction material), and the shims with disc brake lubricant.

NOTE
When purchasing new pads, check with your dealer to make sure the friction

compound of the new pad is compatible with the disc material. Remove any roughness from the backs of the new pads with a fine-cut file.

9. When new pads are installed in the caliper, the master cylinder brake fluid level will rise as the

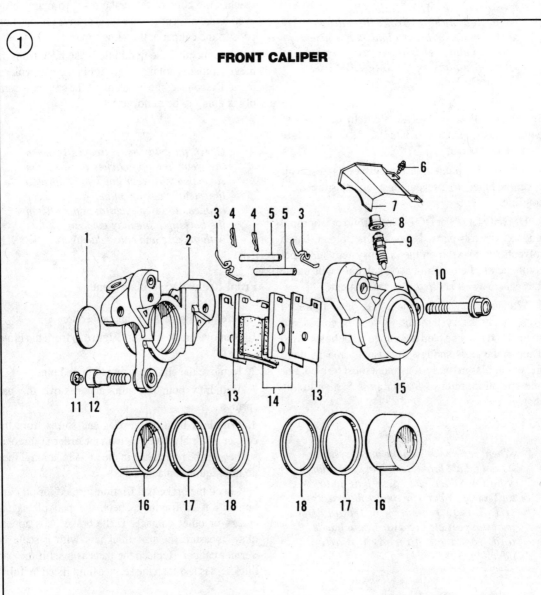

FRONT CALIPER

1. Trim cap	7. Dust cover	13. Shim
2. Caliper outer body	8. Cap	14. Brake pads
3. Spring	9. Bleed screw	15. Caliper inner body
4. Clip	10. Housing bolt	16. Piston
5. Pad pin	11. Trim cap	17. Dust seal
6. Screw	12. Mounting bolt	18. Piston seal

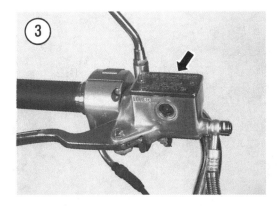

caliper pistons are repositioned. Perform the following:

   a. Clean the top of the master cylinder of all dirt and foreign matter.

   b. Remove the screws securing the cover (**Figure 3**). Remove the cover and the diaphragm from the master cylinder.

   c. Slowly push the caliper pistons into the caliper. Constantly check the reservoir to make sure brake fluid does not overflow. Remove brake fluid, if necessary, before it overflows.

   d. The pistons should move freely. If they don't and there is evidence of them sticking in the cylinder, the caliper should be removed and serviced as described later in this chapter.

10. Push the caliper pistons in all the way to allow room for the new pads.

11. Partially install both pad pins (**Figure 4**) into the caliper.

12. Position a shim against the back of each brake pad and install the spring (**Figure 5**) to hold the 2 parts together.

13. Install the outboard pad into the caliper (**Figure 6**). Push it all the way down until it stops then push both pad pins through the outboard shim and pad (**Figure 7**). Make sure the spring ends are below both pad pins. This is necessary for proper brake operation

14. Install the inboard pad (**Figure 8**) into the caliper. Push it all the way down until it stops (A, **Figure 9**).

15. Push both pad pins part way through the inboard pad and shim (B, **Figure 9**). Make sure the spring ends are below both pad pins. This is necessary for proper brake operation.

16. Rotate both pad pins until the clip holes are facing up, then push both pad pins in until they stop.

12

17. Use needlenose pliers and install the clip (**Figure 10**) into the hole in the lower pad pin. Push the clip in until it seats completely on the pad pin.

18. Install the remaining clip (**Figure 11**) into the hole in the upper pad pin. Push the clip in until it seats completely on the pad pin.

19. Install the dust cap. Make sure it snaps into place; otherwise it will fly off when you hit the first bump in the road.

20. Roll the bike back and forth and activate the front brake lever as many times as it takes to refill the cylinders in the caliper and correctly locate the brake pads.

> *WARNING*
> *Use brake fluid clearly marked DOT 3 or DOT 4 from a sealed container. Other types may cause brake failure. Always use the same brand name; do not intermix as many brands are not compatible. Do not intermix silicone based (DOT 5) brake fluid as it can cause brake component damage leading to brake system failure.*

21. Refill the master cylinder reservoir, if necessary, to maintain the correct fluid level as seen through the viewing port (**Figure 12**) on the side. Install the diaphragm and cover. Tighten the screws securely.

> *WARNING*
> *Do not ride the motorcycle until you are sure the brakes are operating correctly with full hydraulic advantage. If necessary, bleed the brake as described under **Bleeding the System** in this chapter.*

22. Bed the pads in gradually for the first 10 days of riding by using only light pressure as much as possible. Immediate hard application will glaze the new friction pads and greatly reduce the effectiveness of the brake.

FRONT BRAKE CALIPER

Removal/Installation

Refer to **Figure 1** for this procedure.

It is not necessary to remove the front wheel to remove the caliper assembly.

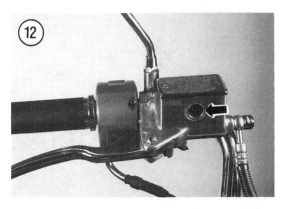

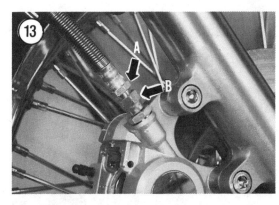

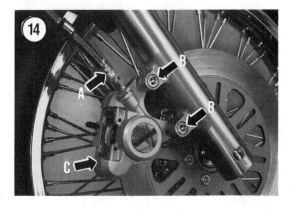

CAUTION
Do not spill any brake fluid on the front fork or front wheel. Wash off any spilled brake fluid immediately, as it will destroy the finish. Use soapy water and rinse completely.

1. Clean the top of the master cylinder of all dirt and foreign matter.

2. If the caliper assembly is going to be disassembled for service, carefully insert a socket extension through the spokes and loosen the caliper housing bolts securing the caliper bodies together.

3. Loosen the screws securing the master cylinder cover (**Figure 3**). Slightly loosen the cover and the diaphragm. This will allow air to enter the reservoir and allow the brake fluid to drain out more quickly in the next step.

4. Hold the brake hose fitting (A, **Figure 13**) with an open-end wrench. Loosen the brake hose adapter nut (B, **Figure 13**) securing the brake hose to the caliper assembly.

5. Remove the brake hose (A, **Figure 14**) and sealing washer from the brake hose adapter nut and let the brake fluid drain out into the container. Dispose of this brake fluid-never reuse brake fluid.

6. Loosen, then remove the bolts (B, **Figure 14**) securing the brake caliper assembly to the front fork.

7. Remove the caliper assembly (C, **Figure 14**) from the brake disc.

8. Place the loose end of the brake hose in a reclosable plastic bag to prevent brake fluid from draining out.

9. If necessary, disassemble, inspect and assemble the front caliper as described under *Brake Caliper (All Models)* later in this chapter.

10. Install by reversing these removal steps while noting the following:

    a. Carefully install the caliper assembly onto the disc being careful not to damage the leading edge of the brake pads.

    b. Install the bolts (B, **Figure 14**) securing the brake caliper assembly to the front fork and tighten to the torque specifications listed in **Table 1**.

    c. Install the brake hose (A, **Figure 14**) and new sealing washer onto the caliper.

    d. Screw the brake hose into the brake hose adapter nut on the caliper.

    e. Hold onto the brake hose fitting (A, **Figure 13**) with an open-end wrench. Tighten the

12

brake hose adapter nut (B, **Figure 13**) securing the brake hose to the caliper assembly. Tighten the brake hose adapter nut securely.

f. Bleed the brake as described under *Bleeding the System* in this chapter.

FRONT MASTER CYLINDER

Removal/Installation

> *CAUTION*
> *Cover the surrounding areas with a heavy cloth or plastic tarp to protect them from accidental brake fluid spills. Wash brake fluid off any painted or plated surfaces or plastic parts immediately, as it will destroy the finish. Use soapy water and rinse completely.*

1. Clean the top of the master cylinder of all dirt and foreign matter.

2. Remove the screws securing the cover (**Figure 3**). Remove the cover and the diaphragm.

3. If you have a shop syringe, draw all of the brake fluid out of the master cylinder reservoir.

4. Disconnect the brake light switch electrical connector (**Figure 15**) from the brake switch.

5. Place a shop cloth under the banjo bolt to catch any spilled brake fluid that will leak out.

6. Unscrew the banjo bolt (A, **Figure 16**) securing the brake hose to the master cylinder. Don't lose the sealing washer on each side of the hose fitting. Tie the loose end of the hose up to the handlebar and cover the end to prevent the entry of moisture and foreign matter.

7. Unscrew the rear view mirror (B, **Figure 16**) from the master cylinder.

8. Remove the clamping bolts and clamp (C, **Figure 16**) securing the master cylinder to the handlebar.

9. Remove the master cylinder (D, **Figure 16**) from the handlebar.

10. Install by reversing these removal steps, noting the following:

a. Install the master cylinder, clamp and bolts. Tighten the upper bolt (A, **Figure 17**) first, then the lower (B, **Figure 17**) so there will be a slight gap (C, **Figure 17**) at the bottom. Tighten the bolts to the torque specification listed in **Table 1**.

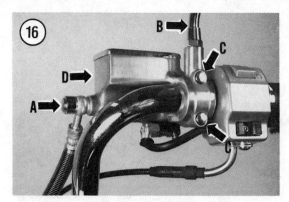

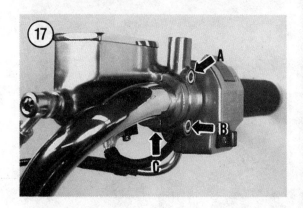

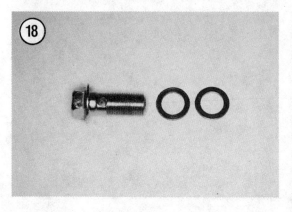

b. Place a new sealing washer on each side of the brake hose fitting (**Figure 18**) and install the banjo bolt.

c. Tighten the banjo bolt to the torque specification listed in **Table 1**.

d. Bleed the front brakes as described under *Bleeding the System* in this chapter.

Disassembly

Refer to **Figure 19** for this procedure.

1. Remove the master cylinder as described in this chapter.

2. Remove the bolt and nut (A, **Figure 20**) securing the hand lever and remove the hand lever (B, **Figure 20**).

3. Remove the rubber dust boot (**Figure 21**) from the area where the hand lever actuates the piston assembly.

4. Using circlip pliers, remove the circlip (**Figure 22**) from the body.

5. Remove the piston assembly (**Figure 23**) and the spring.

6. If necessary, remove the screw (A, **Figure 24**) securing the brake light switch to the master cylinder and remove the switch assembly (B, **Figure 24**).

Inspection

1. Clean all parts in fresh brake fluid.

2. Inspect the body cylinder bore (**Figure 25**) surface for signs of wear and damage. If less than perfect, replace the master cylinder assembly. The body cannot be replaced separately.

3. Measure the cylinder bore with a bore gauge. Replace the master cylinder if its inside diameter exceeds the service limit listed in **Table 2**.

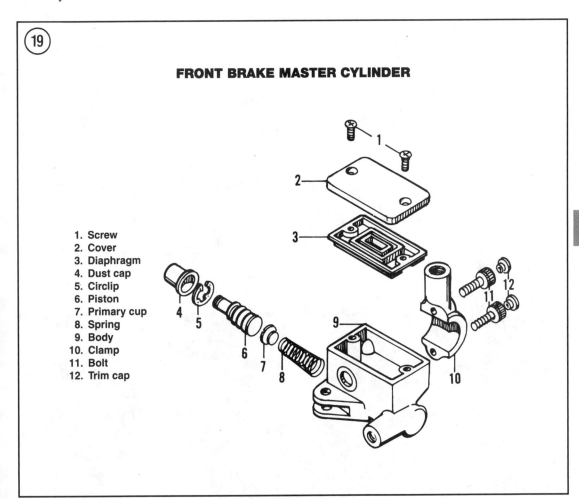

FRONT BRAKE MASTER CYLINDER

1. Screw
2. Cover
3. Diaphragm
4. Dust cap
5. Circlip
6. Piston
7. Primary cup
8. Spring
9. Body
10. Clamp
11. Bolt
12. Trim cap

12

4. Make sure the passage (**Figure 26**) in the bottom of the master cylinder body is clear. Clean out if necessary.

5. Inspect the piston contact surfaces (A, **Figure 27**) for signs of wear and damage. If less than perfect, replace the piston assembly.

6. Check the end of the piston (**Figure 28**) for wear caused by the hand lever. If worn, replace the piston assembly.

7. Measure the diameter of the piston with a micrometer (**Figure 29**). Replace the piston assembly if its diameter is less than the service limit listed in **Table 2**.

8. Replace the piston assembly if either the primary (B, **Figure 27**) or secondary cups (C, **Figure 27**) require replacement. The cups cannot be replaced separately.

9. Check the hand lever pivot lugs (**Figure 30**) on the master cylinder body for cracks or elongation. If damaged, replace the master cylinder assembly.

10. Inspect the pivot hole in the hand lever. If worn or elongated the lever must be replaced.

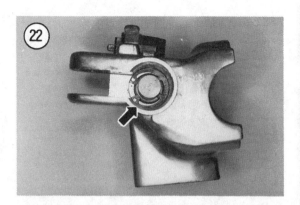

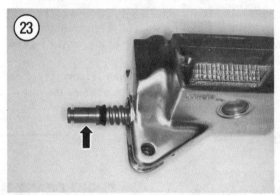

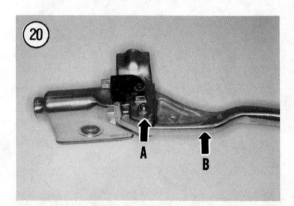

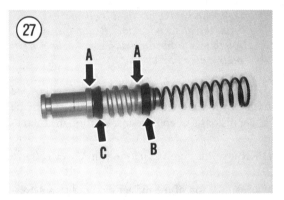

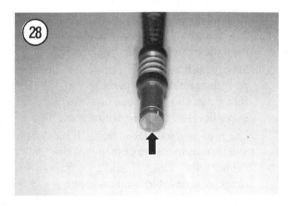

11. Inspect the threads in the bore (**Figure 31**) for the banjo bolt. If damaged, replace the master cylinder assembly.

Assembly

1. Soak the new cups in fresh brake fluid for at least 15 minutes to make them pliable. Coat the inside of the cylinder bore with fresh hydraulic fluid prior to the assembly of parts.

CAUTION
When installing the piston assembly, do not allow the cups to turn inside out as they will be damaged and allow brake fluid to leak within the cylinder bore.

2. Position the spring with its tapered end going in last, facing toward the primary cup on the piston (**Figure 32**).
3. Install the spring, primary cup and piston assembly into the cylinder (**Figure 23**). Push them in until they bottom in the cylinder bore.
4. Install the circlip (**Figure 22**) and slide in the rubber boot (**Figure 21**).

12

5. Install the hand lever, the bolt and nut and tighten securely.

6. If removed, install the brake light switch and screws to the master cylinder. Tighten the screw securely.

7. Install the master cylinder as described in this chapter.

REAR BRAKE PAD REPLACEMENT

There is no recommended mileage interval for changing the friction pads in the disc brakes. Pad wear depends greatly on riding habits and conditions. The pads should be checked for wear every 6 months and replaced when the wear indicator reaches the edge of the brake disc. To maintain an even brake pressure on the disc, always replace both pads in the caliper at the same time.

Disconnecting the hydraulic brake hose from the brake caliper is not necessary for brake pad replacement. Disconnect the hose only if the caliper assembly is going to be removed.

> *CAUTION*
> *Check the pads more frequently when the wear line approaches the disc. On some pads the wear line is very close to the metal backing plate. If pad wear happens to be uneven for some reason the backing plate may come in contact with the disc and cause damage.*

Rear Brake Pad Replacement

Refer to **Figure 33** for this procedure.

1. Remove the dust cover (**Figure 34**) from the brake caliper.

2. Remove the clips (**Figure 35**) securing both pad pins, then withdraw both pad pins (**Figure 36**).

3. Withdraw both brake pads, shims and pad spring assemblies from the caliper assembly. Keep them in the order of removal so they can be reinstalled in the same location if they do not require replacement.

4. Check the brake pad friction surface for oil contamination or fraying. Check the pad plates for cracks or other damage. If the brake pads appear okay, measure the friction thickness with a scale or Vernier caliper. Replace the pads as a set if the friction thickness is less than the service limit listed in **Table 2**.

5. Clean the pad recess and the end of the pistons with a soft brush. Do not use solvent, a wire brush or any hard tool which would damage the cylinders or pistons.

6. Carefully remove any rust or corrosion from the disc.

7. Lightly coat the end of the pistons, the backs of the new pads (not the friction material), and the shims with disc brake lubricant.

> *NOTE*
> *When purchasing new pads, check with your dealer to make sure the friction compound of the new pad is compatible with the disc material. Remove any roughness from the backs of the new pads with a fine-cut file.*

8. When new pads are installed in the caliper, the master cylinder brake fluid level will rise as the caliper pistons are repositioned. Perform the following:

a. Remove the screws and the trim cover (**Figure 37**).

b. Clean the top of the master cylinder remote reservoir of all dirt and foreign matter.

c. Remove the screws securing the cover (**Figure 38**). Remove the cover and the diaphragm from the master cylinder remote reservoir.

d. Slowly push the caliper pistons into the caliper. Constantly check the reservoir to make sure brake fluid does not overflow. Remove brake fluid, if necessary, before it overflows.

e. The pistons should move freely. If they don't and there is evidence of them sticking in the cylinder, the caliper should be removed and serviced as described in this chapter.

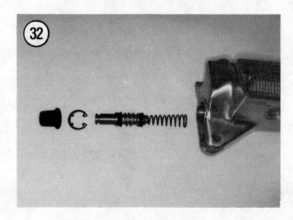

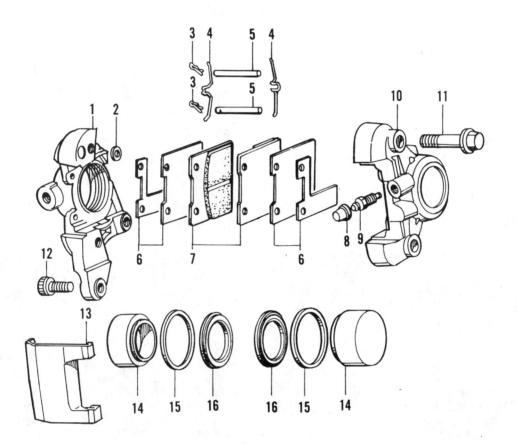

REAR CALIPER

1. Caliper outer body
2. O-ring
3. Clip
4. Spring
5. Pad pin
6. Shims
7. Brake pads
8. Cap
9. Bleed screw
10. Caliper inner body
11. Housing bolt
12. Mounting bolt
13. Dust cap
14. Piston
15. Dust seal
16. Piston seal

12

9. Push the caliper pistons in all the way to allow room for the new pads.

NOTE
Be sure to assemble the brake pad and
*shims as shown in **Figure 39**.*

10. Position the shims against the back of each brake pad and install the spring to hold the 3 parts together (**Figure 40**).

11. Partially install both pad pins (A, **Figure 41**) into the caliper.

12. Install the outboard pad into the caliper (B, **Figure 41**). Push it all the way down until it stops.

13. Push the ends of the outboard pad spring down, then push both pad pins through the shims and outboard brake pad (**Figure 42**). Make sure the spring ends are below both pad pins. This is necessary for proper brake operation.

14. Install the inboard pad (**Figure 43**) into the caliper. Push it all the way down until it stops.

15. Push the ends of the inboard pad spring down, then push both pad pins through the shims and inboard brake pad. Make sure the spring ends are

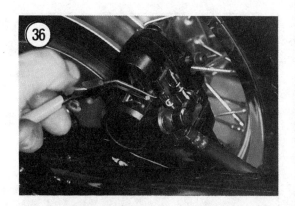

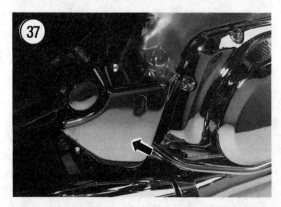

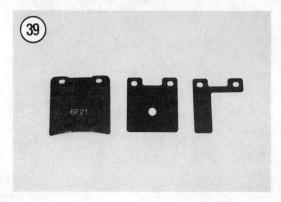

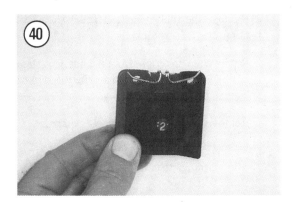

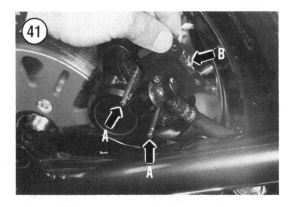

below both pad pins (**Figure 44**). This is necessary for proper brake operation.

16. Rotate both pad pins until the clip holes are facing up, then push both pad pins in until they stop.

17. Use needlenose pliers and install the clip (**Figure 45**) into the hole in the upper pad pin. Push the clip in until it seats completely on the pad pin.

18. Install the remaining clip into the hole in the lower pad pin. Push the clip in until it seats completely on the pad pin.

19. Install the dust cap. Make sure it snaps into place otherwise it will fly off when you hit the first bump in the road.

20. Roll the bike back and forth and activate the front brake lever as many times as it takes to refill the cylinders in the caliper and correctly locate the brake pads.

> *WARNING*
> *Use brake fluid clearly marked DOT 3 or DOT 4 from a sealed container. Other types may cause brake failure. Always use the same brand name; do not intermix as many brands are not compatible. Do not intermix silicone*

12

based (DOT 5) brake fluid as it can cause brake component damage leading to brake system failure.

21. Refill the master cylinder remote reservoir, if necessary, to maintain the correct fluid level as seen through the side of the reservoir (**Figure 46**). Install the diaphragm and cover. Tighten the screws securely.

22. Install the trim cover and tighten the screws securely.

> ### WARNING
> *Do not ride the motorcycle until you are sure the brakes are operating correctly with full hydraulic advantage. If necessary, bleed the brake as described under **Bleeding the System** in this chapter.*

23. Bed the pads in gradually for the first 10 days of riding by using only light pressure as much as possible. Immediate hard application will glaze the new friction pads and greatly reduce the effectiveness of the brake.

REAR BRAKE CALIPER

Removal/Installation

Refer to **Figure 33** for this procedure.

It is not necessary to remove the rear wheel in order to remove the caliper assembly.

> ### CAUTION
> *Do not spill any brake fluid on the swing arm or rear wheel. Wash off any spilled brake fluid immediately, as it will destroy the finish. Use soapy water and rinse completely.*

1. Remove the brake pads as described in this chapter.

2. Remove the screws and the trim cover (**Figure 37**).

3. Clean the top of the master cylinder remote reservoir of all dirt and foreign matter.

4. Remove the screws securing the cover (**Figure 38**). Slightly loosen the cover and the diaphragm. This will allow air to enter the reservoir and allow the brake fluid to drain out more quickly.

5. To disconnect the brake caliper torque link from the swing arm, perform the following:

a. Remove the rubber cap from the Allen bolt nut.

b. Remove the cotter pin from the nut and Allen bolt. Discard the cotter pin as a new one must be installed during assembly.

c. Remove the trim cap from the Allen bolt.

d. Secure the Allen bolt (**Figure 47**) to keep it from turning, then loosen the nut from the Allen bolt.

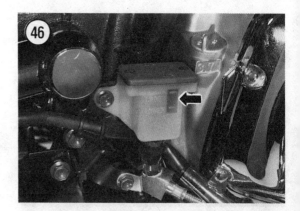

e. Remove the nut and washer and withdraw the Allen bolt from the torque link and swing arm bracket.

f. Reinstall the washer and nut onto the Allen bolt to avoid misplacing them. Place the bolt assembly rubber cap and trim cap in a recloseable plastic bag.

6. Remove the trim cap from the banjo bolt.

7. Loosen, then remove the banjo bolt and sealing washers (A, **Figure 48**) securing the brake hose to the caliper assembly.

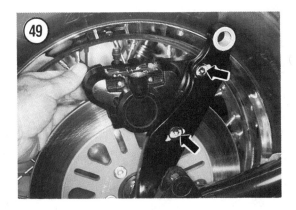

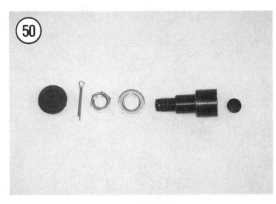

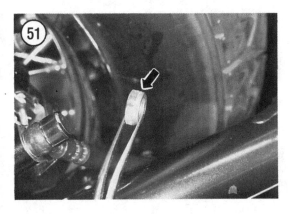

8. Remove the brake hose (B, **Figure 48**) and sealing washers from the brake hose and let the brake fluid drain out into the container. Dispose of this brake fluid—never reuse brake fluid.

9. Place the loose end of the brake hose in a reclosable plastic bag to prevent brake fluid from draining out.

10. Pivot the torque link up to access the caliper mounting bolts.

11. Loosen, then remove the bolts (**Figure 49**) securing the brake caliper assembly to the torque link.

12. Remove the caliper assembly from the brake disc and torque link.

13. If the caliper is not going to be serviced, place it in a reclosable plastic bag to keep it clean.

14. If necessary, disassemble, inspect and assemble the rear caliper as described under *Brake Caliper (All Models)* later in this chapter.

15. Install by reversing these removal steps while noting the following:

a. Carefully install the caliper assembly onto the disc being careful not to damage the leading edge of the brake pads.

b. Install the Allen bolt and nut assembly in the order shown in **Figure 50**.

c. Align the bolt holes of the torque link and the swing arm.

d. Install the bolt through the swing arm and torque link and install the washer.

e. Position the nut with the shoulder side (**Figure 51**) going on first. This shoulder locates the inner end of the bolt within the swing arm mounting bracket.

f. Tighten the Allen bolt and nut to the specification listed in **Table 1**.

g. Install a new cotter pin and bend the ends over completely.

h. Install the rubber cap over the nut and cotter pin.

i. Bleed the brake as described under *Bleeding the System* in this chapter.

12

BRAKE CALIPER DISASSEMBLY/INSPECTION/ASSEMBLY (ALL MODELS)

This procedure represents a typical caliper disassembly, inspection and assembly. Where major differences occur among the various caliper assemblies they are identified.

1. Remove the caliper and brake pads as described in this chapter.

2. Remove the caliper housing bolts (**Figure 52**) securing the caliper inner body to the caliper outer body.

3. Separate the 2 caliper bodies.

4. Remove the O-ring seal (**Figure 53**) from the caliper outer body. Discard this O-ring seal as it must be replaced every time the caliper is disassembled.

5. On the front caliper assembly, unscrew and remove the brake hose adapter nut (**Figure 54**) and washer from the caliper outer body.

6. Place a piece of flat rubber stock (A, **Figure 55**) over the fluid passageway (B, **Figure 55**) to block off the air flow in the next step.

7. Place a shop cloth (A, **Figure 56**) or piece of soft wood over the end of the piston.

8. Perform this step over a workbench top. Hold the caliper body with the piston facing down and away from you.

> ### WARNING
> *Removing the piston with compressed air forces the piston out of its bore like a bullet. In the next step, keep your hands and fingers out of the way. Wear shop gloves and safety goggles when using compressed air to remove the piston.*

9. Apply compressed air pressure through the fitting (B, **Figure 56**) and remove the piston.

10. Repeat Steps 6-9 and remove the piston from the other caliper body half.

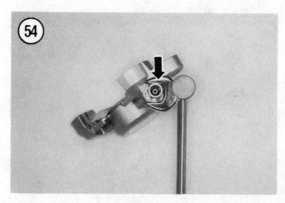

> ### CAUTION
> *In the following step, do not use a sharp tool to remove the dust and piston seals from the caliper cylinders. Do not damage the cylinder surface.*

11. Use a piece of plastic or wood and carefully push the dust seal and the piston seal in toward the caliper cylinder and out of their grooves. Remove the dust (A, **Figure 57**) and piston seal (B, **Figure 57**) from the cylinder.

12. Repeat Step 11 for the other caliper half and discard all seals.

13. Unscrew and remove the bleed bolt.

14. Inspect the caliper as described in this chapter.

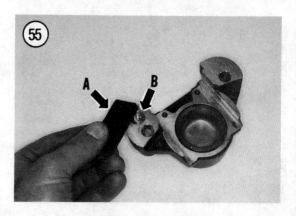

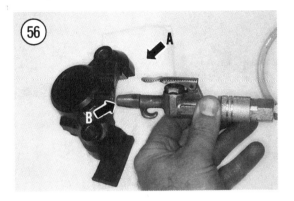

15. On the front brake caliper, install the brake hose adapter nut and washer (**Figure 58**) into the caliper outer body and tighten securely.

NOTE
Never reuse the old dust seals or piston seals. Very minor damage or age deterioration can make the seals useless.

16. Soak the new dust seals and piston seals in fresh DOT 3 or DOT 4 brake fluid.

17. Carefully install the new piston seal and new dust seal in the grooves in each caliper cylinder. Make sure the seals are properly seated in their respective grooves (**Figure 59**).

18. Coat the pistons and caliper cylinders with fresh DOT 3 or DOT 4 brake fluid.

19. Position the pistons with the open sends facing out toward the brake pads and install the pistons into the caliper cylinders. Push the pistons in until they bottom out.

20. Make sure the mating surfaces of the caliper bodies (A, **Figure 60**) are clean to ensure a good seal between the two parts. Clean the housing bolt threads (B, **Figure 60**).

21. Install a new O-ring seal (C, **Figure 60**) onto the caliper outer body.

22. Assemble the 2 caliper bodies and install the caliper housing bolts (**Figure 52**). Tighten the bolts to the torque specification listed in **Table 1**.

23. Install the caliper and brake pads as described in this chapter.

12

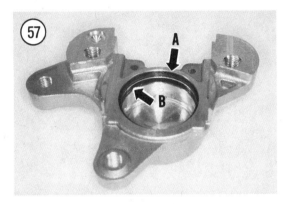

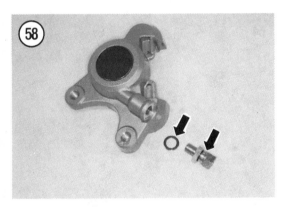

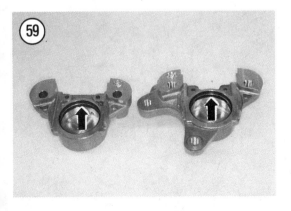

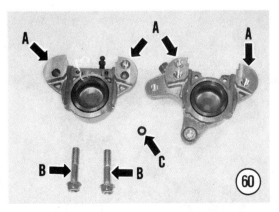

Caliper Inspection

1. Clean all parts in fresh DOT 3 or DOT 4 brake fluid or isopropyl alcohol and dry with compressed air.

2. Inspect the piston and dust seal groove in each caliper body (**Figure 61**) for damage. If damaged or corroded, replace the caliper assembly.

3. Inspect each caliper body (A, **Figure 62**) for cracks or damage. Replace the caliper assembly if either is damaged.

4. Inspect the hydraulic fluid passageway (A, **Figure 63**) at the end of the caliper body and in the passageway in the base of the piston bore. Apply compressed air to the openings and make sure they are clear. Clean out if necessary with fresh brake fluid.

5. Inspect the cylinder walls (B, **Figure 63**) and the pistons (B, **Figure 62**) for scratches, scoring or other damage.

6. Measure the cylinder bore with a bore gauge or vernier caliper (**Figure 64**). Replace the brake caliper if the bore diameter(s) exceeds the service limit dimension listed in **Table 2**.

7. Measure the outside diameter of the pistons with a micrometer or vernier caliper (**Figure 65**). Replace the brake piston(s) if the diameter(s) is less than the service limit listed in **Table 2**.

8. Inspect the caliper mounting bolt hole threads on the outer body (**Figure 66**) for wear or damage. Clean up with a suitable size metric tap or replace the caliper assembly.

9. Inspect the caliper housing bolt holes on the outer body (**Figure 67**). If worn or damaged, replace the caliper assembly.

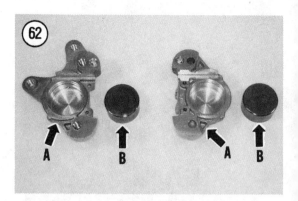

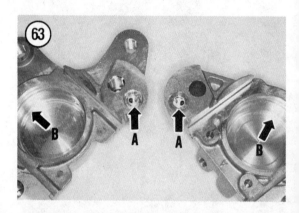

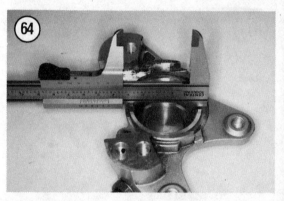

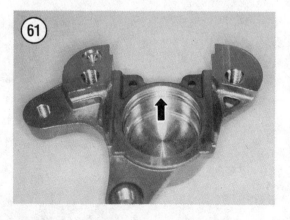

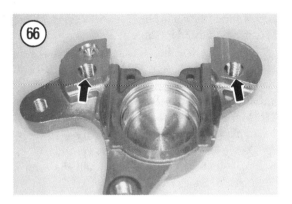

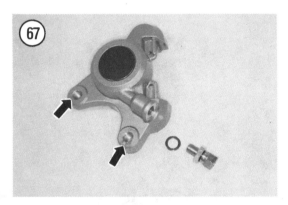

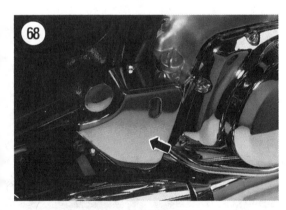

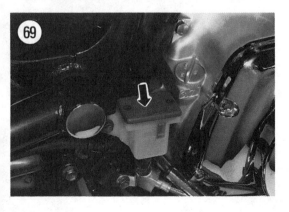

10. If still in place, remove the bleed screw. Apply compressed air to the opening and make sure it is clear. Clean out if necessary with fresh brake fluid.

11. On the front brake caliper, if still in place, remove the brake hose adapter nut (**Figure 58**) from the caliper body. Apply compressed air to the opening and make sure it is clear. Clean out if necessary with fresh brake fluid. Also, make sure the opening in the caliper is clean and open.

REAR MASTER CYLINDER

Removal/Installation

CAUTION
Cover the surrounding areas with a heavy cloth or plastic tarp to protect them from accidental brake fluid spills. Wash brake fluid off any painted or plated surfaces or plastic parts immediately, as it will destroy the finish. Use soapy water and rinse completely.

1. Remove the mounting bolts and remove the remote reservoir cover (**Figure 68**).

2. Clean the top of the master cylinder of all dirt and foreign matter.

3. Remove the screws securing the cover (**Figure 69**). Remove the cover and the diaphragm.

4. If you have a shop syringe, draw all of the brake fluid out of the master cylinder reservoir.

5. Remove the front footpeg assembly as described in Chapter Thirteen and lower it to the ground.

6. Remove the screws securing the brake light switch (A, **Figure 70**) to the master cylinder.

7. Carefully move the switch away and remove the spring and washer (**Figure 71**).

12

8. Place a shop cloth under the banjo bolt to catch any spilled brake fluid that will leak out.

9. Unscrew the banjo bolt (B, **Figure 70**) securing the rear caliper brake hose to the master cylinder. Do not lose the sealing washer on each side of the hose fitting. Tie the loose end of the hose up to the frame and cover the hose end to prevent the entry of moisture and foreign matter.

10. Unscrew the banjo bolt (**Figure 72**) securing the remote reservoir hose to the master cylinder. Do not lose the sealing washer on each side of the hose fitting. Remove the remote reservoir and hose. Cover the hose end to prevent the entry of moisture and foreign matter.

11. Remove the screws (A, **Figure 73**) securing the master cylinder/brake pedal support bracket and remove the bracket (B, **Figure 73**).

12. Remove the master cylinder (C, **Figure 73**) from the front footpeg assembly.

13. Inspect and service the master cylinder as described in this chapter.

14. Apply a couple of drops of oil onto the brake pedal pivot shaft.

15. Carefully install the master cylinder into position on the footpeg assembly. Index the rubber dust boot opening (A, **Figure 74**) under the brake pedal actuating arm (B, **Figure 74**) and move the master cylinder into position and align the bolt holes.

16. Install the master cylinder/brake pedal support bracket and screws (A, **Figure 75**). Tighten the screws securely.

17. Make sure the brake light switch is contacting the brake lever arm correctly (B, **Figure 75**).

CAUTION
*There are 2 different size banjo bolts (10 mm and 12 mm) used to connect the brake hoses to the master cylinder. Refer to the correct torque specification listed in **Table 1** when tightening these bolts to avoid damage to either the bolts or the master cylinder body.*

NOTE
*Be sure to attach the brake hoses to the correct fittings on the master cylinder. The remote reservoir hose attaches to the top fitting (A, **Figure 76**) and the rear caliper hose (B) to the side fitting.*

18. Place a new sealing washer on each side of the remote reservoir hose fitting and install the banjo

bolt. Tighten the banjo bolt (**Figure 72**) to the torque specification listed in **Table 1**.

19. Place a new sealing washer on each side of the remote reservoir hose fitting and install the banjo bolt. Tighten the banjo bolt (**Figure 70**) to the torque specification listed in **Table 1**.

20. Make sure the spring and washer (**Figure 71**) are in place on the brake light switch.

21. Move the brake light switch into position on the master cylinder receptacle and install the screws. Tighten the screws securely.

22. Install the front footpeg assembly as described in Chapter Thirteen.

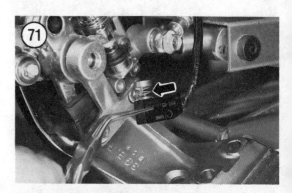

23. Bleed the rear brake as described under *Bleeding the System* in this chapter.

Disassembly

Refer to **Figure 77** for this procedure.

1. Remove the master cylinder as described in this chapter.

2. If still in place, remove the spring and washer from the brake light switch receptacle.

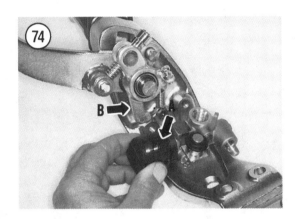

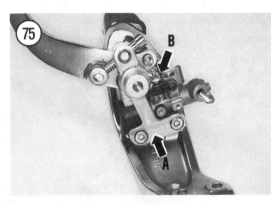

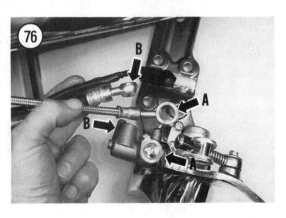

3. Remove the screw and remove the brake light switch (**Figure 78**) from the master cylinder body.

4. Remove the rubber dust boot (**Figure 79**) from the end of the master cylinder.

5. Remove the rubber dust boot (**Figure 80**) from the area where the brake pedal actuating arm rides on the piston assembly.

6. Using circlip pliers, remove the circlip (**Figure 81**) from the body.

7. Remove the piston assembly and the spring.

Inspection

1. Clean all parts in fresh brake fluid.

2. Inspect the body cylinder bore (**Figure 82**) surface for signs of wear and damage. If less than perfect, replace the master cylinder assembly. The body cannot be replaced separately.

3. Measure the cylinder bore with a bore gauge. Replace the master cylinder if the bore diameter exceeds the service limit listed in **Table 2**.

4. Make sure the passage in the bottom of the master cylinder body is clear. Clean out if necessary.

5. Inspect the piston contact surfaces (A, **Figure 83**) for signs of wear and damage. If less than perfect, replace the piston assembly.

6. Check the end of the piston (B, **Figure 83**) for wear caused by the brake pedal actuating arm. If worn, replace the piston assembly.

7. Measure the diameter of the piston with a micrometer (**Figure 84**). Replace the piston assembly if its diameter is less than the service limit listed in **Table 2**.

8. Replace the piston assembly with a kit if either the primary or secondary cups (C, **Figure 83**) require replacement. The cups cannot be replaced separately.

9. Inspect the threads in the bore (**Figure 85**) for both banjo bolts. If worn or damaged, clean out with a metric thread tap or replace the master cylinder assembly.

10. Inspect the banjo bolt threads for damage. Make sure the fluid hole is clear. Check the sealing washers for flatness, wear or damage, replace if necessary.

11. Check all of the components of the brake light switch plunger assembly for wear, deterioration or damage and replace the assembly if necessary.

12

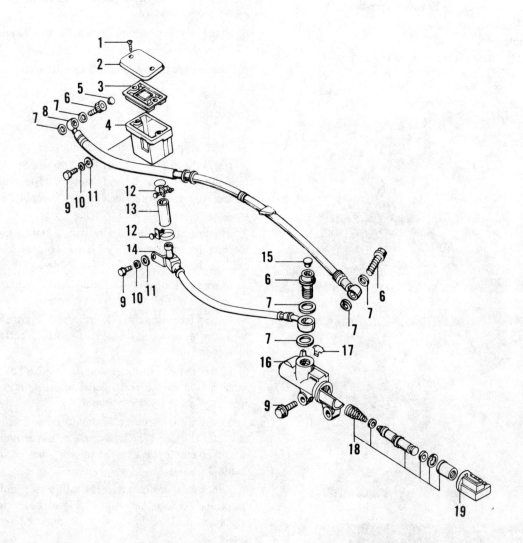

⑦

REAR CALIPER

1. Screw
2. Cover
3. Diaphragm
4. Remote reservoir
5. Trim cap
6. Banjo bolt

7. Sealing washer
8. Caliper hose
9. Bolt
10. Lockwasher
11. Washer
12. Hose clamp

13. Hose
14. Remote reservoir hose
15. Trim cap
16. Master cylinder body
17. Plate
18. Piston/spring assembly
19. Dust boot

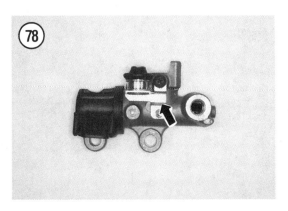

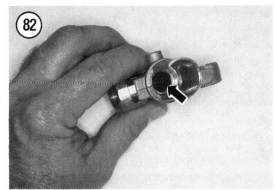

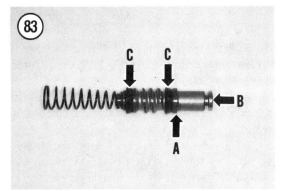

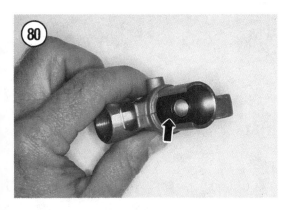

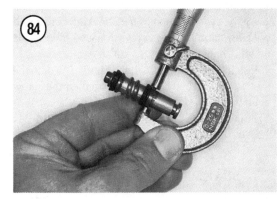

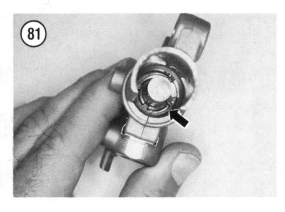

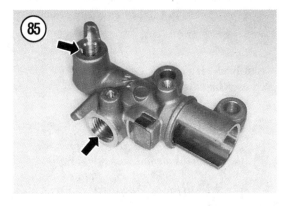

12

Assembly

1. Soak the new cups in fresh brake fluid for at least 15 minutes to make them pliable. Coat the inside of the cylinder bore with fresh hydraulic fluid prior to the assembly of parts.

> **CAUTION**
> *When installing the piston assembly, do not allow the cups to turn inside out as they will be damaged and allow brake fluid leakage within the cylinder bore.*

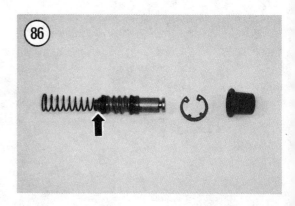

2. Position the spring with the tapered end going in last, facing toward the primary cup on the piston (**Figure 86**).
3. Install the spring, primary cup and piston assembly into the cylinder (**Figure 87**). Push them in until they bottom out.
4. Install the circlip (**Figure 81**) and slide in the rubber boot (**Figure 88**). Make sure it is completely seated.
5. Position the long dust boot with the opening facing up to expose the open channel in the master cylinder (**Figure 89**). This alignment is necessary to allow the brake pedal actuating arm to contact the end of the piston.
6. Apply a small mount of theadlocking compound to the switch mounting screw threaded hole in the master cylinder body.
7. Install the brake light switch (**Figure 78**) onto the master cylinder body. Install and tighten the screw securely.
8. Install the master cylinder as described in this chapter.

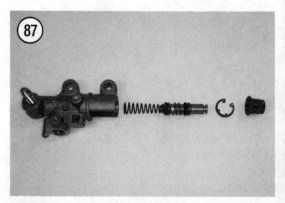

BRAKE HOSE REPLACEMENT

Suzuki recommends replacing the brake hoses every 4 years or sooner if they show any evidence of cracking or damage.

Front Brake Hose
Removal/Installation

> **CAUTION**
> *Cover the surrounding area with a heavy cloth or plastic tarp to protect them from accidental brake fluid spills. Wash brake fluid off any painted or plated surfaces or plastic parts*

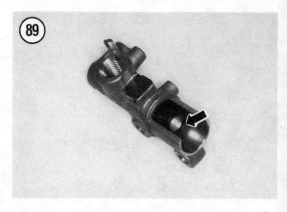

immediately, as it will destroy the finish. Use soapy water and rinse completely.

1. Remove the cap from the bleed screw (A, **Figure 90**) on the front caliper.
2. Attach a piece of hose to the bleed screw and place the loose end in a container.

3. Open the bleed screw and operate the front brake lever to pump the brake fluid out of the master cylinder, the brake hose and the caliper assembly. Operate the lever until the system is clear of brake fluid.

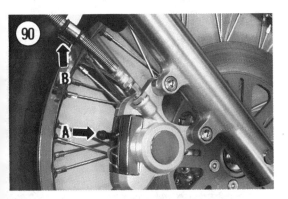

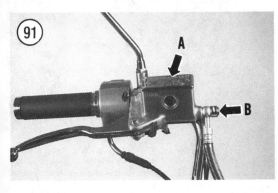

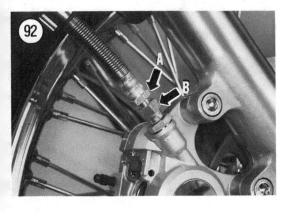

4. Clean the top of the master cylinder of all dirt and foreign matter.
5. Remove the screws securing the cover (A, **Figure 91**). Remove the cover and the diaphragm.
6. If you have a shop syringe, draw all of any residual brake fluid from the master cylinder reservoir.
7. Unscrew the banjo bolt (B, **Figure 91**) securing the brake hose to the master cylinder. Do not lose the sealing washer on each side of the hose fitting.
8. At the brake caliper, hold onto the brake hose fitting (A, **Figure 92**) with an open-end wrench. Loosen the brake hose adapter nut (B, **Figure 92**) securing the brake hose to the caliper assembly.
9. Remove the brake hose and sealing washer from the brake hose adapter nut and let the brake fluid drain out into the container. Dispose of this brake fluid—never reuse brake fluid.
10. Unhook the brake hose from the clamp (B, **Figure 90**) on the right-hand fork leg.
11. Remove the bolt and nut securing the brake hose assembly to the fender support clamp. The clamp is part of the hose assembly.
12. Pull the brake hose assembly up through the lower fork bridge and the upper fork bridge and remove the brake hose from the frame.
13. Install a new hose, sealing washers and banjo bolts in the reverse order of removal while noting the following:

    a. Be sure to install new sealing washers and in their correct positions.
    b. Hold the brake hose fitting (A, **Figure 92**) with an open-end wrench. Tighten the brake hose adapter nut (B, **Figure 92**) securing the brake hose to the caliper assembly. Tighten the brake hose adapter nut securely.
    c. Make sure the rubber grommet (**Figure 93**) around the hose is in place on both the upper and lower fork bridge locations.
    c. Tighten the fittings and banjo bolt to the torque specifications listed in **Table 1**.
    d. Bleed the brake as described under *Bleeding the System* in this chapter.

Rear Brake Hoses
Removal/Installation

Refer to **Figure 77** for this procedure.

12

Cover the surrounding area with a heavy cloth or plastic tarp to protect them from accidental brake fluid spills. Wash brake fluid off any painted or plated surfaces or plastic parts immediately, as it will destroy the finish. Use soapy water and rinse completely.

1. Remove the cap from the bleed screw (A, **Figure 94**) on the rear caliper.

2. Attach a piece of hose to the bleed screw and place the loose end in a container.

3. Open the bleed screw and operate the rear brake pedal to pump the brake fluid out of the master cylinder, the brake hose and the caliper assembly. Operate the lever until the system is clear of brake fluid. Close the bleed screw.

4. Loosen the mounting bolts and remove the remote reservoir cover (**Figure 95**).

5. Clean the top of the master cylinder of all dirt and foreign matter.

6. Remove the screws securing the cover (**Figure 96**). Remove the cover and the diaphragm.

7. If you have a shop syringe, draw all of any residual brake fluid from the master cylinder reservoir.

8. Remove the front footpeg assembly as described in Chapter Thirteen and lower it to the ground.

9. To remove the master cylinder-to-rear caliper hose, perform the following:

   a. Unscrew the banjo bolt (A, **Figure 97**) securing the rear caliper brake hose to the master cylinder. Do not lose the sealing washer on each side of the hose fitting.

   b. Unscrew the banjo bolt (B, **Figure 94**) securing the brake hose to the rear caliper assembly.

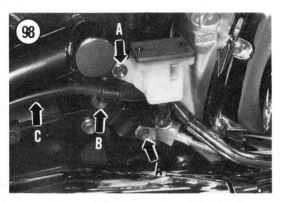

Do not lose the sealing washer on each side of the hose fitting.

c. Remove the bolts (A, **Figure 98**) securing the remote reservoir to the frame. Unhook the brake hose from the bracket (B, **Figure 98**).

d. Unhook the brake hose from any remaining hook, or tie-wraps, on the frame.

e. Remove the brake hose (C, **Figure 98**) from the frame.

10. To remove the master cylinder-to-remote reservoir hose, perform the following:

a. Unscrew the banjo bolt (B, **Figure 97**) securing the brake hose to the master cylinder. Do not lose the sealing washer on each side of the hose fitting.

b. Remove the bolts securing the remote reservoir (A, **Figure 99**) to the frame.

c. Remove the brake hose (B, **Figure 99**) and remote reservoir from the frame.

11. Install new hoses, sealing washers and banjo bolts in the reverse order of removal while noting the following:

CAUTION
*There are 2 different size banjo bolts (10 mm and 12 mm) used to connect the brake hoses to the master cylinder. Refer to the correct torque specification listed in **Table 1** when tightening these bolts to avoid damage to either the bolts or the master cylinder body.*

a. Place a sealing washer on each side of the remote reservoir hose fitting and install the banjo bolt. Tighten the banjo bolt (**Figure 100**) to the torque specification listed in **Table 1**.

b. Place a sealing washer on each side of the remote reservoir hose fitting and install the banjo bolt. Tighten the banjo bolt (**Figure 101**) to the torque specification listed in **Table 1**.

c. Bleed the brake as described under *Bleeding the System* in this chapter.

12

BRAKE DISC

The brake discs are separate from the wheel hubs and can be removed once the wheels are removed from the bike.

Inspection

It is not necessary to remove the disc from the wheel to inspect it. Small nicks and marks on the disc are not important, but radial scratches deep enough to snag a fingernail reduce braking effectiveness and increase brake pad wear. If these grooves are evident, and the brake pads are wearing rapidly, the disc should be replaced.

The Suzuki factory specifications are listed in **Table 2**. Each disc is also marked with the minimum (MIN) thickness. If the specification marked on the disc differs from that listed in **Table 2**, refer to the specification marked on the disc.

When servicing the brake discs, do not have the discs reconditioned (ground) to compensate for any warpage. The discs are thin and grinding will only reduce their thickness, causing them to warp quite rapidly. If the disc is warped, the brake pads may be dragging on the disc, causing the disc to overheat. Overheating can also be caused when there is unequal pad pressure on both sides of the disc. replace any warped discs.

The main causes of unequal brake pad pressure are:

a. The brake caliper piston seal(s) is worn or damaged.

b. The small master cylinder relief is plugged.

c. The primary cup on the master cylinder piston is worn or damaged.

> *NOTE*
> *It is not necessary to remove the wheel to measure the disc thickness. The measurement can be performed with the wheel installed or removed from the bike.*

1. Measure the thickness of the disc at several locations around the disc with a vernier caliper of a micrometer (**Figure 102**). The disc must be replaced if the thickness in any area is less than that specified in **Table 2** (or the MIN thickness marked on the disc).

2. Make sure the disc mounting bolts are tight prior to running this check. Check the disc runout with a dial indicator as shown in **Figure 103**.

3. Slowly rotate the wheel and watch the dial indicator. If the runout exceeds that listed in **Table 2** the disc must be replaced.

4. Clean the disc of any rust or corrosion and wipe clean with lacquer thinner. Never use an oil-based solvent that may leave an oil residue on the disc.

Removal/Installation

1. Remove the front or rear wheel as described in Chapter Ten or Eleven.

> *NOTE*
> *Place a piece of wood or vinyl tube in the caliper in place of the disc. Then, if the brake lever is inadvertently squeezed the pistons will not be forced out of the cylinders. If this does happen, the caliper must be disassembled to reseat the pistons and the system will have to be bled.*

> *CAUTION*
> *Do not set the wheel down on the disc surface, as it may get scratched or*

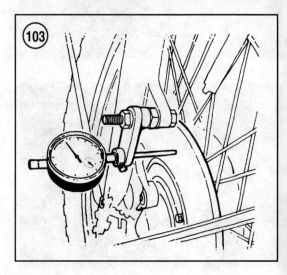

warped. Set the wheel on 2 wooden blocks.

2. Remove the bolts (**Figure 104**) securing the brake disc to the hub and remove the disc.

3. Install by reversing these removal steps while noting the following:

    a. If the disc is marked with a directional arrow, install it so that the arrow faces in the direction of tire rotation.

> *CAUTION*
> *The disc mounting bolts are made from a harder material than similar bolts. Always replace these bolts with Suzuki brake disc bolts – never compromise and use a cheaper bolt as they will not properly retain the disc to the hub.*

    b. Use a small amount of a locking compound such as ThreeBond TB1303 or Loctite No. 242 on the brake disc bolts prior to installation.

    c. Tighten the disc mounting bolts to the torque specification listed in **Table 1**.

BLEEDING THE SYSTEM

This procedure is not necessary unless the brakes feel spongy, there has been a leak in the system, a component has been replaced or the brake fluid has been replaced.

Brake Bleeder Process

This procedure uses a brake bleeder that is available from a motorcycle dealership, an automotive supply stores or from mail order outlets.

> *NOTE*
> *This procedure is shown on the front wheel. The same steps apply to the rear brake assembly.*

1. Remove the dust cap from the bleed valve on the caliper assembly.

2. Connect the brake bleeder and wrench to the bleed screw on the caliper assembly (**Figure 105**).

> *CAUTION*
> *Cover the wheels with a heavy cloth or plastic tarp to protect them from the accidental spilling of brake fluid. Wash any brake fluid off of any plastic, painted or plated surface immediately; as it will destroy the finish. Use soapy water and rinse completely.*

3A. For the front brakes system, perform the following:

> *NOTE*
> *The handlebar angle is so severe on most models it is difficult to position the handlebar so the front master cylinder is level. The level position is desirable so the reservoir can be filled with sufficient brake fluid for this procedure.*

    a. Loosen the master cylinder clamp bolts (A, **Figure 106**).

    b. Carefully slide the master cylinder up onto the top of the curve of the handlebar (B, **Figure 106**). This will position the master cylinder reservoir almost horizontal.

    c. Clean the top of the front master cylinder of all dirt and foreign matter.

12

d. Remove the screws securing the cover. Remove the cover and the diaphragm from the master cylinder.

3B. For the rear brake system, perform the following:

a. Loosen the mounting bolts and remove the remote reservoir cover (**Figure 95**).

b. Clean the top of the rear master cylinder remote reservoir of all dirt and foreign matter.

c. Remove the screws securing the cover (**Figure 96**). Remove the cover and the diaphragm from the reservoir.

4. Fill the reservoir almost to the top lip. Install the cover loosely. Leave the cover in place during this procedure to prevent the entry of dirt.

NOTE
By performing Step 5, the air located within the master cylinder will be eliminated at the beginning instead of forcing the air bubbles all the way through the entire hydraulic system.

WARNING
Use brake fluid from a sealed container marked DOT 3 or DOT 4 only (specified for disc brakes). Other types may cause brake failure. Do not intermix different brands or types as they may not be compatible.

5. If the front master cylinder was drained, it must be bled before bleeding the entire system. Perform the following:

a. Remove the brake hose (C, **Figure 106**) from the master cylinder.

b. Hold your thumb over the brake hose hole in the master cylinder and fill the reservoir with DOT 3 or DOT 4 brake fluid. Do not remove your thumb.

c. While holding your thumb over the hole, pump the brake lever several times. Then hold the lever in the depressed position.

d. Reduce thumb pressure on the brake hose hole. Some air bubbles will leak out. Reapply thumb pressure.

e. Repeat sub-steps c and d until no air bubbles bleed out of the hole and you can feel resistance at the lever or pedal.

f. Check the reservoir fluid level and top it off if necessary.

g. Reconnect the brake hose onto the master cylinder. Be sure to install a sealing washer on each side of the hose fitting. Tighten the banjo bolt to the torque specification listed in **Table 1**.

h. Wash off any spilled brake fluid before continuing.

6. Open the bleed valve about one-half turn and pump the brake bleeder (**Figure 107**).

NOTE
If air is entering the brake bleeder hose from around the bleed screw, apply several layers of Teflon tape to the bleed screw. This should make a good seal between the bleed screw and the brake bleeder hose.

7. As the fluid enters the system and exits into the brake bleeder the level will drop in the reservoir. Maintain the level at about 3/8 inch from the top of the reservoir to prevent air from being drawn into the system.

8. Continue to pump the lever on the brake bleeder until the fluid emerging from the hose is completely free of bubbles. At this point, tighten the bleed valve.

NOTE
Do not allow the reservoir to empty during the bleeding operation or more air will enter the system. If this occurs, the entire procedure must be repeated.

9. When the brake fluid is free of bubbles, tighten the bleed screw, remove the brake bleeder tube and install the bleed screw dust cap.

10. If necessary, add fluid to correct the level in the reservoir. It should be to the upper level line.

11. On the front brake, install the diaphragm and the cover and tighten the screws securely. Move the

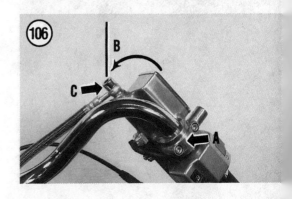

master cylinder back to the original position and tighten the clamping bolts to the torque specification in **Table 1**.

12. On the rear brake, install the diaphragm and cover and tighten the screws securely.

13. Test the feel of the brake lever or pedal. It should be firm and should offer the same resistance each time it's operated. If it feels spongy, it is likely that there is still air in the system and it must be bled again. When all air has been bled from the system and the fluid level is correct in the reservoir, double-check for leaks and tighten all fittings and connections.

WARNING
Before riding the bike, make certain that the brake is operating correctly.

14. Test ride the bike slowly at first to make sure that the brakes are operating properly.

Without a Brake Bleeder

1. Remove the dust cap from the bleed valve on the caliper assembly.

2. Connect a length of clear tubing and wrench to the bleed screw on the caliper assembly.

3. Place the other end of the tube into a clean container. Fill the container with enough fresh brake fluid to keep the end submerged. The tube should be long enough so that a loop can be made higher than the bleed screw to prevent air from being drawn into the caliper during bleeding.

CAUTION
Cover the wheel with a heavy cloth or plastic tarp to protect it from the accidental spilling of brake fluid. Wash any brake fluid off of any plastic, painted or plated surface immediately;

as it will destroy the finish. Use soapy water and rinse completely.

4A. For the front brakes system, perform the following:

NOTE
The handlebar angle is so severe on most models it is difficult to position the handlebar so the front master cylinder is level. The level position is desirable so the reservoir can be filled with sufficient brake fluid for this procedure.

   a. Loosen the master cylinder clamp bolts (A, **Figure 106**).

   b. Carefully slide the master cylinder up onto the top of the curve of the handlebar (B, **Figure 106**). This will position the master cylinder reservoir almost horizontal.

   c. Clean the top of the front master cylinder of all dirt and foreign matter.

   d. Remove the screws securing the cover. Remove the cover and the diaphragm from the master cylinder.

4B. For the rear brake system, perform the following:

   a. Remove the mounting bolts and the remote reservoir cover (**Figure 95**).

   b. Clean the top of the rear master cylinder remote reservoir of all dirt and foreign matter.

   c. Remove the screws securing the cover (**Figure 96**). Remove the cover and the diaphragm from the reservoir.

5. Fill the reservoir almost to the top lip, install the cover loosely. Leave the cover in place during this procedure to prevent the entry of dirt.

NOTE
By performing Step 6, the air located within the master cylinder will be eliminated at the beginning instead of forcing the air bubbles all the way through the entire hydraulic system.

WARNING
Use brake fluid from a sealed container marked DOT 3 or DOT 4 only (specified for disc brakes). Other types may cause brake failure. Do not intermix different brands or types as they may not be compatible.

12

6. If the front master cylinder was drained, it must be bled before bleeding the entire system. Perform the following:

   a. Remove the brake hose (C, **Figure 106**) from the master cylinder.

   b. Hold your thumb over the brake hose hole in the master cylinder and fill the reservoir with DOT 3 or DOT 4 brake fluid. Do not remove your thumb.

   c. While holding your thumb over the hole, pump the brake lever several times. Then hold the lever in the depressed position.

   d. Reduce thumb pressure on the brake hose hole. Some air bubbles will leak out. Reapply thumb pressure.

   e. Repeat substeps c and d until no air bubbles bleed out of the hole and you can feel resistance at the lever or pedal.

   f. Check the reservoir fluid level and top it off if necessary.

   g. Reconnect the brake hose onto the master cylinder. Be sure to install a sealing washer on each side of the hose fitting. Tighten the banjo bolt to the torque specification listed in **Table 1**.

   h. Wash off any spilled brake fluid before continuing.

7. Slowly apply the brake lever, or brake pedal, several times as follows:

   a. Pull the lever in. Hold the lever in the applied position or the pedal in the depressed position.

   b. Open the bleed screw about one-half turn. Allow the lever or pedal to travel to its limit.

   c. When this limit is reached, tighten the bleed screw.

8. As the fluid enters the system, the level will drop in the reservoir. Maintain the level at about 3/8 inch from the cover of the reservoir to prevent air from being drawn into the system.

9. Continue to pump the lever or pedal and fill the reservoir until the fluid emerging from the hose is completely free of bubbles.

NOTE
Do not allow the reservoir to empty during the bleeding operation or more air will enter the system. If this occurs, the entire procedure must be repeated.

10. Hold the lever in, or pedal down, tighten the bleed screw, remove the bleed tube and install the bleed valve dust cap.

11. If necessary, add fluid to correct the level in the reservoir. It should be to the upper level line.

12. On the front brake, install the diaphragm and the cover and tighten the screws securely. Move the master cylinder back to the original position and tighten the clamping bolts to the torque specification in **Table 1**.

13. On the rear brake, install the diaphragm and cover and tighten the screws securely.

14. Test the feel of the brake lever or pedal. It should be firm and should offer the same resistance each time it's operated. If it feels spongy, it is likely that there is still air in the system and it must be bled again. When all air has been bled from the system and the fluid level is correct in the reservoir, double-check for leaks and tighten all fittings and connections.

WARNING
Before riding the bike, make certain that the brake is operating correctly.

15. Test ride the bike slowly at first to make sure that the brakes are operating properly.

Reverse Flow Bleeding

This bleeding procedure can be used if you are having a difficult time freeing the system all of bubbles. Using this procedure, the brake fluid will be forced into the system in a reverse direction. The fluid will enter the caliper, flow through the brake hose and into the master cylinder reservoir. If the system is already filled with brake fluid, the existing fluid will be flushed out of the top of the master cylinder by the new brake fluid being forced into the caliper. Siphon the fluid from the reservoir, then hold a shop cloth under the master cylinder reservoir to catch any additional fluid.

A special reverse flow tool called the EZE Bleeder is available or a tool can be fabricated for this procedure.

To fabricate this tool, perform the following:

NOTE
The brake fluid container must be plastic–not metal. Use vinyl tubing of

the correct inner diameter to ensure a tight fit on the caliper bleed valve.

a. Purchase a 12 oz. (345 ml) plastic bottle of DOT 3 or DOT 4 brake fluid.
b. Remove the cap, drill an appropriate size hole and adapt a vinyl hose fitting onto the cap.
c. Attach a section of vinyl hose to the hose fitting on the cap and secure it with a hose clamp. This joint must be a tight fit as the plastic brake fluid bottle will be squeezed to force the brake fluid out past this fitting and through the hose.
d. Remove the moisture seal from the plastic bottle of brake fluid and screw the cap and hose assembly onto the bottle.

1. Remove the dust cap from the bleed screw on the caliper assembly.
2. Clean the top cover of the master cylinder of all dirt and foreign matter.
3. Remove the screws securing the cover. Remove the cover and the diaphragm.
4. Attach the vinyl hose to the bleed screw on the caliper. Make sure the hose is tight on the bleed valve.
5. Open the bleed screw and squeeze the plastic bottle forcing this brake fluid into the system.

NOTE
If necessary, siphon brake fluid from the reservoir to avoid overflow of fluid.

6. Observe the brake fluid entering the master cylinder reservoir. Continue to apply pressure from the tool, or bottle, until the fluid entering the reservoir is free of all air bubbles.
7. Close the bleed valve and disconnect the bleeder or hose from the bleed valve.
8. Install the dust cap onto the bleed screw on the caliper.
9. At this time the system should be free of bubbles. Apply the brake lever or pedal and check for proper brake operation. If the system still feels spongy, perform the typical bleeding procedure in the beginning of this section.

WARNING
Before riding the bike, make certain that the brake is operating correctly.

10. Test ride the bike slowly at first to make sure the brakes are operating properly.

REAR BRAKE PEDAL

Removal/Installation

Refer to **Figure 108** for this procedure.

1. Remove the front footpeg assembly as described in Chapter Thirteen and lower it to the ground.
2. Remove the master cylinder/brake pedal support bracket and screws (A, **Figure 109**) and the rear master cylinder (B, **Figure 109**) from the footpeg assembly as described in this chapter.
3. On models so equipped, remove the cotter pin and washer securing the brake pedal to the pivot post on the footpeg assembly.
4. Remove the screw (A, **Figure 110**) and brake pedal return spring (B, **Figure 110**).
5. Slide the brake pedal off the pivot shaft (C, **Figure 110**).
6. Inspect the pivot shaft (**Figure 111**) on the front footpeg assembly for wear or damage.
7. Check the brake pedal bushing (A, **Figure 112**) for wear or damage.
8. Check the return spring (B, **Figure 112**) for sagging or damage.
9. Apply clean engine oil to the pivot shaft and bushing prior to installing any parts and again after all parts have been installed.
10. Slide the brake pedal onto the pivot shaft (C, **Figure 110**).
11. Install the screw (A, **Figure 110**) and brake pedal return spring (B, **Figure 110**).
12. On models so equipped, install a new cotter pin—never reuse a cotter pin as the ends may break off and the cotter pin could fall out disabling the brake system.
13. Install the rear master cylinder and the master cylinder/brake pedal support bracket onto the footpeg assembly as described in this chapter.
14. Install the front footpeg assembly as described in Chapter Thirteen.

12

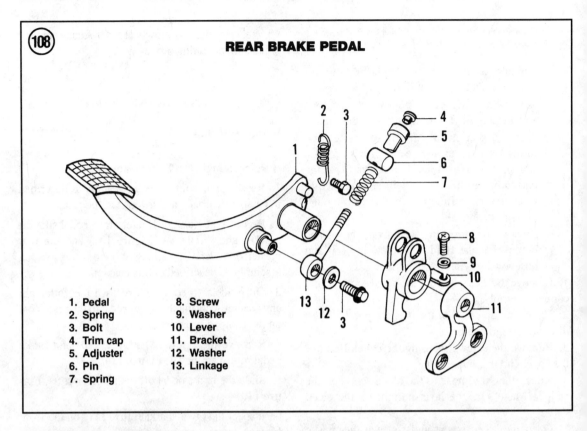

REAR BRAKE PEDAL

1. Pedal
2. Spring
3. Bolt
4. Trim cap
5. Adjuster
6. Pin
7. Spring
8. Screw
9. Washer
10. Lever
11. Bracket
12. Washer
13. Linkage

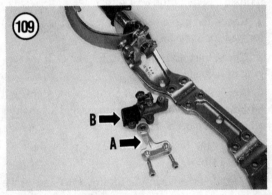

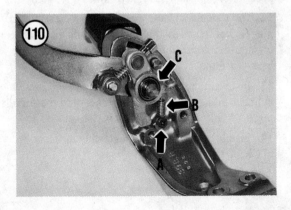

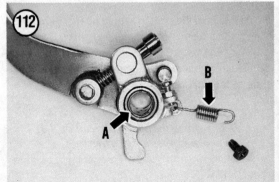

Table 1 BRAKE SYSTEM TIGHTENING TORQUES

Item	N•m	in.-lb.	ft.-lb.
Brake disc bolts and nuts			
Front and rear wheels	15-25	–	11-18
Front caliper			
Mounting bolts	25-40	–	18-29
Body assembly bolts	15-20	–	11-15
Front moster cylinder clamp bolts	8-12	71-106	–
Rear caliper			
Mounting bolts	40-60	–	29-44
Body assembly botls	25-40	–	18-29
Rear caliper torque link bolt and nut	40-60	–	29-44
Rear master cylinder mounting bolt	15-25	–	11-18
Rear master cylinder reservoir			
mounting bolt	8-12	71-106	–
Front footrest mounting bolt	15-25	–	11-18
Front brake hose banjo bolts	20-25	–	15-18
Rear brake hose banjo bolts			
10 mm	20-25	–	15-18
12 mm	30-35	–	22-25
Bleed valves	6-9	53-79	–

Table 2 BRAKE SPECIFICATIONS

	New mm (in.)	Service limit mm (in.)
Front brake master cylinder		
Bore diameter	12.700-12.743 (0.5000-0.5017)	–
Piston diameter	12.657-12.684 (0.4983-0.4994)	–
Front brake caliper		
Bore diameter	42.850-42.926 (1.6870-1.6900)	–
Piston diameter	42.770-42.820 (1.6839-1.6858)	–
Rear brake master cylinder		
Bore diameter	12.700-12.743 (0.50000-0.5017)	–
Piston diameter	12.657-12.684 (0.4983-0.4994)	–
Rear brake caliper		
Bore diameter	42.850-42.926 (1.6870-1.6900)	–
Piston diameter	42.770-42.820 (1.6839-1.6858)	–
Brake disc minimum thickness		
Front	4.8-5.1 (0.189-0.201)	4.5 (0.18)
Rear	5.8-6.2 (0.228-0.244)	5.5 (0.22)
Maximum disc runout (front and rear)	–	0.30 (0.012)
Brake pad lining thickness	–	1.5 (0.06)

12

CHAPTER THIRTEEN

BODY AND FRAME

This chapter contains removal and installation procedures for all body panels and frame components.

SEATS

Refer to **Figure 1** for this procedure.

1. Carefully pull on both sides of the backrest pad and disengage it from the locating bosses on the tool box cover on the rear handle.

2. Insert the ignition key into the tool box cover, unlock and remove the cover (**Figure 2**).

3. Remove the tool bag and the pillion seat mounting bolt rubber protective pad.

4. Remove the bolt and washer (**Figure 3**) securing the rear portion of the pillion seat and retaining bracket to the rear fender.

5. Pull up on the rear of the seat and remove the pillion seat from the rider's seat mounting bracket on the rear fender.

6. Remove the bolts, lockwashers and washers securing the seat mounting bracket (**Figure 4**) at the rear of the rider's seat.

7. Pull up on the rear of the rider's seat and move the seat toward the rear to disengage it from the front retaining bracket on the frame.

8. Partially remove the seat and turn it over. Carefully disconnect the electrical connectors (A, **Figure 5**) from the igniter unit attached to the base of the seat.

9. Remove the rider's seat assembly.

10. If the seats are going to be left off the bike for any length of time, wrap each one in a blanket or towel, then in a plastic bag and place them in a cardboard box to protect from damage.

11. Connect the electrical connectors onto the igniter unit and make sure the connectors are locked into place.

12. Install the rider's seat and insert the seat's front locating tab under the retaining loop (B, **Figure 5**) on the frame. Push the seat forward and make sure the tab is located correctly under the loop.

13. Push the rear of the seat down and align the rear mounting bracket holes with the mounting holes in the frame. Be careful not to trap any of the electrical wires under the mounting bracket. Install the washers, lockwashers and bolts (**Figure 6**) and tighten securely.

①

SEATS

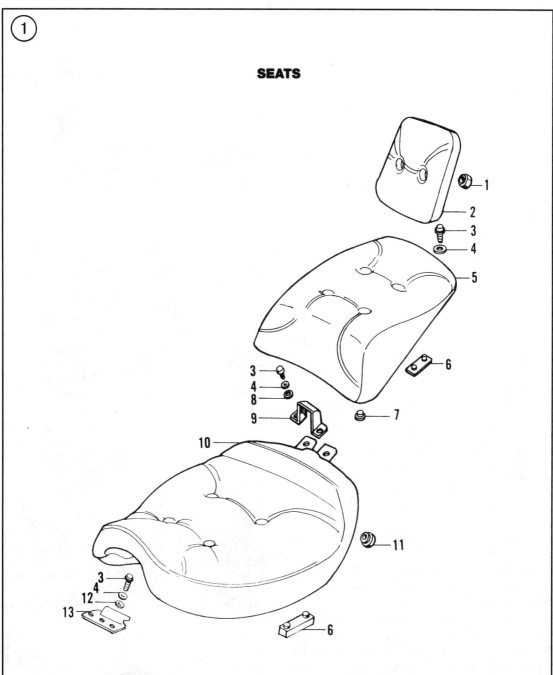

1. Cushion
2. Backrest pad
3. Bolt
4. Washer
5. Pillion seat
6. Retainer
7. Cushion
8. Lockwasher
9. Retaining bracket
10. Rider's seat
11. Cushion
12. Lockwasher
13. Bracket

13

14. Move the seat from side to side to make sure it is firmly locked in place.

WARNING
After the seat is installed, pull up on it firmly and move it from side to side to make sure it is securely locked into place. If the seat is not correctly locked into place it may slide to one side or the other when riding the bike. This could lead to the loss of control and a possible accident.

15. Install the pillion seat and hook it onto the rider's seat mounting bracket on the rear fender.
16. Install the bolt and washer securing the rear portion of the pillion seat and retaining bracket to the rear fender. Tighten the bolt securely.
17. Install the rubber protective pad onto the pillion seat mounting bolt.
18. Install the tool bag.
19. Install the tool box cover and push it closed, then lock it closed.
20. Correctly position the backrest pad and tap it into place into locating bosses on the tool box cover on the rear handle. Make sure the pad is secure.

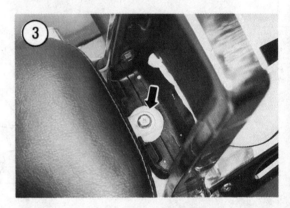

FRAME SIDE COVERS

Removal/Installation

1. Remove the rider's seat as described in this chapter.
2. Remove the screws (**Figure 7**) securing the frame side cover to the frame rail.
3. Carefully lift up the front section of the frame side cover and disconnect the side cover from the locating bracket tab. Remove the cover(s).
4. Make sure the rubber grommet is in place on the locating bracket tabs.
5. Install the side cover onto the bracket tab, align the screw holes with the frame and install the screws.
6. Tighten all screws securely.
7. Install the rider's seat as described in this chapter.

FRAME HEAD SIDE COVERS

Removal/Installation

1. Remove the fuel tank as described in Chapter Eight.

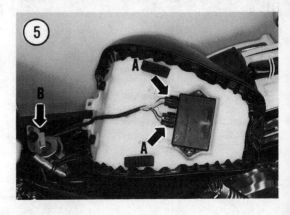

2. Remove the front 2 screws (A, **Figure 8**) and the lower single screw securing the left-hand frame head side cover.

3. Pull the cover (B, **Figure 8**) straight off the frame and remove it.

4. Repeat for the other cover if necessary.

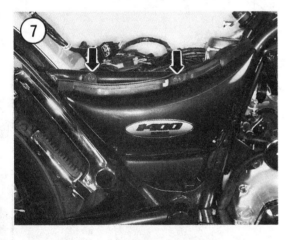

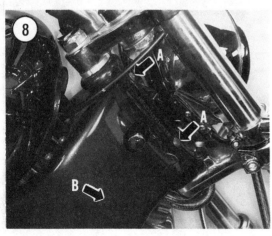

5. Install by reversing these removal steps.

FOOTPEGS

Front Footpeg Assembly Removal/Installation

Refer to **Figure 9** for this procedure.

> *NOTE*
> *The front footpeg assembly cannot be completely removed from the frame without first removing the rear brake master cylinder assembly from the footpeg assembly.*

1. Place a suitable size jack or wooden block(s) under the engine to support the bike securely. The sidestand is part of the front footpeg assembly and cannot be used to support the bike.

2. Remove the clamping bolt (**Figure 10**) securing the rear end of the shift rod to the shift shaft. Slide the shift rod and connector off the shift shaft and reinstall the clamping bolt to avoid misplacing it.

3. Remove the clips, or cotter pins, from the 2 outboard bolts (A, **Figure 11**) on each side, securing the front footpeg assembly to the frame.

4. Remove the Allen bolts and lower the footpeg assembly (B, **Figure 11**).

5. Remove the rear brake master cylinder, and if necessary, the rear brake pedal, as described in Chapter Twelve. It is not necessary to disconnect any of the hydraulic brake hoses, just move the master cylinder assembly out of the way.

6. Remove the footpeg assembly.

7. To remove the individual footpeg from the assembly, perform the following:

  a. Remove the inner screw, lockwasher and washer (A, **Figure 12**) securing the footpeg.

  b. Remove the footpeg (B, **Figure 12**) from the assembly.

8. Install by reversing these removal steps, noting the following:

  a. Tighten the mounting bolts to 15-25 N•m (11-18 ft.-lb.) and install the clips, or new cotter pins, on the 2 outboard bolts on each side. If new cotter pins are used, bend the ends over completely.

  b. Make sure all electrical connectors are free of corrosion and are tight.

13

⑨

FRONT FOOTPEG ASSEMBLY

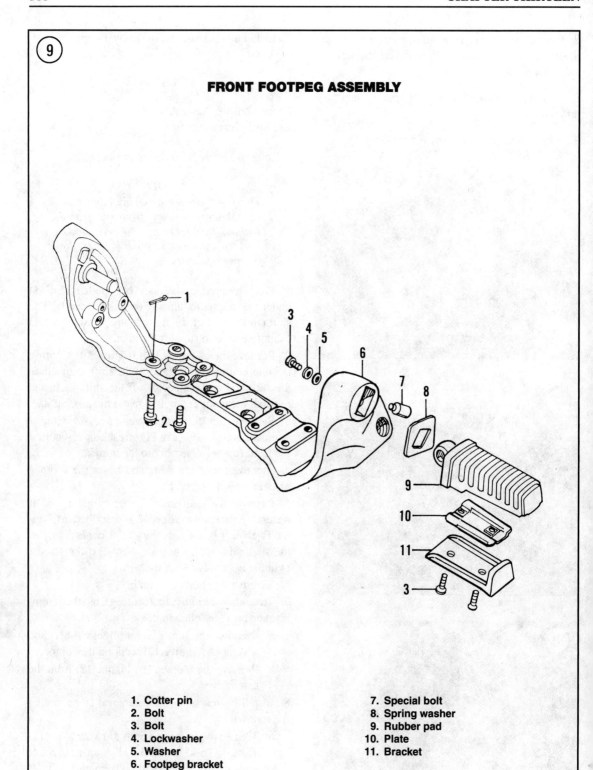

1. Cotter pin
2. Bolt
3. Bolt
4. Lockwasher
5. Washer
6. Footpeg bracket
7. Special bolt
8. Spring washer
9. Rubber pad
10. Plate
11. Bracket

Rear Footpeg Removal/Installation

1. Remove the bolt securing the footpeg to the mounting tab on the frame

2. Remove the footpeg and shim from the frame.

3. Do not lose the spring and the two steel ball detents.

4. Install by reversing these removal steps, noting the following:

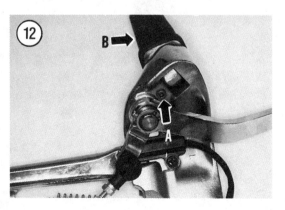

a. Make sure the shim is installed correctly.

b. Tighten the mounting bolt securely.

SIDESTAND

Removal/Installation

1. Remove the front footpeg assembly as described in this chapter, lower the footpeg assembly.

2. Use locking pliers and disconnect the return springs (A, **Figure 13**) from the pin on the sidestand.

3. Remove the screws securing the sidestand switch (B, **Figure 13**) and remove the switch.

4. Remove the trim cap from the special Allen bolt.

5. Remove the nut from the Allen bolt securing the sidestand to the front footpeg assembly.

6. Withdraw the bolt and remove the sidestand (C, **Figure 13**) and shim from the footpeg assembly.

7. Install by reversing these removal steps, noting the following:

a. Apply a light coat of multipurpose grease to the pivot points on the footpeg assembly, the sidestand and pivot bolt prior to installation.

b. Tighten the bolt and nut securely. Install the trim cap onto the bolt head.

FRONT FENDER

Removal/Installation

1. Remove the front wheel as described in Chapter Ten.

2. Remove the bolt securing the fender (A, **Figure 14**) and speedometer cable and bracket (B, **Figure 14**) to the fork slider.

3. To protect the bracket, place a piece of vinyl tubing over the cable bracket (**Figure 15**).

13

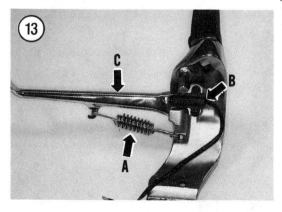

4. Remove the bolt securing the fender (A, **Figure 16**) and speedometer cable and bracket (B, **Figure 16**) to the fork slider.

5. To protect the bracket, place a piece of vinyl tubing over the cable bracket.

6. Remove the front fender (C, **Figure 16**).

7. Install by reversing these removal steps, noting the following:

    a. Be sure to install the speedometer bracket and front brake hose bracket to the fork assemblies along with the front fender.

    b. Tighten all mounting bolts securely.

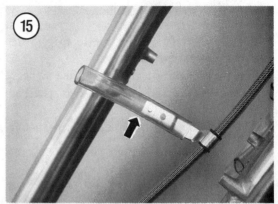

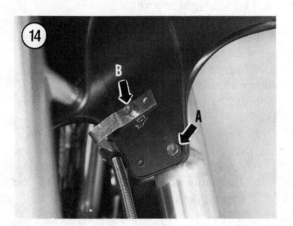

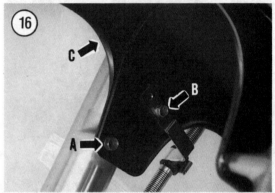

INDEX

14

14

1987 VS1400 (U.S. AND CANADA)

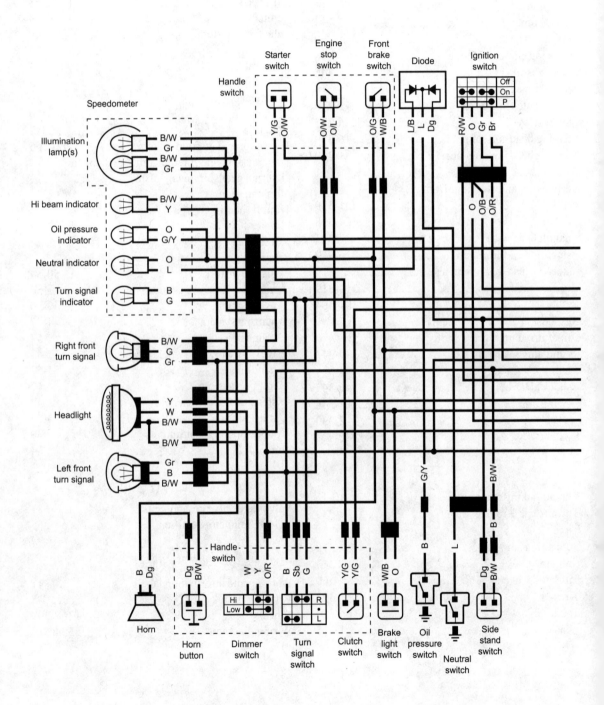

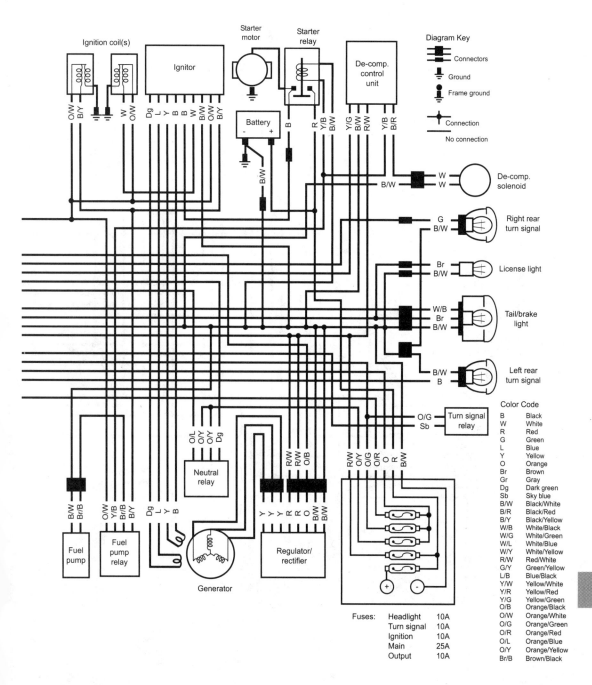

Diagram Key

Connectors

Ground

Frame ground

Connection

No connection

Color Code

B	Black
W	White
R	Red
G	Green
L	Blue
Y	Yellow
O	Orange
Br	Brown
Gr	Gray
Dg	Dark green
Sb	Sky blue
B/W	Black/White
B/R	Black/Red
B/Y	Black/Yellow
W/B	White/Black
W/G	White/Green
W/L	White/Blue
W/Y	White/Yellow
R/W	Red/White
G/Y	Green/Yellow
L/B	Blue/Black
Y/W	Yellow/White
Y/R	Yellow/Red
Y/G	Yellow/Green
O/B	Orange/Black
O/W	Orange/White
O/G	Orange/Green
O/R	Orange/Red
O/L	Orange/Blue
O/Y	Orange/Yellow
Br/B	Brown/Black

Fuses:		
	Headlight	10A
	Turn signal	10A
	Ignition	10A
	Main	25A
	Output	10A

15

1987 VS1400 (U.K. AND BELGIUM)

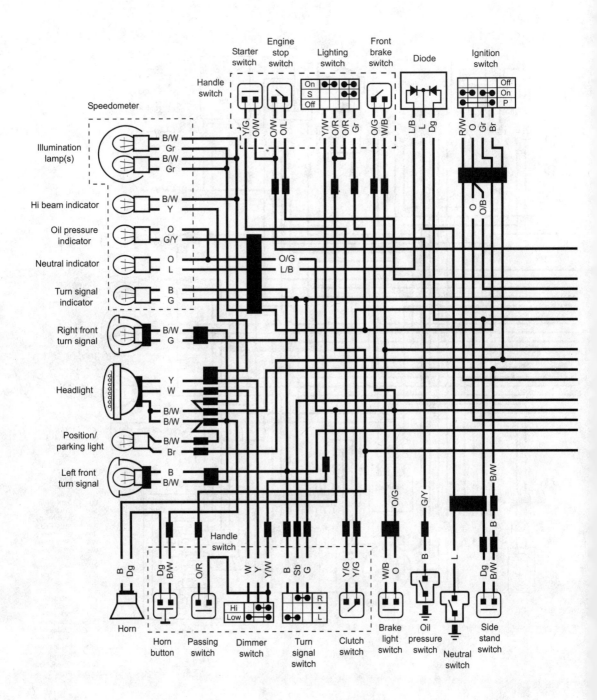

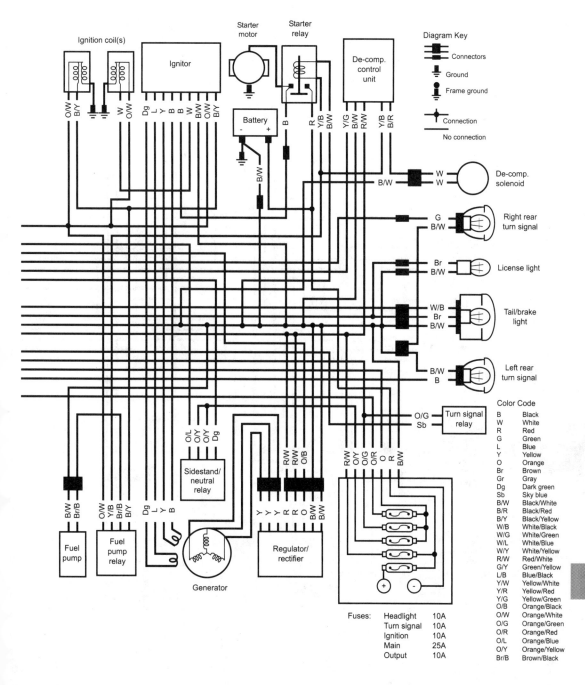

Ignition coil(s)

Ignitor

Starter motor

Starter relay

De-comp. control unit

Diagram Key
- Connectors
- Ground
- Frame ground
- Connection
- No connection

Battery

De-comp. solenoid

Right rear turn signal

License light

Tail/brake light

Left rear turn signal

Turn signal relay

Sidestand/ neutral relay

Regulator/ rectifier

Generator

Fuel pump

Fuel pump relay

Color Code	
B	Black
W	White
R	Red
G	Green
L	Blue
Y	Yellow
O	Orange
Br	Brown
Gr	Gray
Dg	Dark green
Sb	Sky blue
B/W	Black/White
B/R	Black/Red
B/Y	Black/Yellow
W/B	White/Black
W/G	White/Green
W/L	White/Blue
W/Y	White/Yellow
R/W	Red/White
G/Y	Green/Yellow
L/B	Blue/Black
Y/W	Yellow/White
Y/R	Yellow/Red
Y/G	Yellow/Green
O/B	Orange/Black
O/W	Orange/White
O/G	Orange/Green
O/R	Orange/Red
O/L	Orange/Blue
O/Y	Orange/Yellow
Br/B	Brown/Black

Fuses:		
	Headlight	10A
	Turn signal	10A
	Ignition	10A
	Main	25A
	Output	10A

15

1987-ON VS1400 (WEST GERMANY)

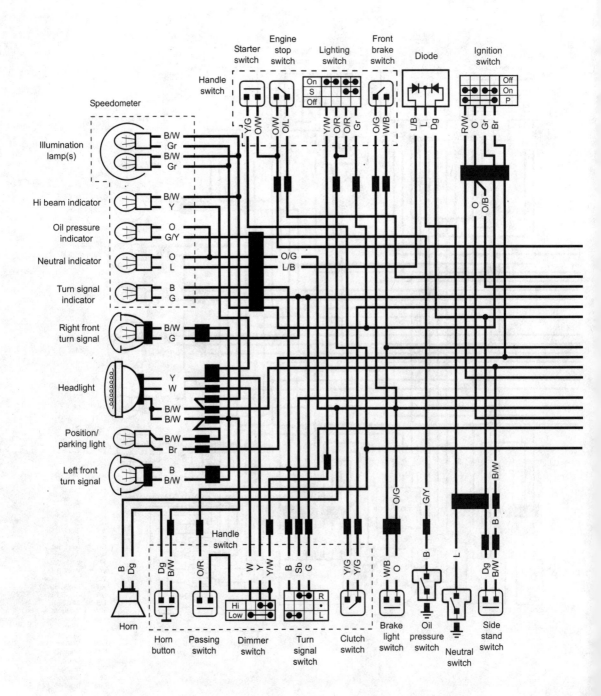

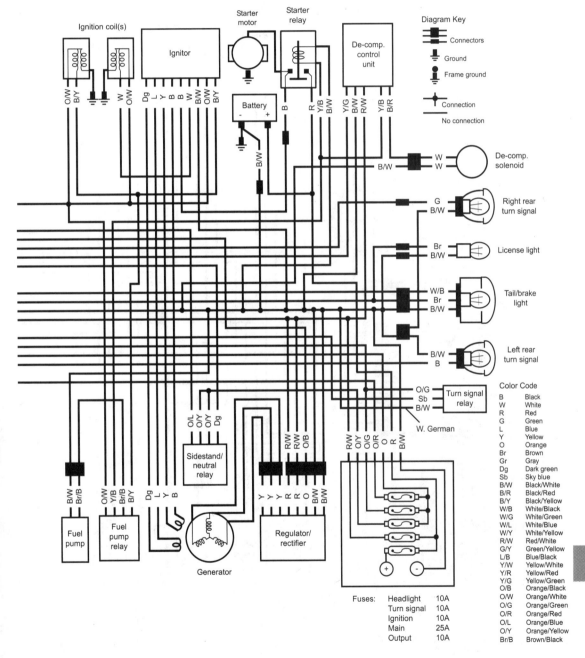

Ignition coil(s)

Ignitor

Starter motor

Starter relay

De-comp. control unit

Battery

Diagram Key
- Connectors
- Ground
- Frame ground
- Connection
- No connection

De-comp. solenoid

Right rear turn signal

License light

Tail/brake light

Left rear turn signal

Turn signal relay

W. German

Sidestand/ neutral relay

Fuel pump

Fuel pump relay

Generator

Regulator/ rectifier

Fuses:

Headlight	10A
Turn signal	10A
Ignition	10A
Main	25A
Output	10A

Color Code

B	Black
W	White
R	Red
G	Green
L	Blue
Y	Yellow
O	Orange
Br	Brown
Gr	Gray
Dg	Dark green
Sb	Sky blue
B/W	Black/White
B/R	Black/Red
B/Y	Black/Yellow
W/B	White/Black
W/G	White/Green
W/L	White/Blue
W/Y	White/Yellow
R/W	Red/White
G/Y	Green/Yellow
L/B	Blue/Black
Y/W	Yellow/White
Y/R	Yellow/Red
Y/G	Yellow/Green
O/B	Orange/Black
O/W	Orange/White
O/G	Orange/Green
O/R	Orange/Red
O/L	Orange/Blue
O/Y	Orange/Yellow
Br/B	Brown/Black

15

1987 VS1400 (EXCEPT U.S., CANADA, U.K. AND BELGIUM)

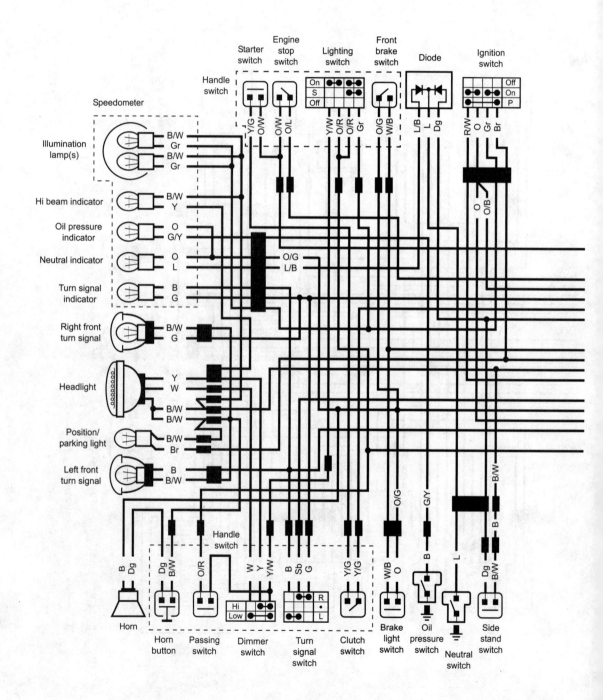

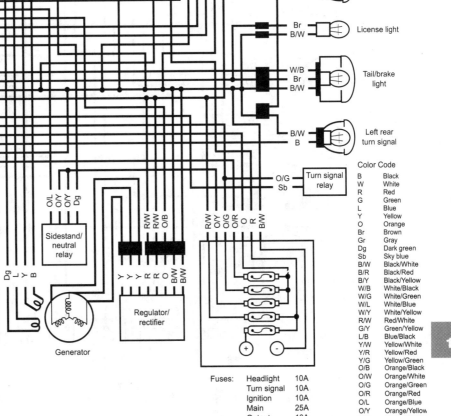

Diagram Key

Connectors
Ground
Frame ground
Connection
No connection

Ignition coil(s)
Ignitor
Starter motor
Starter relay
De-comp. control unit

Battery

De-comp. solenoid

Right rear turn signal

License light

Tail/brake light

Left rear turn signal

Turn signal relay

Fuel pump
Fuel pump relay
Generator
Sidestand/ neutral relay
Regulator/ rectifier

Fuses:
Headlight	10A
Turn signal	10A
Ignition	10A
Main	25A
Output	10A

Color Code

B	Black
W	White
R	Red
G	Green
L	Blue
Y	Yellow
O	Orange
Br	Brown
Gr	Gray
Dg	Dark green
Sb	Sky blue
B/W	Black/White
B/R	Black/Red
B/Y	Black/Yellow
W/B	White/Black
W/G	White/Green
W/L	White/Blue
W/Y	White/Yellow
R/W	Red/White
G/Y	Green/Yellow
L/B	Blue/Black
Y/W	Yellow/White
Y/R	Yellow/Red
Y/G	Yellow/Green
O/B	Orange/Black
O/W	Orange/White
O/G	Orange/Green
O/R	Orange/Red
O/L	Orange/Blue
O/Y	Orange/Yellow
Br/B	Brown/Black

15

1988-1989 VS1400 (U.S.)

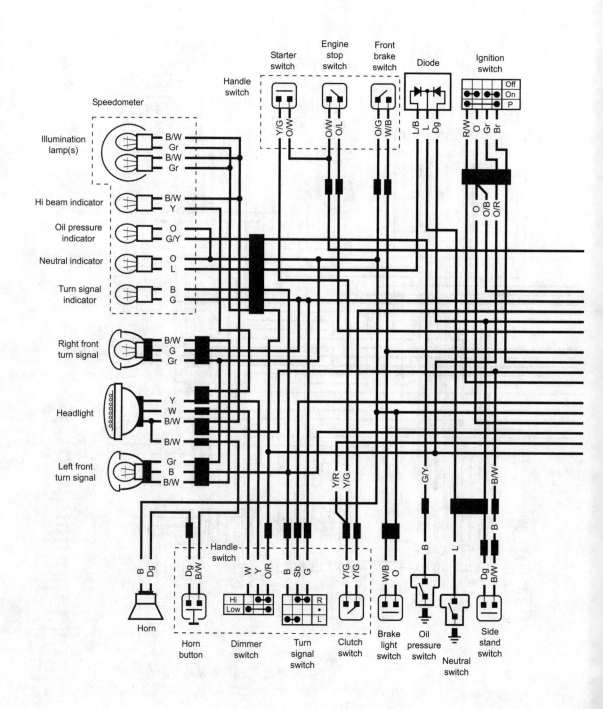

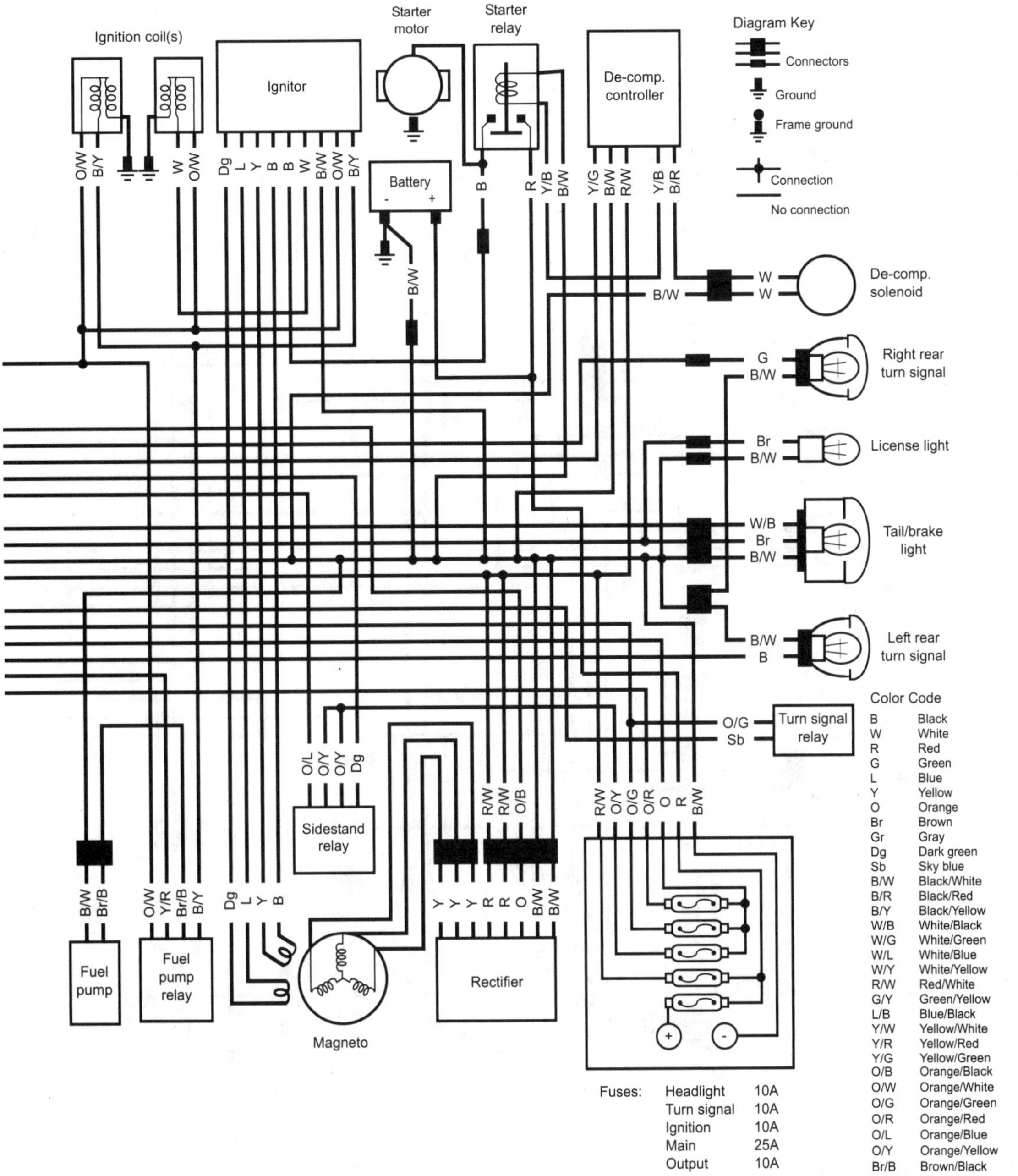

Ignition coil(s)

Starter motor

Starter relay

Ignitor

De-comp. controller

Diagram Key

Connectors

Ground

Frame ground

Connection

No connection

Battery − +

De-comp. solenoid
W
W
B/W

G
B/W
Right rear turn signal

Br
B/W
License light

W/B
Br
B/W
Tail/brake light

B/W
B
Left rear turn signal

O/G
Sb
Turn signal relay

Sidestand relay

Magneto

Rectifier

Fuel pump

Fuel pump relay

Fuses:
Headlight 10A
Turn signal 10A
Ignition 10A
Main 25A
Output 10A

Color Code
B Black
W White
R Red
G Green
L Blue
Y Yellow
O Orange
Br Brown
Gr Gray
Dg Dark green
Sb Sky blue
B/W Black/White
B/R Black/Red
B/Y Black/Yellow
W/B White/Black
W/G White/Green
W/L White/Blue
W/Y White/Yellow
R/W Red/White
G/Y Green/Yellow
L/B Blue/Black
Y/W Yellow/White
Y/R Yellow/Red
Y/G Yellow/Green
O/B Orange/Black
O/W Orange/White
O/G Orange/Green
O/R Orange/Red
O/L Orange/Blue
O/Y Orange/Yellow
Br/B Brown/Black

15

1988-1989 VS1400 (CANADA)

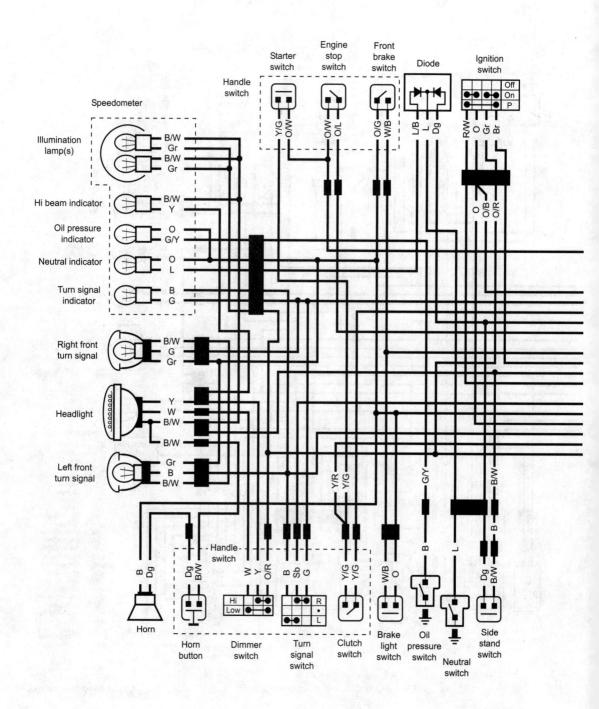

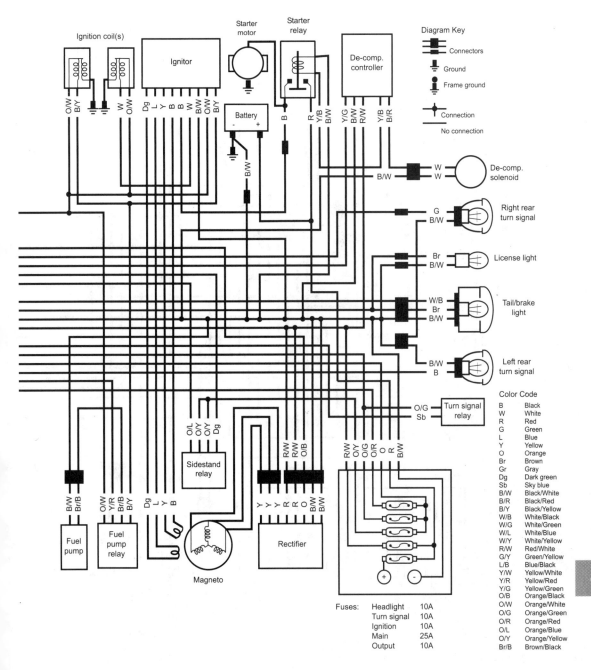

1988-1989 VS1400 (EXCEPT U.S. AND CANADA)

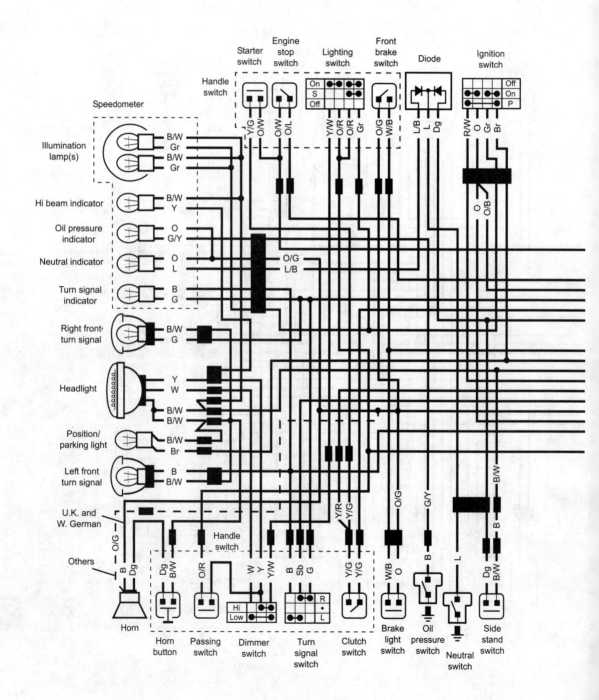

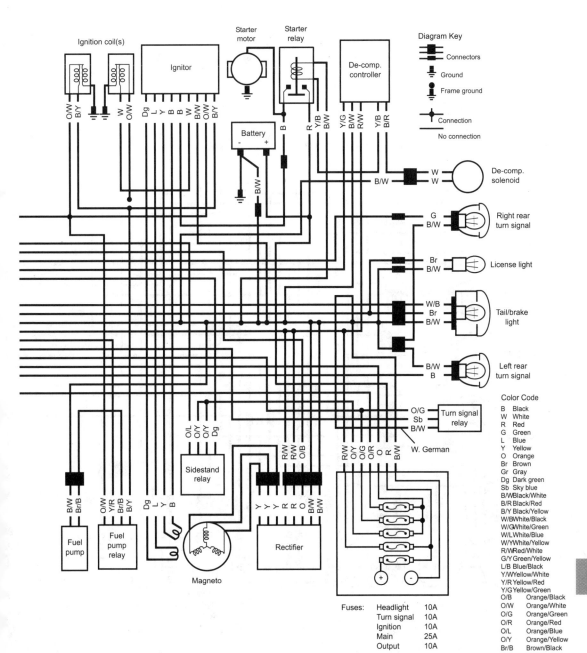

Ignition coil(s)

Ignitor

Starter motor

Starter relay

De-comp. controller

Diagram Key

Connectors
Ground
Frame ground
Connection
No connection

Battery

De-comp. solenoid

Right rear turn signal

License light

Tail/brake light

Left rear turn signal

Turn signal relay

W. German

Sidestand relay

Magneto

Rectifier

Fuel pump

Fuel pump relay

Color Code

B   Black
W   White
R   Red
G   Green
L   Blue
Y   Yellow
O   Orange
Br Brown
Gr Gray
Dg Dark green
Sb Sky blue
B/W Black/White
B/R Black/Red
B/Y Black/Yellow
W/B White/Black
W/G White/Green
W/L White/Blue
W/Y White/Yellow
R/W Red/White
G/Y Green/Yellow
L/B Blue/Black
Y/W Yellow/White
Y/R Yellow/Red
Y/G Yellow/Green
O/B Orange/Black
O/W Orange/White
O/G Orange/Green
O/R Orange/Red
O/L Orange/Blue
O/Y Orange/Yellow
Br/B Brown/Black

Fuses: Headlight   10A
         Turn signal   10A
         Ignition   10A
         Main   25A
         Output   10A

15

1990-1991 VS1400 (U.S. AND ALL OTHER MODELS EXCEPT CANADA)

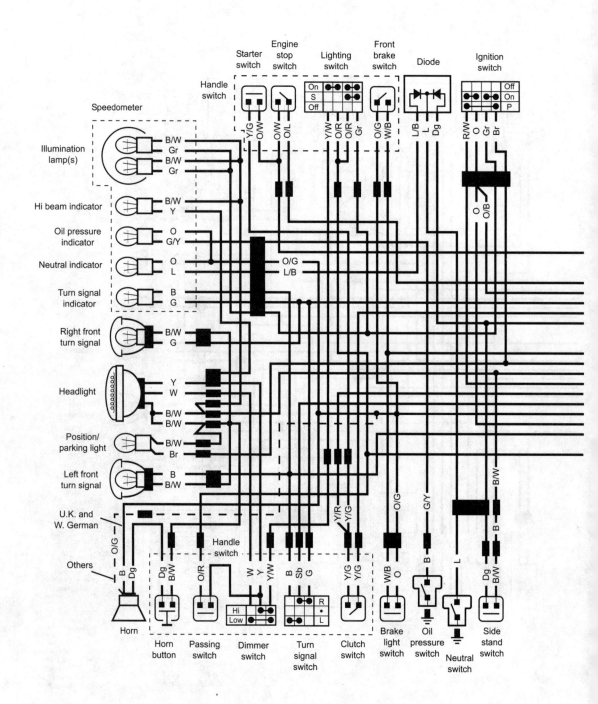

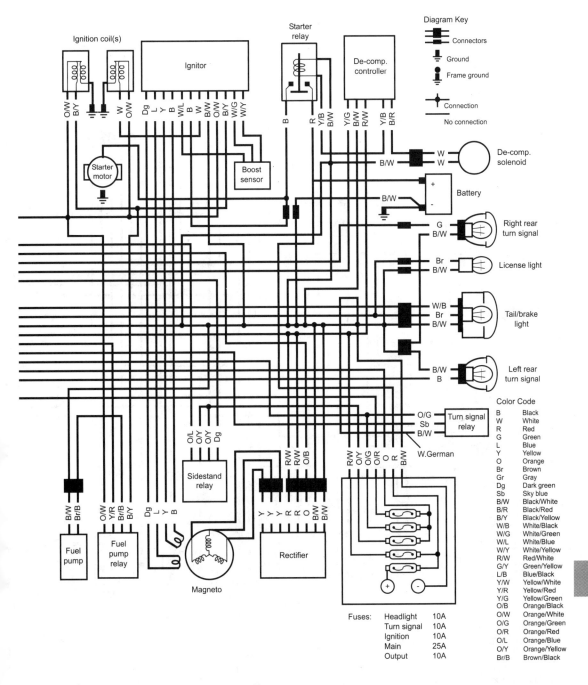

Diagram Key
- Connectors
- Ground
- Frame ground
- Connection
- No connection

Ignition coil(s)

Ignitor

Starter relay

De-comp. controller

Starter motor

Boost sensor

De-comp. solenoid

Battery

Right rear turn signal

License light

Tail/brake light

Left rear turn signal

Turn signal relay

W.German

Sidestand relay

Fuel pump

Fuel pump relay

Magneto

Rectifier

Fuses:
Headlight	10A
Turn signal	10A
Ignition	10A
Main	25A
Output	10A

Color Code
B	Black
W	White
R	Red
G	Green
L	Blue
Y	Yellow
O	Orange
Br	Brown
Gr	Gray
Dg	Dark green
Sb	Sky blue
B/W	Black/White
B/R	Black/Red
B/Y	Black/Yellow
W/B	White/Black
W/G	White/Green
W/L	White/Blue
W/Y	White/Yellow
R/W	Red/White
G/Y	Green/Yellow
L/B	Blue/Black
Y/W	Yellow/White
Y/R	Yellow/Red
Y/G	Yellow/Green
O/B	Orange/Black
O/W	Orange/White
O/G	Orange/Green
O/R	Orange/Red
O/L	Orange/Blue
O/Y	Orange/Yellow
Br/B	Brown/Black

15

1990-1991 VS1400 (CANADA)

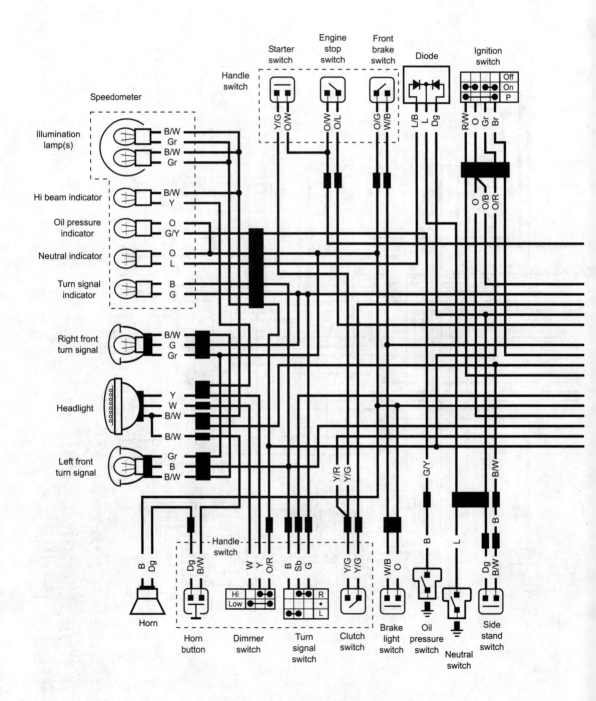

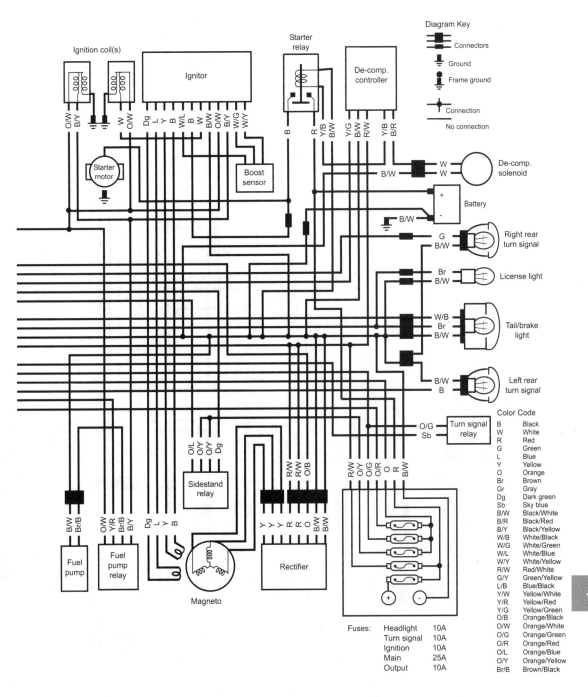

Diagram Key

- Connectors
- Ground
- Frame ground
- Connection
- No connection

Color Code

B	Black
W	White
R	Red
G	Green
L	Blue
Y	Yellow
O	Orange
Br	Brown
Gr	Gray
Dg	Dark green
Sb	Sky blue
B/W	Black/White
B/R	Black/Red
B/Y	Black/Yellow
W/B	White/Black
W/G	White/Green
W/L	White/Blue
W/Y	White/Yellow
R/W	Red/White
G/Y	Green/Yellow
L/B	Blue/Black
Y/W	Yellow/White
Y/R	Yellow/Red
Y/G	Yellow/Green
O/B	Orange/Black
O/W	Orange/White
O/G	Orange/Green
O/R	Orange/Red
O/L	Orange/Blue
O/Y	Orange/Yellow
Br/B	Brown/Black

Fuses:

Headlight	10A
Turn signal	10A
Ignition	10A
Main	25A
Output	10A

15

1992-1995 VS1400 (U.S. AND CANADA)

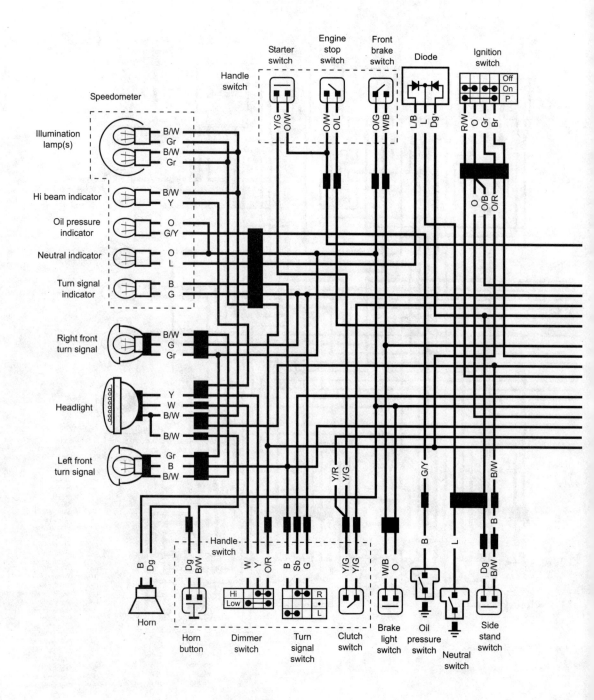

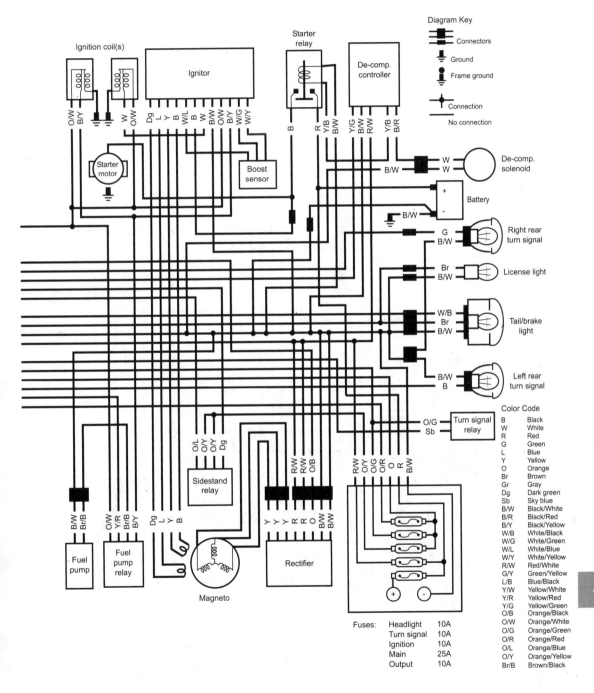

1992-1999 VS1400 (EXCEPT U.S. AND CANADA)

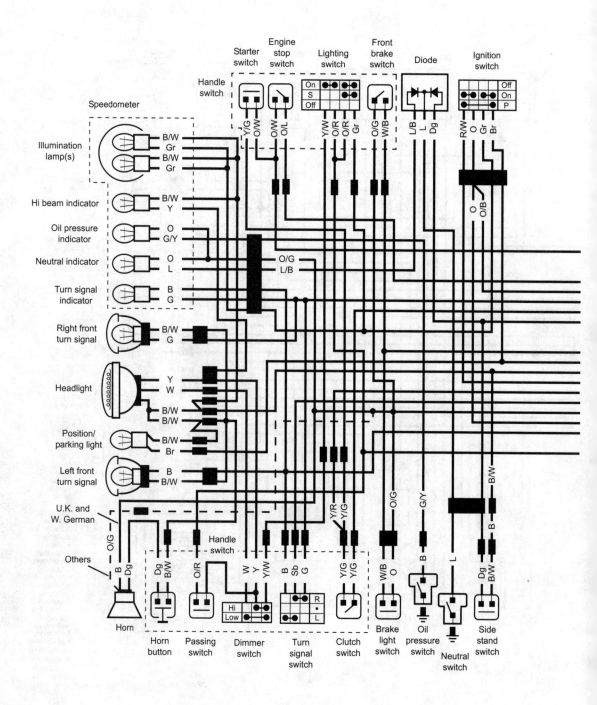

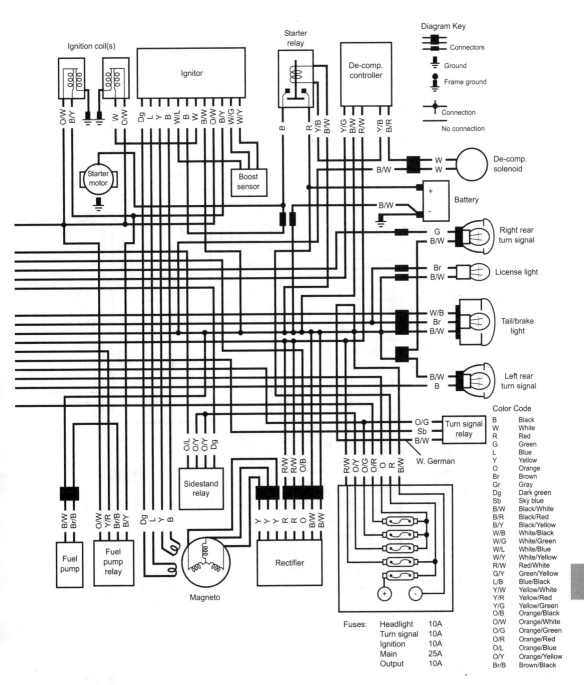

Diagram Key

- Connectors
- Ground
- Frame ground
- Connection
- No connection

Ignition coil(s)

Ignitor

Starter relay

De-comp. controller

Starter motor

Boost sensor

De-comp. solenoid

Battery

Right rear turn signal

License light

Tail/brake light

Left rear turn signal

Turn signal relay

W. German

Sidestand relay

Fuel pump

Fuel pump relay

Magneto

Rectifier

Color Code	
B	Black
W	White
R	Red
G	Green
L	Blue
Y	Yellow
O	Orange
Br	Brown
Gr	Gray
Dg	Dark green
Sb	Sky blue
B/W	Black/White
B/R	Black/Red
B/Y	Black/Yellow
W/B	White/Black
W/G	White/Green
W/L	White/Blue
W/Y	White/Yellow
R/W	Red/White
G/Y	Green/Yellow
L/B	Blue/Black
Y/W	Yellow/White
Y/R	Yellow/Red
Y/G	Yellow/Green
O/B	Orange/Black
O/W	Orange/White
O/G	Orange/Green
O/R	Orange/Red
O/L	Orange/Blue
O/Y	Orange/Yellow
Br/B	Brown/Black

Fuses:		
	Headlight	10A
	Turn signal	10A
	Ignition	10A
	Main	25A
	Output	10A

15

1993-1997 VS1400 (AUSTRALIA)

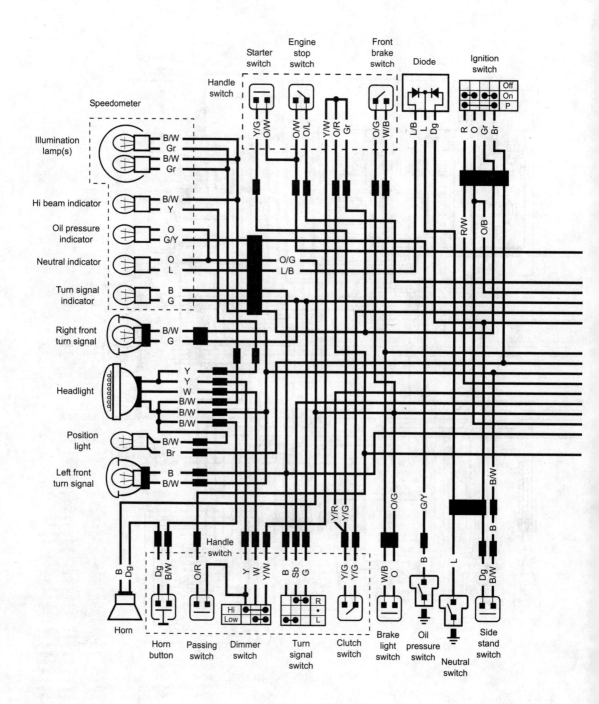

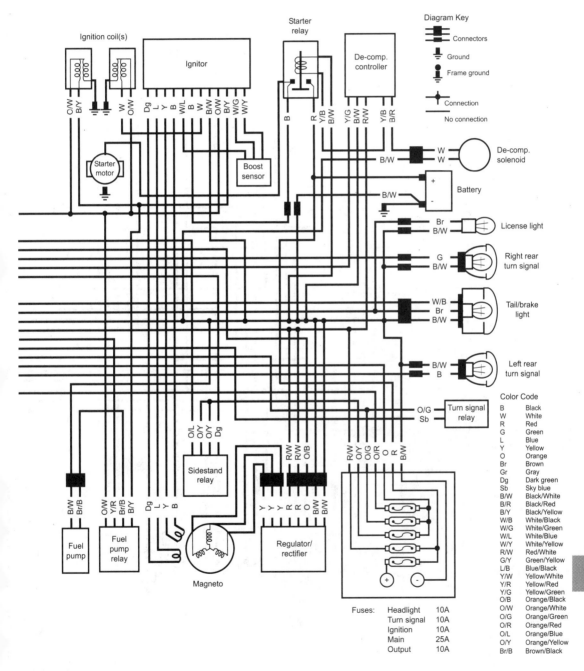

Starter
relay

Diagram Key

Connectors

Ground

Frame ground

Connection

No connection

Ignition coil(s)

Ignitor

De-comp.
controller

De-comp.
solenoid

Battery

License light

Right rear
turn signal

Tail/brake
light

Left rear
turn signal

Starter
motor

Boost
sensor

Turn signal
relay

Sidestand
relay

Fuel
pump

Fuel
pump
relay

Magneto

Regulator/
rectifier

Color Code	
B	Black
W	White
R	Red
G	Green
L	Blue
Y	Yellow
O	Orange
Br	Brown
Gr	Gray
Dg	Dark green
Sb	Sky blue
B/W	Black/White
B/R	Black/Red
B/Y	Black/Yellow
W/B	White/Black
W/G	White/Green
W/L	White/Blue
W/Y	White/Yellow
R/W	Red/White
G/Y	Green/Yellow
L/B	Blue/Black
Y/W	Yellow/White
Y/R	Yellow/Red
Y/G	Yellow/Green
O/B	Orange/Black
O/W	Orange/White
O/G	Orange/Green
O/R	Orange/Red
O/L	Orange/Blue
O/Y	Orange/Yellow
Br/B	Brown/Black

15

Fuses:		
	Headlight	10A
	Turn signal	10A
	Ignition	10A
	Main	25A
	Output	10A

1996-ON VS1400 (U.S. AND ALL OTHER MODELS EXCEPT AUSTRALIA)

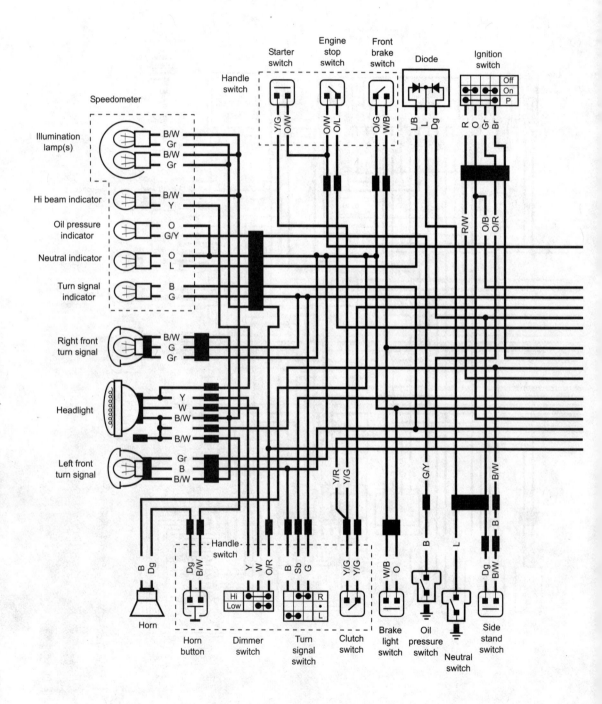

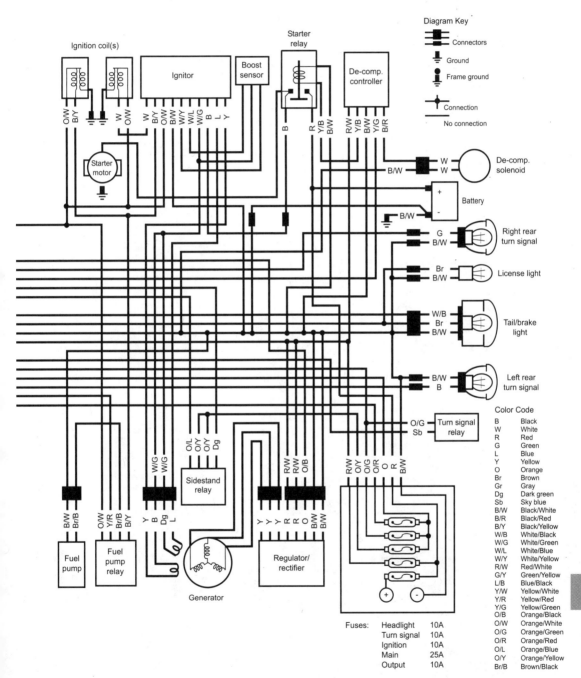

NOTES

MAINTENANCE LOG

Date	Miles	Type of Service

BMW

M308	500 & 600 CC Twins, 55-69
M309	F650, 1994-2000
M500-3	BMW K-Series, 85-97
M501	K1200RS, GT & LT, 98-05
M502-3	BMW R50/5-R100 GSPD, 70-96
M503-3	R850, R1100, R1150 and R1200C, 93-05

HARLEY-DAVIDSON

M419	Sportsters, 59-85
M428	Sportster Evolution, 86-90
M429-4	XL/XLH Sportster, 91-03
M427-1	Sportster, 04-06
M418	Panheads, 48-65
M420	Shovelheads, 66-84
M421-3	FLS/FXS Evolution, 84-99
M423-2	FLS/FXS Twin Cam, 00-05
M422-3	FLH/FLT/FXR Evolution, 84-99
M430-4	FLH/FLT Twin Cam, 99-05
M424-2	FXD Evolution, 91-98
M425-3	FXD Twin Cam, 99-05

HONDA

ATVs

M316	Odyssey FL250, 77-84
M311	ATC, TRX & Fourtrax 70-125, 70-87
M433	Fourtrax 90 ATV, 93-00
M326	ATC185 & 200, 80-86
M347	ATC200X & Fourtrax 200SX, 86-88
M455	ATC250 & Fourtrax 200/250, 84-87
M342	ATC250R, 81-84
M348	TRX250R/Fourtrax 250R & ATC250R, 85-89
M456-3	TRX250X 87-92; TRX300EX 93-04
M215	TRX250EX, 01-05
M446-2	TRX250 Recon & ES, 97-04
M346-3	TRX300/Fourtrax 300 & TRX300FW/Fourtrax 4x4, 88-00
M200-2	TRX350 Rancher, 00-06
M459-3	TRX400 Foreman 95-03
M454-3	TRX400EX 99-05
M205	TRX450 Foreman, 98-04
M210	TRX500 Rubicon, 98-04

Singles

M310-13	50-110cc OHC Singles, 65-99
M319-2	XR50R, CRF50F, XR70R & CRF70F, 97-05
M315	100-350cc OHC, 69-82
M817	Elsinore, 125-250cc, 73-80
M442	CR60-125R Pro-Link, 81-88
M431-2	CR80R, 89-95, CR125R, 89-91
M435	CR80, 96-02
M457-2	CR125R & CR250R, 92-97
M464	CR125R, 1998-2002
M443	CR250R-500R Pro-Link, 81-87
M432-3	CR250R, 88-91 & CR500R, 88-01
M437	CR250R, 97-01
M352	CRF250, CRF250X & CRF450R, CRF450X, 02-05
M312-13	XL/XR75-100, 75-03
M318-4	XL/XR/TLR 125-200, 79-03
M328-4	XL/XR250, 78-00; XL/XR350R 83-85; XR200R, 84-85; XR250L, 91-96
M320-2	XR400R, 96-04
M339-7	XL/XR 500-650, 79-03

Twins

M321	125-200cc, 65-78
M322	250-350cc, 64-74
M323	250-360cc Twins, 74-77
M324-5	Twinstar, Rebel 250 & Nighthawk 250, 78-03
M334	400-450cc, 78-87
M333	450 & 500cc, 65-76
M335	CX & GL500/650 Twins, 78-83
M344	VT500, 83-88
M313	VT700 & 750, 83-87
M314-2	VT750 Shadow (chain drive), 98-05
M440	VT1100C Shadow, 85-96
M460-3	VT1100C Series, 95-04

Fours

M332	CB350-550cc, SOHC, 71-78
M345	CB550 & 650, 83-85
M336	CB650, 79-82
M341	CB750 SOHC, 69-78
M337	CB750 DOHC, 79-82
M436	CB750 Nighthawk, 91-93 & 95-99
M325	CB900, 1000 & 1100, 80-83
M439	Hurricane 600, 87-90
M441-2	CBR600F2 & F3, 91-98
M445-2	CBR600F4, 99-06
M434-2	CBR900RR Fireblade, 93-99
M329	500cc V-Fours, 84-86
M438	Honda VFR800, 98-00
M349	700-1000 Interceptor, 83-85
M458-2	VFR700F-750F, 86-97
M327	700-1100cc V-Fours, 82-88
M340	GL1000 & 1100, 75-83
M504	GL1200, 84-87
M508	ST1100/PAN European, 90-02

Sixes

M505	GL1500 Gold Wing, 88-92
M506-2	GL1500 Gold Wing, 93-00
M507-2	GL1800 Gold Wing, 01-05
M462-2	GL1500C Valkyrie, 97-03

KAWASAKI

ATVs

M465-2	KLF220 & KLF250 Bayou, 88-03
M466-4	KLF300 Bayou, 86-04
M467	KLF400 Bayou, 93-99
M470	KEF300 Lakota, 95-99
M385	KSF250 Mojave, 87-00

Singles

M350-9	Rotary Valve 80-350cc, 66-01
M444-2	KX60, 83-02; KX80 83-90
M448	KX80/85/100, 89-03
M351	KDX200, 83-88
M447-3	KX125 & KX250, 82-91 KX500, 83-04
M472-2	KX125, 92-00
M473-2	KX250, 92-00
M474-2	KLR650, 87-06

Twins

M355	KZ400, KZ/Z440, EN450 & EN500, 74-95
M360-3	EX500, GPZ500S, Ninja R, 87-02
M356-4	Vulcan 700 & 750, 85-04
M354-2	Vulcan 800 & Vulcan 800 Classic, 95-04
M357-2	Vulcan 1500, 87-99
M471-2	Vulcan Classic 1500, 96-04

Fours

M449	KZ500/550 & ZX550, 79-85
M450	KZ, Z & ZX750, 80-85
M358	KZ650, 77-83
M359-3	900-1000cc Fours, 73-81
M451-3	1000 &1100cc Fours, 81-02
M452-3	ZX500 & 600 Ninja, 85-97
M453-3	Ninja ZX900-1100 84-01
M468-2	Ninja ZX-6, 90-04
M469	ZX7 Ninja, 91-98
M453-3	Ninja ZX900, ZX1000 & ZX1100, 84-01
M409	Concours, 86-04

POLARIS

ATVs

M496	Polaris ATV, 85-95
M362	Polaris Magnum ATV, 96-98
M363	Scrambler 500, 4X4 97-00
M365-2	Sportsman/Xplorer, 96-03

SUZUKI

ATVs

M381	ALT/LT 125 & 185, 83-87
M475	LT230 & LT250, 85-90
M380-2	LT250R Quad Racer, 85-92
M343	LTF500F Quadrunner, 98-00
M483-2	Suzuki King Quad/ Quad Runner 250, 87-98

Singles

M371	RM50-400 Twin Shock, 75-81
M369	125-400cc 64-81
M379	RM125-500 Single Shock, 81-88
M476	DR250-350, 90-94
M384-3	LS650 Savage, 86-04
M386	RM80-250, 89-95
M400	RM125, 96-00
M401	RM250, 96-02

Twins

M372	GS400-450 Twins, 77-87
M481-4	VS700-800 Intruder, 85-04
M482-2	VS1400 Intruder, 87-01
M484-3	GS500E Twins, 89-02
M361	SV650, 1999-2002

Triple

M368	380-750cc, 72-77

Fours

M373	GS550, 77-86
M364	GS650, 81-83
M370	GS750 Fours, 77-82
M376	GS850-1100 Shaft Drive, 79-84
M378	GS1100 Chain Drive, 80-81
M383-3	Katana 600, 88-96 GSX-R750-1100, 86-87
M331	GSX-R600, 97-00
M478-2	GSX-R750, 88-92 GSX750F Katana, 89-96
M485	GSX-R750, 96-99
M377	GSX-R1000, 01-04
M338	GSF600 Bandit, 95-00
M353	GSF1200 Bandit, 96-03

YAMAHA

ATVs

M499	YFM80 Badger, 85-01
M394	YTM/YFM200 & 225, 83-86
M488-5	Blaster, 88-05
M489-2	Timberwolf, 89-00
M487-5	Warrior, 87-04
M486-5	Banshee, 87-04
M490-3	Moto-4 & Big Bear, 87-04
M493	YFM400FW Kodiak, 93-98
M280-2	Raptor 660R, 01-05

Singles

M492-2	PW50 & PW80, BW80 Big Wheel 80, 81-02
M410	80-175 Piston Port, 68-76
M415	250-400cc Piston Port, 68-76
M412	DT & MX 100-400, 77-83
M414	IT125-490, 76-86
M393	YZ50-80 Monoshock, 78-90
M413	YZ100-490 Monoshock, 76-84
M390	YZ125-250, 85-87 YZ490, 85-90
M391	YZ125-250, 88-93 WR250Z, 91-93
M497-2	YZ125, 94-01
M498	YZ250, 94-98 and WR250Z, 94-97
M406	YZ250F & WR250F, 01-03
M491-2	YZ400F, YZ426F, WR400F WR426F, 98-02
M417	XT125-250, 80-84
M480-3	XT/TT 350, 85-00
M405	XT500 & TT500, 76-81
M416	XT/TT 600, 83-89

Twins

M403	650cc, 70-82
M395-10	XV535-1100 Virago, 81-03
M495-4	V-Star 650, 98-05
M281-2	V-Star 1100, 99-05
M282	Road Star, 99-05

Triple

M404	XS750 & 850, 77-81

Fours

M387	XJ550, XJ600 & FJ600, 81-92
M494	XJ600 Seca II, 92-98
M388	YX600 Radian & FZ600, 86-90
M396	FZR600, 89-93
M392	FZ700-750 & Fazer, 85-87
M411	XS1100 Fours, 78-81
M397	FJ1100 & 1200, 84-93
M375	V-Max, 85-03
M374	Royal Star, 96-03
M461	YZF-R6, 99-04
M398	YZF-R1, 98-03
M399	FZ1, 01-05

VINTAGE MOTORCYCLES

Clymer® Collection Series

M330	Vintage British Street Bikes, BSA, 500-650cc Unit Twins; Norton, 750 & 850cc Commandos; Triumph, 500-750cc Twins
M300	Vintage Dirt Bikes, V. 1 Bultaco, 125-370cc Singles; Montesa, 123-360cc Singles; Ossa, 125-250cc Singles
M301	Vintage Dirt Bikes, V. 2 CZ, 125-400cc Singles; Husqvarna, 125-450cc Singles; Maico, 250-501cc Singles; Hodaka, 90-125cc Singles
M305	Vintage Japanese Street Bikes Honda, 250 & 305cc Twins; Kawasaki, 250-750cc Triples; Kawasaki, 900 & 1000cc Fours